ultimate

This man looks like he's about to fall into a crevasse. But he's actually standing on a 3-D chalk painting that artist Edgar Mueller drew on the sidewalk

NATIONAL GEOGRAPHIC KIDS™

ultimate weird but true

WASHINGTON, D.C.

contents

CHAPTER 1 GOING TO EXTREMES 6

CHAPTER 2 SEEING IS BELIEVING 26

CHAPTER 3 WHO'S COUNTING? 46

CHAPTER 4 FREAKS OF NATURE 66

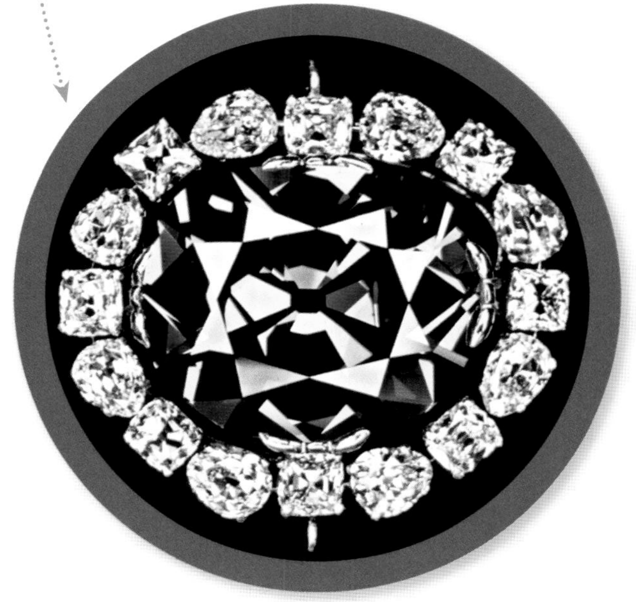

ROBOVIE

Tillman the skateboarding dog can travel 328 feet (100 m) in 19.68 seconds. Check out more awesome animals in action on pages 20 and 21.

CHAPTER 1

Going to Extremes

EXTREME-LY Odd Sports

Sky Surfing

SPECIAL GEAR:
skyboard and parachute

WHY IT'S WEIRD:
Surfing on air and doing 360s, cartwheels, half twists, and flips while **falling** from **13,000 feet** (3,962 m) in the **air** make this sport a combination of skateboarding, snowboarding, and skydiving.

Parkour

SPECIAL GEAR:
none, just a lot of guts

WHY IT'S WEIRD:
Using cities as their playgrounds, athletes do **flips** off buildings, scale walls, and leap across **rooftops** in a single bound.

Wingsuit Flying

SPECIAL GEAR:
wingsuit and parachute

WHY IT'S WEIRD:
Skydivers wear special **jumpsuits** with built-in "wings," allowing them to **glide** at 100 miles an hour (160 kph) before releasing a parachute.

Extreme Ironing

SPECIAL GEAR:
iron, ironing board, and wrinkled clothes

WHY IT'S WEIRD:
Thrill seekers iron their **laundry** while climbing snowy mountain peaks, scuba diving, water-skiing, bungee jumping, or performing almost any extreme sport.

Skyaking

SPECIAL GEAR:
kayak and parachute

WHY IT'S WEIRD:
Skyakers ride the air **instead of** white-water **rapids,** free-falling for some 8,000 feet (2400 m) before opening a parachute and **targeting** a **water** landing.

Globe Riding

SPECIAL GEAR:
globe ball

WHY IT'S WEIRD:
Like a **hamster** inside its wheel, a globe rider runs inside a giant **inflated** ball cushioned with a layer of air as it **rolls** across water or down a steep hillside.

Mountain Unicycling

SPECIAL GEAR:
unicycle with extra-wide, knobby tires

WHY IT'S WEIRD:
Cyclists **climb** boulders, teeter on rocky ledges, and pedal through streams on one wheel—with **no brakes!**

Space Vacation

TAKING A **SPACE-CATION** WILL BE POSSIBLE IN YOUR LIFETIME. HERE ARE SOME WEIRD THINGS TO LOOK FORWARD TO AT YOUR ORBITAL RESORT:

WATCH the **EVER-CHANGING** view of **EARTH** as the **HOTEL ROTATES** around it every **90 minutes.**

Play **ZERO-GRAVITY SPORTS!**

BLAST OFF after **BREAKFAST AND BE** at your **SPACE DESTINATION** by **LUNCHTIME.**

Ride a **SPACE ELEVATOR 22,000** miles (35,400 km) **FROM EARTH** into **SPACE.**

TAKE a **141.6-MILLION-MILE** (227.9-million-km) **CRUISE** to **MARS.**

EXPLORE outer **SPACE** on **EXCITING SPACE** walks.

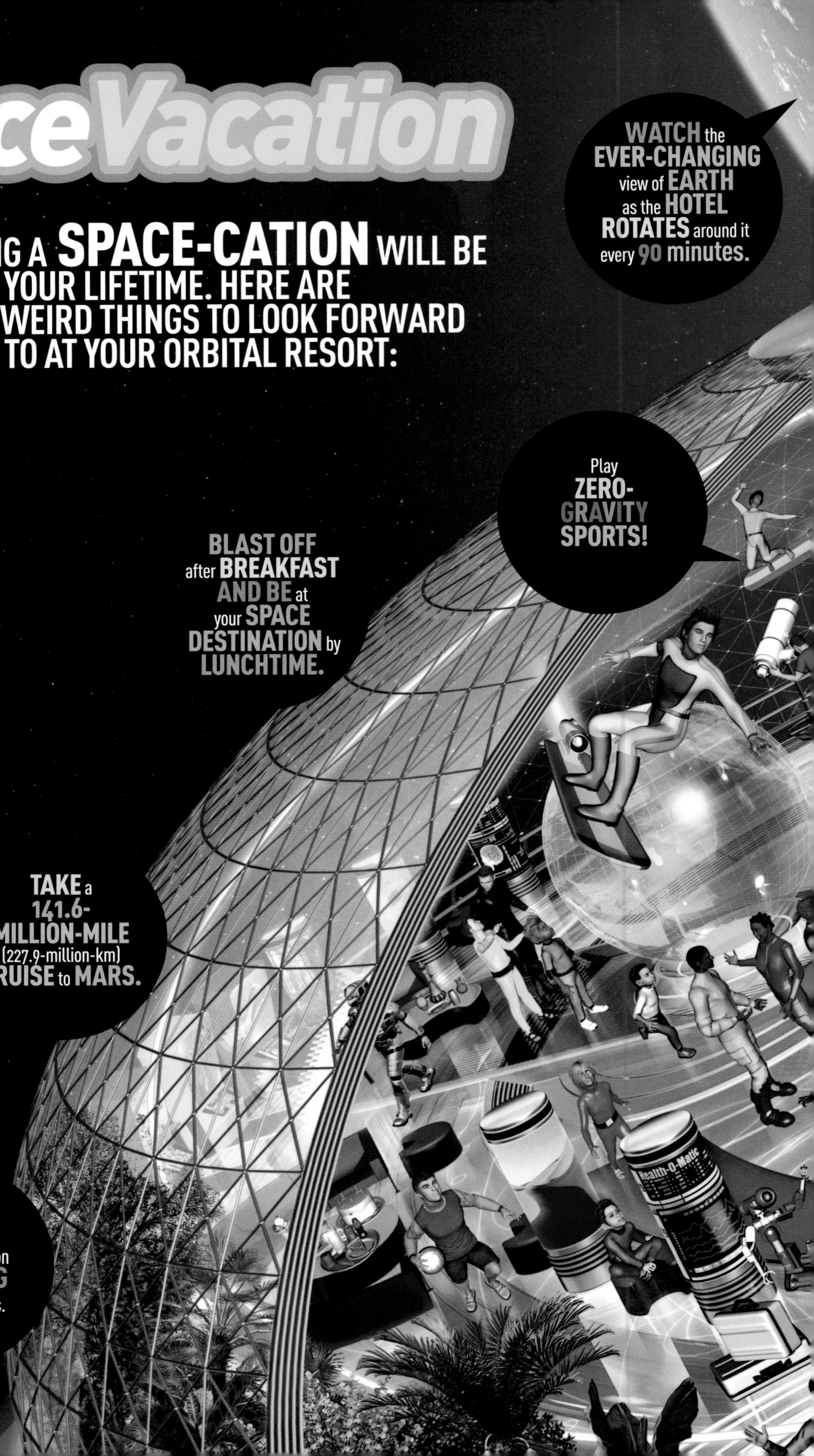

Health-O-Matic

ENJOY a CLOSE-UP VIEW of the STARS.
Have FUN DODGING blobs of FLYING WATER in the WATER ROOM attraction.
WATER WORLD
ROBOTS help TAKE CARE of GUESTS' NEEDS.
AFRAID OF FLYING? Travel anywhere in the universe without LEAVING HOME with the latest HOLOGRAPHIC VACATION app.
03

GREEN Extremes

THESE OVER-THE-TOP IDEAS TAKE **ECO-FRIENDLY** TO A WHOLE NEW LEVEL. FIND OUT HOW FAR SOME PEOPLE WILL GO TO **REDUCE**, **REUSE**, AND **RECYCLE**.

Air Pod

This tiny car runs on compressed air rather than fuel and weighs only as much as four 12-year-olds.

Solar Flight

On a long summer day, this solar-powered plane flew for more than 26 hours and reached a height of more than 5 miles (8.5 km), using only energy from the sun.

Energy Boost

At a hotel in Denmark, guests can eat a free meal if they ride a stationary bike for 15 minutes, producing 10 watts of energy to help power the building.

Cave Dwelling

This house was built inside a cave to save energy—the temperature stays the same year-round.

Walking House

This house stores rainwater and runs on wind and solar power—and if your neighbors are noisy, it can *walk* to a new location!

Pooch Power

A public dog park in Massachusetts, U.S.A., was the first to use a street lamp powered by the dogs' droppings!

Bottle Boat

To raise awareness about smarter use of plastic waste, a crew sailed from California, U.S.A., to Sydney, Australia, in a boat made from 12,500 plastic bottles!

ON THE EDGE

THE 2,345-FOOT (715-M)-TALL KJERAG WATERFALL IS ONE OF THE TALLEST IN THE WORLD.

THE UNITARD WAS FIRST WORN BY SWIMMER AND ACTRESS ANNETTE KELLERMAN IN 1905.

MORE THAN 33,000 BASE JUMPS HAVE BEEN MADE FROM KJERAG PLATEAU.

IT'S A STEEP THREE-HOUR HIKE TO REACH THIS SPOT.

DARING HIKERS OFTEN WALK ACROSS THIS BOULDER.

KJERAGBOLTEN IS ABOUT 6.5 FEET (2 M) ACROSS—AS WIDE AS THREE PEOPLE STANDING SIDE BY SIDE.

This EXTREME **acrobat** is BALANCING **3,280 feet** (1,000 m) **ABOVE** the ground—that's as **HIGH** as **three** EIFFEL TOWERS stacked on top of **each other.**

NORWAY'S MOUNTAINS WERE FORMED SOME 400 MILLION YEARS AGO.

FastFACTS

WHO: Acrobat Eskil Rønningsbakken

WHERE: Kjerag Mountain in Norway

NAME OF BOULDER: Kjeragbolten

HOW HE GOT STARTED: Rønningsbakken once worked in a circus.

BalancingACTS

This acrobat's other stunts include:

- balancing on a giant steel ring on a different cliff in Norway;
- riding a bicycle across a canyon on a tightrope;
- doing a handstand on a ladder while balancing on a cliff;
- walking a tightrope between two hot-air balloons.

WHICH IS HOTTER?

A KERNEL OF **POPCORN** WHEN IT POPS 356°F (180°C)

THE TEMPERATURE A **SIDEWALK** MUST BE TO **FRY** AN EGG 158°F (70°C)

WINNER!

MARS AT NIGHT -200°F (-130°C)

OUTSIDE AN AIRPLANE AT 30,000 FEET (9,144 M) -49°F (-45°C)

BOILING **WATER** TURNING TO **ICE** IN MIDAIR -63°F (-53°C)

WINNER!

THE **SUN'S** CORE
27,000,000°F
(15,000,000°C)

WHICH IS COLDER?

REAL-LIFE SPiDER-MAN

HE HAS HAD TWO SERIOUS FALLS AND BROKEN MULTIPLE BONES.

ROBERT HAS VERTIGO—A CONDITION THAT CAUSES THE FEELING THAT YOU OR YOUR SURROUNDINGS ARE MOVING.

This daredevil, known as the **FRENCH SPIDER-MAN,** climbed for **six hours** to reach the top of the **WORLD'S TALLEST skyscraper!**

IT TOOK ROBERT ABOUT SIX HOURS TO CLIMB TO THE TOP.

THIS SKYSCRAPER, CALLED THE BURJ KHALIFA, HAS MORE THAN 160 STORIES!

THE ELEVATORS INSIDE THIS BUILDING TRAVEL FARTHER THAN ANY OTHERS IN THE WORLD.

THE FIRST URBAN CLIMBER, HARRY H. GARDINER, CLIMBED MORE THAN 700 BUILDINGS IN THE EARLY 1900S.

FastFACTS

CLIMBER'S NAME: Alain Robert

TALLEST SKYSCRAPER: Burj Khalifa

WHERE: Dubai, United Arab Emirates

HOW TALL: 2,717 feet (828 m)

DON'T TRY THIS AT HOME: It is illegal to climb buildings in many places. Robert sometimes gets arrested after his climbs.

BUILDERING IS ANOTHER NAME FOR THIS SPORT.

Awesome ANiMALS in Action!

Motoring Mouse

NAME: **Bunsen**

WHY HE'S AWESOME:
Bunsen plays **captain** aboard his boat, which his owner **navigates** by remote control.

FUN FACT:
More than **two million** people have also watched him surf on YouTube.

Flying Dog

NAME: **Patch**

WHY HE'S AWESOME:
Patch **soars** 2,500 feet (762 m) in the **air**—as high as a **250-story** building.

FUN FACT:
Patch also likes riding a **motorcycle** with his owner.

Scootering Macaw

NAME: **Zachary**

WHY HE'S AWESOME:
He likes riding his scooter almost as much as **flying.**

FUN FACT:
Zachary also **skateboards** and **rides a bike** on a **high wire.**

Surfer Cat

NAME: **Ice Breaker**

WHY HE'S AWESOME:
This cool cat **loves** the water. He **catches waves** at a beach in Florida, U.S.A.

FUN FACT:
When he's not surfing, Ice Breaker is at home **playing** in the **shower.**

Go-al Fish!

NAME: **Albert Einstein**

WHY HE'S AWESOME:
This **"fintastic"** goldfish dribbles the ball with his **mouth**—and SCORES!

FUN FACT:
Albert also does the limbo, **plays football**, swims through a hoop, and **starred** in a **TV commercial!**

Snowboarding Dog

NAME: **ROSE**

WHY SHE'S AWESOME:
Rose **shreds** the bunny **slopes** at a ski resort near Los Angeles, California, U.S.A., with her bulldog **friend Tillman** (see page 6).

FUN FACT:
During a **parade** in Pasadena, California, Rose snowboarded on a specially designed **float.**

A BLUE WHALE is almost as LOUD as a JET ENGINE

(but you can't always hear it)

A *2-inch (5-cm)* pistol shrimp is even LOUDER than a blue whale!

There's no doubt about it: Blue whales are loudmouths. But some of their vocals are too low for humans to hear. Humans can generally hear sounds as low as about 20 Hertz, but whales broadcast at 15 to 20 Hertz—or lower. These giants of the sea are solitary creatures, and scientists suspect their low vibrations help them communicate with other blue whales up to 300 miles (483 km) away. Now that's a long-distance call!

A MAN TREKKED 17,000 FEET (5,300 M) UP MOUNT EVEREST TO SWIM IN A LAKE, RAISING AWARENESS ABOUT CLIMATE CHANGE.

A TEAM OF TORNADO CHASERS BUILT A 14,000-POUND (6,350-KG) VEHICLE THAT CAN DRIVE INTO TORNADOES WITH WIND SPEEDS UP TO 300 MILES AN HOUR (483 KPH).

SOME 50 PEOPLE SPEND THE WINTER AT THE SOUTH POLE EVERY YEAR.

A 16-YEAR-OLD GIRL SAILED AROUND THE WORLD NONSTOP BY HERSELF.

EXPLORERS TRAVELED FOR MORE THAN TWO WEEKS TO REACH THE BOTTOM OF THE WORLD'S DEEPEST CAVE.

A MAN RODE HiS BiKE 20,000 MILES (32,187 KM) FROM THE ARCTiC TO ARGENTINA.

SURFERS JUMP FROM HELICOPTERS TO RIDE 60-FOOT (18-M)-TALL MONSTER WAVES IN HAWAII.

ADVENTURERS HAVE CLiMBED INSIDE ERUPTiNG VOLCANOES.

The Philippine tarsier has the biggest eyes relative to its size of any animal. This tiny primate—only three to six inches (8 to 15 cm) long, not including its tail—lives in the forest of southeastern Philippines. For more *eye*-popping facts, turn to page 40.

CHAPTER 2

Seeing is Believing

AMAZiNG Animals

Reading Dog

WHERE SHE LIVES:
New York, New York, U.S.A.

WHY SHE'S AMAZING:
Willow the English terrier mix doesn't just **hear** her owner's commands—she also **reads** them. The pooch raises her paw when she sees the word **"wave"** and sits up when she sees the phrase **"sit up"!**

Tortoise Friend

WHERE HE LIVES:
Cornwall, England, U.K.

WHY HE'S AMAZING:
Showing any kind of affection is **rare** for a reptile, but Timmy the tortoise has loved Tanya, the **plastic toy** tortoise, for **several years.** Who knows, maybe Tanya really brings Timmy out of his shell!

Pig in Boots

WHERE SHE LIVES:
Thirsk, England, U.K.

WHY SHE'S AMAZING:
Not all pigs love the **mud.** Cinders—who has a mysterious **fear** of dirt—wore doll-size boots to **protect** her, uh, little piggies from the muck.

Mother Hen

WHERE SHE LIVES:
Shrewsbury, England, U.K.

WHY SHE'S AMAZING:
When it comes to her **mothering** instincts, Mabel the hen clucks for pups! She looks after a litter of tiny **dogs** as if they are her own **chicks**—when their mom goes outside for a break, Mabel snuggles up and keeps the puppies toasty.

Backseat Bison

WHERE HE LIVES:
Spruce Grove, Alberta, Canada

WHY HE'S AMAZING:

Forget hooves—Bailey Jr. the **bison** gets around in the comforts of a **car.** To make room for this mammoth mammal, his owner removed the roof and front and rear passenger seats of a four-door car and **reinforced** the bottom. Now that's what you call **riding** in style!

Bionic Cat

WHERE HE LIVES:
Surrey, England, U.K.

WHY HE'S AMAZING:
After losing his **back paws** in an accident, doctors fit Oscar with the **first-ever** realistic cat paws. Oscar can now jump on beds, crawl up curtains, and even scratch his ears with his **plastic feet.** Hope there aren't any mice in this house!

WHERE SHE LIVES:
Istanbul, Turkey

WHY SHE'S AMAZING:
Sara pretends to **play** a toy sax while **swaying** along to jazz music and flapping her flippers to the **beat.** That's one rockin' walrus!

BASILISK
LIZARDS
are the only lizards that
run on
water.

→ Basilisks can stay underwater for 30 minutes.

→ Basilisks live mostly in the rain forests of Central and South America.

→ These lizards can **run** on water for more than **15 feet** (4.5 m) before dropping to all fours and swimming.

→ What makes a basilisk **defy gravity?** Large feet, widespread toes, and the ability to **windmill** its hind legs and feet so fast that it creates a **tiny air pocket** to keep it from sinking.

→ Baby basilisks can **climb, swim, and run** on land and water as soon as they **hatch**.

SHAPE-SHIFTERS

Check out these totally wild **animal transformations!**

LOVEBIRDS

WHAT IT IS: frigate bird

WHERE IT LIVES: tropical ocean coastlines

EXTREME MAKEOVER:
When trying to attract a female, the male inflates a heart-shaped sac that's half the size of the bird's body!

STOP, DROP, AND ROLL!

WHAT IT IS: three-banded armadillo

WHERE IT LIVES: South America

EXTREME MAKEOVER:
Sensing danger, this stocky mammal ducks into its armorlike shell and rolls up into a predator-proof ball.

LIGHT SHOW

WHAT IT IS: blue-ringed octopus

WHERE IT LIVES: warm, shallow waters off the coasts of Asia and Australia

EXTREME MAKEOVER:
Don't make this octopus angry! It will light up with electric blue rings in warning, and its bite is venomous enough to kill a human.

IT'S A BIRD, IT'S A . . .

WHAT IT IS: flying squirrel

WHERE IT LIVES: forests of North America and Central America

EXTREME MAKEOVER:
These strange squirrels look normal until they spread out winglike skin flaps and soar from tree to tree. They don't really fly, but they can glide more than 150 feet (45 m).

FISH BALL

WHAT IT IS: pufferfish

WHERE IT LIVES: tropical ocean waters; some species in freshwater

EXTREME MAKEOVER:
Predators beware! When this petite fish gets scared, it gulps down enough water to balloon to twice its size and then sticks out its prickly spines.

ALL THAT Glitters

THIS **CUPCAKE** IS **SPRINKLED** WITH AROUND **25 KARATS OF DIAMONDS** AND COSTS MORE THAN **$150,000**— ABOUT AS MUCH AS **FIVE CARS.**

SOME HIGH-END **SPAS** OFFER **$500 MUD MASKS** MADE WITH **24-KARAT GOLD.**

INSTEAD OF **MONEY,** THIS "CASH" MACHINE IN ABU DHABI, UNITED ARAB EMIRATES, DISPENSES **24-KARAT GOLD BARS** AND **COINS.**

BEDAZZLED WITH 300,000 CRYSTALS, THIS MERCEDES-BENZ IS WORTH $1 MILLION. >>>

"POTTY" LIKE A ROCK STAR WITH A SOLID-GOLD TOILET WORTH ABOUT $37 MILLION. <<<

THIS $70,000 TEDDY BEAR HAS DIAMOND-AND-SAPPHIRE EYES, GOLD LEAF IN ITS FUR, AND A 24-KARAT GOLD NOSE! >>>

Can you see me?
BOLIN PAINTS HIS BODY, FACE, AND CLOTHES TO BLEND INTO ALMOST ANY SETTING.
PEOPLE OFTEN WALK RIGHT BY WITHOUT SEEING THIS CAMOUFLAGED MAN.

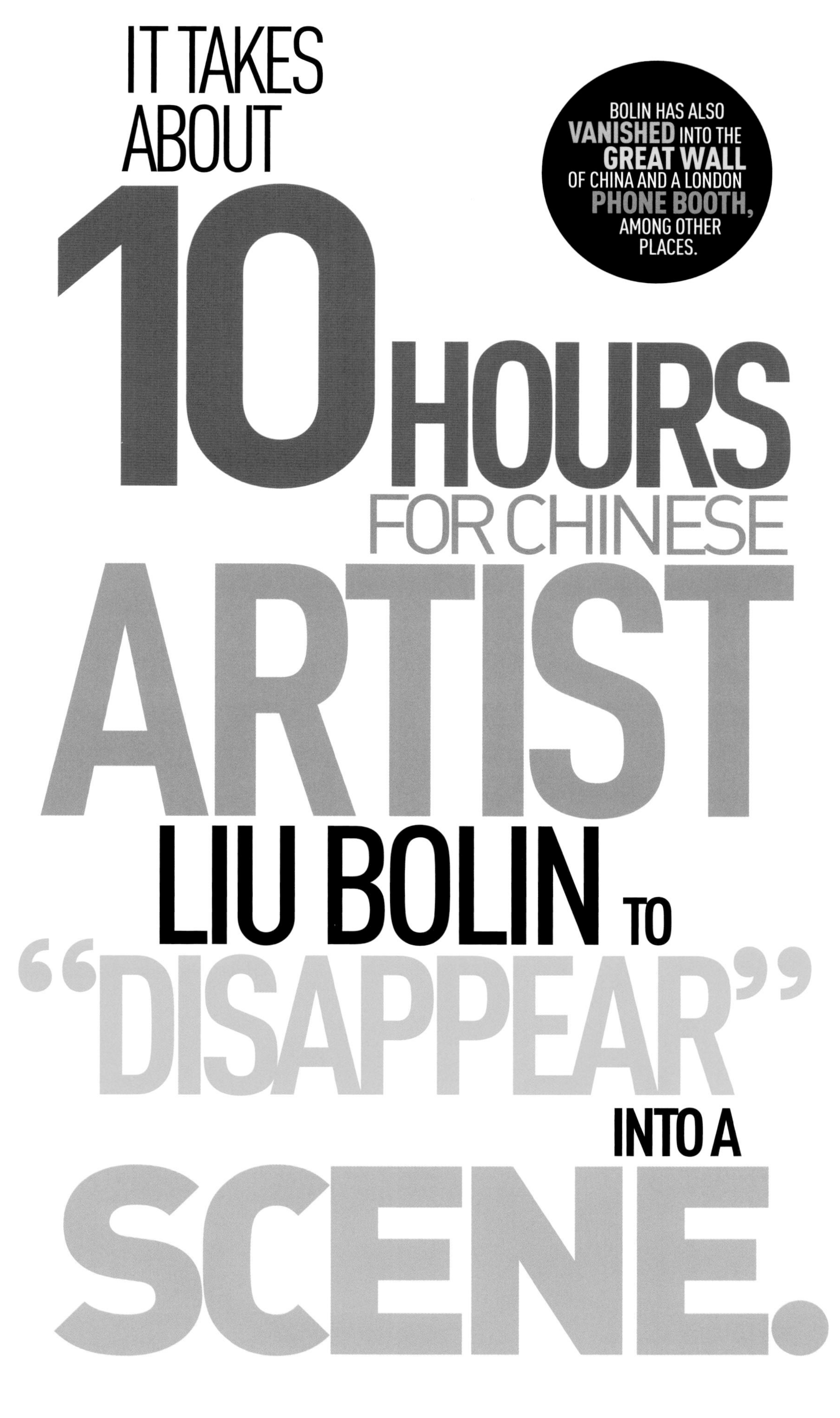

IT TAKES ABOUT 10 HOURS FOR CHINESE ARTIST LIU BOLIN TO "DISAPPEAR" INTO A SCENE.

BOLIN HAS ALSO **VANISHED** INTO THE **GREAT WALL** OF CHINA AND A LONDON **PHONE BOOTH**, AMONG OTHER PLACES.

Wacky HOUSES

Alien Invasion

WHERE:
Chattanooga, Tennessee, U.S.A.

WHY IT'S WACKY:
This **UFO-shaped** house definitely looks like it's from another planet! Instead of a front door, you enter the home on a **retractable staircase** that lowers to the ground with the push of a button.

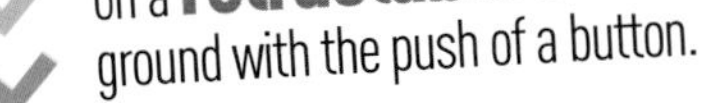

A Home with Sole

WHERE:
Hellam, Pennsylvania, U.S.A.

WHY IT'S WACKY:
Built by a **shoe**-store owner to promote his business, this three-bedroom home has **five** levels. Guess that makes it a **high-top!**

Gone Fishing

WHERE:
Mexico City, Mexico

WHY IT'S WACKY:
Tunnels connect curvy rooms inside this **shark-shaped** house. Lights inside change from pink to yellow to orange.

CARchitecture

WHERE:
Salzburg, Austria

WHY IT'S WACKY:
This **car-shaped** house, a tribute to the original Volkswagen Beetle, features **headlight-shaped** windows and giant "tires" on the outside. The architect who built the house also built a VW-shaped restaurant!

Rock On

WHERE:
Brittany, France

WHY IT'S WACKY:
Squeezed between **two boulders,** this tiny stone house was built in **1755** and was once a home for a **village fisherman.**

Up a Tree

WHERE:
Olympia, Washington, U.S.A.

WHY IT'S WACKY:
Talk about living the **high** life: This two-level tree house—spread out across **seven** trees—has its own **electricity** and heat!

Flipped Out

WHERE:
Trassenheide, Germany

WHY IT'S WACKY:
No wonder tons of tourists **flip** for this house: **Everything** is upside-down inside—including the **toilet!**

11 EYE-POPPING

GOLDFISH CAN'T CLOSE THEIR EYES.

A squid's eyes are each about the size of a **watermelon.**

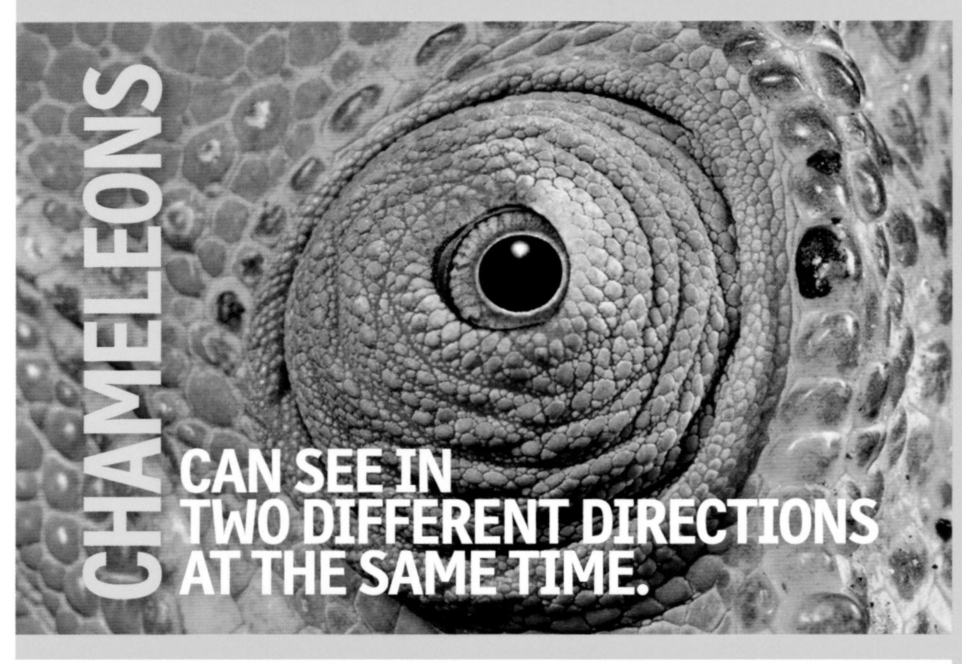

CHAMELEONS CAN SEE IN TWO DIFFERENT DIRECTIONS AT THE SAME TIME.

Ostriches' eyes are **bigger** than their brains.

YOU **BLINK** MORE THAN **10,000** TIMES A DAY.

Some people can **HEAR THEIR EYEBALLS MOVING.**

A BUTTERFLY CAN SEE **ULTRAVIOLET** LIGHT.

YOU CAN GET A **SUNBURN** ON YOUR EYES.

DOLPHINS **SLEEP** WITH ONE EYE **OPEN.**

THE HUMAN EYEBALL WEIGHS ABOUT AS MUCH AS FIVE QUARTERS.

THE BLINK OF AN EYE **EQUALS** ABOUT TWO-FIFTHS OF A SECOND.

FANTASY ISLAND

THE TOTAL AMOUNT OF ROCKS AND SAND USED TO BUILD THE PALM ISLAND COULD FORM A 6-FOOT-TALL (2-M) WALL LONG ENOUGH TO CIRCLE THE GLOBE THREE TIMES.

THERE'S A MONORAIL TRAIN THAT TRANSPORTS PEOPLE FROM THE ISLAND'S "TRUNK" TO THE CRESCENT.

SOME YEARS, IT NEVER RAINS ON THE PALM JUMEIRAH.

28 BOTTLENOSE DOLPHINS WERE FLOWN FROM THE SOLOMON ISLANDS TO FILL DOLPHIN BAY, AN 11-ACRE LAGOON ON THE PALM'S CRESCENT.

THE 7-MILE (11-KM) CRESCENT SURROUNDING THE ISLAND IS MADE FROM MORE THAN 7 MILLION TONS OF ROCKS.

This massive palm-tree-shaped island can be seen from the International Space Station, some 220 miles (354 km) above Earth!

A LUXURY VILLA ON ONE OF THE ISLAND'S "FRONDS" SELLS FOR ABOUT $5 MILLION.

THERE ARE ENOUGH HOMES AND HOTEL ROOMS ON THE ISLAND TO FIT

Fast FACTS

NAME: The Palm Jumeirah

WHAT: One of three man-made islands in the Arabian Gulf that are shaped like palm trees!

WHERE: Dubai, United Arab Emirates

SIZE: 12 square miles (31 sq km)—as big as 5,800 football fields

COST TO BUILD: $12 billion

ISLANDS TAKE SHAPE

FEDERATION ISLAND This yet-to-be-built island in the Black Sea will look like a map of Russia.

THE WORLD This collection of 300 man-made islands in Dubai is shaped like a world map and cost $14 billion ($14,000,000,000) to build.

GALESNJAK This tiny natural island in the Adriatic Sea off the coast of Croatia is perfectly heart shaped.

CRAZY ART

ARTISTS MADE A **10-FOOT** (3-m) **HOT DOG** USING **6,300** CANS OF BAKED BEANS, VIENNA SAUSAGES, AND MORE.

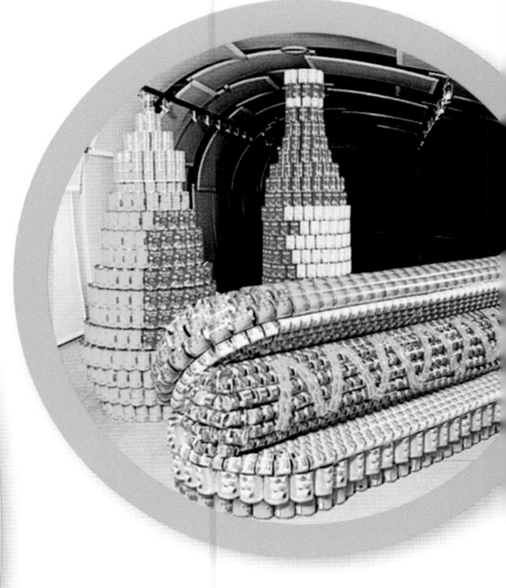

A **DUTCH** ARTIST SPENT TWO DAYS **SPRAY-PAINTING** GIANT FRIED **EGGS** ON A LARGE CITY SQUARE.

THIS 10-FOOT-TALL (3-m) **BALLOON DOG**—ACTUALLY COLORED STAINLESS STEEL—IS FEATURED IN THE MOVIE *NIGHT AT THE MUSEUM 2.*

BALLOON DOG B

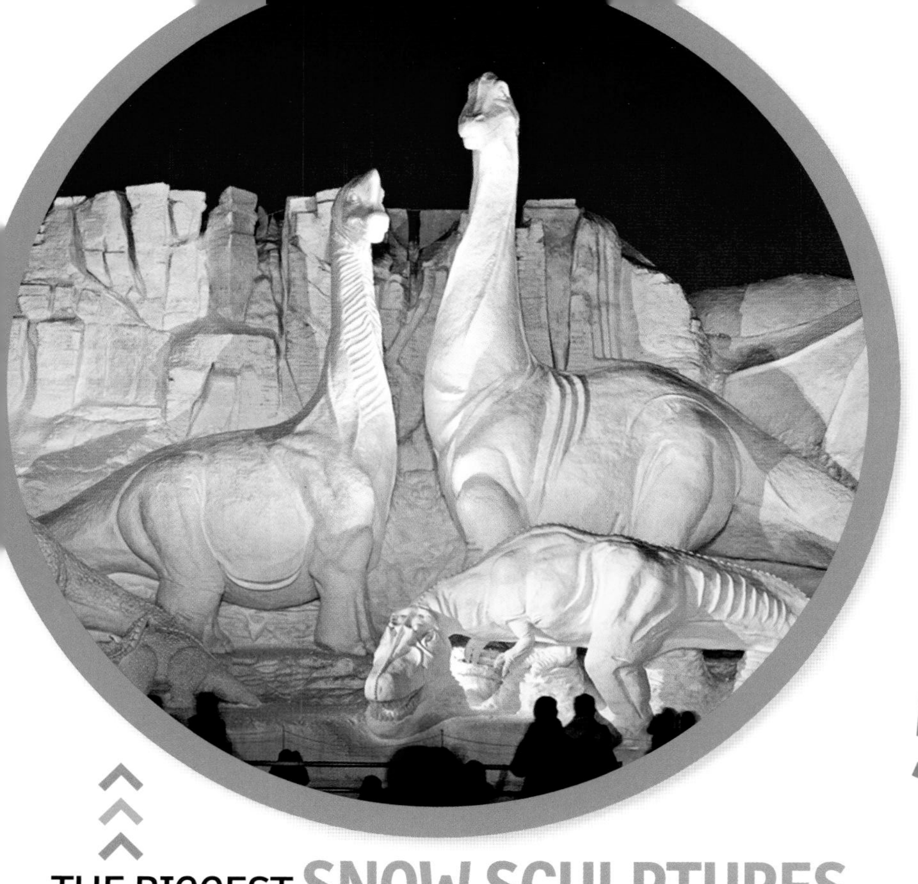

THE BIGGEST **SNOW SCULPTURES,** **LIKE THESE DINOS, CAN** **WEIGH** UP TO **100 TONS** (90 t)—THAT'S MORE THAN **30** HIPPOS.

THIS **TIGER** IS SCULPTED ENTIRELY FROM **SUGAR.** THE ART OF SUGAR SCULPTURE BEGAN IN **CHINA** MORE THAN **500** YEARS AGO.

THE ART OF CREATING **IMAGES** OUT OF RUBIK'S CUBES, LIKE THIS **PAC-MAN GHOST,** IS CALLED **RUBIK'S CUBISM.**

All five types of rhinos have at least one horn, excellent hearing, and a fancy for rolling in the mud. Find out what weighs as much as 160 million rhinos on page 55.

CHAPTER 3

Who's Counting?

Scientists have **determined** that every animal **pictured** here has at least a basic **ability** to count.

Chickens

Baby chicks have been shown to have an **inborn** sense of numbers and can **perform** simple addition and subtraction.

Counting CRiTTERS

Honeybees

In exchange for a **sweet** treat, bees can learn to **distinguish** among patterns containing 2, 3, and 4 dots.

Red-Backed Salamander

When given the choice among **fruit fly-filled** tubes, these salamanders could tell the **difference** among 1, 2, and 3 flies.

Rhesus Monkeys

These primates show a number sense that's similar to our own. In some computer tests, researchers found that rhesus monkeys and college students earned similar results.

These finned math whizzes can tell the difference among groups of 1 to 4 fish.

Mosquito Fish

American Coots

These birds tally the number of eggs they lay in their nests. When an invading bird tries to sneak an egg in, the coot knows there's an extra and rejects it.

In tests, lemurs can put groups of dots in order according to number.

Ring-tailed Lemurs

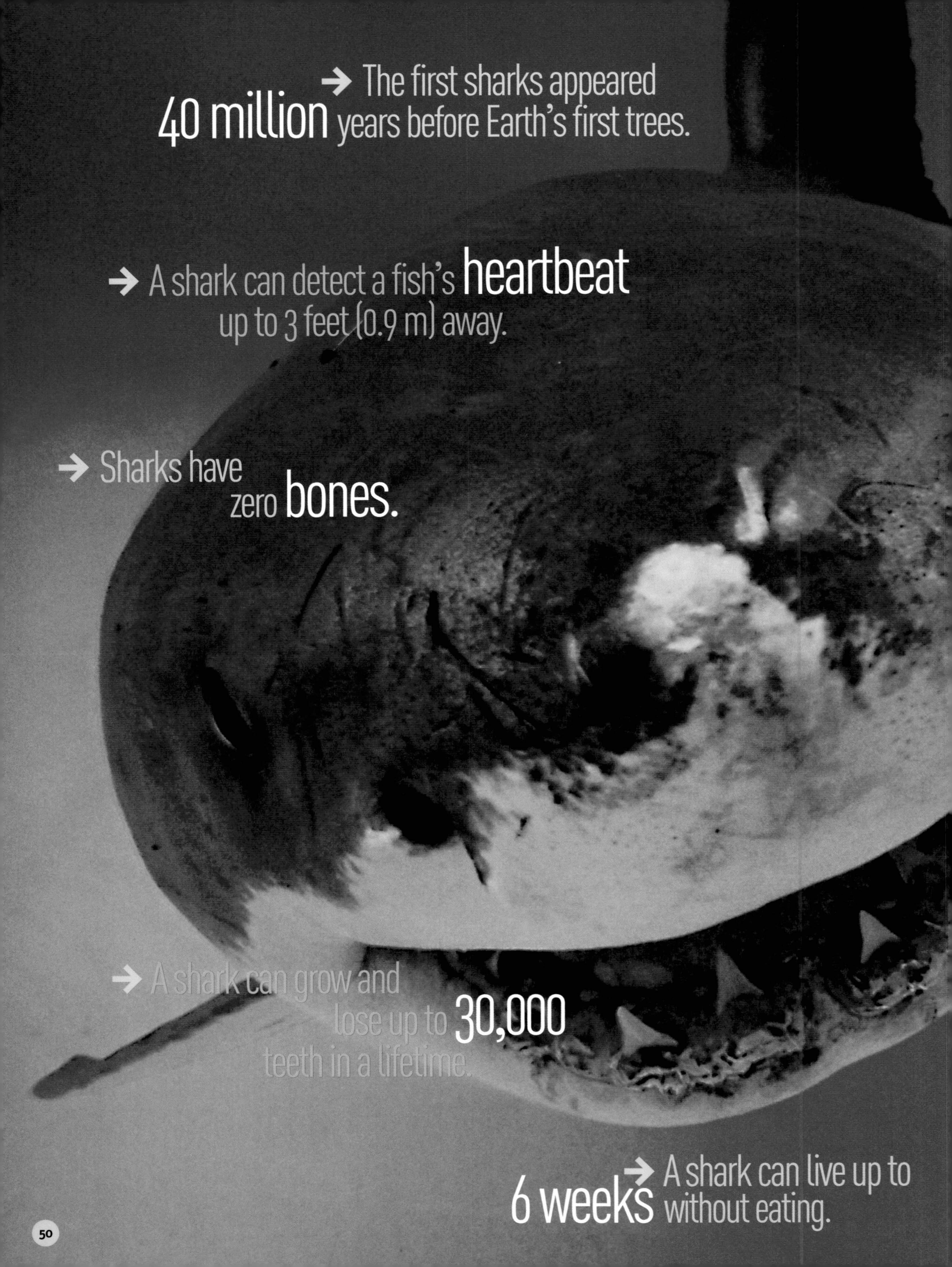

→ The first sharks appeared **40 million** years before Earth's first trees.

→ A shark can detect a fish's **heartbeat** up to 3 feet (0.9 m) away.

→ Sharks have zero **bones.**

→ A shark can grow and lose up to **30,000** teeth in a lifetime.

→ A shark can live up to **6 weeks** without eating.

A GREAT WHITE SHARK

can weigh as much as

15 gorillas.

[POPULATION EXPLOSION]

BY THE END OF 2011, YOU WILL BE ONE OF

7 BILLION

PEOPLE LIVING ON EARTH.

IF ALL 7 BILLION GOT TOGETHER TO HAVE A **PARTY** (COMPLETE WITH SPACE TO DANCE), WE WOULD NEED A VENUE THE SIZE OF **RHODE ISLAND!**

ABOUT EVERY **SECOND,** 5 PEOPLE ARE **BORN** AND 2 PEOPLE **DIE.**

IF ALL **7 BILLION PEOPLE** ON EARTH STOOD SHOULDER TO SHOULDER TO TAKE A GROUP PHOTO, WE WOULD **FILL** THE ENTIRE CITY OF **LOS ANGELES.**

IN 1975, ONLY **3** CITIES WORLDWIDE TOPPED **10 MILLION** RESIDENTS. TODAY, **21** OF THESE **MEGACITIES** EXIST.

IT WOULD TAKE **200 YEARS** JUST TO COUNT TO 7 BILLION OUT LOUD.

IN **1800**, THE **WORLD'S** POPULATION WAS **1 BILLION**. BY 2045, IT COULD BE **NINE BILLION**

CURRENTLY, THE **HUMAN POPULATION** IS GROWING BY **80** MILLION **PEOPLE** A YEAR.

Storm WARNING!

FastFACTS

A hurricane can weigh 100 billion pounds (454 million kg)—that's the same as 160 million rhinos.

A storm cloud weighs as much as 24 million rhinos.

A hurricane is also known as a typhoon or a cyclone depending on where in the world it forms.

Hurricanes can unleash more than 2.4 trillion gallons (9.1 trillion l) of rain a day.

The largest land animal that ever lived was a hornless rhinoceros called *Indricotherium*. It lived 30 million years ago, weighed at least 15 tons (13.6 t), and was as tall as a modern-day giraffe.

[JUMPING CONTEST]

WHICH ONE HAS THE LONGEST LEAP?

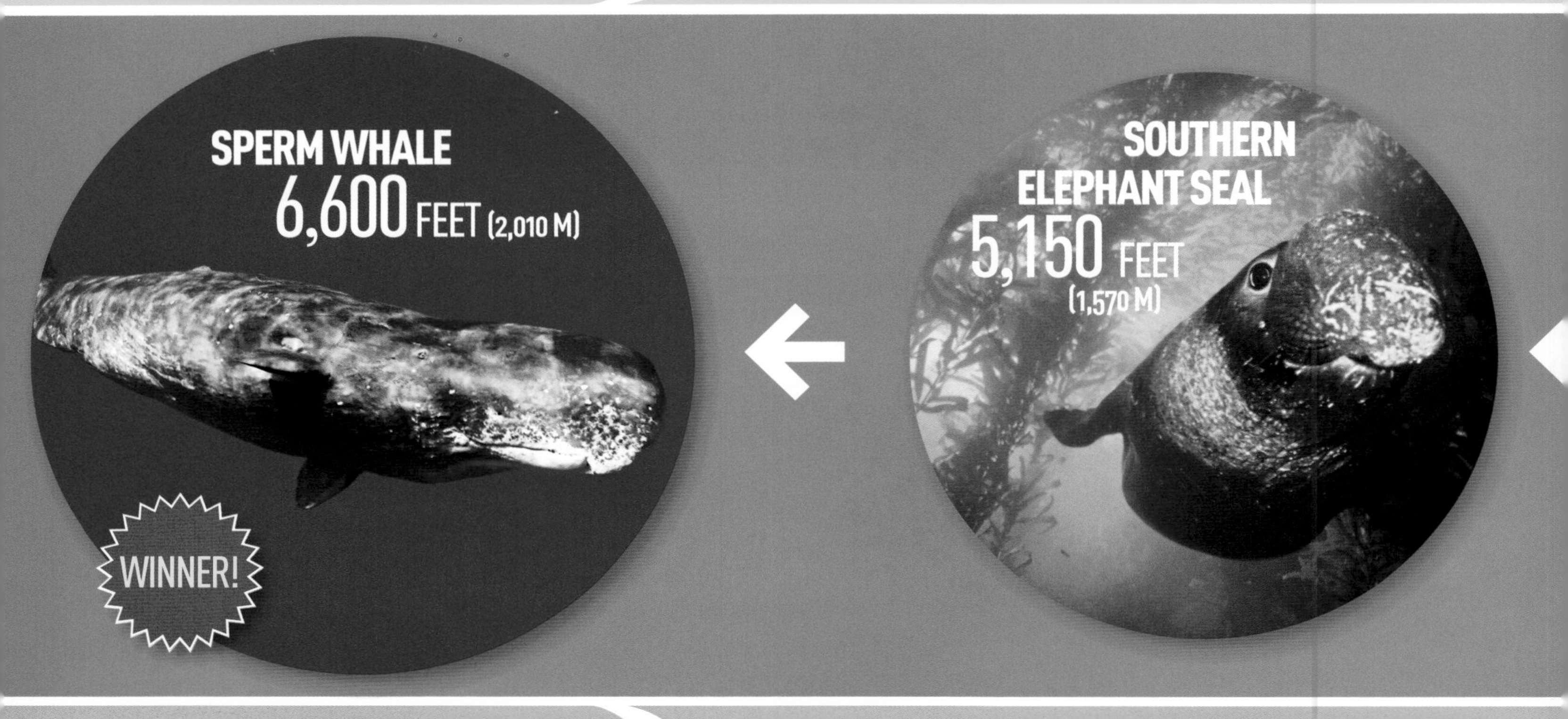

[CHOMP WARS]

WHICH ONE HAS THE STRONGEST BITE?

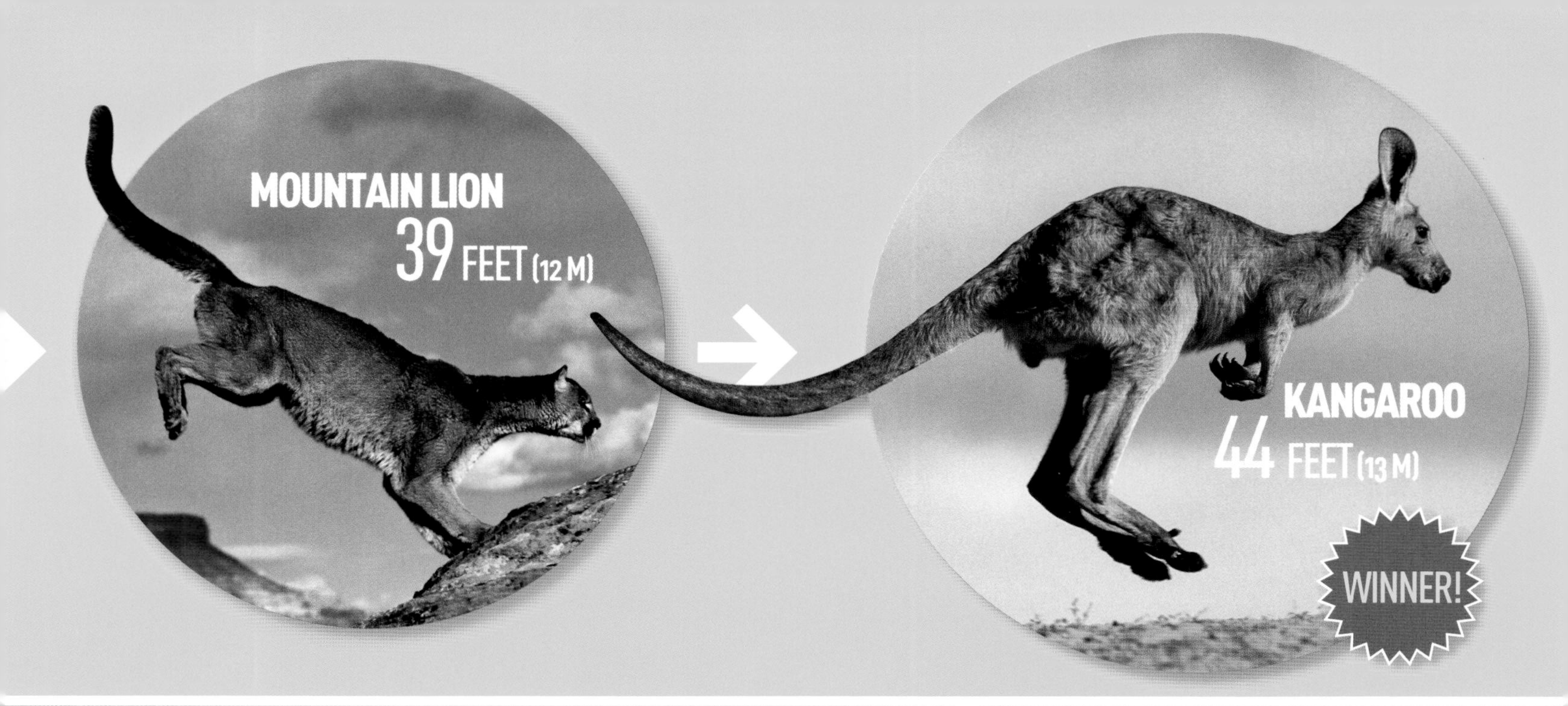

DIVING CHALLENGE

WHICH ONE TAKES THE DEEPEST PLUNGE?

8 Cool Facts ABOUT

NAKED **MOLE RATS** LIVE ALMOST **TEN TIMES** LONGER **THAN THEIR MOUSE** OR STREET **RAT** COUSINS.
(THEIR SECRET: THEY APPARENTLY NEVER GET CANCER.)

A GALÁPAGOS **TORTOISE** IN AN AUSTRALIAN ZOO LIVED TO BE ABOUT **175** YEARS OLD.

A FRENCH WOMAN HAD THE **LONGEST** DOCUMENTED **LIFE SPAN** EVER RECORDED. SHE LIVED FOR **122 YEARS** AND **164 DAYS.**

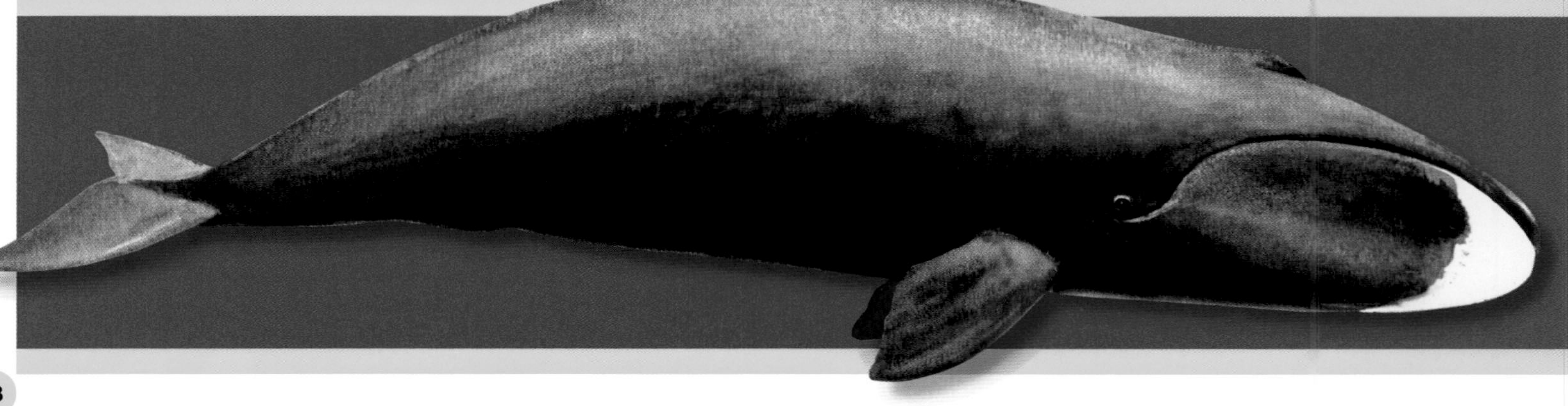

LIFE SPANS

A **405**-YEAR-OLD **CLAM**

FOUND IN **2007** WAS **ALIVE** WHEN **SHAKESPEARE** WAS **WRITING** ***MACBETH.***

THE **GIANT SEQUOIA** TREES OF **CALIFORNIA'S REDWOOD FORESTS** CAN LIVE FOR MORE THAN **3,000** YEARS.

TODAY THE **AVERAGE PERSON** LIVES **67** YEARS.

THE LIFE SPAN OF AN ADULT MAYFLY IS ONE DAY!

SCIENTISTS WERE **SHOCKED** TO FIND **STONE-TIPPED HARPOONS** FROM THE **1800s** IN SOME BOWHEAD WHALES' BODIES. NOW THEY BELIEVE THE WHALES CAN LIVE UP TO **200 YEARS.**

A GIRAFFE IS AS TALL AS A STACK OF 3 OSTRICHES, 9 KOALAS, OR 36 CHIPMUNKS.

KOALA = 2 FEET (0.6 m)
GIRAFFE = 18 FEET (5.5 M)
OSTRICH = 6 FEET (1.8 m)
CHIPMUNK = ½ FOOT (0.2 m)

Time in the Tub

Fast FACTS

All the things you use, do, and eat in your lifetime add up. There are some other numbers that show an American's average human footprint—the mark you make on the Earth.

You'll drink 13,056 pints (6, 178 liters) of milk.

You'll eat 4,476 loaves of bread.

You'll use 656 bars of soap and 198 bottles of shampoo.

You'll guzzle 43,371 cans of soda.

You'll spend $52,972 on clothes.

This parade
of 28,433
rubber ducks
represents the number of
showers
you'll take
in your lifetime.

If humans had the metabolism of a hummingbird, we would need to eat about 400 [hamburgers] a day.

Some HUMMINGBIRDS consume up to 8 times their body weight in nectar each day.

Why would an animal that can be as small as a thumb need to pig out in such proportions? Hummingbirds are the only birds that can hover like a helicopter or a bee. In order to achieve this aerial balancing act, they beat their flexible wings up to 200 times a second. This allows them to accomplish feats such as flying in one place, backward, and even upside down. Most importantly, hovering allows the birds to feed on the nectar of flowers. But because hummingbirds' in-flight aerobatics require so much energy, these tiny birds have big appetites to fuel.

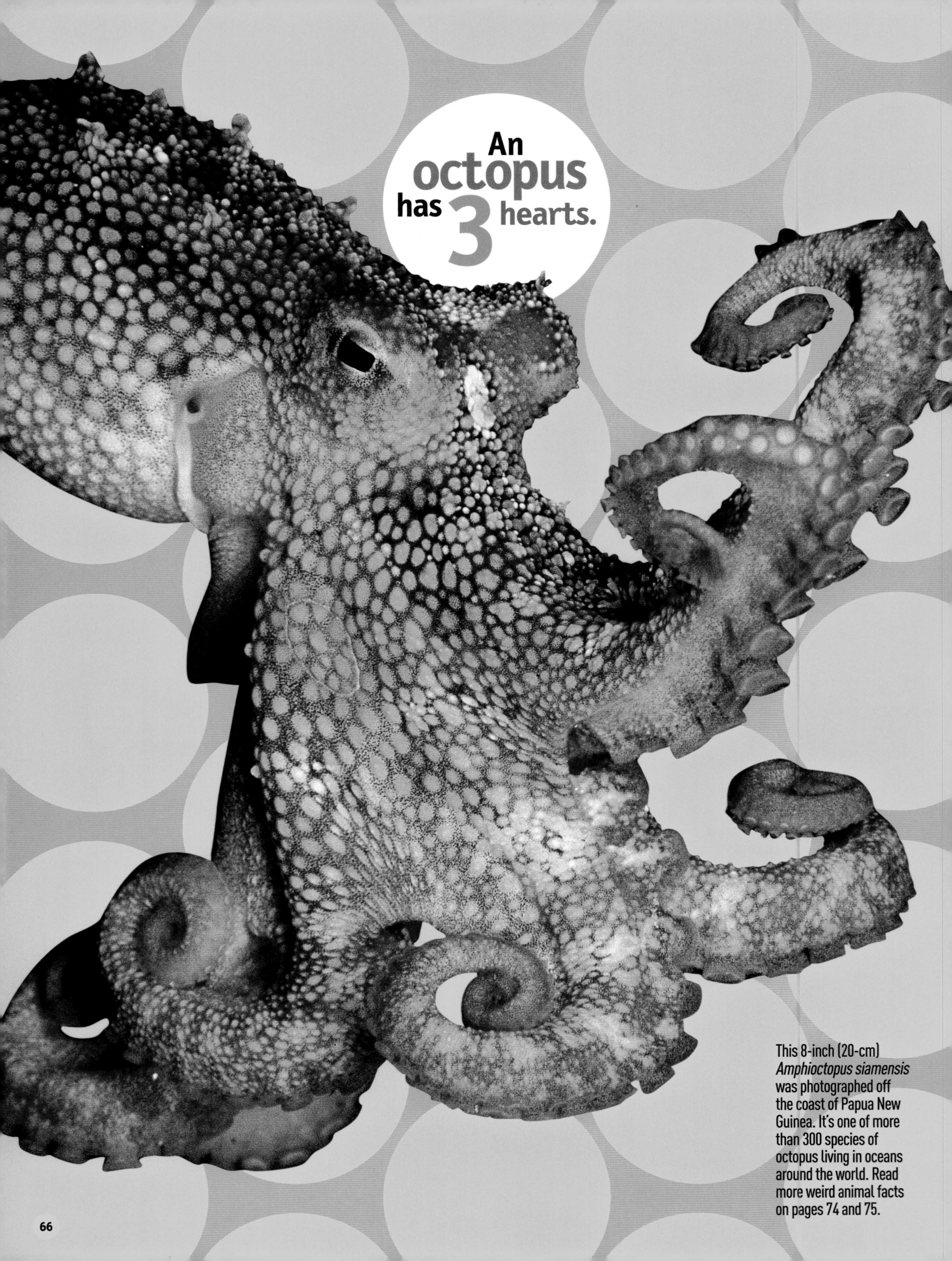

This 8-inch (20-cm) *Amphioctopus siamensis* was photographed off the coast of Papua New Guinea. It's one of more than 300 species of octopus living in oceans around the world. Read more weird animal facts on pages 74 and 75.

CHAPTER 4

FREAKS OF NATURE

It *once* RAINED FROGS in Kansas City, Missouri, U.S.A.

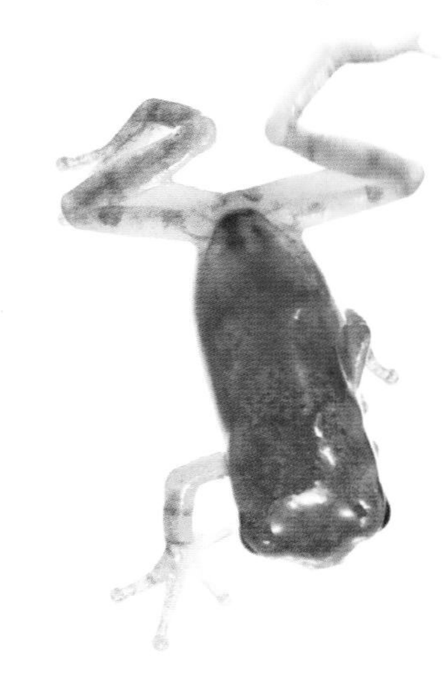

It has *also* RAINED worms, fish, toads, tadpoles, and birds in other places around the world.

(But, as far as we know, it has never rained cats and dogs!)

Last time we checked, frogs couldn't fly.

But tornadoes and powerful storms sometimes vacuum up the surface of ponds, including frogs, fish, and other animals that live in and near the water. When the storm breaks up, the animals fall from the sky.

TOOTHY TALLY

WHICH HAS MORE TEETH?

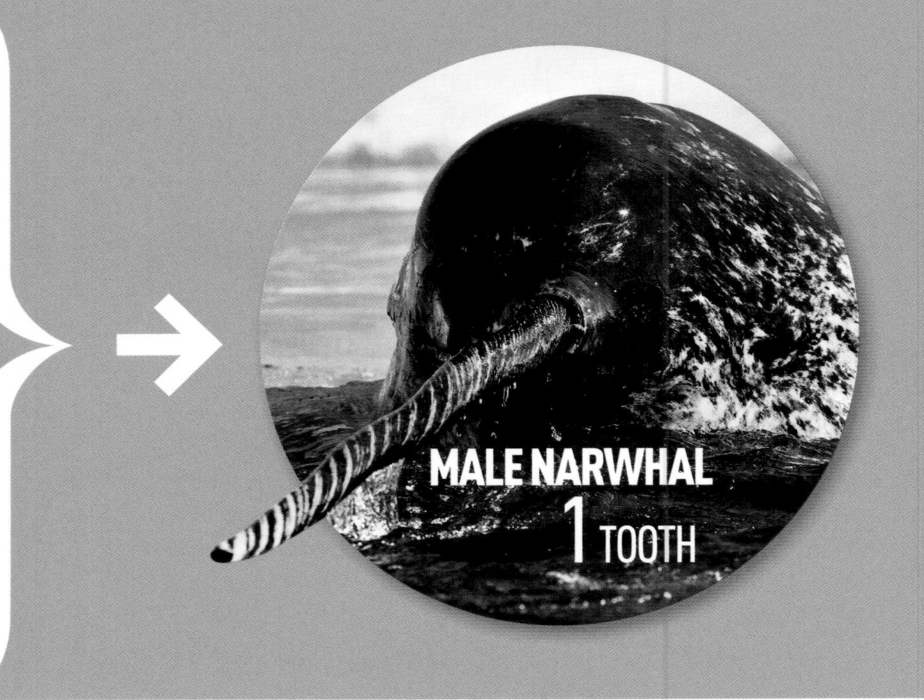

FUR-ST PLACE

WHICH ONE IS HAIRIEST?

[MEGA MUNCHERS]

WHICH ONE EATS THE MOST?

Over the Moon

THESE AMAZING FACTS ABOUT THE MOON WILL MAKE YOU AS SMART AS A ROCKET SCIENTIST.

It's IMPOSSIBLE to WHISTLE on the MOON.

A 100-pound (45-kg) PERSON WEIGHS about 17 pounds (8 kg) on the MOON.

There is NO WIND or SOUND on the MOON.

WITHOUT a SPACE SUIT, an astronaut's BLOOD would BOIL INSTANTLY.

JAMES B. IRWIN, an astronaut on APOLLO 15, became the EIGHTH person to WALK ON the moon on JULY 30, 1971.

The LAST PERSON to STAND on the moon was THERE in 1972.

More PEOPLE have TRAVELED to the MOON than to the DEEPEST part of the OCEAN.

APOLLO 15 ASTRONAUTS BLASTED back to the SPACECRAFT in the TOP of this LUNAR MODULE.
The MOON is moving 1.5 INCHES (3.8 cm) AWAY from EARTH every YEAR.
UNITED STATES
The BOTTOM of this LUNAR MODULE is STILL on the MOON.
APOLLO 15 astronauts DROVE this LUNAR ROVING VEHICLE a TOTAL of 17.5 MILES (28 km).
The SURFACE of the MOON is SMALLER than ASIA.
The MOON was likely CREATED when a CELESTIAL BODY the SIZE of MARS COLLIDED with EARTH!
It's a MYTH that PEOPLE act STRANGELY during a FULL MOON.

Furless Cat

WHERE IT LIVES:
in homes

WHY IT'S WEIRD:
Born with almost **no fur,** these cats can cost as much as **$3,000.**

World's WEiRDEST Animals

Liger

WHERE IT LIVES:
only in zoos

WHY IT'S WEIRD:
This half lion, half tiger has a **lion's face** and a **tiger's stripes**—a big cat combo that would never occur in nature.

Zedonk

WHERE IT LIVES:
wildlife preserve

WHY IT'S WEIRD:
Her mom is a **donkey,** and her dad is a **zebra.** The result? A donkey's brown **coat** on top and a zebra's **striped** legs.

Star-nosed Mole

WHERE IT LIVES:
North America

WHY IT'S WEIRD:
Twenty-two pink **tentacles** on its **nose** help the mole feel its way around.

Bubble-eye Goldfish

WHERE IT LIVES:
aquariums only

WHY IT'S WEIRD:
The fluid-filled sacs around its **eyes** are so **big** and **heavy** that the fish can barely lift its **head.**

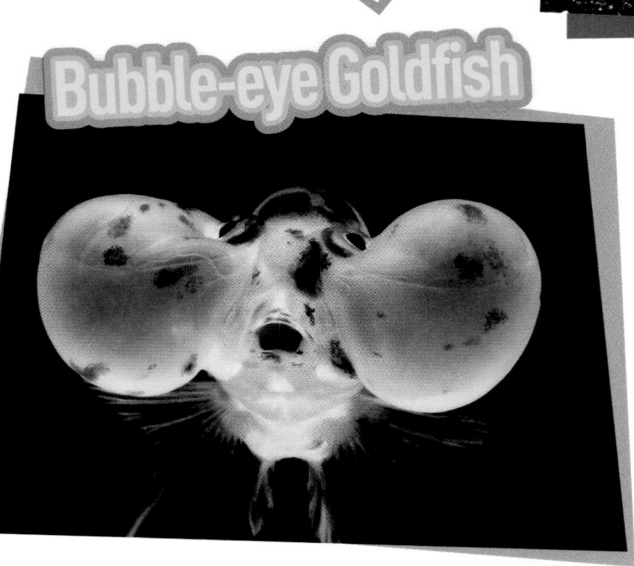

Proboscis Monkey

WHERE IT LIVES:
Borneo

WHY IT'S WEIRD:
A male's **nose** can be 7 inches (18 cm) long—as long as a pencil. Scientists think the supersized **schnoz** attracts females.

Frilled Lizard

WHERE IT LIVES:
Australia and New Guinea

WHY IT'S WEIRD:
When this lizard gets freaked out, its hood **flares** out, its mouth opens **wide,** and it stands up on two back legs. Then it **sprints** for the nearest tree.

CATS CANNOT TASTE SWEET FLAVORS.

A SHARK COULD SMELL A DROP OF BLOOD IN A SWIMMING POOL.

SOME MOTHS DROP FROM THE AiR WHEN THEY HEAR A BAT NEARBY.

KiDS CAN HEAR SOUNDS SOME ADULTS CANNOT.

THE NEARLY 9-FOOT (2.74-M)-TALL CORPSE FLOWER SMELLS LIKE ROTTEN MEAT AND WEIGHS 170 POUNDS (77 KG).

THE OCEAN MAKES A SOUND CALLED A BLOOP THAT CAN BE HEARD MORE THAN 3,100 MILES (5,000 KM) AWAY.

WALRUSES FEEL WITH THEIR WHISKERS, LIKE WE DO WITH OUR FINGERTIPS.

A SPiDER HEARS USING TiNY HAIRS ON ITS LEGS.

PEOPLE HAVE TASTE RECEPTORS IN THEIR LUNGS.

You DRINK the same
WATER
as the
dinosaurs!

You *also* DRINK the same water as woolly mammoths, the first humans, and King Tut.

Earth has been recycling water for more than four billion years. Earth has no more or less water now than at any other time, including when George Washington, Cleopatra, or the dinosaurs were around. Water constantly evaporates from streams, rivers, and oceans into the sky. Some water even stays trapped in ice sheets. Rain, snow, and sleet bring evaporated water back to Earth. Then the whole process starts over again. So all of the water on Earth now has been here since Earth began.

This LIGHTHOUSE turned into a giant ice sculpture during a WINTER STORM— and stayed that way for two weeks!

Fast FACTS

NAME: Cleveland Harbor West Pierhead Lighthouse

LOCATION: Lake Erie and Cuyahoga River, Cleveland, Ohio, U.S.A.

HEIGHT: 67 feet (20 m)

BUILT: 1911

FROZE: 2010

DEEP FREEZE

En-*light*-ening TRIVIA

1. Sailors can hear the lighthouse's foghorn 12 miles (19 km) away and see its light from 10 miles (16 km) away.
2. The lighthouse operates on solar power.
3. The first lighthouse was built between 300 B.C. and 280 B.C. in Egypt.

WIND AND WAVES POUNDED AGAINST THE BUILDING, AND WATER FROZE AS IT HIT THE LIGHTHOUSE.

THE LIGHT INSIDE WAS AUTOMATED IN 1965, SO THERE'S NO ONE INSIDE.
THIS IS THE FOG SIGNAL BUILDING.
CANADA IS 50 MILES (80 KM) NORTH.
THE LIGHTHOUSE IS ACCESSIBLE ONLY BY BOAT.

FREAKY Weather

Snow Rollers

WHY IT'S FREAKY:
Snowballs **roll themselves.**

HOW IT HAPPENS: Strong **winds** can roll **snowballs** when new snow falls and can't stick to slippery ice underneath.

Super Tornado

WHY IT'S FREAKY:
With **winds of up to 300 miles** an hour (480 kph), these high-speed tornadoes are so destructive they can **rip pavement** off the streets and derail trains.

HOW IT HAPPENS:
Supercell **thunderstorms** sometimes spin into huge horizontal cyclones, called **mesocyclones.** If these spinning storms tip down and **touch down** on the ground, they become terrifying twisters!

Confused Rainbows

WHY IT'S FREAKY:
Called **circumzenithal** arcs, these rainbows are **upside down!**

HOW IT HAPPENS:
They are usually seen in **colder** areas because they are caused by the refraction of light through **ice crystals** rather than raindrops.

Tube-Shaped Clouds

WHY IT'S FREAKY:
Every year these **odd** clouds form over northern Australia and stretch for **620 miles** (1,000 km).

HOW IT HAPPENS:
The tube shape clouds form when a sea breeze **collides** with a shallow layer of **cold air.**

WHY IT'S FREAKY:
Ten-story-tall waves form in the middle of the ocean, even in **mild weather** conditions.

HOW IT HAPPENS:
What causes a **freak wave** is a complete **mystery.**

Rogue Waves

Fire Whirls

WHY IT'S FREAKY:
It's a **tornado** made of **fire!**

HOW IT HAPPENS:
When heat from a **wildfire** causes air to rise and fresh air swoops in, it can create a fire **tornado** that can be 50 feet (15 m) wide and **40 stories tall.**

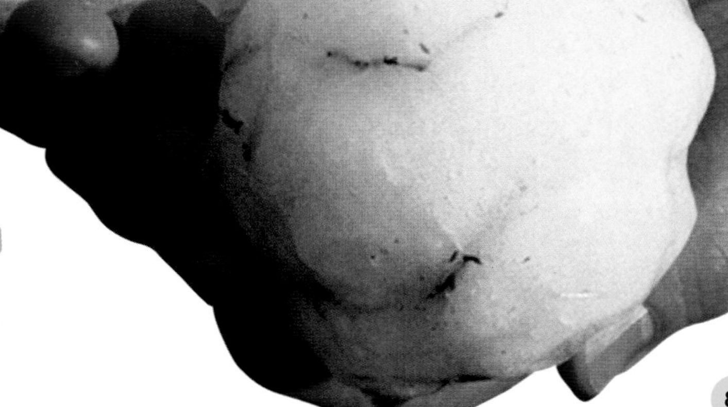

Grapefruit-size Hail

WHY IT'S FREAKY:
Giant hailstones **plummet** to Earth at about a hundred miles an hour (160 kph).

HOW IT HAPPENS:
Huge hail is created when updrafts carry raindrops as high as **50,000** feet (15,240 m). The **longer** the hail is carried by the wind, the more **ice crystals** it collects and the more **supersized** it becomes.

A FLEA JUMPS more than 130 TIMES its height.

BOTTLENOSE DOLPHIN—1,560 FEET (476 M)

If other **ANIMALS** could jump that **HIGH**, they would leap...

10-YEAR-OLD KID—
590 FEET (180 M)

EMPEROR PENGUIN—
490 FEET (150 M)

FRENCH BULLDOG—
130 FEET (40 M)

Cheetahs can change direction in midair when chasing prey.

What's faster than a cheetah? Not much! The world's fastest land mammals, cheetahs live in parts of Africa and Iran. These cool cats have existed on Earth for about four million years! For more fast facts, turn to page 100.

CHAPTER 5

On the Move

SiNK OR SWiM?

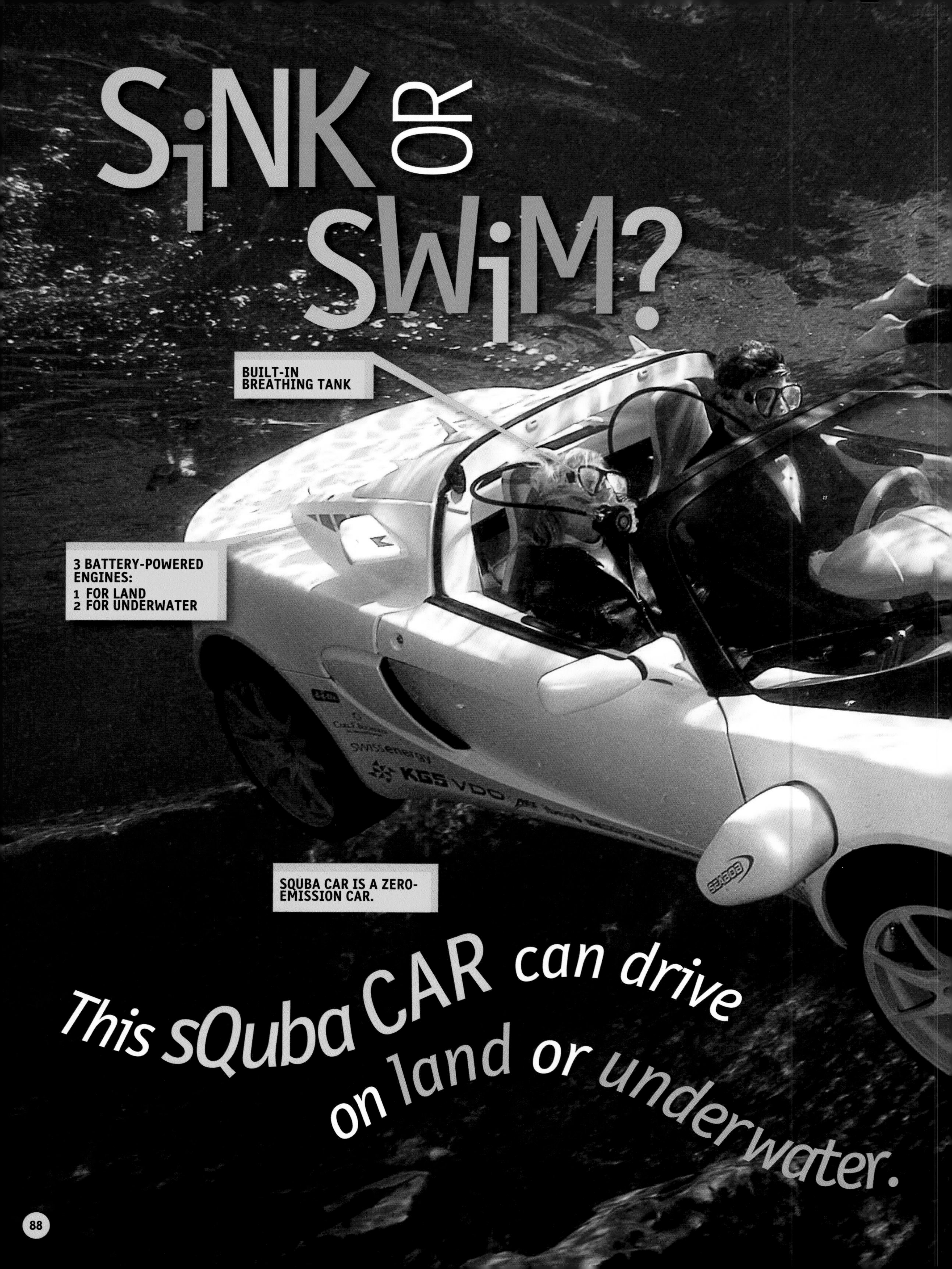
BUILT-IN BREATHING TANK
3 BATTERY-POWERED ENGINES:
1 FOR LAND
2 FOR UNDERWATER
SQUBA CAR IS A ZERO-EMISSION CAR.
SWISSenergy
KGS VDO
SEABOB

This sQuba CAR can drive on land or underwater.

My scooter is 5x faster than your car!

WHY A CONVERTIBLE? THE OPEN ROOF DOUBLES AS AN EMERGENCY EXIT!

INTERIOR DECORATED WITH MOTHER-OF-PEARL AND DIAMONDS

FastFACTS

NAME: sQuba car

COST: $1.75 million

MAX. LAND SPEED: 75 mph (120 kph)

MAX. WATER SURFACE SPEED: 4 mph (6 kph)

MAX. UNDERWATER SPEED: 1.8 mph (3 kph)

INSPIRED BY: aquatic car in the classic James Bond movie *The Spy Who Loved Me*

HOW TO PASS A DRIVER'S TEST

1. Put on a breathing mask.
2. Buckle up to avoid floating away.
3. Drive into the ocean.
4. Open doors to let in water and begin to sink.
5. Accelerate, plunging 30 feet (9 m).
6. Adjust the thrust to make the car resurface.
7. Back on land? A laser system can drive the car... without a driver!

THIS MOUSE HITCHED A RIDE ON A FROG'S BACK TO ESCAPE A FLOODED STREET IN LUCKNOW, INDIA.

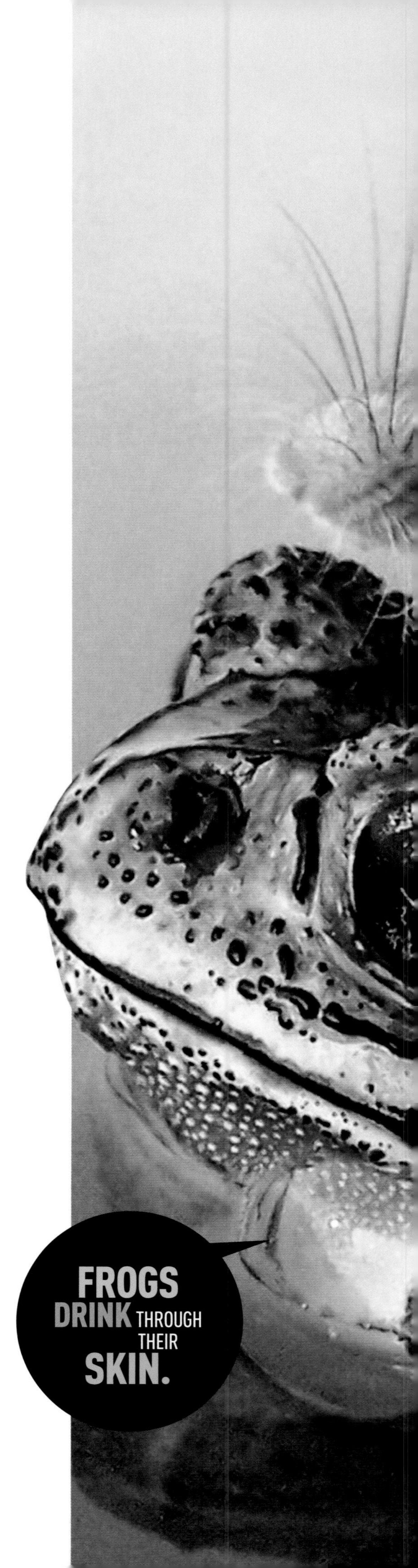

FROGS DRINK THROUGH THEIR SKIN.

WHEN **MICE SWIM** THEY USE THEIR **TAILS** LIKE MOTORS TO PROPEL THEM IN THE **WATER.**

FROG BONES GROW NEW **RINGS** AS THEY AGE, JUST LIKE **TREES.**

FASTER THAN THE SPEED OF SOUND

AS THE JET BREAKS THROUGH THE CLOUD, THE RELEASE OF AIR PRESSURE SENDS SHOCK WAVES TO THE GROUND, CAUSING A THUNDEROUS NOISE ALSO KNOWN AS A SONIC BOOM.

THE CLOUD IS A CLUSTER OF CONDENSATION THAT CAN FORM JUST AS THE JET BREAKS THE SOUND BARRIER.

SOUND TRAVELS MORE SLOWLY IN COLDER TEMPERATURES.

THE SPEED OF SOUND IS FASTER IN WATER THAN IN AIR.

TWO POWERFUL ENGINES HELP THIS JET REACH A TOP SPEED OF MACH 1.8—ALMOST TWICE THE SPEED OF SOUND.

WHEN AN OBJECT REACHES MACH 1, IT IS TRAVELING AT THE SPEED OF SOUND.

FastFACTS

NAME: Boeing F/A-18F Super Hornet

COST: $57 million

MAX. AIR SPEED: 1,190 mph (1,915 kph)

MAX. FLYING ALTITUDE: 50,000 feet (15,240 m)

This AIRCRAFT is breaking the SOUND BARRIER at 741 MILES (1,193 kph) an hour.

Full SPEED AHEAD

Space shuttles in orbit travel at around Mach 22—23.35 times the speed of sound.

A jet-powered car called the ThrustSSC can top 764 mph (1,229 kph)—slightly more than one percent faster than the speed of sound.

An airforce pilot came close to breaking the sound barrier when he skydived from 102,800 feet (31,333 m) above Earth at a speed of 614 mph (988 kph), or Mach 0.83.

WeiRd WayS TO GET ArOUND

THIS DRIVABLE HIGH-HEELED **SHOE** IS MADE OUT OF SPARE **MOTORCYCLE PARTS.**

FIFI, THE 13-FOOT-TALL (4-m), 1,500-POUND (680-kg) **POODLE,** CAN TRAVEL ON LAND, WATER, AND THROUGH MUD.

THE **TOP BUN** OF THIS **"HAMBURGER HARLEY"** FLIPS OPEN FOR EASY ACCESS TO THE DRIVER'S **SEAT.**

A TEAM PEDALED 1,159.7 MILES (1,866.4 km) IN 28 DAYS ON THIS TRICYCLE BUILT FOR SEVEN.

THE HORN OF THIS "COWASAKI" MOTORCYCLE MAKES A MOOING SOUND.

EVERY PART OF THIS MONOWHEEL—FROM THE HANDLEBARS TO THE ENGINE—SITS INSIDE A GIANT WHEEL MADE FROM MOTORCYCLE TIRES.

UNLIKE A SKATEBOARD, THESE WHIRRING ORBITWHEEL SKATES LET YOU SKATE EVEN ON GRASS!

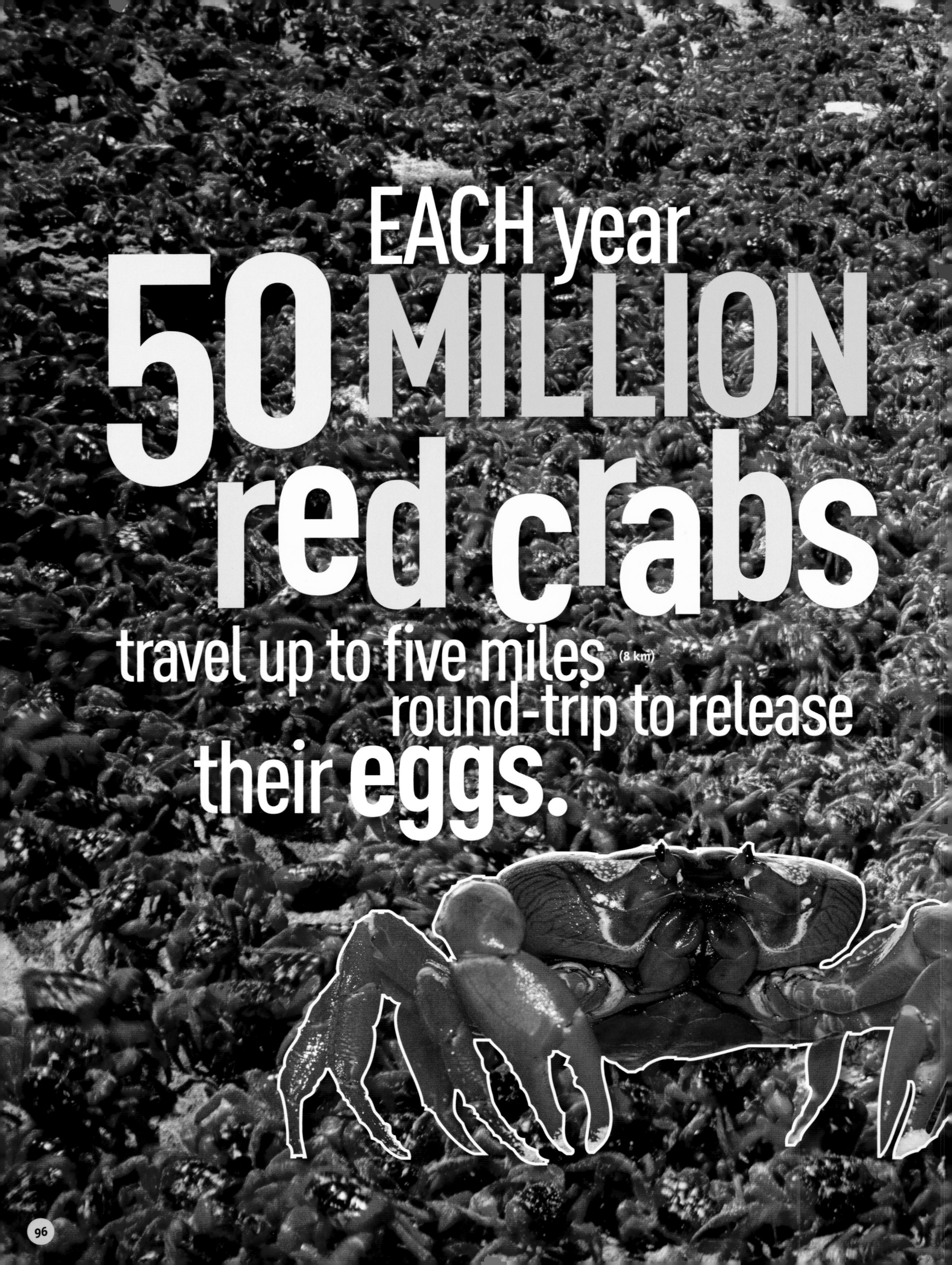

EACH year 50 MILLION red crabs travel up to five miles (8 km) round-trip to release their **eggs.**

WILDEBEESTS, monarch butterflies, JELLYFISH, army ANTS, and MANY other ANIMALS also MIGRATE in groups of more than a MILLION.

ultimate secret revealed!

So what's up with this massive movement of crabs?

The crabs live in the rain forest on Christmas Island, located in the Indian Ocean, northwest of Australia. The journey to the coast takes about ten days. Traveling in a giant group for protection from predators, the salad-plate-size crabs scale steep cliffs and face threats from cars and yellow crazy ants. When they finally reach the beach where they were born, the females lay up to 100,000 eggs each before trekking back to their forest home.

SKY WARS

WHAT FLIES THE HIGHEST?

ROUND & ROUND

WHAT SPINS THE FASTEST?

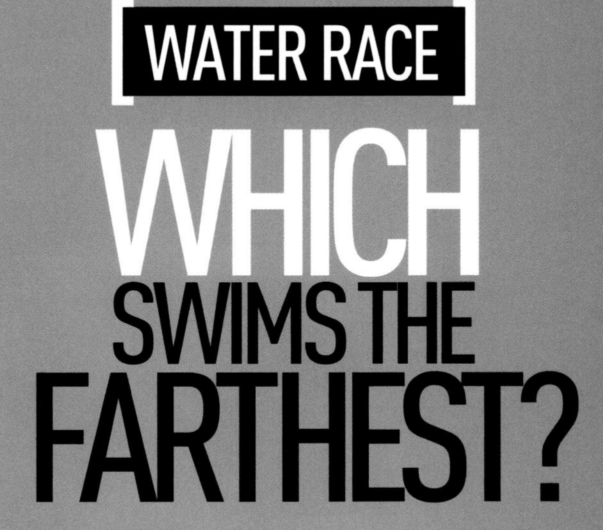

FASTEST RECORDED TORNADO
318 MILES AN HOUR
(512 kph)

THE FASTEST MAN ALIVE CAN SPRINT AS FAST AS 27 MILES AN HOUR. (43 kph)

ONE OF THE WORLD'S FASTEST SNAKES, THE BLACK

A SWORDFISH CAN SWIM ABOUT AS FAST AS A CHEETAH CAN RUN.

WITH SPEEDS REACHING 150 MILES (240 kph) AN HOUR, A ROLLER COASTER IN THE UNITED ARAB EMIRATES IS SO FAST RIDERS HAVE TO WEAR SAFETY GOGGLES TO PROTECT THEIR EYES.

CHEETAHS CAN ACCELERATE TO 70 MILES AN HOUR— (112 kph) THAT'S AS FAST AS A CAR SPEEDING ON A HIGHWAY.

THE SUPERFAST ELEVATORS IN TAIWAN'S TAIPEI 101 TOWER ZOOM 84 STORIES IN 37 SECONDS.

MAMBA, SLITHERS UP TO **12** MILES (19 kph) AN HOUR

A TRAIN IN CHINA CAN TOP **300 MILES** (483 kph) AN HOUR.

JET.

THE SR-71 BLACKBIRD MILITARY AIRCRAFT COULD FLY FROM NEW YORK TO LONDON IN JUST UNDER TWO HOURS—MORE THAN FOUR HOURS FASTER THAN A PASSENGER

PATAS MONKEYS CAN **SPRINT** FROM 0 TO 33 MILES AN HOUR IN JUST THREE SECONDS

THE FASTEST **TENNIS SERVES** REACH SPEEDS OF MORE THAN **150 MILES AN HOUR.** (240 kph)

WiLD Rides

Double Trouble

NAME:
Mirror Image

WHY IT'S WILD:
The shell of one Volkswagen is turned **upside down** on top of the other. And those legs sticking out? They belong to **inflatable dolls.**

Bugged Out!

NAME:
The Glass Quilt

WHY IT'S WILD:
About **10,000 marbles** and thousands of pieces of stained glass have been **glued** onto this car.

Auto Tune

NAME:
Pico de Gallo

WHY IT'S WILD:
A salute to **Mexican mariachi** music, this car has guitars, drums, a trumpet, a saxophone, an accordion, and hundreds of **bells** attached to it.

Cruise Control

NAME:
Titanic

WHY IT'S WILD:
With the **help** of some plywood and paint, this boat of a car was transformed into the **Titanic,** the famous sunken cruise ship.

Lobsterfest

NAME:
Art the Lobster

WHY IT'S WILD:
This **crustacean creation** has a giant fiberglass lobster on its roof. And its tail opens like a **car trunk.**

Road Show

NAME:
Mondrian Car

WHY IT'S WILD:
The owner of this art car **painted** the vehicle in the style of modern artist **Piet Mondrian,** and then made a matching roof sculpture and clothing.

Wagon Wheels

NAME:
Radio Flyer Wagon

WHY IT'S WILD:
This car is a **grown-up** version of a Radio Flyer wagon and doubles as **Santa's sleigh** in the winter—complete with a fake reindeer in the front.

In the MINUTE
it takes a
sloth
to move
5 FEET...
(1.5 m)

a human can walk 220 FEET.
(67 m)
a cockroach can crawl 295 FEET.
(90 m)
a greyhound can run 2,112 FEET.
(644 m)
a horse can gallop 2,677 FEET.
(816 m)

The British Imperial State Crown contains 2,868 diamonds, 273 pearls, 17 sapphires, 11 emeralds, and 5 rubies. It's stored with the rest of the Crown Jewels in the Tower of London. How long has this bling been there? Find out on page 116.

Britain's jewel-studded **IMPERIAL STATE CROWN** weighs more than a **FULL-GROWN** guinea pig.

CHAPTER 6

CLAIM to FAME

STRANGEST Restaurants

Want to **spice** up your **dining** experience? These **wacky** restaurants take eating **out** to the **extreme!**

Red Sea Star

This glass-roofed **underwater** restaurant in Israel allows diners to **gaze** at fish **before** they end up on a **plate.**

Modern Toilet

At this bathroom-themed restaurant in Taiwan, **toilets** double as **chairs** and the walls are covered with **showerheads.** Food is **served** in toilet-shaped dishes.

Dalu Robot Restaurant

A team of robots provides **service** with an **electronic** smile at this Chinese eatery. The robots **move** along a white **track** that passes all of the restaurant's **21** tables.

Here's a restaurant that can be **packed** up and **shipped,** stored, or saved for a sunny day. A Canadian company **recycles** old shipping containers by turning them into **cafés.**

Shipping Container Restaurant

Talk about a table with a view! A crane in Brussels, Belgium, lifts a table **160** feet (49 m) off the **ground** so patrons practically dine in **midair.** Diners are **buckled** into their seats for **safety.**

Dinner in the Sky

Carter balances on nylon webbing that's anchored between points. The line has some bounce, like a trampoline. Tightropes, on the other hand, are pulled rigidly taut.

Carter's fancy footwork is actually known as slacklining.

Thrill seeker Darrin Carter balanced his way across California's Lost Arrow Spire, 2,890 feet (881 m) off the ground.

Don't Look Down!

FastFACTS

Adili Wuxor walked a tightrope strung over the Bird's Nest stadium in Beijing, China, for 5 hours a day for 60 days.

In 1974, Philippe Petit walked a tight-rope wire between the World Trade Center towers. He was arrested for trespassing immediately afterward.

In 1867, Maria Spelterini became the first woman to tightrope walk across Niagara Falls. For added drama, she tried it blindfolded and then again with her feet fastened inside beach baskets.

Furry & Fabulous!

Party Animals

Some pets have birthday bashes that would put Hollywood stars to shame. One pup's party featured pony rides, a canine-safe cake, and a DJ spinning jams. Her birthday present: a diamond necklace!

CHALK IT UP TO PUPPY LOVE!

LAST YEAR, U.S. PET OWNERS SPENT ABOUT **$48 BILLION** ON THEIR PETS. HERE ARE SOME OF THE MOST OUTRAGEOUS WAYS PETS HAVE BEEN **PAMPERED.**

Clips & Curls

At pet spas, pooches can get a massage, have their nails done, or get a rainbow-colored dye job. One doggy ranch even has a bone-shaped pool!

Designer Duds

One pet owner says her cat refuses to wear anything but a rhinestone-studded leather collar. Dogs can get in on the act with $200 cashmere sweaters and $100 raincoats.

Dream Decor

Some felines live in the lap of luxury with $600 hand-carved furniture sets, such as four-poster beds and custom-built dressers. (A kitty has to have somewhere to keep her jeweled tiaras!)

Tropical Vacations

Many hotels offer special services for four-legged guests (on their owners' bill, of course). One Mexican resort has pooch-only pool cabanas. Some hotels have room service offering doggy delights.

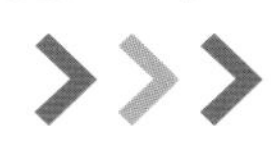

Pet Estates

You'll want to be in the doghouse with these posh doggy pads. One pooch has a two-story doghouse with floor-to-ceiling windows, air-conditioning, and heated floors.

8 Frightening

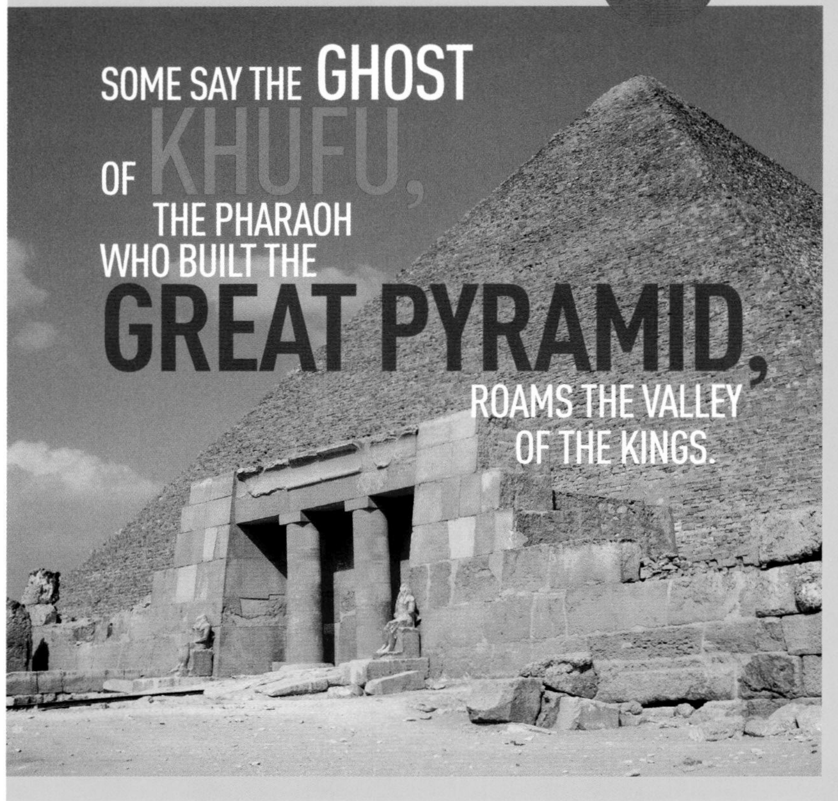

SOME SAY THE GHOST OF KHUFU, THE PHARAOH WHO BUILT THE GREAT PYRAMID, ROAMS THE VALLEY OF THE KINGS.

ACCORDING TO LEGEND THE GHOST OF ABIGAIL ADAMS, THE WIFE OF THE 2ND PRESIDENT OF THE UNITED STATES, DOES LAUNDRY IN THE WHITE HOUSE'S EAST ROOM.

WHEN PARIS'S GRAVEYARDS BECAME OVERCROWDED, SKELETONS WERE PILED HIGH IN THE CATACOMBS DURING THE 18TH & 19TH CENTURIES.

FACTS ABOUT CREEPY PLACES

THE **SKELETONS** OF AS MANY AS **40,000** PEOPLE

DECORATE **SEDLEC OSSUARY,** A CHAPEL IN THE **CZECH** REPUBLIC.

BRAN CASTLE IN **ROMANIA** BRIEFLY HOUSED **"VLAD DRACULA,"** A **15TH-CENTURY** TYRANT AND THE INSPIRATION FOR **THE MOVIE** ***DRACULA.***

DURING ITS **29** YEARS AS A **FEDERAL PRISON,** NO **INMATE** MANAGED TO SUCCESSFULLY **ESCAPE** ALCATRAZ ISLAND.

AT THE **CATACOMBS** OF THE **CAPUCHINS** IN **SICILY,** THOUSANDS OF **MUMMIES**—FULLY CLOTHED AND ARRANGED IN POSES—**FILL ROCK-CARVED TUNNELS.**

IN A **FRENZY** OF FEAR, VILLAGERS IN **SALEM, MASSACHUSETTS,** U.S.A., ONCE ACCUSED **185** YOUNG MEN AND WOMEN OF BEING **WITCHES.**

FunkyFortress
CHECK OUT THESE COOL FACTS ABOUT THE TOWER OF LONDON!
England's CROWN JEWELS are still GUARDED in the Tower's JEWEL HOUSE, a collection that goes back HUNDREDS of years.
The 35 Yeomen Warders and their FAMILIES are among the few still allowed to LIVE at the Tower. The Warders were established in 1509 as bodyguards.
The ghost of Queen ANNE BOLEYN, who was BEHEADED on ORDERS of her husband, KING HENRY VIII, is said to WANDER the GROUNDS.
During HENRY VIII's reign, the Tower housed the ROYAL MINT, which PRODUCED England's silver COINS.
Called the "WORD," the password changes every 24 HOURS and is a must-have to ENTER the Tower AFTER hours.
JESTER WAZ HERE
LONDON TOURS
HENRY WUZ HERE

In the 1400s, KING HENRY VI hosted huge TOURNAMENTS in which KNIGHTS with lances JOUSTED on horses.
A GOLDSMITH named John Barkstead supposedly HID more than $40,000 worth of stolen GOLD on the Tower grounds. It has NEVER been found.
Legend says if the RAVENS that live on the Tower grounds ever LEAVE, the Tower will CRUMBLE and a DISASTER will befall England.
JOHN SM
An imprisoned PRIEST once hacked through the STONE of his cell, SLID down a rope across the MOAT, and ESCAPED in a boat up the RIVER.
PROP OF KING
In 1204, King John kept a COLLECTION of ANIMALS, including lions, leopards, and elephants. King Henry III received a POLAR BEAR as a GIFT.

Going out of **town?** Take your **vacation** to the **extreme** with these **offbeat** accommodations.

Giraffes use their long **necks** to peek in on **guests** enjoying **breakfast** at this Kenya hotel.

Giraffe Manor

EXTREME Hotels

Dog lovers can satisfy their craze for canines at this **dog-shaped** hotel in Idaho, U.S.A. Inside a giant **wooden** beagle, you'll find a **sleeping** loft and a **reading** nook.

Dog Bark Park Inn

In this hotel in Berlin, Germany, an eight-story aquarium contains more than 1,500 fish. Guests can see the sea life up close by taking a glass elevator through the cylindrical tank.

Fans of J. R. R. Tolkien's *Lord of the Rings* trilogy (or the recent film versions) will love this New Zealand hideaway. It's based on the fictional houses of pint-size characters called hobbits.

Hobbit Motel

AquaDom

Alpha Resort-Tomamu

Sleep on an ice bed and dine from ice plates at this igloo-like inn in northern Japan. All rooms, including bathrooms, are made out of ice.

At this Costa Rican rain-forest getaway, a 1965 Boeing jet has been converted to a two-bedroom suite.

Hotel Costa Verde

Baseball Card MVPs

Honus Wagner

SHORTSTOP / PIRATES

Hall of Famer Honus Wagner was a shortstop in the early 1900s. Only 60 baseball cards were produced.

HIS HOTTEST CARD:
A card in near-perfect condition auctioned for **$2.8 million,** a record for a baseball card.

VALUE RATING: ★★★★★

AMERICANS SPEND UP TO $40 MILLION ON BASEBALL CARDS EACH YEAR.

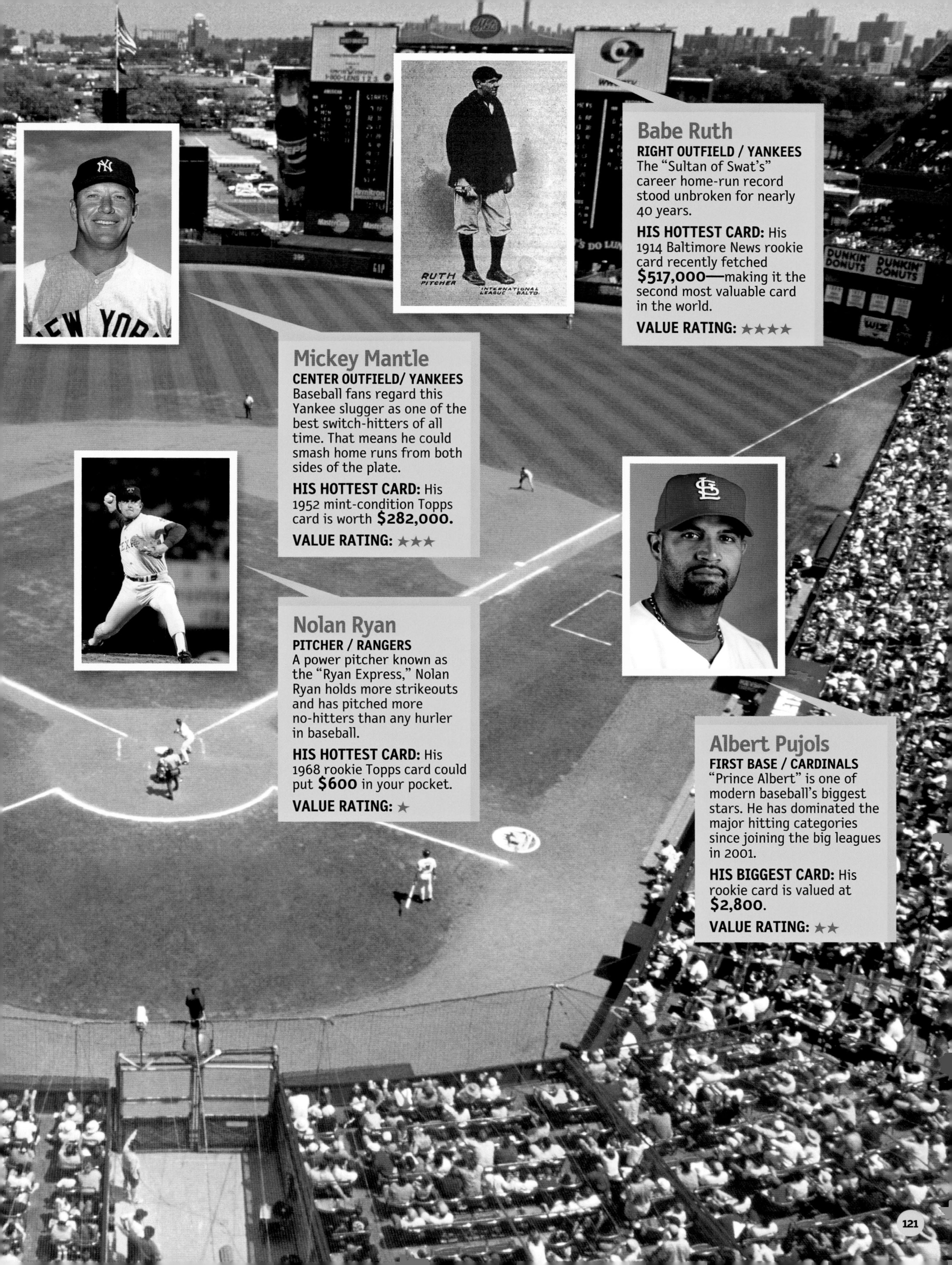

Babe Ruth

RIGHT OUTFIELD / YANKEES
The "Sultan of Swat's" career home-run record stood unbroken for nearly 40 years.

HIS HOTTEST CARD: His 1914 Baltimore News rookie card recently fetched **$517,000**—making it the second most valuable card in the world.

VALUE RATING: ★★★★

Mickey Mantle

CENTER OUTFIELD/ YANKEES
Baseball fans regard this Yankee slugger as one of the best switch-hitters of all time. That means he could smash home runs from both sides of the plate.

HIS HOTTEST CARD: His 1952 mint-condition Topps card is worth **$282,000.**

VALUE RATING: ★★★

Nolan Ryan

PITCHER / RANGERS
A power pitcher known as the "Ryan Express," Nolan Ryan holds more strikeouts and has pitched more no-hitters than any hurler in baseball.

HIS HOTTEST CARD: His 1968 rookie Topps card could put **$600** in your pocket.

VALUE RATING: ★

Albert Pujols

FIRST BASE / CARDINALS
"Prince Albert" is one of modern baseball's biggest stars. He has dominated the major hitting categories since joining the big leagues in 2001.

HIS BIGGEST CARD: His rookie card is valued at **$2,800**.

VALUE RATING: ★★

THE WORLD-FAMOUS HOPE DIAMOND IS RUMORED TO BE CURSED!

(AND IT'S NOT THE ONLY BAUBLE WITH BAD VIBES.)

BLACK ORLOV DIAMOND

Other **treasures** believed to bring their finders misfortune include **King Tut's tomb**, the **Black Orlov diamond**, and the **Delhi Purple Sapphire.**

DELHI PURPLE SAPPHIRE

Can priceless treasure really be cursed? Or is this myth just a gem of a tale?

KING TUT'S TOMB

In the case of the priceless blue Hope Diamond, bad luck seemed to have plagued its series of owners for more than 300 years. After the French royal family bought the stone in 1668, tragedy struck several members of the royal court, including King Louis XVI and Marie Antoinette. They were beheaded in the French Revolution. The families of later owners were plagued with debt, mental illness, and personal disaster. Yet today, the Hope Diamond resides safely in a museum, where thousands of people a year see it—without harm!

After King Tut's treasure-filled tomb was found, one of its discoverers died. The death sparked a flurry of rumors that the boy king cursed the tomb. In reality, the stricken man was killed as a result of an infected bug bite.

8 Weird FACTS ABOUT

EMPEROR JULIUS CAESAR THREW HUGE PARTIES ON THE STREETS OF ROME WITH AS MANY AS 22,000 TABLES PILED HIGH WITH FOOD.

IVAN THE TERRIBLE HAD A SECRET POLICE FORCE OF 6,000 BLACK-UNIFORMED GUARDS ON ALL-BLACK HORSES.

EMPRESS CIXI ROSE FROM A MIDDLE-CLASS FAMILY to be one of the MOST POWERFUL WOMEN IN THE HISTORY OF CHINA.

GREEK CONQUEROR

KINGS AND QUEENS

ACCORDING TO LEGEND,

ATTILA THE HUN, THE GREAT CONQUEROR, **DIED** OF A **NOSEBLEED** ON HIS **WEDDING NIGHT.**

NEIGHBORS PREDICTED THAT **GENGHIS KHAN** WOULD GROW UP TO BE A **GREAT LEADER** BECAUSE OF A **DARK MARK** ON HIS PALM at BIRTH. HIS **EMPIRE** BECAME THE **LARGEST** **EVER CREATED.**

The **UNITED KINGDOM'S** CURRENT MONARCH, **QUEEN ELIZABETH,** has a royal **YOUTUBE** CHANNEL.

MARY TUDOR, THE FUTURE **MARY, QUEEN OF SCOTS,** WAS **CROWNED QUEEN** WHEN SHE WAS **9 MONTHS OLD.**

ALEXANDER THE GREAT FOUNDED AN **ASIAN CITY** IN HONOR OF HIS **FAVORITE** HORSE, BUCEPHALUS.

Mexican axolotls are endangered and live only in the wetlands of Xochimilco, Mexico. Unlike most salamanders, they stay in a tadpole-like state into adulthood, and very few ever go on dry land. What's their cutest feature? A permanent smile! Read about more strange water creatures on pages 132 and 133.

CHAPTER 7

WHAT on EARTH?

CONJOINED TWINS OCCUR IN ALL SPECIES, INCLUDING FISH, SNAKES, COWS, AND EVEN PEOPLE.
THESE CONJOINED TWINS FORMED INSIDE THE EGG. THE EMBRYO STARTED TO SPLIT INTO TWO TURTLES, BUT DIDN'T SEPARATE COMPLETELY.
How about some frog legs?
TURTLES DO NOT HAVE TEETH AND SIMPLY SWALLOW THEIR FOOD WHOLE OR TEAR IT WITH THEIR BEAK OR CLAWS.

THESE TURTLE HEADS SHARE ONE BODY BUT THEY EAT ENOUGH FOR TWO.

→ Called Bracken Cave, this bat **hideout** is located near San Antonio, Texas, U.S.A.

→ It can take more than **three hours** for all of the bats to **exit** the cave.

→ The bats fly out every summer evening to feed, then return at **dawn.**

→ The **giant cloud** of bats shows up on the radar at a nearby airport.

→ Inside the cave, as many as **500 baby** bats squeeze into one square foot (30.5 cubic cm) to stay warm.

20 MILLION BATS LIVE in the WORLD'S LARGEST bat colony!

Strangest FISH in the Sea

Deep-Sea Anglerfish

WHERE IT LIVES:
Eastern and Northern Atlantic Ocean

WHY IT'S STRANGE:
This freaky-looking fish lives so deep in the ocean that it swims in complete **darkness**. A "fishing rod" juts out of its **forehead** with a lure at the end that is **luminous** to attract prey.

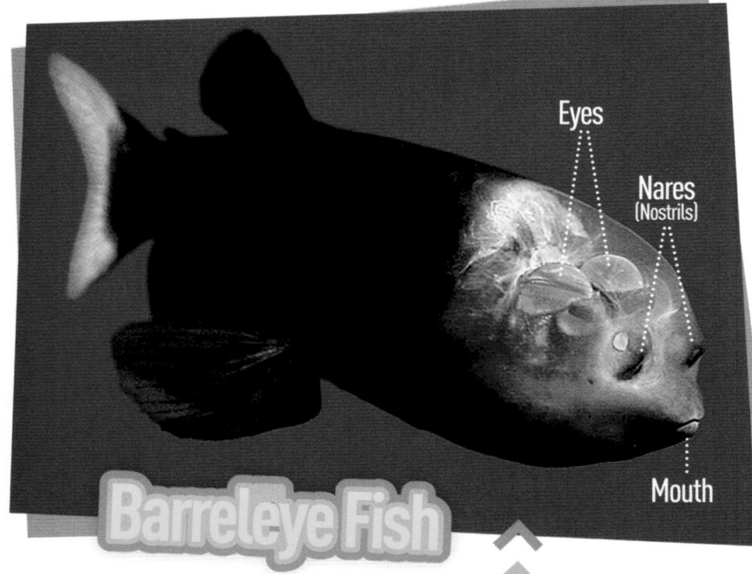

Barreleye Fish

WHERE IT LIVES:
Pacific Ocean

WHY IT'S STRANGE:
Its head is **see-through!** The fish's eyes **swivel** up and down, so it can look through its own head to **scope** out prey.

Wolf Eel

WHERE IT LIVES:
North Pacific

WHY IT'S STRANGE:
This **slinky** sea creature got its name because it **slithers** through the water like an eel, but it's actually a fish.

Leafy Sea Dragon

WHERE IT LIVES:
off the coast of Australia

WHY IT'S STRANGE:
The leafy sea dragon's plantlike look **camouflages** the fish in seaweed, where it can **hide** from predators.

Goblin Shark

WHERE IT LIVES:
worldwide in deep coastal waters

WHY IT'S STRANGE:
The shark's **bizarre beak** helps it sense prey. Then it **impales** its catch with those fang-like **teeth.**

Rosy-Lipped Batfish

WHERE IT LIVES:
tropical Western Atlantic Ocean

WHY IT'S STRANGE:
This "glamorous" fish looks like it's wearing **lipstick,** but that's not really makeup. The bright color may help members of the species **recognize** each other.

Blobfish

WHERE IT LIVES:
New Zealand coast

WHY IT'S STRANGE:
Officially called a **fathead** sculpin fish, this species was only recently discovered. The fish became an instant Internet sensation and even has a **Facebook** page.

This isn't really a nose; it's a flap of flabby skin.

This MUSHROOM GLOWS 24 HOURS a day and is BRIGHT enough to read by at night.

Fireflies, glow worms, click beetles, railroad worms, Malaysian land snails, fire centipedes, and other animals also glow!

ultimate secret revealed!

How do these mushrooms and animals turn on the light without flipping a switch? They are bioluminescent, which means they generate "cold light," or light that does not create heat. This natural glow is created when two natural chemicals, luciferin and luciferase, are combined within living things. Now that's an *illuminating* fact!

FROM SECRETS CARVED IN STONE TO HIDDEN MESSAGES SCRATCHED INTO THE EARTH, THE DISCOVERY OF SOME OF HISTORY'S MOST INTRIGUING MYSTERIES LEADS TO MORE QUESTIONS THAN ANSWERS.

EARTH'S Greatest Mysteries

Stonehenge

(Wiltshire, England, U.K.) About 4,500 years ago, people began creating this mysterious circle of stones. No one knows exactly how or why these ancient people transported the enormous stones, some as heavy as ten large African elephants, to this site.

Great Sphinx of Giza

(Giza, Egypt) For thousands of years no one knew who built the massive Sphinx statue near Egypt's two largest pyramids. Recent archaeological excavations found that it may be a self-portrait of Pharaoh Khafre—who built one of the pyramids—in the shape of the Egyptian god Horus.

Machu Picchu

(Near Cusco, Peru) The mountaintop city of Machu Picchu, built around 1460, was home to some 700 Inca, a group of South American Indians, until the people suddenly fled. Experts suspect the city was a sacred place, but exactly why it was built and then abandoned remains a mystery.

Nasca Lines

(Nasca, Peru) Alien landing strips? Mystical calendars? These are some of the far-fetched explanations for the 2,000-year-old giant drawings—best viewed from the air—of animals, people, and shapes etched into the plains. No one knows for sure, but the ancient Nasca people may have created the drawings to pray for rain.

Terra Cotta Warriors

(near Xi'an, China) When archaeologists unearthed a pit filled with thousands of life-size clay soldiers and other artifacts in 1974, they knew this was the work of China's first emperor, Qin Shi Huang Di. But they didn't know *why* he built this clay army 2,200 years ago. One possibility? Protection from his enemies' ghosts in the afterlife.

Moai Statues

(Easter Island, South Pacific) When Europeans discovered Easter Island in 1722, they found giant stone heads, now called moai statues. But where did the carvers of these 887 statues go? No people lived on the remote island, 2,300 miles (3,700 km) off the coast of South America. To this day, no one knows what happened to them.

Fast FACTS

NAME: Cave of Crystals
LOCATION: Near Chihuahua, Mexico
DEPTH: Almost 1,000 feet (300 m)
DISCOVERED: In 2000

CRYSTAL CAVES

Crystal CREATIONS

This underground crystal palace formed over hundreds of thousands of years. Groundwater mixed with minerals trickled through the cave and was heated by magma, or molten rock, from below Earth's surface. When the mixture cooled to about 136°F (58°C), the minerals began converting to selenite, which slowly formed the gigantic crystals.

THE LARGEST CRYSTALS ARE ABOUT 600,000 YEARS OLD.

This cave contains the WORLD'S LARGEST known natural crystals—one is as LONG as a school bus!

THESE EXPLORERS ARE WEARING SPECIAL COOLING SUITS SO THEY DON'T GET OVERHEATED.

SOME OF THE CRYSTAL BEAMS WEIGH AS MUCH AS 24 TONS (22 T)—THAT'S MORE THAN 3 AFRICAN ELEPHANTS.

A FINGERNAIL CAN EASILY SCRATCH THESE DELICATE CRYSTALS, WHICH ARE MADE OF A NATURAL SUBSTANCE CALLED SELENITE.

THE TEMPERATURE INSIDE THE CAVE IS A STEAMY 136°F (58°C).

IF 28 MILLION 10-YEAR-OLDS HELD HANDS, THEY COULD CIRCLE THE EARTH.

IF YOU WERE STANDING AT THE EQUATOR, YOU WOULD BE TRAVELING AT ABOUT 1,000 MILES AN HOUR (1,600 KPH).

YOU CAN SEE BRIGHT METEORITES, CALLED FIREBALLS, IN GREATER NUMBERS IN THE SPRING.

THE EARTH TRAVELED MORE THAN 5,000 MILES (8,000 KM) IN THE PAST 5 MINUTES.

THERE ARE SOME 50 EARTHQUAKES EVERY DAY ON OUR PLANET, BUT MOST ARE TOO WEAK TO FEEL.

THE EARTH ISN'T PERFECTLY ROUND. IT'S WIDER IN THE MIDDLE.

IT TAKES 23 HOURS, 56 MINUTES, AND 4 SECONDS FOR EARTH TO ROTATE, NOT 24 HOURS.

ABOUT ONE-SIXTH OF EARTH IS MADE OF IRON.

THE STUNNING STRIPES WERE EXPOSED WHEN THE OUTER ICE MELTED AWAY.

MOST ICEBERGS ARE WHITE, BUT SOME ARE GREEN OR BLUE.

AN ICEBERG IS A GIANT CHUNK OF ICE THAT BREAKS OFF OF A GLACIER OR ICE SHEET.

ICEBERGS CAN BE MORE THAN 5,000 YEARS OLD.

BLUE STRIPES CAN FORM IN ICEBERGS WHEN WATER FILLS CRACKS IN THE ICE AND THEN FREEZES.

LONG-LOST RELATIVES

Check out these totally *wild* cousins!

CHICKEN AND *T. REX*

WHAT'S THE CONNECTION?
Comparisons recently confirmed chickens and *T. Rex* share similar collagen proteins—components of the strong fibers in tissues such as tendons, ligaments, and cartilage. That's a strong sign they share the same genetic makeup.

FAMILY SECRETS: Shake a dinosaur's family tree and a bird falls out! Modern birds, such as chickens, are the living descendants of dinosaurs, such as the *Tyrannosaurus rex*!

PIG AND CAMEL

WHAT'S THE CONNECTION?
These two share a rabbit-size ancestor that lived 50 to 55 million years ago.

FAMILY SECRETS: To see the family resemblance, look at their toes. Pigs and camels both come from a long family line with an even number of toes on each foot. Also in the family? Cows and hippos.

WHALE, DOLPHIN, AND HIPPOPOTAMUS

WHAT'S THE CONNECTION?
They are all related to a four-footed and hoofed mammal that lived 50 to 60 million years ago.

FAMILY SECRETS: Over time, the family split. Whales (dolphins are part of the whale family) lost their hooves and stayed in the sea, while hippos became amphibious animals that now live in water and on land.

MANATEE AND ELEPHANT

WHAT'S THE CONNECTION?
They have a common relative that was about the size of a small dog and lived more than 60 million years ago.

FAMILY SECRETS: Though elephants and manatees don't look like long-lost twins, the structure of their hearts and the arrangement of their teeth are similar.

You can spot this fierce *T. rex* statue in a museum in Drumheller, Alberta, Canada. What else attracts dino-loving road trippers to the town? Find out on page 164.

CHAPTER 8

WILD & WACKY

FREAKY FOODS

Giant Cupcake

WHY IT'S FREAKY:
It took **24 hours** and 240 pounds (109 kg) of eggs to bake this **four-and-a-half foot** (1.4-m)-tall cupcake, which weighs more than two motorcycles!

The Big Cheese

WHY IT'S FREAKY:
A sculptor spent **40 hours** carving Abraham Lincoln out of a **1,000-pound** (454-kg) block of cheddar cheese.

Scorpions On Sticks

WHY IT'S FREAKY:
Though they may seem freaky to some, these **skewered** scorpions—deep-fried and sprinkled with spices—are considered a **delicacy** in China.

Bite-size Fast Food

WHY IT'S FREAKY:
Hope you're **not hungry.** The cheeseburger in this mini-meal is only an **inch** (2.5 cm) wide!

Square Watermelon

WHY IT'S FREAKY:
The melons, grown inside a **cube-shaped** glass box to get their square shape, cost about **$75 each.**

Jell-O Architecture

WHY IT'S FREAKY:
To create this **wiggly** replica of the Palace of Fine Arts in San Francisco, California, an artist filled special **rubber molds** with different colors of Jell-O. Each sculpture took a few **months** to complete.

WHY IT'S FREAKY:
At more than **200 pounds** (91 kg), this cake is a complete replica of a giant octopus, right down to the **tentacles** and suckers.

Octopus Cake

PEANUT BUTTER can be converted into a

ultimate secret revealed!

Anything that's made of carbon can be turned into a diamond. And every plant and animal on Earth is made up of some carbon. One recipe?

1. Squeeze peanut butter between two diamonds.
2. Expose to extremely high pressure at 3,632°F (2,000°C).
3. Take cover in case of explosion.
4. The catch? Only highly trained scientists in a special laboratory have ever done this.

DIAMOND.

So can
broccoli, flower petals,
butterfly wings,
& pencils

(and most natural things on Earth).

StreetWise
COOL FACTS ARE HANGING OUT AROUND EVERY CORNER OF THIS NEIGHBORHOOD. TAKE A TOUR TO IMPROVE YOUR STREET SMARTS.
Some CARS can run on used FRENCH-FRY oil.
A DOG can make about 100 different facial EXPRESSIONS.
Some FISH can WALK on LAND!
The ODDS that an average GOLFER will make a HOLE IN ONE during a game are 12,000 to 1.
POPSICLES were INVENTED by an 11-YEAR-OLD.
PARKING
ICE CREAM

The world's OCEANS contain enough GOLD to give 2 pounds (0.9 kg) to each person on the PLANET.
A SPACE SUIT weighs 280 POUNDS (127 kg) without an ASTRONAUT in it.
Your BRAIN is sometimes more ACTIVE when you SLEEP than when you are AWAKE.
An elephant's HEAD weighs up to 1,000 pounds (454 kg).
Traffic LIGHTS were invented BEFORE cars.
A dairy COW produces 100,000 glasses of MILK in a lifetime.
PARK
HELLO
Joe's
moo
moo

Festival FuN

ON INTERNATIONAL **PILLOW FIGHT DAY**—USUALLY IN MARCH OR APRIL—PEOPLE IN MORE THAN **130 CITIES** HOLD GIANT OUTDOOR PILLOW FIGHTS.

AT THE **LEMON FESTIVAL** IN MENTON, FRANCE, AN ARTIST MADE THIS REPLICA OF EGYPT'S GREAT **SPHINX STATUE** FROM ORANGES AND LEMONS.

YOU'LL SEE **DOUBLE** WHEN THOUSANDS OF TWINS GATHER AT THE **TWINS DAYS FEST,** HELD IN — WHERE ELSE?— TWINSBURG, OHIO, U.S.A.

AT THE **MONKEY FESTIVAL** IN LOP BURI, THAILAND, TOWNSPEOPLE SEEKING **GOOD FORTUNE** HONOR **MONKEYS** WITH FRESH FLOWERS AND FEASTS OF FRUIT, VEGGIES, AND SWEETS.

EACH **HALLOWEEN,** DOZENS OF DOGS DRESS UP IN THEIR **CUTEST COSTUMES** FOR A **PET PARADE** IN NEW YORK CITY, NEW YORK, U.S.A.

REVELERS AT **LA TOMATINA FESTIVAL** IN SPAIN **SLING** 100 TONS OF TOMATOES AT (90 t) EACH OTHER IN THE WORLD'S BIGGEST **FOOD FIGHT!**

8 Amazing FEATS BY

A woman in India danced for 123 hours and 15 minutes without stopping.

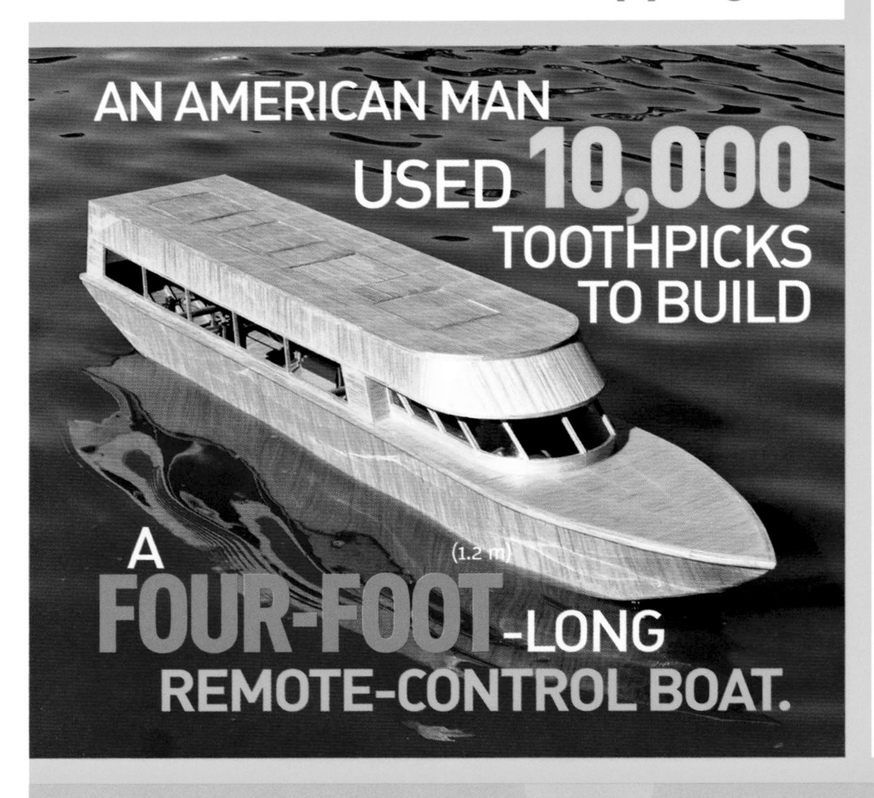

AN AMERICAN MAN USED 10,000 TOOTHPICKS TO BUILD A FOUR-FOOT (1.2 m) -LONG REMOTE-CONTROL BOAT.

A MAN WALKED ON HIS HANDS FROM VIENNA, AUSTRIA, TO PARIS, FRANCE. THE TRIP TOOK 55 DAYS!

AN ARTIST IN OHIO USED 26,666 bars of soap to sculpt a MASSIVE WINGED PIG named Sudsie.

WILD & WACKY PEOPLE

A SKYDIVER Indiana, U.S.A., parachuted out of an airplane 640 times in 24 hours.

A MAN IN THE U.K. GREW A GIANT ZUCCHINI THAT WEIGHED AS MUCH AS A LARGE SHEEPDOG.

A SCULPTOR created a statue of HIMSELF using his own HAIR, TEETH, and NAILS.

A NEW ZEALAND WOMAN RAN 100 METERS (328 FT) IN 18.5 SECONDS WEARING FLIPPERS ON HER FEET.

PEOPLE WHO COLLECT PEZ DISPENSERS ARE CALLED "PEZHEADS."
THE WORLD'S LARGEST PEZ-DISPENSING MACHINE STANDS 7 FEET, 10 INCHES (2.4 M) TALL AND HAS A SNOWMAN HEAD.
STAR WARS FIGURES ARE THE MOST POPULAR MOVIE-CHARACTER PEZ DISPENSERS.
AMERICANS EAT MORE THAN THREE BILLION PEZ CANDIES EVERY YEAR.
PEZ CANDY COMES IN TEN FLAVORS, SUCH AS CHERRY, CHOCOLATE, COLA, AND SOUR WATERMELON.
ONE MAN OWNS 5,000 PEZ DISPENSERS—ONE OF THE WORLD'S LARGEST COLLECTIONS OF THE PRODUCT.

A museum in CALIFORNIA, U.S.A., DISPLAYS MORE THAN 900 PEZ dispensers—ONE OF EVERY DESIGN EVER SOLD.

THE NAME PEZ IS A SHORTENED VERSION OF THE GERMAN WORD FOR PEPPERMINT, *PFEFFERMINZ.*

Silly Styles

THIS **SKIRT** DOUBLES AS A **VENDING MACHINE** DISGUISE WHEN YOU WANT TO **GO UNDERCOVER.**

>>>

THIS **ECO-FRIENDLY BAG** IS MADE FROM

365 RECYCLED COMPUTER KEYBOARD KEYS.

A SPANISH DESIGNER GLUED TOGETHER MORE THAN **200** COLORFUL **PLASTIC BALLS** TO CREATE THIS **"BALL GOWN."**

THESE **WEDDING GOWNS** ARE MADE OF TOILET PAPER. THEY COULD BE HANDY HANKIES IF THE BRIDE GETS **CHOKED UP.**

EVER GET SO HUNGRY YOU COULD EAT YOUR SHOES? **THESE "LOAFERS"** ARE MADE FROM **REAL BREAD** AND COME IN **WHITE AND WHOLE WHEAT.**

THIS HEADPIECE, MADE FROM CRUSHED AND CUT **SODA CANS** AND WIRE, IS HARD TO **TOP!**

THE ARTIST WHO MADE THESE AP-*PEAL*-ING **SHOES** CONSIDERS THEM **WEARABLE** SCULPTURES.

GREAT WhiTE Gator!

Anyone have sunscreen?

BOUYA BLAN IS NOT ALBINO. ALBINO ANIMALS HAVE RED OR PINK EYES; BOUYA'S EYES ARE BLUE.

THIS RARE REPTILE PROBABLY WOULDN'T SURVIVE IN THE WILD BECAUSE IT LACKS NATURAL CAMOUFLAGE TO HELP IT HIDE FROM PREDATORS.

BOUYA BLAN IS ONE OF 19 WHITE ALLIGATORS COLLECTED AS HATCHLINGS FROM A NEW ORLEANS, LOUISIANA, U.S.A., SWAMP. ONLY A FEW SURVIVED.

FastFACTS

NAME: Bouya Blan

WHAT: A 24-year-old alligator born with leucism, a genetic condition that produces little pigmentation, resulting in white skin and blue eyes.

WHERE: Gatorland theme park in Orlando, Florida

SIZE: 11 feet (3.4 m) long
500 pounds (227 kg)

WHITE GATORS CAN GET SUNBURNED.

BOUYA BLAN MEANS "WHITE FOG" IN LOUISIANA CREOLE.

There are only 15 known WHITE ALLIGATORS in the world.

Zany ROAD TRIP!

Peachoid Water Tower

WHERE:
Gaffney, South Carolina, U.S.A.

WHY IT'S ZANY:
It took **50 gallons** (189 l) of paint in 20 colors to get the perfect **peach** shade for this four-story water tower.

Dinosaur Capital of the World

WHERE:
Drumheller, Alberta, Canada

WHY IT'S ZANY:
This town is dizzy with dinos! Its land is rich in fossils, and prehistoric animals greet you wherever you go, from an 82-foot (25-m)-tall roadside dinosaur statue to the *T. rex* statue (above) at the town's paleontology museum.

The Leaning Tower of Niles

WHERE:
Niles, Illinois, U.S.A.

WHY IT'S ZANY:
Built in honor of scientist Galileo Galilei, this **water tower** looks—and leans—just like the real deal in Italy, only it's **half** the size!

Signpost Forest

WHERE:
Watson Lake, Yukon, Canada

WHY IT'S ZANY:
What started with **one sign** tacked to a post in 1942 has grown to a collection of **64,000 signs** today.

Fremont Troll

WHERE:
Seattle, Washington, U.S.A.

WHY IT'S ZANY:
Litterbugs, **beware!** This 18-foot (5.5-m)-tall troll's "job" is to stop people from **dumping trash** under a bridge.

Big Gumboot

WHERE:
Tully, Queensland, Australia

WHY IT'S ZANY:
The town of Tully built this 26-foot (8-m)-high **rain boot** to celebrate its title as the **wettest** place in Australia. The green tree frog is a nod to Tully's abundant amphibians, which thrive in the wet weather.

Cadillac Ranch

WHERE:
Amarillo, Texas, U.S.A.

WHY IT'S ZANY:
These spray-painted Cadillacs are stuck **hood-first** in a pasture.

This **LIFE-SIZE** transformer was made of parts from **100** of London's double-decker **BUSES.**

More than 60,000 Twitter users voted for the creation of the 13-foot (4-m) Transformer—called Bendy-Bus Prime—to celebrate the DVD release of a Transformers film. Check out another mind-boggling bot on page 182.

CHAPTER 9

INTELLIGENT LIFE

8 ANIMAL GENIUSES

AN ORCHESTRA OF 16 ELEPHANTS IN THAILAND CRANKS OUT TUNES ON JUMBO-SIZE XYLOPHONES, DRUMS, & CHIMES.

NORA, A PIANO-PLAYING TABBY, BEGAN MAKING "MUSIC" AFTER HOPPING ON A PIANO BENCH AND PUTTING HER PAWS TO THE KEYS.

TALK ABOUT FORTUNE-TELLING TENTACLES! AN OCTOPUS NAMED PAUL CORRECTLY PREDICTED THE OUTCOMES OF EIGHT 2010 WORLD CUP MATCHES.

in ACTION

BY ITS FIRST BIRTHDAY, A DOLPHIN CHOOSES A "SIGNATURE WHISTLE" THAT FUNCTIONS AS ITS NAME.

MANY ZOO ANIMALS "PAINT" TO WARD OFF BOREDOM, BUT A BONOBO NAMED KANZI ACTUALLY NAMES HIS PAINTINGS AS A HUMAN ARTIST WOULD.

CROWS FORM HOOKS OUT OF LEAF STEMS TO FISH GRUBS FROM HARD-TO-REACH PLACES.

MARGAYS, WILD CATS OF THE AMAZON, IMITATE THE CALLS OF MONKEYS TO DRAW THEM NEAR FOR A SNACK.

WHEN HONEYBEES NEED A NEW BEEHIVE, BEE "SCOUTS" COMMUNICATE NEW ADDRESS OPTIONS WITH DANCES. THEIR HIVE MATES VOTE ON A WINNER.

High-tech POLICE STATIONS will soar through the SKIES like airborne cruise SHIPS.
POLICE
Spaceport
Aquarium
Science Museum
One day, flying DRONES will deliver PACKAGES and PIZZAS.
BODY SHOP
HAMBURGER
ICE CREAM
TOURS
ROBO PET
BREAKFAST
OPEN
JAPANESE FOOD
TRAVEL
Cities will CREATE lanes for speedy PERSONAL transportation vehicles such as MOTORIZED CHAIRS and hoverboards.
Your CLOSET will contain just ONE all-purpose OUTFIT that can CHANGE shape and color depending on what you feel like WEARING that day.
2MORO

FutureWorld
FAR-OUT THINGS YOU CAN LOOK FORWARD TO!
CLONING technology could bring EXTINCT ANIMALS back to life.
HUMANS will call on ROBOTS to handle ROUTINE CHORES like walking the DOG.
POLICE will use HI-TECH "truth-sensing" GLASSES to help them know if a SUSPECT was involved in a CRIME.
DINOVERSE!
MEXICAN FOOD
ENJOY SAUCER CRISPS
Drive-Thru
OPEN
POLICE

COOL Inventions

These six amazing gizmos could ride the wave of the future.

Jetting Around

Blast off with a jetpack that sends its wearer aloft with two powerful fans. Controls on the jetpack's arms allow the pilot to adjust speed and direction, and an emergency parachute is included (just in case!).

Green Air Travel

This sleek, seamless airplane is a promising design for Earth-friendly flights. The lightweight, aerodynamic design of this blended-wing plane could cut fuel use in half.

Brain Games

By measuring brain activity, a device called MindSet allows you to control video games with your thoughts.

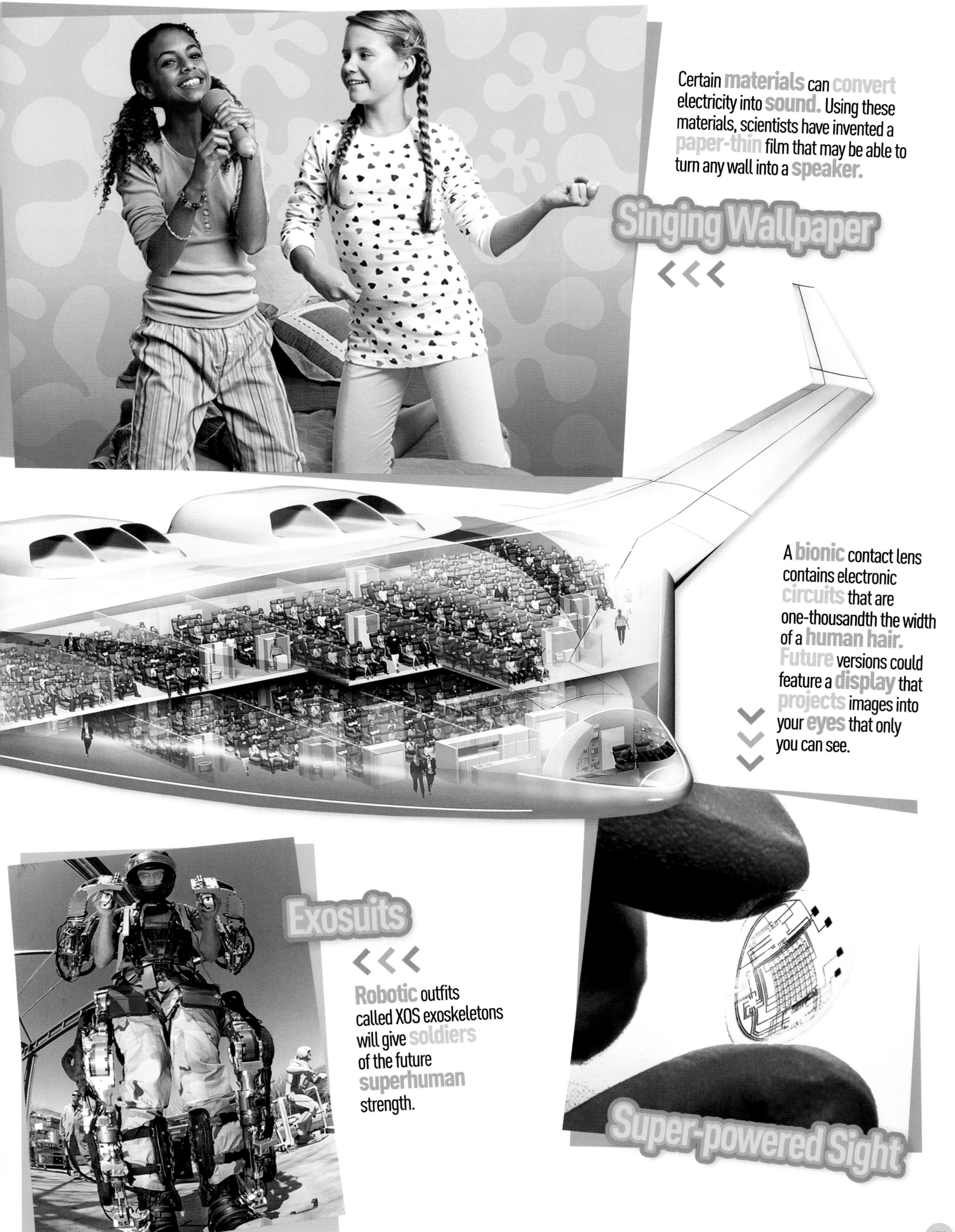
Certain materials can convert electricity into sound. Using these materials, scientists have invented a paper-thin film that may be able to turn any wall into a speaker.
Singing Wallpaper
A bionic contact lens contains electronic circuits that are one-thousandth the width of a human hair. Future versions could feature a display that projects images into your eyes that only you can see.
Exosuits
Robotic outfits called XOS exoskeletons will give soldiers of the future superhuman strength.
Super-powered Sight

GREENING the RED PLANET

One day humans might live on Mars. Here's how it could become the new Earth in 1,000 years.

YEAR ZERO
The project might begin with a series of missions to set up living quarters.

YEAR 100
Human-built factories that spew potent greenhouse gases work to boost Mars's atmosphere. The global warming that results from the greenhouse gas buildup will thaw the frozen planet.

YEAR 200
Rain would fall and water would flow once enough carbon dioxide had been released. Microbes, algae, and lichens could start growing on rocks.

Fast FACTS

Living in space can cause some weird side effects. By monitoring astronauts on shuttle flights and on the International Space Station, researchers have been studying the effects that being away from Earth can have on the body. Here are a few out-of-this-world observations.

NEW HEIGHTS: Decreased pressure on the spine causes most space travelers to grow two or more inches (5+ cm).

QUEASY FEELING: Nearly every astronaut experiences space sickness, which includes nausea and headaches.

SLEEPY SILENCE: Astronauts who snored on Earth have been found to sleep silently in space.

PASS THE TISSUES: A weightless environment causes the body's fluids to shift upward, resulting in nasal congestion and facial puffiness.

GRAVITY AGAIN: Some space station veterans say that the hardest thing to get used to after returning to Earth is gravity—when an object is released in midair and falls.

YEAR 600

Microbes would create organic soil and add oxygen to the atmosphere. Introduced flowering plants and evergreen forests might take root.

YEAR 1,000

Since oxygen levels would remain low, humans on Mars would require scuba gear to breathe outside. Energy for cities might come from nuclear power and wind turbines.

Doggone Funny

To rob a grocery store, a thief attempted to disguise himself by wearing a mask that looked like Pluto, the cartoon dog. But the clerk took one look at the goofy disguise and burst out laughing. The humiliated bad guy fled the scene—without any cash.

Stupid Criminals BUSTED!

FORGET THE PERFECT CRIME!

THESE BUNGLING BURGLARS WERE PRACTICALLY BEGGING TO BE CAUGHT. HERE ARE **SIX** FAILED CRIME ATTEMPTS THAT ARE POSITIVELY **CRIMINAL.**

Dumpster Diving

When a thief wriggled underneath a Dumpster to steal some valuable copper wiring, he wasn't planning on spending time there. But after squeezing underneath, the robber got stuck and couldn't get out! He spent the whole night there. The copper caper mastermind was probably grateful to see the police—who rescued him—even though it meant being arrested.

Steal & Snooze

After a department store break-in, police officers followed a trail of stolen items. The trail led to a field near the store's parking lot. There, the officers found two thieves fast asleep. One rested his head on a stolen chair cushion; the other snuggled on a swiped hammock. The thieves learned a hard lesson: Don't fall asleep on the job.

All Wet

A business owner thought he was being robbed—until he saw the thief's "gun" dripping water. The thief was armed with a water pistol! When the owner realized that he wasn't in any danger, he refused to hand over any cash. The thief ran away with the police hot on his trail.

Tight Squeeze

A would-be robber tried to squeeze through a shop window—the problem was, the window was no bigger than this book and the robber got stuck! After hearing his cries for help, the shop owner called the police to pull the trapped thief out.

Slow-Speed Chase

You've heard of a getaway car. But a getaway lawn mower? That's exactly what one criminal tried to use to escape the scene of a crime. After trashing a building, a vandal puttered away on a riding lawn mower. Police busted the gardening gangster when a cruiser blocked the mower's path.

→ Marvey calls this stunt **the Ultimate Cut.**

→ An **illusion** is something that appears to be different from the way it is in reality.

→ The **sawing** trick has been performed at magic shows for nearly **100 years.**

MIND GAMES

Magician Peter Marvey's bottom half appears to ride a unicycle around the stage, while his top half stays put!

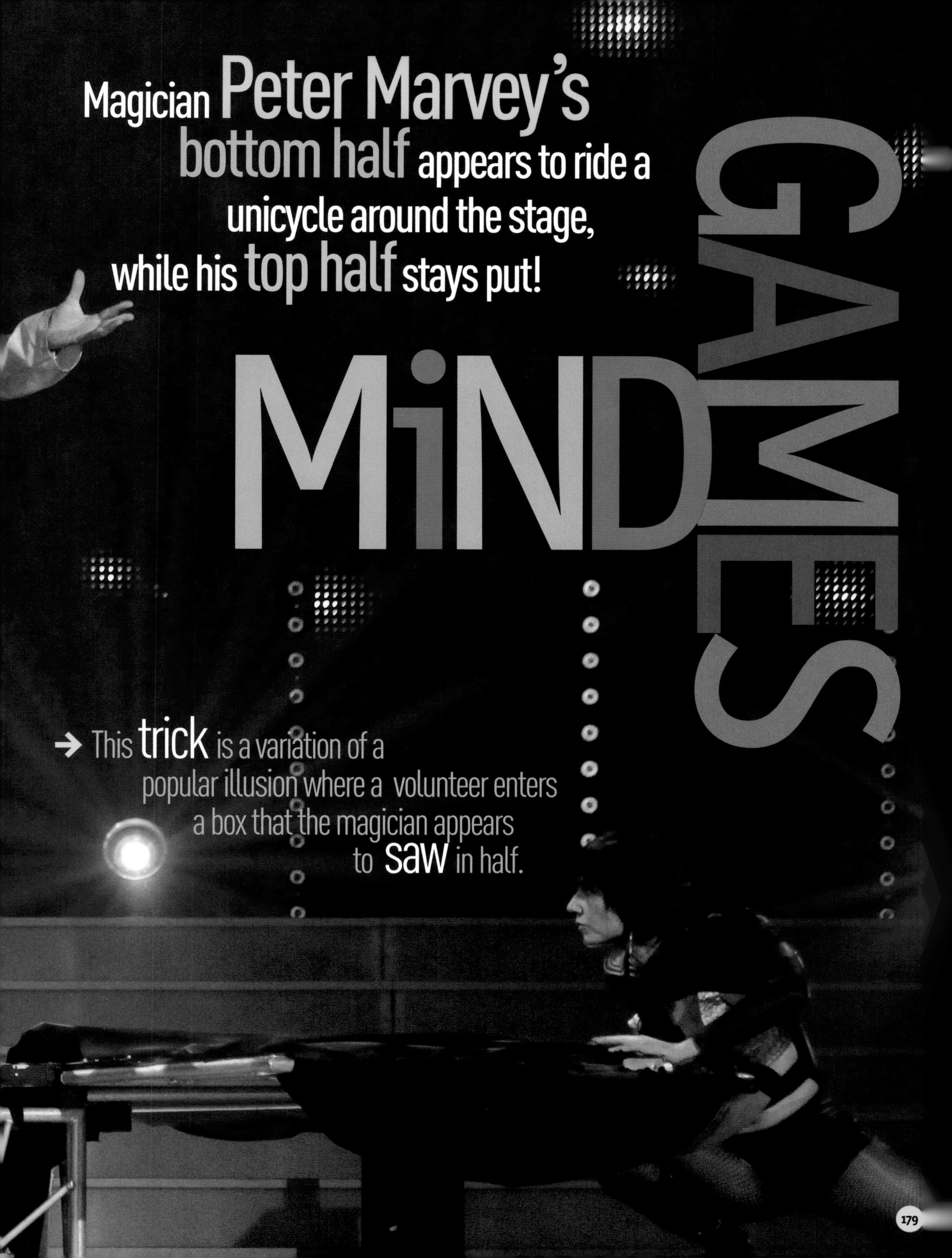

→ This trick is a variation of a popular illusion where a volunteer enters a box that the magician appears to saw in half.

ANIMALS Acting Like Us!

Maybe animals aren't so different from humans after all . . .

Ten Hut!

King penguin Nils Olav is an honorary colonel-in-chief in the Norwegian King's Guard.

Stinging Security

Venomous scorpions keep precious jewels safe from shifty fingers at a Michigan, U.S.A., jewelry store.

Best-Dressed Hens

When stressed-out chickens lost their plumage, a United Kingdom woman had jumpers (sweaters) knitted for the balding birds.

Camera Ham

Photographer **Paul Nicklen** made an **unexpected** best friend while snapping **pictures** of **leopard seals in Antarctica.** This seal brought Nicklen **"gifts"** of **penguins.**

Baby Doll Love

Young **female** chimps **play** with sticks and logs as if they're **infants,** probably as **practice** for motherhood.

Love Your Cologne

Cats dig cool scents just like people do. Zookeepers in the U.S.A. **spray** men's **cologne** around the cats' **enclosures** to exercise their noses.

This ROBOT NAMED ROBOViE helps you shop for groceries!

The head contains two cameras housed within Robovie's large, round eyes. Motors within the camera generate humanlike eye movements.

Two microphones pick up human voices.

That lettuce looks tasty! The salad dressing is in aisle 5.

ROBOVIE

ATR

Three wheels keep Robovie on a roll while roaming the supermarket aisles.

SHOP bOt

Hinged arms are equipped with touch sensors so they can detect and carry shopping baskets.

From home, shoppers upload their shopping lists to a store's Robovie through a mobile phone app. When shoppers arrive at the store, Robovie is waiting to greet them.

FastFACTS

ROBOVIE BY THE NUMBERS

Stands 4 feet (1.2 m) tall

Weighs 88 pounds (40 kg)

Operates for 4 hours before needing a recharge

Includes 24 ultrasonic sensors for navigating around obstacles

BOTS DO IT ALL!

What else can robots do? Check out some of their latest feats!

TOPIO plays table tennis.

ROTi teaches English in elementary schools.

Moroman SDA10 flips pancakes.

Robonaut 2 helps astronauts aboard the International Space Station.

Watson plays *Jeopardy!*—and WINS!

This DOG KNOWS 1,000 WORDS!

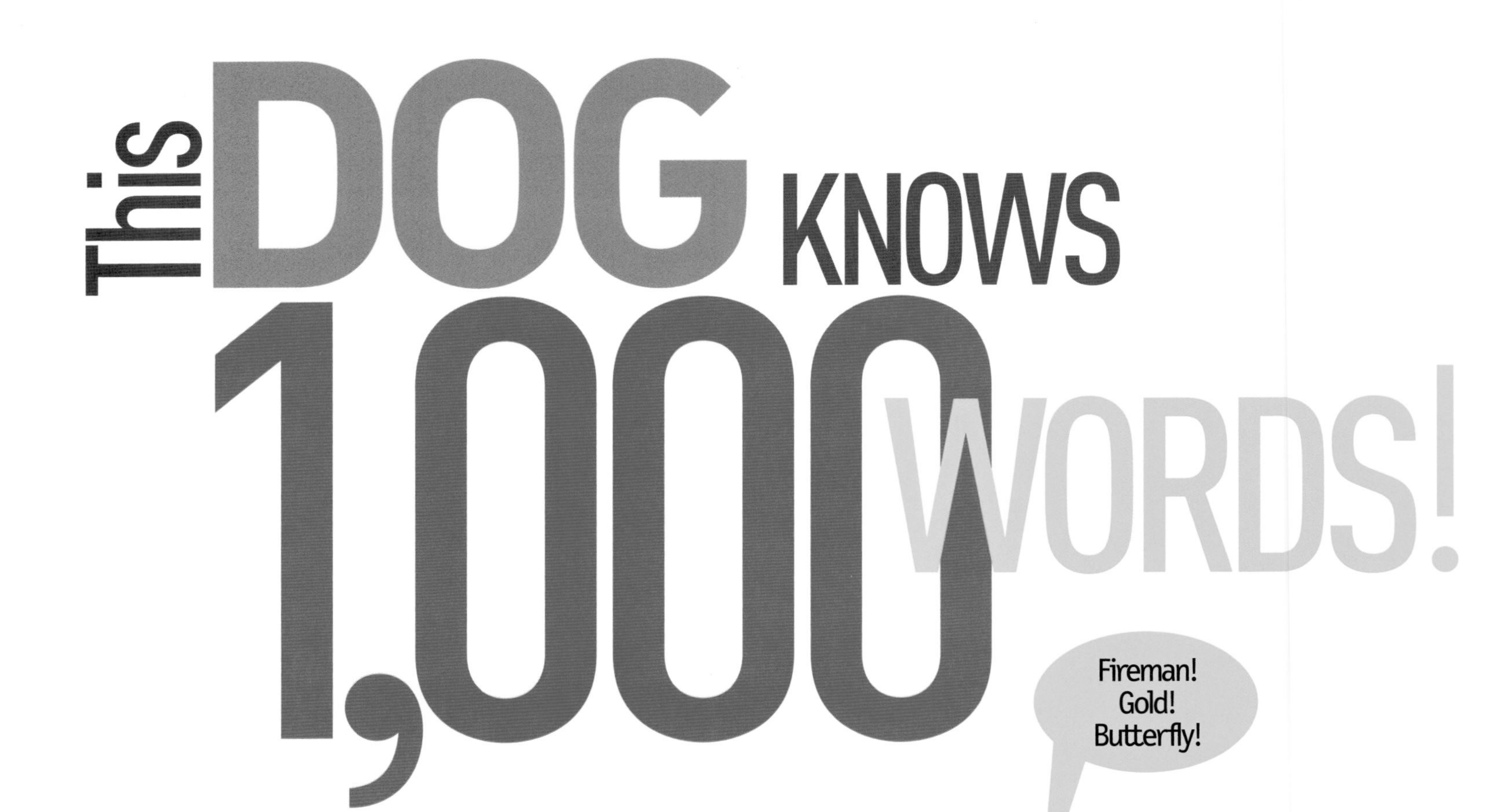

→ Chaser's trainers worked with her 4 to 5 hours every day.

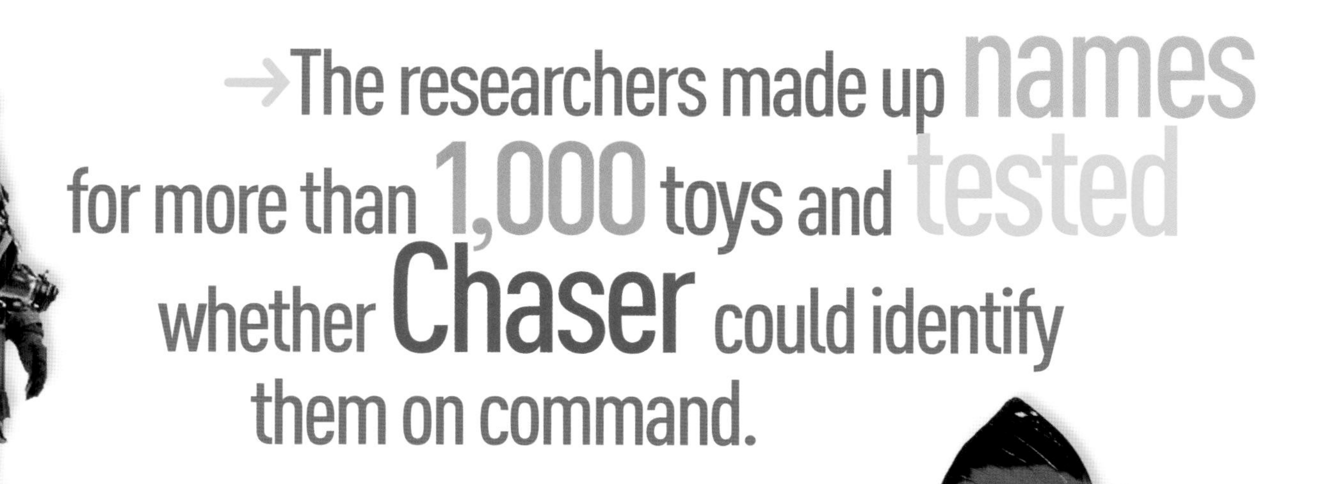

→ The researchers made up names for more than 1,000 toys and tested whether Chaser could identify them on command.

→ Chaser completed 838 of these tests over 3 years.

She never got fewer than 18 out of 20 correct.

Some dogs can understand the meanings of new words as quickly as toddlers. How can canines have this ability? Experts say it all has to do with their origins. More than 15,000 years ago, humans tamed wolves to be the world's first domesticated animal—the dog. Humans and dogs began living side by side.

Like their wolf ancestors, dogs' brains are wired for obeying a pack leader. So most dogs are happy to listen to their human masters' commands. Over the years people have bred dogs for specific tasks like guarding, herding, and companionship. Dogs became naturally skilled at working closely with their owners, particularly picking up on voice commands and body language.

Today's dogs can be trained to do all kinds of tasks. They serve as guide dogs for people who can't see. They can help search for lost people after a disaster. Some dogs help police officers catch criminals.

fact finder

Boldface indicates illustrations.

fact finder

fact finder

COVER
(turtle), ChinaFotoPress/Getty Image; (jetpack), Courtesy of Martin Jetpack; (salamander), Jane Burton/naturepl.com; (robot), Marco Secchi/Getty Images for Paramount Home Entertainment; (dog), Ryan Cardone/Tidalstock; (cat), Tim Flach/Getty Images

BACK COVER
(gorillas), Eric Isselée/Shutterstock; (shark), Michael Patrick O'Neill/Alamy

2-3, Edgar Mueller/Getty Images; 4 (top), Jump Run Productions/Getty Images; 4 (bottom), Zhang Peng/Onasia .com; 5 (left), Dane Penland/Smithsonian Institution/Associated Press; 5 (right), Randy Olson/NationalGeographicStock.com

CHAPTER 1: GOING TO EXTREMES
6, Ryan Cardone; 8 (top), Jump Run Productions/Getty Images; 8 (bottom left), Andy Day/actionplus sports images/ Newscom; 8 (bottom right), Thomas Senf/Sportsandnews/ Sipa; 9, Gareth Lock; 9 (left center), Sergei Karpukhin/Reuters; 9 (right center), Jimmy Halliday/Getty Images; 9 (bottom), Harrison Shull/Aurora Photos/Corbis; 10-11, Mondolithic Studios Inc.; 12 (top), P. Psaïla/DoubleVue; 12 (bottom right), Denis Balibouse/Reuters; 12 (bottom left), courtesy of Crown Plaza, Copenhagen Towers; 13 (top), Lars Tunbjörk/ Agence Vu/Aurora Photos; 13 (left center), N55, Walking House, 2008. Commissioned by Wysing Arts Centre, England; 13 (right center), Tim Wimborne/Reuters; 13 (bottom), y60/ ZumaPress/Newscom; 14-15, Sindre Lundvold/Barcroft Meida/ Getty Images; 16 (top right), Creatas Images/Jupiterimages; 16 (top left), Photolibrary.com; 16 (bottom left), Detlev van Ravenswaay/Photo Researchers, Inc; 16 (bottom), Bryan and Cherry Alexander; 16 (bottom right), SuperStock; 17 (top), Frans Lanting/NationalGeographicStock.com; 17 (top left), Lawrence Lawry/PhotoDisc/PictureQuest; 17 (top right), NASA; 17 (bottom right), Todd White/NationalGeographicStock.com; 17 (bottom left), Shaffer–Smith/Getty Images; 18-19, Aguirre Emmanuel/Sipa/Newscom; 20 (top), Mark Clifford/Barcroft Media Ltd; 20 (bottom right), Karine Aigner/NG Staff; 20 (bottom left), Brian Cassey Photography; 21 (top right), Dean Pomerleau; 21 (top left), Peter Langone; 21 (bottom), Splash News/Newscom; 22-23, David B. Fleetham/SeaPics.com; 22, Alexander Hafemann/iStockphoto; 23, Fred Bavendam/ Minden/NationalGeographicStock.com; 24-25, Gregg Bleakney/ GBleakney.com

CHAPTER 2: SEEING IS BELIEVING
26, FLPA; 28 (top left), Karine Aigner/NG Staff; 28 (top right), Adam Gerrard/SWNS.com; 28 (bottom), Ross Parry Agency; 29 (bottom right), Murad Sezer/Associated Press; 29 (top), Adam Hartnett/Caters; 29 (top right), Courtesy of L. Sautner; 29 (bottom left), Jim Incledon; 30-31, Bence Mate/naturepl .com; 32 (bottom left), DLILLC/Corbis; 32 (top left), Tui De Roy/Minden Pictures; 32 (bottom center), Mark Payne–Gill/ naturepl.com; 32 (top center), Mark Payne–Gill/naturepl.com; 33 (bottom right), Constantinos Petrinos/naturepl.com; 33 (top right), Gary Bell/oceanwideimages.com; 33 (bottom left), Glaucomy Volans/naturepl.com; 33 (top left), Glaucomy Volans/ naturepl.com; 33 (bottom center), SuperStock; 33 (top center), SuperStock; 34 (top), ROX/rox.co.uk; 34 (right), Randy Olson/ NationalGeographicStock.com; 34 (bottom left), Joe Skipper/ Reuters; 35 (top), Issei Kato/Reuters; 35 (bottom left), Mike Clark/AFP/Getty Images; 35 (bottom right), WENN/Newscom; 36-37, YU Gallery, Paris, France; 38 (top right), Franck Fotos/ Alamy; 38 (top left), Franck Fotos/Alamy; 38 (bottom), Courtesy of Javier Senosiai; 39 (top), Franz Neumayr/Getty Images; 39 (center left), Johan De Meester/Ardea; 39 (center right), Julia Kuskin; 39 (bottom), Sean Gallup/Getty Images; 40 (left), Nick Garbutt/naturepl.com; 40 (right), Michael Nichols/ NationalGeographicStock.com; 41 (top), Ingram; 41 (center), Brandon Cole; 41 (bottom), Rob Friedman/iStockphoto.com; 42-43, Paul Macleod; 44 (right), Kevin Wick/Canstruction/0NC/ Newscom; 44 (left), Rex Features/Rex USA; 44 (bottom), Benoit Tessier/Reuters/Corbis; 45 (top), JTB Photo/ Photolibrary; 45 (bottom right), Zhang Peng/Onasia.com; 45 (bottom left), Invader/space–invaders.com

CHAPTER 3: WHO'S COUNTING?
46, Life on white/Alamy; 48 (top), Dorling Kindersley/Getty Images; 48 (bottom left), Chris Alleaume/National Geographic Your Shot; 48 (bottom right), Animals Animals/SuperStock; 49 (top left), Pete Oxford/Minden Pictures; 49 (top right), blickwinkel/Alamy; 49 (center), Werner Bollmann/Photolibrary .com; 49 (bottom), Cyril Ruoso/JH Editorial/Minden Pictures/ NationalGeographicStock.com; 50-51, David Fleetham/Getty Images; 51 (right), Eric Isselée/Shutterstock; 52-53, Yann Arthus–Bertrand/Altitude Henderson; 54-55, Hal Pierce/NASA's Goddard Space Flight Center; 54-55 (rhinos), Life on white/ Alamy; 56 (top), Richard Du Toit/Getty Images; 56 (center left), Masa Ushioda/SeaPics.com; 56 (center right), Bob Cranston/ SeaPics.com; 56 (bottom), Photodisc/Getty Images; 57 (top left), Jeremy Woodhouse/Photodisc Green/Getty Images; 57 (top right), Jean–Paul Ferrero/Minden Pictures; 57 (center), Tui De Roy/Minden Pictures; 57 (bottom left), imagebroker/ Alamy; 57 (bottom right), Superstock/Photolibrary.com; 58 (top left), Joel Sartore/NationalGeographicStock.com; 58 (top right), Tui De Roy/NationalGeographicStock.com; 58 (bottom), Wildlife GmbH/Alamy; 59 (left), Bangor University; 59 (right), Cisca Castelijns/Foto Natura/Minden Pictures/ NationalGeographicStock.com; 60-61 (giraffe), age fotostock/ SuperStock; 60-61 (ostriches), Four Oaks/Shutterstock; 60-61 (koalas), Life on white/Alamy; 60-61 (squirrel), Ingram; 62-63, Roy Gumpel/Touch Productions Ltd.; 64-65, Bill Draker/ Photolibrary.com; 64, Ingram

CHAPTER 4: FREAKS OF NATURE
66, Minden Pictures/SuperStock; 68, Yuji Sakai/Digital Vision/ Getty Images; 69 (top left), Milos Luzanin/Shutterstock; 69 (top right), saiko3p/Shutterstock; 69 (bottom left), Geoff Brightling/ Getty Images; 69 (bottom right), Jan Castricum/Minden Pictures; 70 (top), Paul Nicklen/NationalGeographicStock .com; 70 (left center), Winfried Wisniewski/Getty Images; 70 (right center), Konrad Wothe/Minden Pictures/ NationalGeographicStock.com; 70 (bottom), Frans Lanting Studio/Alamy; 71 (top left), Mike Anich/SuperStock; 71 (top right), Brandon Cole/Getty Images; 71 (center), Gerry Ellis/ Minden Pictures; 71 (bottom left), Buck Forester/Getty Images; 71 (bottom right), Suzi Eszterhas/Minden Pictures; 72-73, NASA; 74 (top), Biosphoto/Cèdric Girard; 74 (bottom left), Danita Delimont/Alamy; 74 (bottom right), Wesley A. Carr; 75 (top right), Ken Catania/Visuals Unlimited/Corbis; 75 (top left), Bruno Cavignaux/Biosphoto; 75 (bottom right), Ian Cruickshank/Alamy; 75 (bottom left), David A. Northcott/ Corbis; 76-77, Ultra_Generic/iStockphoto.com; 78 (left), Franco Tempesta; 78 (right), Maria Toutoudaki/Getty Images; 79 (top), Warren Photographic/Photo Researchers, Inc.; 79 (center), Digital Vision/Getty Images; 79 (frame), Ingram; 79 (bottom), F. G. Mayer/Photo Researchers, Inc.; 80-81, Petty Officer 2nd Class Lauren Jorgensen/U.S. Coast Guard/Associated Press; 82 (top), Spectrum Photofile/All Rights Reserved; 82 (center), Paul Hellstern/The Daily Oklahoman/Associated Press; 82 (bottom), Andrew G. Saffas; 83 (top left), Lyn Battle; 83 (top right), U.S. Navy, Official Photograph; 83 (bottom left), Spectrum Photofile/All Rights Reserved; 83 (bottom right), Jim Reed/Photo Researchers, Inc; 84 (bottom), Steve Hopkin/ Ardea.com; 84 (top left), Mike Hill/Getty Images; 84-85 (top right), Photodisc/Getty Images; 84-85 (Background), Dynamic Graphics/Creatas Images/Jupiter Images; 85 (left), Martha Holmes/NPL/Minden Pictures; 85, Tierfotoagentur/Alamy

CHAPTER 5: ON THE MOVE
86-87, Andy Rouse/naturepl.com; 88-89, Joffet Emmanuel/ Sipa; 90-91, STR News/Reuters; 92-93, Dr. Andreas Zeitler; 94 (top), Peter Mackay; 94 (center), David Kone/The American Visionary Art Museum; 94 (bottom), Harrod Blank; 95 (top left), Conference Bike by Eric Staller.com; 95 (top right), Harrod Blank; 95 (bottom left), Transtock/Corbis; 95 (bottom right), Inventist.com; 96-97, NGT; 96, Jean–Paul Ferrero/Auscape/ Minden Pictures; 97 (left), Joe McDonald/Woodfall/Photoshot; 97 (right), Beata Slonecka/NationalGeographicStock.com; 98 (top), Martin Ruegner/Getty Images; 98 (center left), Photolibrary.com; 98 (center right), Masa Ushioda/Alamy; 98 (bottom), Robert Kyllo/Shutterstock; 99 (top left), Juniors Bildarchiv/Alamy; 99 (top right), Punchstock; 99 (center), Michael Kevin Daly/Getty Images; 99 (bottom left), William Radcliffe/Science Faction/Corbis; 99 (bottom right), A.T. Willett/ Alamy; 100-101, Nikada/iStockphoto.com; 102-103 (all), Harrod Blank; 104-105, Wayne Lynch/Corbis; 105 (top right), Amy Lane/Getty Images; 105 (top left), Marcus Jones/iStockphoto. com; 105 (bottom left), Henri Simon Faure/iStockphoto.com; 105 (bottom right), Ron Kimball/www.kimballstock.com

CHAPTER 6: CLAIM TO FAME
106, Adrian Dennis/Associated Press; 108 (top), Anthony Pidgeon/Lonely Planet; 108 (bottom left), c40/c40/ZUMA Press/Newscom; 108 (bottom right), Cui jian–Imaginechina/ Associated Press; 109 (top), Courtesy of Muvbox Concept; 109 (bottom), Courtesy of Events in the Sky; 110-111, Tyler Stableford/Getty Images; 112 (top), Courtesy of Teacups Puppies and Boutique; 112, (bottom) Courtesy of Las Ventanas al Paraiso, A Rosewood Resort; 113 (top right), Tim Flach/ Getty Images; 113 (top left), Melissa Pearcy; 113 (bottom right), Courtesy of La Petite Maison; 113 (bottom left), Candace Zynda; 114 (top), Corbis Premium RF/Alamy; 114 (bottom), gapper/Alamy; 115, Stephen Saks Photography/Alamy; 116-117, Clayton Hanmer; 118 (top), Stevie Mann; 118 (bottom), CB2/ZOB/Newscom; 119 (top), CB2/ZOB/WENN.com/ Newscom; 119 (center left), Kurt Vinion/Getty Images; 119 (center right), Kim Kyung–Hoon/Reuters/Corbis; 119 (bottom), Mr. Vincent Costello; 120, Kathy Willens/Associated Press; 120-121 (Background), Visions of America/SuperStock; 121 (top left), Associated Press; 121 (top right), Gary Sussman/ Associated Press; 121 (bottom left), Kevork Djansezian/ Associated Press; 121 (bottom right), Rob Carr/Associated Press; 122, Dane Penland/Smithsonian Institution/Associated Press; 123 (top left), Kristy Wigglesworth/Associated Press; 123 (top right), The Natural History Museum, London; 123 (bottom), ClassicStock/Alamy; 124 (top), Ancient Art & Architecture Collection Ltd/Alamy; 124 (bottom), Yiannis Papadimitriou/ Alamy; 125 (left), Paul Helm/Alamy; 125 (right), Michael Kappeler/Associated Press

CHAPTER 7: WHAT ON EARTH?
126, Jane Burton/naturepl.com; 128, ChinaFotoPress/Getty Images; 130-131, Bat Conservation; 132 (top), Darlyne A. Murawski/NationalGeographicStock.com; 132 (bottom left), courtesy of the Monterey Bay Aquarium Research Institute (c) 2004 MBARI; 132 (bottom right), Bruno Guenard/Photolibrary; 133 (top), Alexander Mustard; 133 (left center), Fred Bavendam/Minden Pictures; 133 (right center), David Shen/ Seapics.com; 133 (bottom), cs9/ZUMA Press/Newscom; 134-135, Ben Nottidge/Alamy; 135 (top), Phil Degginger/Alamy; 135 (bottom), Jason Edwards/NationalGeographicStock .com; 136 (left), Scott E. Barbour/Getty Images; 136 (right), Glow Images/SuperStock; 137 (top), Jon Warburton Lee; 137 (center left), Yoshio Tomii Photo Studio/Photolibrary.com; 137 (center right), James P. Blair/NationalGeographicStock.com; 137 (bottom), O. Luis Mazzatanta/NationalGeographicStock. com; 138-139, Carsten Peter/Speleo Research & Films/ NationalGeographicStock.com; 140-141, Design Pics/ SuperStock; 142, Photolibrary.com; 144 (left center), Armin Floreth/SuperStock; 144 (top), Franco Tempesta; 144 (bottom), Mark Horn/Getty Images; 144 (right center), DLILLC/Corbis; 145 (left center), AlaskaStock/Corbis; 145 (top), Christian Heinrich/SuperStock; 145 (bottom), SuperStock; 145 (right center), Doug Perrine/SeaPics.com

CHAPTER 8: WILD & WACKY
146-147, Buddy Mays/Corbis; 148 (top left), Zuma Press/ Newscom; 148 (top right), Rex USA; 148 (bottom), Quirky China News/Rex/Rex USA; 149 (top right), AFP/Getty Images; 149 (top left), Nadia Caffesse/Fulltiltphotography.com; 149 (bottom), Karen Portaleo/Highland Bakery; 149 (center), Liz Hickok; 150, Sean Wandzilak/iStockphoto.com; 151 (top), AptTone/Shutterstock; 151 (bottom), andersphoto/Shutterstock; 152-153, Mondolithic Studios Inc.; 154 (top), Shen Hong/ ZUMA Press; 154 (bottom right), Lionel Cironneu/Asssociated Press; 154 (bottom left), Mike Simons/Getty Images; 155 (top left), Mario Tama/Getty Images; 155 (bottom), Alberto Saiz/Associated Press; 155 (top right), Natthawat Wongrat/ ZUMA Press; 156, Steven J. Backman; 157 (top), Charles Whitehouse/*Yuma Daily Sun*/Associated Press; 157 (bottom), Stock Connection/SuperStock; 158, ZUMA Press/Corbis; 160 (top, both), Polaris; 160 (bottom left), Joao Sabino/Solent News/Rex/Rex USA; 160 (bottom right), Maria C. Valentino/ MCV Photo; 161 (top left), Rex/Rex USA; 161 (top right), Quirky China News/Rex/Rex USA; 161 (bottom right), Casey Gutteridge, CPG Photography; 161 (bottom left), Kobi Levi/ Solent News/Rex/Rex USA; 162-163, Barry Bland/Barcroft Media LTD; 164 (top left), PhotriMicroStock/L. Howe; 164 (top right), Buddy Mays/Corbis; 164 (bottom left), James P. Rowan; 164-165, Richard Cummins; 165 (top), Natalia Bratslavsky/ Alamy; 165 (center left), Dave and Sigrun Tollerton/Alamy; 165 (center right), David Barnes/Danita Delimont

CHAPTER 9: INTELLIGENT LIFE
166, Marco Secchi/Getty Images for Paramount Home Entertainment; 168 (top), Peter Charlesworth/OnAsia; 168-169, Chris Alleaume/National Geographic Your Shot; 169 (top left), Stuart Westmorland/DanitaDelimont.com; 169 (top right), Daniel Sambraus/Getty Images; 169 (center right), C. Dani/I. Jeske/De Agostini Picture Library/Getty Images; 169 (bottom), iStockphoto.com; 170-171, Mondolithic Studios Inc.; 172 (top), Courtesy of Martin Jetpack; 172 (bottom), NeuroSky, Inc. All Rights Reserved; 172-173, Kevin Hand; 173 (top), Brand X Pictures/Jupiter Images; 173 (bottom right), Courtesy of University of Washington; 173 (bottom left), Courtesy of Jonathan Black, Raytheon Company; 174-175, Stephan Morrell/NationalGeographicStock.com; 176-177 (all), Tom Nick Cocotos; 178-179, Image/Zuma Press; 180 (top left), David Cheskin–pa/Associated Press; 180 (top right), Jeffrey Sauger/WPN; 180 (bottom), Mason News Service; 181 (top), Paul Nicklen/National Geographic Stock; 181 (left), Corbis Premium RF/Alamy; 181 (right), Ron Kimball/Kimball Stock; 182-183, Randy Olson/NationalGeographicStock.com; 184, Mark Olencki/Wofford College; 185 (top left), Design Pics/ SuperStock; 185 (top right), fStop/SuperStock; 185, fStop/ SuperStock

PUBLISHED BY THE NATIONAL GEOGRAPHIC SOCIETY

John M. Fahey, Jr., *Chairman of the Board and Chief Executive Officer*
Tim T. Kelly, *President*
Declan Moore, *Executive Vice President; President, Publishing*
Melina Gerosa Bellows, *Executive Vice President; Chief Creative Officer, Books, Kids, and Family*

PREPARED BY THE BOOK DIVISION

Nancy Laties Feresten, *Senior Vice President, Editor in Chief, Children's Books;* Jonathan Halling, *Design Director, Books and Children's Publishing;* Jay Sumner, *Director of Photography, Children's Publishing;* Jennifer Emmett, *Editorial Director, Children's Books;* Carl Mehler, *Director of Maps;* R. Gary Colbert, *Production Director;* Jennifer A. Thornton, *Managing Editor*

STAFF FOR THIS BOOK

Robin Terry, *Project Editor*; Jennifer Emmett, Mary Varilla Jones, *Additional Editors*; James Hiscott, Jr., *Art Director*; Lori Epstein, Kelley Miller, Jay Sumner, *Illustrations Editors*; James Hiscott, Jr., Dawn McFadin, Rachael Hamm Plett, *Designers*; Julie Beer, Michelle Harris, *Researchers*; Kate Olesin, *Editorial Assistant*; Kathryn Robbins, *Design Production Assistant*; Hillary Moloney, *Illustrations Assistant*; Elizabeth Carney, Sarah Wassner Flynn, Ruth Musgrave, *Contributing Writers*; Grace Hill, *Associate Managing Editor*; Lewis R. Bassford, *Production Manager*; Susan Borke, *Legal and Business Affairs*

MANUFACTURING AND QUALITY MANAGEMENT

Christopher A. Liedel, *Chief Financial Officer;* Phillip L. Schlosser, *Senior Vice President;* Chris Brown, *Technical Director;* Rachel Faulise, Nicole Elliot, and Robert L. Barr, *Managers*

Library of Congress Cataloging-in-Publication Data

Ultimate weird but true.
p. cm. -- (Weird but true)
Includes index.
ISBN 978-1-4263-0864-2 (hardcover : alk. paper) --
ISBN 978-1-4263-0895-6 (library binding : alk. paper)
1. Curiosities and wonders--Juvenile literature.
AG243.U45 2011
031.02--dc23

2011020506

Scholastic ISBN: 978-1-4263-0978-6

Printed in U.S.A.
11/LPH-RRDW/1

ACKNOWLEDGMENTS

National Geographic Kids gratefully acknowledges Karine Aigner, Madeline Franklin, Marilyn Terrell, Jeffrey Wandel, and Erin Whitmer for their contributions to *Ultimate Weird But True.* We would also like to thank the many scientists and experts who helped ensure that our facts are not only weird, but also true. While there are far too many to mention by name, the following people truly went the extra mile:

Jerry Bonnell, NASA's Goddard Space Flight Center; Richard Carlson, Carnegie Institution for Science; Dennis Desjardin, Department of Biology, San Francisco State University; Michael E. Dillon, Department of Zoology and Physiology, University of Wyoming; Paolo Forti, Italian Institute of Speleology, University of Bologna; Sharon Gursky-Doyen, Department of Anthropology, Texas A & M University; Andrea Heydlauff, Panthera; Lauren Jorgensen, 9th District Public Affairs, United States Coast Guard; Dave Mellinger, NOAA/PMEL VENTS Program, Hatfield Marine Science Center, Oregon State University; Chris Orban, Brown University; Michael Reeder, School of Mathematical Sciences, Monash University; Frank M. Rinderknecht, Rinspeed, Inc.; Rosa Rugani, Department of Psychology, University of Padova; Bill Sanders, Museum of Paleontology, University of Michigan; J. G. M. "Hans" Thewissen, Department of Anatomy and Neurobiology, Northeastern Ohio Universities Colleges of Medicine and Pharmacy; Chih-Shiue Yan, Geophysical Laboratory, Carnegie Institution of Washington.

National Geographic's net proceeds support vital exploration, conservation, research, and education programs.

For more information, please call 1-800-NGS LINE (647-5463) or write to the following address:
National Geographic Society
1145 17th Street N.W.
Washington, D.C. 20036-4688 U.S.A.

Visit us online at nationalgeographic.com/books
For librarians and teachers: ngchildrensbooks.org
More for kids from National Geographic: kids.nationalgeographic.com

For information about special discounts for bulk purchases, please contact National Geographic Books Special Sales: ngspecsales@ngs.org

For rights or permissions inquiries, please contact National Geographic Books Subsidiary Rights: ngbookrights@ngs.org

ANATOMY OF A WEIRD-BUT-TRUE FACT

How does a fact make it into a Weird But True book?

First, it has to be WEIRD. Our team of editors and writers scour the news, the latest discoveries, Internet gems, urban legends, wacky myths, and tantalizing tidbits to find a fact that's really weird.

It also has to be TRUE. So our researchers check every single word to make sure the fact is 100% accurate.

It has to LOOK COOL. Our photo editors and designers find the perfect weird picture or the most dazzling weird design to make each fact jump out at you.

It has to BE FUN by itself and also as a book. So we put it all together in an amazing-looking book that's so much fun you can't put it down.

Here's a weird-but-true fact about *Ultimate Weird But True:* It took an ultimate team of 5 editors, 3 writers, 4 designers, 4 photo editors, 2 researchers, more than 20 experts, and at least 10 others to make it the weirdest, truest, most ultimate book around.

Social Security

4th Edition

by Jonathan Peterson
Award-winning journalist

Social Security For Dummies®, 4th Edition

Published by: **John Wiley & Sons, Inc.,** 111 River Street, Hoboken, NJ 07030-5774, www.wiley.com

Published simultaneously in Canada

For general information on our other products and services, please contact our Customer Care Department within the U.S. at 877-762-2974, outside the U.S. at 317-572-3993, or fax 317-572-4002. For technical support, please visit https://hub.wiley.com/community/support/dummies.

Wiley publishes in a variety of print and electronic formats and by print-on-demand. Some material included with standard print versions of this book may not be included in e-books or in print-on-demand. If this book refers to media such as a CD or DVD that is not included in the version you purchased, you may download this material at http://booksupport.wiley.com. For more information about Wiley products, visit www.wiley.com.

Library of Congress Control Number: 2020945328

ISBN 978-1-119-68992-8 (pbk); ISBN 978-1-119-68996-6 (ebk); ISBN 978-1-119-68995-9 (ebk)

Manufactured in the United States of America

SKY10021096_092120

Contents at a Glance

Table of Contents

Introduction

You're reading this book, so you're probably thinking about the future — for yourself or for your loved ones. You probably want to know more about the Social Security benefits that could go to you and your family one day and how that money will meet your needs. You may also be thinking about the next phase of your life. Will it be financially comfortable? Will it be a struggle? If you're like many people, you wonder whether you're going to outlive your savings. Will Social Security keep you afloat? Can you count on your Social Security benefits? What should you know about the program? How can you find the information you need?

Despite its significance in modern life, Social Security is rarely explained clearly in one place. Not in a way that lays out the program and explains how you fit in, all the protections Social Security offers, and what they mean for you and your loved ones. Not in a way that empowers you to plan right and face the bureaucracy with your eyes open. Not in a way that tells you what you need to know about the rules that affect benefit amounts and eligibility. But understanding this stuff is important — for you and for those who depend on you.

That's why I wrote this book: to explain the important protections of Social Security in a way that makes sense to the people who earn them and pay for them. (That means you!)

Social Security is big, and it can be confusing. It has an endless assortment of rules, variations on the rules, exceptions to the rules, and exceptions to the exceptions to the rules. The fine print is a big deal. Decisions you make about retirement benefits can have a financial impact for many years, in ways you may not recognize today. Certain areas, such as disability, are especially complicated. No wonder you may be uncertain. It's not like they teach you this stuff in school.

Everybody has questions about Social Security — questions like these:

- What's the best age for me to start claiming benefits?
- Can I work and also collect Social Security?
- How does my divorce affect my eligibility for benefits?
- Will it help my spouse if I wait until 70 to start collecting Social Security?

» Is the retirement age changing?

» What's the best way to contact Social Security?

» What kind of benefits can go to a spouse or child?

» Can I solve my problem online?

» What should I bring with me when I apply for benefits?

» Will Social Security be there when I need it?

You deserve helpful answers to these important questions and many others — answers that are clear and accurate. After all, Social Security is *your* program. You own it through the taxes you pay and the benefits you earn. You should know how your personal finances and your work history affect the benefits that land in your bank account. You should know what to expect from the bureaucracy and how to deal with it effectively. And you can find the answers in these pages.

About This Book

Social Security For Dummies walks you through the basics of this critical program: what Social Security is, how you qualify, when to file, how much you'll get, how much goes to your dependents, and how to contact the Social Security Administration (SSA) to get the information you need. And it does all this in easy-to-understand plain English.

Above all, this book is a reference, which means that you don't have to read it from beginning to end, nor do you have to read every word, every chapter, or every part. Keep this book on your desk or kitchen counter and pull it out when you need an answer to a specific question. Feel free to skip anything marked with the Technical Stuff icon and anything in a shaded box (called a sidebar); that information is interesting but not essential to understanding Social Security.

This edition makes use of the latest statistics available at the time of writing in 2020 and includes updated information on claiming strategies for married couples, as well as Social Security policy on same-sex marriages and details on personal "*my* Social Security" accounts.

Within this book, you may note that some web addresses break across two lines of text. If you're reading this book in print and want to visit one of these web pages, simply key in the web address exactly as it's noted in the text, pretending as though the line break doesn't exist. If you're reading this as an e-book, you've got it easy — just click the web address to be taken directly to the web page.

Foolish Assumptions

This book makes a few assumptions about you, the reader:

- You probably don't know a whole lot about Social Security. You've been busy living your life, and you haven't had time to dig into the details yet. (Don't worry: If you already have a solid knowledge base, you'll still find lots to chew on in these pages.)
- You may be starting to plan for retirement and want a better idea of how Social Security fits into the picture. Or maybe you already are receiving Social Security but want a better understanding of your benefits.
- You may be trying to help an older parent or other relative navigate the Social Security system.

Icons Used in This Book

Throughout this book, I use the following icons to draw your attention to certain kinds of information.

The Tip icon draws your attention to information that can save you time and money, or just make your life easier as you navigate the Social Security system.

You don't have to commit this book to memory, but when you see the Remember icon, you want to pay attention because it flags information that's so important, it's worth remembering.

The Warning icon signals important information that helps you avoid potentially costly or time-consuming pitfalls.

I use the Technical Stuff icon when I veer into highly technical information — information that adds insight but isn't critical to your understanding of the topic at hand.

Beyond the Book

In addition to the material in the print or e-book you're reading right now, this book comes with some bonus information on the web that you can access from anywhere. If you want some answers quickly on some of the most basic parts of Social Security, you can go to the *Social Security For Dummies* Cheat Sheet. To view this book's Cheat Sheet, simply go to `www.dummies.com` and enter "Social Security For Dummies Cheat Sheet" in the Search box.

Where to Go from Here

You can skip around this book any way you want. If you're the sort who reads every word of every book, you can start with Chapter 1 and read all the way through to the end. If you're looking for information on a particular topic, use the table of contents and the index to find what you need. For example, if you're not sure when you should start collecting Social Security retirement benefits, turn to Chapter 3. If you're disabled and need information on Social Security Disability Insurance, turn to Chapter 11. Or if you want to know what the future may hold for Social Security, turn to Chapter 17. No matter where you dive in, this book has you covered.

You've earned your Social Security benefits. Knowing what you have is always a good idea, and this book provides the information you need.

1 Getting Started with Social Security

IN THIS PART . . .

Get an overview of the Social Security program and the protections that go to practically everyone: retirees and their dependents, surviving family members, and disabled workers, as well as those who rely on them financially.

Take note, in simple terms, of what you need to know to file for various kinds of benefits.

Discover details on what to consider when deciding to claim benefits.

Find guidance on protecting your Social Security card and number from identity thieves.

» Looking at the value of Social Security

» Considering where your contributions go

» Getting all you can out of Social Security

» Contacting the Social Security Administration

Chapter 1

What Social Security Is and Why You Need It

Social Security is the foundation of long-term financial support for almost every American. If you're like most people, you'll depend on Social Security to help you survive in your later years (if not sooner). In fact, its protections are becoming even more important as an answer to growing insecurity in old age.

Look around you. If you're in the workforce, you know that good jobs are hard to come by. If you're an older worker who loses a job, you may also know it can take a long time to get a new one. Have you been able to set aside money for the future? Saving is essential, but many Americans save little, if anything. Maybe you contribute to a 401(k) at work, if your employer offers one, but who knows how much your investments will be worth next week or next month, let alone many years in the future?

Some of the people who read this book will live to be 100. Maybe you're one of them. Many people will make it into their 80s and even their 90s. Those years cost money. In a future of risks and unknowns, Social Security is one thing you can count on. Your benefit is guaranteed by law and protected against inflation. But that doesn't mean it takes care of itself or that you should be a passive participant in Social Security. You have decisions to make, and you can make them better if you have some working knowledge of the benefits you've earned. You may also have actions to perform, such as informing the Social Security Administration (SSA) about things that could affect your benefits.

This chapter provides an overview of Social Security and a broad-brush description of benefits. Here, I explain why Social Security was created and why those reasons are highly relevant to Americans today.

Understanding What Social Security Means for You

So, what is this U.S. institution that — sooner or later — plays a role in virtually all our lives?

You can think of Social Security as a set of protections against things that threaten your ability to survive financially — things like getting older and retiring, or having a serious accident or illness that leaves you unable to work. When such things happen, family members who depend on you may not be able to pay for the basic necessities of life.

That's why Social Security offers a range of benefits. These protections can provide crucial financial security for workers, their immediate family members, and even divorced spouses. For example, Social Security benefits may go to

- People who retire and their dependents, typically spouses, but potentially children and grandchildren
- People who are disabled and the immediate family members who depend on them
- Spouses, children, and even the parents of breadwinners who die

REMEMBER

Social Security's guaranteed monthly payments, set by legal formulas, stand out in a world of vanishing pensions, risky financial markets, rising healthcare costs, and increasing longevity. Although the program faces a potential financial shortfall in the future, its most fundamental features enjoy broad public support.

In the following sections, I look at specific groups of people who benefit from Social Security.

Benefits for retirees

More than 47 million retirees and their spouses get retirement benefits every month. These benefits help millions of people stand on their own two feet instead of relying on their kids or charity or scrambling every month to pay the bills. Social Security provides at least 90 percent of the income for almost half of single people and a fifth of married couples. But even for people who don't rely so heavily on Social Security, it provides a solid floor of income in later life.

Although Social Security benefits are generally modest, they help keep 15 million seniors above the poverty line, including many hardworking, middle-class Americans who otherwise would have little to fall back on.

REMEMBER

Social Security isn't intended to be your sole source of income. Instead, it gives you a foundation to build on with personal savings and other income.

If you're already retired (and not rich), you understand the role these payments play in your monthly budget. If you're still in the workforce but thinking about that next phase of life, here are a few things to reflect on:

- **Social Security is reliable.** Its payments don't rise and fall with the markets on Wall Street or depend on how your company is faring or how well you selected investments. Social Security income lasts a lifetime.
- **Social Security is accessible.** Almost all workers are covered. To put this in perspective, about half of workers are covered by an employer retirement plan, and many of these workers do not even participate.
- **Social Security is protected against inflation, a crucial safeguard.** Rising prices can slash the value of fixed income over time, driving down your standard of living in retirement.
- **Social Security is especially important for older women.** Women tend to live longer than men do, and they have less income to draw on in old age. Elderly widows are exceptionally vulnerable to poverty.
- **Social Security gives a boost to the least affluent.** That's because the benefit is progressive. Poorer individuals get back a larger share of earnings than their higher-paid peers. Social Security benefits replace about 40 percent of the earnings of an average worker.

THE ROOTS OF SOCIAL SECURITY

You may think of Social Security as part of life in the United States, but it wasn't always this way. Social Security was a foreign idea — literally. Americans by and large never expected their national government to rescue them in hard times. This was a country shaped by pioneer culture, a society that expected people to pull themselves up by their own bootstraps. Back on the farm, extended families took care of their own and struggled together. But as more Americans migrated to cities for work, traditional supports of family and close-knit communities began to unravel.

The Great Depression of the 1930s transformed attitudes. Unemployment rocketed to 25 percent. People's life savings vanished in a tsunami of bank failures. More than half of older Americans were poor. In desperation, people turned to Washington for help, and Washington looked overseas for ideas. President Franklin D. Roosevelt and his advisors, including Labor Secretary Frances Perkins, considered an idea known as *social insurance,* which had gained popularity in Europe. The idea was that governments could adapt insurance principles to protect their populations from economic risks. Unlike private insurance arrangements, which are supposed to protect individuals, social insurance programs are supposed to help *all* of society.

In 1889, German Chancellor Otto von Bismarck pioneered the idea with a system of old-age insurance that required contributions from workers and employers. By the time of the Great Depression, dozens of nations had launched some sort of social insurance effort. U.S. leaders, eager to ease the economic pain engulfing the nation, took a more serious look at social insurance from Europe. Others viewed social insurance as radical and un-American.

After a lengthy debate, Congress passed the Social Security Act, and President Roosevelt signed it into law on August 14, 1935. The law provided unemployment insurance as well as help for seniors and needy children. Title II of the act, "Federal Old-Age Benefits," created the retirement benefits that many people now see as the essence of Social Security.

"We can never insure 100 percent of the population against 100 percent of the hazards and vicissitudes of life," Roosevelt said at the bill signing, "but we have tried to frame a law which will give some measure of protection to the average citizen and to his family against the loss of a job and against poverty-ridden old age."

Benefits for children

Social Security pays more benefits to children than any other government program. More than 4 million children qualify for their own benefits, as dependents of workers who have retired, died, or become disabled. More than 6 million children live in households where someone gets Social Security.

The program's definition of *eligible children* may include stepchildren and, in some cases, grandchildren and step-grandchildren. Typically, children who qualify may be covered until age 18 — or 19, if they haven't yet graduated from high school and aren't married.

Benefits for survivors

The death of a family breadwinner hits everyone under the same roof. That's why Social Security provides benefits for dependent survivors. Not to overwhelm you with statistics, but this is a significant program with more than 6 million beneficiaries, including children, widows, and widowers. These dependents qualify for benefits if the deceased worker or retiree met certain basic requirements of Social Security. In Chapter 2, I cover the rules, including technicalities that affect widows and widowers.

Benefits for the disabled and their dependents

Almost 11 million Americans get Social Security's disability benefits, a protection that extends to almost 2 million dependent family members. Social Security's disability program is complicated, and it can be difficult to meet the standards required for benefits. I devote Chapter 11 to examining the program, as well as Supplemental Security Income (SSI) benefits for beneficiaries with the least income.

Many applicants for Social Security disability benefits are turned down, but these decisions may be reversed in the appeals process. In Chapter 8, I go over your options if Social Security makes a decision you disagree with.

You may not like to think about the risks you take walking out the door, but they may be higher than you realize. Almost four in ten men entering the labor force will become disabled or die before reaching retirement age; the same fate awaits more than three out of ten women.

Table 1-1 provides probabilities of death or disability for young workers (people born in 1999, in this example).

TABLE 1-1 **Probabilities of Death or Disability**

Probability of . . .	Male	Female	Combined
Death or disability before retirement	35%	31%	33%
Death before retirement (excluding disability)	9%	5%	7%
Disability before retirement (excluding death)	26%	26%	26%

Source: Social Security Administration

Appraising the Value of Social Security

The amount you get in Social Security retirement benefits is based on your earnings history and when you start to collect, factors I examine closely in Chapters 2 and 3. The average retirement benefit is currently about $18,036 per year, and the maximum benefit is more than $36,132 if you claim benefits at full retirement age. You can increase your benefits by taking them after your full retirement age, up to 70, and you reduce them by taking them earlier (typically, as early as 62).

The survivor's benefit of Social Security is really a life-insurance policy that has been valued at $612,000 for a 30-year-old worker who's married with two children and has a median salary. The long-term disability protections are valued at $580,000 in coverage for that same family.

Social Security combines other distinctive features that you usually don't find all in one place. These traits are worth keeping in mind when you're trying to get a handle on what the program is worth to you:

- **Benefits are earned.** After you meet the requirements for eligibility — generally ten years of earnings for retirement, but less than that for certain protections such as disability — you've established your right to a guaranteed benefit, which may also extend to your dependents.
- **Benefits are portable.** You can change jobs with no penalty, unlike traditional pensions. Your benefits reflect earnings in various places of employment during your working life. They aren't typically reduced when you change jobs, because most jobs are covered. (Exceptions include most federal employees hired before 1984, various state and local government workers, and many railroad employees.)
- **Benefit levels are guaranteed.** Unlike 401(k)s, for example, Social Security benefits are paid under legal formulas and don't rise or fall based on your luck with investments, the fortunes of your employer, the direction of interest rates, or other forces over which you have no control.

» **Benefits are universal.** Social Security covers the rich, the poor, and — most of all — the middle class. Social Security is a kind of social insurance for the benefit of individuals *and* society. This makes it very different from a welfare program.

» **Benefits are protected against inflation.** Private pensions generally don't have this feature. But without such protection, rising prices can take a huge toll on fixed income, one that adds up the longer you live.

SOCIAL SECURITY GROWS UP: SOME KEY DEVELOPMENTS

Since President Franklin D. Roosevelt signed Social Security into law in 1935, the program has evolved. Here are some key milestones:

- **1939:** Congress added benefits for retirees' spouses and minor children, as well as dependents of workers who die.
- **1950:** Coverage was extended to farm workers, domestic workers (such as housekeepers and gardeners), employees of nonprofits, and self-employed nonprofessionals.
- **1954:** Coverage was extended to self-employed farmers and certain professionals, such as accountants, architects, and engineers.
- **1956:** Benefits were added for disabled workers ages 50 to 64 and adult disabled children of workers who earned benefits. Social Security introduced early retirement benefits for women only.
- **1960:** Benefits were added for dependents of disabled workers.
- **1961:** Men were given the option of early retirement benefits, five years after this choice was granted to women.
- **1965:** Congress approved Medicare, a program of federal health insurance for people 65 and older, long sought by advocates of Social Security and social insurance.
- **1972:** Congress approved annual cost-of-living increases for Social Security, linked to the rise in consumer prices. (It had previously approved some benefit hikes on an ad hoc basis.)
- **1977:** Congress approved *wage indexing,* which adjusts retirement benefits upward to make sure that they reflect the long-term increase in wages that took place during a worker's lifetime.

(continued)

(continued)

- **1983:** Congress agreed to gradually raise the age for full retirement benefits from its traditional level of 65 to 67. That increase is still being phased in. The full retirement age has reached 66 for people born between 1943 and 1954 and will gradually move up to 67 for people born in 1960 or later. The 1983 law also introduced taxation of Social Security benefits for higher-income retirees, a shift that is causing growing numbers of people to pay income taxes on part of their Social Security income.
- **2014:** The Social Security Administration began to process and approve some claims for benefits related to same-sex marriage, including claims for spousal and survivor benefits in states that recognize such unions as legal. The new policy followed a U.S. Supreme Court ruling in 2013 that Section 3 of the Defense of Marriage Act was unconstitutional.
- **2015:** The Supreme Court ruled that same-sex marriages have a constitutional right in all states. The SSA recognizes same-sex marriage in all states and gives benefits to spouses.

Understanding How You Pay for Social Security

Social Security is paid for through taxes. (No surprise there.) But you're not the only one paying into the Social Security pot: Your employer also pays a portion of your Social Security tax. All that money that's taken out of your paycheck today goes to pay the benefits for today's retirees.

For the lowdown on how much you pay into Social Security and where it goes, read on.

How much you pay

If you're a wage earner, you pay into the Social Security system straight out of your paycheck. This payroll tax is dubbed "FICA," which stands for the Federal Insurance Contributions Act. The Social Security portion of your payroll tax is typically 6.2 percent of earnings up to a certain amount, which is adjusted annually (for 2020, the cap was set at $137,700). Employers also pay 6.2 percent for each employee. In addition, workers and their employers each pay 1.45 percent of *all* earnings for Medicare's Hospital Insurance Trust Fund. As of January 2013, individuals who earn more than $200,000 ($250,000 for married couples filing jointly) pay an additional 0.9 percent in Medicare taxes.

If you're self-employed, you're on the hook for both the employee and employer share, which usually adds up to 12.4 percent for Social Security and 2.9 percent for Medicare. This tax is dubbed "SECA," for the Self-Employed Contributions Act.

Politicians have been willing to ease the payroll-tax burden in response to economic conditions. In 2011, Congress approved a "payroll-tax holiday" to boost the economy; it lowered the worker's tax rate to 4.2 percent instead of the usual 6.2 percent. Employers still paid the usual 6.2 percent. The self-employed paid an overall rate of 10.4 percent. (The payroll-tax holiday expired at the end of 2012.)

Most workers pay Social Security taxes on all their earnings, because most workers don't earn above the cap for Social Security payroll taxes. Well more than half — maybe three-quarters — of U.S. households pay more in Social Security taxes than in federal income taxes. Although no one enjoys paying taxes, people tend to accept the Social Security tax because it enables them to earn important benefits.

Where your money goes

The taxes you pay in your working years pay for the benefits for retirees and other beneficiaries who no longer are working. This approach is called "pay as you go." Think of it as a pipeline that goes from current workers to current beneficiaries.

What the government does with your payroll tax contributions has long been a source of rumor, misunderstanding, and strongly held views. Here are the facts: The Social Security payroll tax deducted from your wages goes into two U.S. Treasury accounts, where it's used to pay for benefits. Most of the money — about 85 percent — goes into the Old-Age and Survivors Insurance Trust Fund; the remainder goes into the Disability Insurance Trust Fund. These combined trust funds are quite large, with assets of slightly more than $2.9 trillion at the end of 2018.

Tax revenues above and beyond what's needed to pay benefits are invested in special Treasury securities. These bonds have historically provided extra income for Social Security. Some critics argue that the trust funds could go belly up if the Treasury doesn't make good on its borrowing. But these bonds are backed by the full faith and credit of the U.S. government, which is still considered a safe investment by investors all over the world.

Although Social Security gets most of its income from payroll taxes, a smaller share comes from interest and some income tax revenues paid by the affluent on their Social Security benefits. (See Chapter 13 for a discussion of income taxes and Social Security.)

A CHANGING OUTLOOK

Large as the trust funds are, they're going to shrink rapidly in the future. Today, more than 47 million Americans are age 65 and older. Does that sound like a lot of older people? Just wait. That number will soar beyond 80 million in the coming decades, bringing vastly higher demand for Social Security benefits. Today, there are 2.8 workers for each person getting Social Security. But by 2035 just 2.3 workers will support each beneficiary, and revenue no longer will be sufficient to fully pay for promised benefits, meaning that revenue won't be able to keep up with benefits. The pay-as-you-go approach will come under increasing pressure, with proportionately fewer workers to support a great many beneficiaries. The trust funds are forecast to run out of money at about that time.

Although that's a problem that must be addressed, it's not as grim as it may sound. The SSA gets most of its revenue from payroll taxes. Even if the trust funds were somehow allowed to dry up, an extremely large amount of money would continue to flow through the system, paying most of what is currently promised.

Keep that in mind, especially if you wonder whether Social Security will be there for you down the road. Social Security should be able to pay three-quarters of promised benefits, even when it no longer has a surplus and if no action is taken. (That's according to the Social Security trustees, who report annually on the system's long-term outlook.)

If you're like most people, you probably believe that the system requires long-term financial stability. But the idea that the SSA can cover three-fourths of promised benefits far into the future gives at least some perspective. With enough political will, lawmakers can put their heads together and come up with a fair and reasonable plan to shore up Social Security for the long term. (In Chapter 17, you can look at the most common proposals to accomplish this goal.)

Getting the Most Out of Your Social Security Benefits

TIP

Today's workers will need all the retirement security they can muster in old age, and for most people Social Security is the centerpiece. Here are some things you can do today to get the most out of Social Security tomorrow:

- **Educate yourself about the program.** By reading this book, you're taking a big step in the right direction. In Appendix B, I connect you with a broader range of resources to further inform you on Social Security and other retirement concerns.

LESSONS FROM AN EARLY BENEFICIARY

Whatever you expect to get from Social Security, it's a pretty safe bet you won't fare as well as Aunt Ida. A retired legal secretary in Vermont, Ida May Fuller, known to friends as "Aunt Ida," earned her place in Social Security history by receiving the first recurring monthly check — for $22.54 on January 31, 1940. (It wasn't the first Social Security payment. That distinction goes to a Cleveland streetcar driver named Ernest Ackerman, who got a "lump sum" of 17 cents three years earlier.)

Aunt Ida's experience can teach today's retirees (and workers who will join them one day) a couple of lessons:

- **You could be depending on Social Security for a very long time.** Aunt Ida lived to 100. She collected benefits for 35 years, starting at age 65.
- **The inflation protection provided by Social Security is critical.** In the course of Aunt Ida's life, her monthly benefit nearly doubled, from $22.54 to $41.30. That increase enabled her purchasing power to hold up, even as the cost of living soared. (Congress added regular inflation increases to the program toward the end of Aunt Ida's life.)

» **Think about when you should claim benefits.** It often makes sense to hold off, which will enable your benefit to grow. I go into that important issue in Chapter 3. For an overview from the SSA, go to `www.ssa.gov/pubs/10147.html`.

» **Consider Social Security's guaranteed benefit the foundation in a larger strategy for retirement security.** Add up your assets. Look hard at your spending habits. Younger people have more time to plan, but older workers may also be able to take steps to improve their finances. If you need more money for the future, think about holding off retirement and working longer, even part time, as a way to stretch out your assets.

Getting in Touch with the Social Security Administration

The SSA has one overriding goal (which may be hard to recognize amid all the rules and complexities): to make sure you end up with the correct benefit amount you're entitled to under the law. Sometimes reaching that goal may not be simple (though it typically is). But whatever the particulars of your case, you may well end up having to contact the SSA to get what you want.

The SSA runs not only the basic Social Security protections for retirement, survivors, and disability, but also SSI for the poor. The SSA also handles applications for Medicare and the deductions in benefits that pay for Medicare premiums. (SSA doesn't run the Medicare program itself, however. That job is handled by the Centers for Medicare and Medicaid Services.)

That's a lot of territory to navigate — many rules, many technicalities, and many areas that can be confusing. But knowledge is power when it comes to bureaucracy. Understanding the rules for your particular situation helps. (I go over filing for benefits in Chapter 5, and I hit the high points of maneuvering through the Social Security bureaucracy in Chapter 7.)

Contacting the SSA isn't difficult. You can go to a local field office, call a toll-free number, or go online:

- **Field offices:** SSA offices are located all over the country — at last count, there were about 1,230 field offices. To find the nearest SSA office, just go to `www.ssa.gov/locator` and enter your zip code, and the address of your nearest office will appear, along with the hours it's open to the public. If you don't have internet access, you can find the address of your local SSA office in your local phone book, where all the U.S. government offices are listed, or you can call the SSA (see the next bullet) to inquire.
- **Phone:** You can contact an SSA representative toll free at 800-772-1213 (TTY 800-325-0778). Both numbers are staffed Monday through Friday, 7 a.m. to 7 p.m.
- **Online:** The SSA website (`www.ssa.gov`) has a great deal of information on benefits and rules that affect you. You can also find forms you may need and begin applications for certain benefits, including retirement.

Social Security has increased its hours and staff at field offices to help shorten the long lines and waiting times on the telephone. As of this writing, field offices are open to the public from 9 a.m. to 4 p.m., Monday through Friday.

TIP

If you're stretched for time and need to deal with the SSA, it helps to keep a couple of things in mind:

- Waiting times on the phone and in offices tend to be longer early in the month and early in the week.
- You can call the toll-free number to make an appointment with a local field office and save time when you arrive.

» Surviving the death of a loved one with help from Social Security

» Relying on Social Security when you can't work

» Seeing how Social Security protects the poorest of the poor

Chapter 2
A Breakdown of Benefits

When you hear about Social Security in the news, it seems like the talk is always about politics. Of course, that matters, but the squabbling in Washington can sound pretty far removed from what really links *you* to Social Security — the benefits for you and your loved ones. The truth is, many people don't know all they're paying for when it comes to Social Security.

In this chapter, I provide a detailed description of the main Social Security benefits: coverage for retirement and a retiree's dependent family members, protections for surviving family members when a loved one dies, and coverage for disability and a disabled worker's dependents. In addition, I go over the program of Supplemental Security Income (SSI) for individuals with extremely little income, which is also administered by the Social Security Administration (SSA).

Social Security's various benefits are meant to address different situations, but they share a common goal: to help individuals and their families meet the fundamental needs of survival. This chapter explains what that means for you.

Bringing Security to Old Age: Retirement Benefits

Retirement benefits were created to help older Americans live in dignity and independence after a lifetime of work. To qualify for these benefits, you have to meet certain earnings requirements. The good news is that these requirements are in relatively easy reach for most healthy people who've worked for a number of years. However, interruptions in earnings — such as for child rearing, caregiving, or long-term unemployment — may leave you with a smaller benefit.

REMEMBER

Benefit levels were established to replace just a *portion* of the income earned by you or the breadwinner you depend on. This is in keeping with Social Security's goal of providing a foundation for you to build on with personal savings, investments, and other income.

In this section, I fill you in on who qualifies for Social Security retirement benefits and when, how you qualify (through work credits), why you may not qualify, and how much you can expect to get.

Who qualifies and when

Retirees may qualify for benefits starting at age 62. Technically, you become eligible on the first full month after your 62nd birthday. Say you turn 62 on July 19. That means you become eligible for benefits on August 1. The August payment arrives in September, however, because Social Security pays with a one-month delay.

REMEMBER

You don't have to take your benefit when you turn 62. The longer you wait, the higher your monthly payment will be, until you reach 70. At that point, there's no payoff in further delay.

If you qualify for retirement benefits, Social Security may also provide benefits to other family members under certain conditions without reducing the benefits that go to you. Eligible dependents may include

- **A spouse age 62 or older:** When you begin collecting retirement benefits, a spouse who has reached 62 may also qualify for a benefit.
- **A spouse of any age who cares for your dependent child:** Spouses may get benefits based on your work record if they're caring for a child who is dependent on you and younger than 16 or disabled.

The SSA tends to follow state guidelines in terms of recognizing common-law marriages, although the rules leave some wiggle room for interpretation. In addition, Social Security now recognizes same-sex marriage in all states and some nonmarital relationships for the purposes of determining entitlement to Social Security and Medicare benefits as well as eligibility and payment amount for Supplemental Security Income (SSI).

» **Children:** In certain cases, your children can get benefits if you're collecting retirement or disability benefits. To qualify, children must fall into one of the following categories:

- Younger than 18 and unmarried
- Full-time students up to age 19 who haven't yet completed high school and are unmarried
- Age 18 or older and severely disabled with a disability that began before age 22

The SSA's definitions of *parent* and *child* are generally inclusive but sometimes a cause of dispute. It recognizes that you may have an adopted child or a stepchild. (See Chapter 10 for some of the technicalities.)

» **Grandchildren:** If the grandchild depends on you financially and the grandchild's parents provide no support (for example, because of death or disability of both parents), the grandchild may qualify for Social Security benefits on your work record.

» **A former spouse:** Your ex may get benefits if the following apply:

- You were married for at least ten years.
- You have been divorced for at least two years, and your ex is 62 or older and has not claimed benefits for him- or herself.
- Your ex is 62 or older, not remarried, and not eligible for a bigger benefit on anyone else's work record. (If a former spouse remarries before turning 60 but that marriage ends, the former spouse may again qualify for benefits on the record of the original partner.)

» ***Note:*** If your former spouse collects Social Security benefits based on your work record, this doesn't reduce the amount of benefits that go to you or your current spouse. The same is true even if you have more than one ex-spouse who qualifies under the rules.

How you qualify

Under the rules, you get *credits* toward eligibility by earning certain amounts of money. Most workers pick up the necessary credits without even thinking about it. Generally, 40 credits — which you can pick up in ten years of covered employment — does the trick. By *covered employment,* I mean a job in which you and your employer pay Social Security taxes. (If you're in business for yourself, you have to pay both the employer and employee shares.) These days, almost all jobs are covered. (For information on which jobs *aren't* covered, see the nearby sidebar "Which jobs aren't covered.")

TECHNICAL STUFF

People born before 1929 need fewer than 40 credits to qualify.

In 2020, Social Security awards you one credit for every $1,410 in earnings, and you can get up to a maximum of four credits per year. (The dollar amount typically rises each year to reflect growth in wages.) For example, say you earned $5,640 in 2020. That means you earned a total of four credits ($1,410 × 4 = $5,640). Now, say you earned $100,000 in 2020. You still earn a total of four credits, because four credits is the yearly maximum no matter how much money you make.

How much you get

Although you have to earn 40 credits to qualify for benefits, that doesn't determine the size of the payment that goes to you or your dependents. The SSA bases the amount of your benefit on your lifetime earnings — specifically (for workers born after 1928), the 35 highest-paid years in which you paid Social Security taxes. Your 35 highest years don't have to be consecutive, and they don't have to be the most recent 35 years, but 35 is an important number. If you have fewer than 35 years of earnings, the SSA adds zeros to reach 35. The impact of those zeros varies depending on your earnings history.

As you may expect, more career earnings mean a bigger benefit. Highly paid workers who contributed more taxes throughout their working careers end up with bigger Social Security payments, although the benefit formula is skewed to provide low earners a larger share of their working wages in retirement than high earners receive.

Social Security benefits rise because of cost-of-living increases that are meant to help retirees keep up with inflation. Congress may debate whether to modify the cost-of-living formula to save money or even to increase payouts, but the importance of inflation protection is widely recognized, and it remains one of the most important and popular features of Social Security.

WHICH JOBS AREN'T COVERED

Most work is covered by Social Security today, but that wasn't always the case. When Social Security was launched in the 1930s, roughly half the economy wasn't part of it. Largely excluded were fields associated with African Americans, women, and low pay (including agriculture, domestic service, and many jobs in education and social work). Critics said the exclusions reflected bias in favor of white, male breadwinners. The self-employed, professionals (such as doctors and lawyers), and most jobs in government and the nonprofit sector were also initially left out.

Today, 94 percent of American jobs are covered by Social Security. Categories of workers who may still not be covered include the following:

- Most federal employees hired before 1984
- Railroad workers with more than ten years of experience or who have worked at least five years with the railroads since 1995
- Some state and local government employees

If you fall into one of these categories, it's possible you will get no Social Security benefits or reduced amounts. (Many people who spend part of their working lives in uncovered employment end up with reduced benefits because of the Windfall Elimination provision and Government Pension Offset provision, which I explain later in this chapter.)

REMEMBER

Other things affect your benefit amount as well, including the following:

- **How old you are when you start collecting benefits:** You can start receiving Social Security as early as age 62, but your payment will be larger the longer you wait to claim, potentially to age 70. (See Chapter 3 for a discussion of when to begin receiving retirement benefits.)
- **If you worked in any jobs that weren't covered by Social Security:** Your full benefit may be reduced by any periods of your working career in which your job wasn't covered by Social Security, a reality for many government workers. (See the earlier sidebar "Which jobs aren't covered.")
- **If you're working while drawing benefits:** Social Security may withhold a portion of your retirement benefits if you earn above a certain amount while receiving benefits and you haven't yet reached the full retirement age, which is currently 66 and 2 months. (See Chapter 13 for a detailed explanation of how benefits may be affected by earnings.)

Social Security also takes money off the top of your retirement benefit to pay for Medicare coverage if you've reached 65 and you're enrolled in Medicare. The monthly premium for Medicare Part B, supplementary medical insurance (doctors' and some other services), is deducted automatically if you've reached 65 and entered Medicare. The standard Part B premium paid by most Medicare enrollees was set at $144.60 for 2020. Premiums — and the Medicare deduction — generally rise with inflation.

In the following sections, I cover how to estimate your benefit, and how much your spouse and children can expect to receive based on your work history.

Estimating your retirement benefit

The average monthly retirement benefit is about $1,503 (in 2020), but the amounts vary. Higher-paid workers who start benefits at full retirement age and have paid the maximum taxable amounts for their entire careers receive about twice that amount ($3,011). If you wait beyond full retirement age, you can get a lot more.

So, what's your number? If there were a quick and easy way to do the math yourself, I'd tell you right here. But there isn't. Fortunately, Social Security makes it easy to get a ballpark estimate by using one of its online tools: the Social Security Quick Calculator (`www.ssa.gov/oact/quickcalc`) or the Retirement Estimator (`www.ssa.gov/estimator`). See Chapter 6 for more discussion about Social Security calculators, including a helpful tool from AARP.

Make sure that your employer's records match up with Social Security. Every year your employer sends a copy of your W-2 to Social Security, which relies on the name and number on that form to put credits on your earnings record. That record determines whether you qualify for benefits and how much you'll get. If your employer and Social Security are using different names or numbers, it could cost you money, so it's smart to pay attention. It's also your responsibility to correct mistakes. If you're incorrectly identified on your work records or if your income is reported incorrectly, let your employer know. You can contact the SSA (see Chapter 1) to correct an error in the name on your Social Security card.

If you're self-employed, you have 3 years, 3 months, and 15 days from the end of the year in which you earned money to correct errors that may turn up on your earnings record. Otherwise, earnings records can be corrected at any time, if satisfactory evidence of wages can be found. If you don't bring errors to the attention of the SSA within that time, it may not fix them.

Your employer is the one who points out W-2 errors to the SSA. If your employer refuses, you should bring the matter to the attention of the Internal Revenue Service (IRS). You can contact the IRS at 800-829-1040.

THE WINDFALL ELIMINATION PROVISION: IF YOU QUALIFY FOR A PENSION AS WELL AS SOCIAL SECURITY

Have you spent part of your life working for an employer who wasn't part of the Social Security system, and are you earning a pension from that employer? If so, you could get hit by the *Windfall Elimination provision,* which means that the SSA uses a different formula to compute your benefit, and your benefit is reduced. The Windfall Elimination provision is complex and has various exceptions, but be aware that it may apply if you turned 62 or became disabled after 1985 and you first qualified for a pension based on work in which you didn't pay Social Security taxes after 1985. Importantly, this provision doesn't apply to federal workers hired after December 31, 1983, because their earnings are automatically covered by Social Security.

Although the Windfall Elimination provision may cost you, it's capped at 50 percent of your uncovered pension. If you have an uncovered pension of $1,000 per month, the most that your Social Security benefit can be reduced by is $500, and depending on the specific facts of your situation, that amount may be a lot less.

Want to find out more? A good place to start is the Social Security website. You can find out more about the impact of a pension from uncovered work on your benefits at `www.ssa.gov/pubs/10045.html`.

Covering your spouse and children with retirement benefits

Social Security benefits for spouses are part of the economic foundation of older households. Under the rules, a spouse may get up to half of the full benefit given to the retired breadwinner.

REMEMBER

The spouse may qualify at 62, but benefits are reduced for every month they're claimed before the spouse reaches full retirement age. If a spouse takes spousal benefits at 62, and the full retirement age is 67, the amount comes to 32.5 percent of the breadwinner's full retirement payment. If the spouse waits until full retirement age, the amount comes to 50 percent of the breadwinner's full payment.

A noteworthy exception is when the spouse is caring for a child who also qualifies. In this case, the spouse gets 50 percent of the breadwinner's full payment regardless of the spouse's age. (For a deeper exploration of spousal benefits, including issues for spouses who qualify based on their own working records, see Chapter 9.)

TECHNICAL STUFF

The reduction for early collections of the spousal benefit works like this: Benefits are reduced by $\frac{25}{36}$ of 1 percent for each month the benefit is claimed before full retirement age — up to 36 months before full retirement age. If a spouse claims the benefit earlier than 36 months ahead of full retirement age, the benefit is further cut by a factor of $\frac{5}{12}$ of 1 percent per month.

Here's an example: Max has just retired at 66 and begun collecting a full retirement benefit of $1,600 per month. Olivia, his wife, who is 63, qualifies for a spousal benefit of half that amount — $800 — if she waits until her full retirement age of 66 to claim it. But that's three years away. If Olivia collects the spousal benefit now, Social Security reduces her benefit by 25 percent, to $600. (Unlike the basic retirement benefit, which continues to increase up to age 70 if you don't claim it at full retirement age, spousal benefits don't grow after the spouse reaches full retirement age.)

TIP

Social Security offers an online calculator that can tell spouses what percentage of the breadwinner's full retirement they'll get, depending on the age at which they begin collecting a spousal benefit. Go to `www.ssa.gov/oact/quickcalc/spouse.html` to use this handy tool.

You may also earn benefits that cover your dependent children if you die, retire, or become disabled. Suppose an older dad has a child. If the father begins to collect Social Security retirement benefits while his child is still young enough to qualify, the child may receive as much as half the father's benefit (75 percent of the benefit if the father dies).

Social Security may make no distinction among biological children, adopted children, and stepchildren. For that matter, a dependent grandchild may also qualify. (See Chapter 10 for more details on child and family benefits.)

Say Johnny is a securities lawyer married to a much younger woman. When Johnny hits 60, his 30-year-old wife, Larissa, gives birth to a daughter, Janniva. Johnny plugs away at the law firm for six more years and then retires at 66, claiming a Social Security retirement benefit of $2,466. Janniva qualifies for a child benefit of $1,233 (half of her father's full retirement benefit), and she gets that benefit as a dependent child until she turns 18. If Johnny dies at age 66, Larissa can also get a benefit, even though she's only 36 years old. As a young surviving spouse who is caring for the deceased worker's dependent child, she gets a monthly payment of $1,850. The SSA applies different time limits to some of the family benefits that involve children. In the preceding example, the money Larissa gets as Janniva's mother ends when her daughter turns 16.

THE GOVERNMENT PENSION OFFSET PROVISION

Say you qualify for spousal or survivor's benefits in Social Security, but you also get a pension because of your own work in local, state, or federal government. If so, your Social Security may be reduced under the *Government Pension Offset provision.* The reduction is significant: It comes to two-thirds of the amount of your government pension. Suppose you have a government pension of $900 per month, and you're eligible for a Social Security widow's benefit of $1,200 per month. In this case, Social Security may reduce your widow's benefit by $600 (two-thirds of $900), leaving you with a Social Security benefit of $1,200 – $600 = $600.

Congress enacted the Government Pension Offset provision to make sure that Social Security benefits for government workers are reduced in a similar manner as for individuals who have worked entirely within the Social Security system. For example, if you qualify for a Social Security spousal or survivor's benefit, but your own work record makes you eligible for an even *larger* benefit, you get only the benefit you've earned yourself. You can't receive both your larger benefit and the smaller spousal or survivor's benefit. In practice, several factors can preserve your full Social Security benefit, such as the following:

- Your government pension isn't based on your earnings.
- Your government pension is based on a job in which you paid Social Security taxes and you filed for Social Security benefits before April 1, 2004, or your job ended before July 1, 2004, or you paid Social Security taxes on your earnings during the last five years of government work.
- You're a federal employee who switched from civil service retirement to the Federal Employees Retirement System (FERS) after December 31, 1987, and you filed for Social Security spousal or widow/widower benefits before April 1, 2004; your job ended before July 1, 2004; or you paid Social Security taxes on five years of earnings for government employment between January 1988 and when you become entitled to benefits.

You can find out more about the Government Pension Offset provision at `www.ssa.gov/pubs/10007.html`.

Surviving the Loss of a Breadwinner

Social Security isn't just about retirement — it also protects Americans when a family breadwinner dies. You can think of these protections as life insurance that helps families carry on when their livelihood has been shattered. Social Security pays benefits to almost 2 million children whose parents have died. Survivor benefits also go to more than 4 million widows, widowers, and elderly parents who had depended on the deceased worker for financial support.

Benefits may be higher for survivors than for those who depend on a living retiree. In cases of multiple beneficiaries, the family maximum may kick in, limiting payments to about 150 percent to 180 percent of the late worker's primary insurance amount (see the nearby sidebar "Social Security's benchmark for benefits: The primary insurance amount"). When that happens, benefits going to dependents are reduced proportionately.

In this section, I fill you in on who qualifies for survivor benefits and how the breadwinner may earn those benefits before he or she dies.

TIP

Besides the regular, recurring benefit payments (discussed in this section), Social Security pays a one-time *lump-sum death benefit* of $255. This payment typically goes to the surviving spouse after the death is reported to the SSA. If the survivor wasn't living with the deceased spouse, the survivor must still be eligible for benefits on the late spouse's earnings record in order to receive the death payment. In cases where there is no surviving spouse, payments may go to a child. The key for a child's eligibility is that the surviving child qualifies for benefits based on the deceased parent's record at the time of death.

Who qualifies

Survivor benefits can help a household get back on its feet after a death, providing long-term support to growing children, surviving spouses, and sometimes older parents of the worker. Here are the most common categories of relatives who may qualify for Social Security survivor benefits upon the death of a breadwinner:

- **Widows and widowers without young children:** In a noteworthy difference from retirement benefits, these benefits may be collected at a reduced level, as early as age 60. Widowed survivors who are disabled may collect benefits starting at age 50.
- **Widows and widowers raising the deceased worker's child who is under 16:** In such cases, the surviving parent can be any age.

SOCIAL SECURITY'S BENCHMARK FOR BENEFITS: THE PRIMARY INSURANCE AMOUNT

The *primary insurance amount* (PIA) is a dollar figure that becomes the basis for benefits that go to you and your family members. The PIA is what you get if you begin collecting Social Security at your full retirement age (currently 66 and 2 months, and gradually increasing to 67 for workers born in 1960 or later). To determine your PIA, the SSA looks at your past earnings and adjusts them upward to reflect today's wage levels. The SSA then goes through a series of mathematical steps and arrives at your PIA.

For an average wage earner, a PIA is around $1,820 per month (as of 2019), although it can be significantly more for high wage earners. You can get a rough idea of your PIA — and get an idea of other potential benefits — by using Social Security's online tools and projecting benefits at your full retirement age: Check out the Social Security Quick Calculator (`www.ssa.gov/oact/quickcalc`) and the Retirement Estimator (`www.ssa.gov/estimator`).

Your actual Social Security benefits may be lower or higher than the PIA for various reasons, but they will be *based* on it. Here are some examples of benefits and their link to the PIA:

- **Retired worker:** You get 100 percent of your PIA if you retire at the full retirement age. You can start collecting as early as age 62, but the amount you receive per month is reduced if you collect before the full retirement age and increased if you delay collecting until after the full retirement age (up to age 70).
- **Disabled worker:** You get 100 percent of your PIA. The benefit isn't reduced for age and automatically switches to a retirement benefit when you reach full retirement age.
- **Spouse of retiree or disabled worker:** You get up to 50 percent of the covered worker's PIA. You can start collecting at age 62, but the amount you receive is reduced if you collect before reaching full retirement age.
- **Spouse with child:** You get 50 percent of the covered worker's PIA if the child is under 16 or disabled. You may be any age, and the benefit isn't reduced if you collect before you reach full retirement age.
- **Divorced spouse:** You get up to 50 percent of the covered worker's PIA. You can start collecting at 62, but the amount you receive is reduced if you collect before reaching full retirement age. A couple of other rules: Your marriage must have lasted at least ten years, and you must be unmarried.

(continued)

(continued)

- **Widow/widower age 60-plus or divorced widow/widower age 60-plus:** You get up to 100 percent or more of the covered worker's PIA, but the amount depends on several factors. It's reduced if you collect before reaching full retirement age, and it's increased if the deceased spouse had built up delayed retirement credits. The amount you receive per month can't exceed what the deceased spouse was collecting.
- **Widow/widower (at any age), caring for a child under 16:** You get 75 percent of the covered worker's PIA.
- **Disabled widow/widower ages 50 to 59:** You get 71.5 percent of the covered worker's PIA.
- **Child survivor under 18 (or up to age 19 if still in high school and unmarried):** You get 75 percent of the covered worker's PIA. The Social Security family maximum (see Chapter 10) may apply in households with multiple beneficiaries. Stepchildren and grandchildren fall into this category, too, subject to the family maximum.
- **Child of retiree under 18 (or up to age 19 if still in high school and unmarried):** You get 50 percent of the covered worker's PIA. Stepchildren and grandchildren fall into this category, too, subject to the family maximum.
- **Disabled adult child of retiree age 18-plus:** You get 50 percent of the covered worker's PIA.
- **Disabled adult child of deceased worker age 18-plus:** You get 75 percent of the covered worker's PIA.
- **Grandchild of retiree:** You get 50 percent of the covered worker's PIA (if you meet rules for eligibility).
- **Grandchild of deceased worker/retiree:** You get 75 percent of the covered worker's PIA (if you meet rules for eligibility).
- **Parents of deceased worker/retiree:** You get 82.5 percent of the covered worker's PIA if one parent is claiming benefits, 75 percent of the covered worker's PIA if two parents are claiming benefits.

» **Children:** To qualify, children must be under 18 or up to 19 if they are full-time students who haven't yet graduated from high school and are unmarried. Disabled children qualify at any age if they were disabled before age 22. Benefits may go to stepchildren, grandchildren, and step-grandchildren as well.

» **Parents:** Surviving parents qualify if they were dependent on the worker for at least half of their financial support.

- **Divorced spouses:** Former partners may qualify for a survivor benefit if the marriage lasted at least ten years and if they don't remarry before age 60.

How much you get

How much you get in survivor benefits varies depending on your situation. In the following sections, I cover the main categories of survivors so you can see how you and your family may fare.

Surviving spouses

Spouses generally are expected to have been married for nine months to qualify for survivor benefits, but exceptions to the nine-month rule can be made if the widow or widower is the parent of the deceased worker's child. (Exceptions to the nine-month marriage rule are also made if a breadwinner dies in an accident or in the line of duty as a member of a uniformed service.)

Surviving spouses who wait until full retirement age to collect survivor benefits could get up to 100 percent of the benefit amount received by the deceased partner. Survivor benefits can be collected as early as age 60, but the benefit is reduced for each month it's taken before full retirement age — a difference that, over time, can add up to many thousands of dollars.

TECHNICAL STUFF

For widow's and widower's benefits, the reduction rate ranges from $^{19}/_{40}$ of 1 percent per month (for a person whose full retirement age is 65) to $^{19}/_{56}$ of 1 percent per month (for a person whose full retirement age is 67). The reduction is computed for the time period starting when benefits are received until the widow or widower reaches his or her full retirement age.

Widowed applicants are asked to sign Form SSA-4111, which discloses that benefits taken before their full retirement age are reduced. You can go to `www.ssa.gov/forms/ssa-4111.pdf` to print the form.

Note: The full retirement age for survivor benefits (for widows and widowers) may be slightly different than the full retirement age for workers and spouses, depending on your date of birth. The full retirement age for survivors is gradually rising to 67 for people born in 1962 or later. The full retirement age for workers and spouses is gradually rising to 67 for people born in 1960 or later.

Benefit amounts for widows and widowers are also affected by whether the deceased partner had begun collecting Social Security benefits:

- **If the deceased hadn't yet begun collecting retirement benefits,** the surviving spouse could get 100 percent of the deceased spouse's full retirement benefit (the PIA; see the earlier sidebar "Social Security's benchmark for benefits: The primary insurance amount" for more information), as computed by Social Security.

- **If the deceased had already begun collecting retirement benefits,** the survivor payment is the lower of the following:
  - The benefit based on 100 percent of the deceased individual's PIA reduced by any months before the survivor's full retirement age
  - The larger of (a) the amount that was going to the deceased or (b) 82.5 percent of the deceased worker's PIA

TIP

The death of a higher-earning spouse may mean higher benefits for the survivor, even if the survivor is already collecting retirement benefits. When a spouse dies, the survivor should remind the SSA that he or she is getting benefits based on his or her own record. The SSA then checks to see whether the amount should be increased because of survivor protections. If that's the case, the SSA provides a combined benefit — the survivor's own retirement benefit plus an extra amount, so the total equals the full survivor benefit under the deceased spouse's record.

What happens if you're a survivor with an earnings record of your own? It depends on whether you've already started collecting retirement benefits:

- **If you haven't yet started collecting your own Social Security retirement benefits on your own work record:** As a surviving spouse, you may choose to collect a survivor's benefit, while allowing your own unclaimed retirement benefits to increase in value. Later, if your unclaimed retirement benefit has exceeded the amount of your survivor's benefit, you may switch to your own retirement benefit. (The SSA doesn't allow you to claim both and simply add them up.) These rules are potentially complex, so it's a good idea to consult with a Social Security representative if you qualify for survivor and retirement benefits.
- **If you're already collecting Social Security retirement benefits on your own work record:** If the survivor benefit you now qualify for is higher than the retirement benefit you're already collecting, the SSA adds a benefit to your retirement amount, creating a combined benefit equal to the higher survivor's benefit. If the amount you would get as a survivor is lower than what you're receiving already as a retiree, the SSA leaves your retirement benefit alone.

Here's an example of this situation in action: Beverly, a public relations executive, always earned more than Marvin, her husband, who retired from his job as a high school English teacher. When Marvin died at 66, his full retirement age, he had already started collecting a Social Security retirement benefit of $1,400 per month. Beverly, 62, was eligible for a reduced widow's benefit of $1,134 (81 percent of $1,400, because of the reduction for Beverly's age). Beverly collects the widow's benefit for several years. Meanwhile, she allows her own, unclaimed retirement benefit to increase, even after she stops working. Her full retirement benefit is $2,300. That means with the reductions for early retirement, she could get $1,725 per month at 62, but she waits eight more years to stop her survivor benefit and claim a delayed retirement benefit of $2,300 × 1.32 = $3,036 at age 70. If Beverly had already started her retirement benefit at the time Marvin died, she still would have received only her retirement benefit, because her own benefit (no matter when she took it) would be larger than her potential survivor's benefit based on Marvin's more modest earnings. That isn't always the case, but it is for Beverly, because her earnings were so much higher than her husband's.

WHAT HAPPENS WHEN YOU TAKE YOUR BENEFIT EARLY

If your Social Security benefit is reduced because you started it early, the reduction lasts for the rest of your life. Here's an example: Frankie's husband suffered a fatal heart attack, and she has to decide when to begin collecting her widow's benefit. She is about to turn 60, and her full retirement age is six years away. If she waits until she's 66 to start the benefit, she'll get $1,140 per month. But if she takes the benefit now, that amount is reduced by $^{19}/_{48}$ of 1 percent for each month she starts prior to reaching full retirement age. Here's a look at two of her options:

- **Take the benefit now.** Frankie is 72 months away from her full retirement age, so she'll receive $72 \times {}^{19}/_{48} = 28.5$ percent less per month. So, $1,140 × 28.5 percent = $324.90, which means she'll get $1,140 – $324.90 = $815.10 per month.
- **Take the benefit when she's 62.** In this case, her benefit is reduced by 48 months, so she'll get $48 \times {}^{19}/_{48} = 19$ percent less per month. So, $1,140 × 19 percent = $216.60, which means she'll get $1,140 – $216.60 = $923.40 per month.

Frankie, who has been out of the labor force for years, knows that her skills in office administration will bring in only a modest income. She also knows that the individual retirement account her husband had set up has gained little over the past several years, and that he never qualified for a pension. Even though she prefers to wait for a higher payment, Frankie decides to start her Social Security widow's benefit as soon as possible.

The decision of whether to start receiving your survivor's benefit early is an individual one. You need to consider your entire financial picture in order to make the choice that's best for you. Sometimes, taking the benefit early is a necessity — just make sure that if you go this route, you're fully aware of how much your monthly payment will be reduced.

Getting remarried can end an adult's survivor benefits, depending on the person's age. If the widow or widower gets remarried before age 60, benefits can be cut off. (Benefits continue for surviving children.) Widows who remarry can qualify for benefits based on their new spouse's earnings record when they reach 62.

Surviving divorced spouses

Divorced spouses may qualify for survivor's benefits that are similar to those for a widow or widower if the marriage lasted at least ten years. That ten-year requirement is lifted in cases where the divorced spouse is caring for the deceased parent's child who is under 16 or disabled. Divorced spouses also lose survivor benefits if they remarry before age 60.

Surviving children younger than 16

Social Security survivor benefits provide critical protection for families with children. When a widow or widower is raising the deceased worker's child, the parent's age doesn't matter to the SSA. Benefits may go to the surviving parent and the surviving child.

Brandon and Samantha are Baby Boomers whose old romance is rekindled on the dance floor at their 40th high school reunion. She's divorced, and he's widowed. Brandon, 58, has a 12-year-old son, Tyler, from his prior marriage. Samantha, 57, has no children. Brandon and Samantha waste no time getting married, and for a while, life is good. He makes $100,000 per year as a contract manager at an aerospace firm. She works part time at the mall. Three years later, Brandon is killed in a car accident. At that point, Samantha and Tyler each qualify for survivor's benefits of about $1,570 per month. Samantha's benefit would be about $2,090 at her full retirement age, but she can't afford to wait. These benefits help the household stay afloat until Tyler graduates from high school and enrolls in college.

Surviving parents

Older parents of a breadwinner potentially qualify for survivor benefits if their adult child dies. To be eligible, they must be at least 62 and must prove that they relied on the child for half of their financial support. Also, surviving parents must not be eligible for their own Social Security benefits that exceed what they might get as survivors. If two living parents both qualify, each may receive 75 percent of the deceased child's basic benefit. If one parent survives, the amount is slightly higher: 82.5 percent.

Disabled survivors

Special rules also apply to disabled survivors, who may be eligible for benefits at a younger age than widows in good health and without dependent children.

Disabled widows and widowers may begin collecting survivor benefits as early as age 50, but such payments are reduced 28.5 percent from what they would be if the beneficiary waited until full retirement age to collect.

How benefits are earned

In order for family members to get survivor's benefits, the deceased worker must have built up credits based on his or her working record. But the rules are somewhat different than for retirement benefits. The exact requirement depends on the age of the worker. For example, workers still in their early and mid-20s may gain survivor's protections by earning just six credits — about one and a half years of work. A 40-year-old worker needs 18 credits — less than five years of work. For a 62-year-old, the requirement is 40 credits. Special rules allow workers with young children to qualify with only six credits (see the nearby sidebar "Getting a boost from Social Security even if you haven't worked much" for more information).

Survivor's coverage has the same dollar requirements for earning credits as retirement does: Workers can earn up to four credits, and the credit amount, which rises over time, was set at $1,410 in 2020.

GETTING A BOOST FROM SOCIAL SECURITY EVEN IF YOU HAVEN'T WORKED MUCH

For most benefits, you need to achieve what the SSA calls *fully insured status* to gain full protection. But the SSA has a kind of safety net for children and parents raising children, which it calls *currently insured status*. This status allows you to earn certain benefits for family members even when you haven't met the usual earnings requirements. You're considered "currently insured" if you've attained at least six Social Security credits in a period of 3 years and 3 months (13 quarters), ending with death, disability, or retirement. Benefits are likely to be modest, and they're restricted to children, as well as a spouse who is caring for a dependent child. Benefits under this status can't go to a spouse without children or to a worker's surviving parents.

Here's an example: Levan hasn't been a model breadwinner. But lately, the single father has started to hunker down, taking a job as a desk clerk in a resort hotel and bringing in steady money for the first time in his life. When he dies in a hang-gliding accident at age 33, Levan has built up seven work credits over the last two years. That wouldn't normally be enough to gain a survivor's benefit. But under Levan's "currently insured status" with the SSA, his young son qualifies for a survivor's benefit. Given his limited earnings history, however, the benefit is modest.

Paying Your Bills When You Can't Work: Disability Benefits

Disability can be devastating to an individual or family's finances. Social Security offers different benefits for disability. The benefits are complex, with sometimes-ambiguous rules for qualifying and many requirements that are distinct from other areas of Social Security.

This section offers an extremely brief overview of Social Security Disability Insurance (SSDI). Turn to Chapter 11 for a detailed examination of this important and complex area, including information on how the SSA defines *disability* and the medical evidence applicants need in order to make a claim.

If you're disabled, you may apply for SSDI benefits or for a separate program called Supplemental Security Income (see the next section), which targets the needy.

The SSA also runs a special federal program for miners who suffer from black lung disease. For more information on the Federal Black Lung Program, you can download the publication available online at `www.dol.gov/owcp/dcmwc/regs/compliance/cm-6.pdf` or go to `www.dol.gov/owcp/dcmwc/`.

Who qualifies

As in other Social Security protections, dependent family members of a disabled worker may also qualify for help if they meet certain requirements. Social Security disability benefits may go to

- **Disabled workers:** To qualify, an individual must have built up the necessary number of credits, through covered work, and must meet a standard of having worked recently.
- **Spouses of disabled workers:** To qualify, a disabled worker's spouse must be caring for a child under 16 or a disabled child of any age, or be at least 62 years old.
- **Children of disabled workers:** To qualify, a child must fall into one of the following categories:
  - Under 18, unmarried, and attending school full time
  - Up to 19 years old and unmarried, if he or she is attending school full time but hasn't yet graduated from high school
  - Adult and disabled but younger than 22

  These standards also apply to stepchildren and possibly grandchildren.

How you qualify

Qualifying for SSDI isn't easy. The SSA says that to get benefits, a person has to be completely disabled — unable to work — or suffering from a condition that may end in death. Disability benefits potentially continue until full retirement age, at which time they're switched to retirement benefits.

How much you get

SSDI payment levels are based on average lifetime earnings. Individuals can qualify with a lower number of credits than is typical for retirement benefits:

- **Workers younger than 24:** You need six credits earned in the three years before the onset of disability. As with other Social Security benefits, you can earn up to four credits per year for covered work.
- **Workers ages 24 to 31:** You need to have worked in Social Security–covered employment 50 percent of the time between age 21 and the onset of the disability.
- **Workers ages 31 and up:** The credit requirements steadily increase. At 31, you're expected to have built up 20 credits, and this moves up to 40 credits for applicants ages 41 and older. Also, applicants generally are expected to have earned 20 credits within the ten years before the onset of disability.

If you meet the strict qualifications for disability insurance, you may receive a benefit that is 100 percent of your primary insurance amount, which is the same as the retirement benefit you qualify for at full retirement age. Significantly, a worker's disability benefit is *not* reduced for age (after all, job-related disability takes place before you retire).

The average monthly benefit for a disabled worker is a bit over $1,255, but if you're disabled with above-average earnings, your benefit is higher. A worker's disability benefit switches automatically to a retirement benefit when the worker reaches full retirement age. The payment level doesn't change.

When a worker qualifies for SSDI, benefits may also go to other family members. Not only does the breadwinner get income, but payments may also be made to a dependent child and spouse. The child's benefit may be 50 percent of the breadwinner's amount (as long as the child is younger than 18, or up to 19 if still in high school and unmarried). A dependent spouse without a child may qualify for 50 percent of the disabled worker's benefit if the spouse has reached full retirement age. If the spouse is younger, the benefit becomes available at 62. If the spouse is caring for the disabled worker's child, the dependent spouse benefit of 50 percent is available at any age. When multiple Social Security benefits are flowing into one household, they may be reduced by the family maximum (see Chapter 10).

When the Need Is Great: Supplemental Security Income

Supplemental Security Income (SSI) targets the neediest Americans — specifically, those who are 65 or older, blind, or disabled — with cash payments to help them survive. Its benefits are designed to pay for life's necessities: food, clothing, and shelter. SSI also has child disability benefits for children under 18.

The SSA runs SSI, but SSI isn't considered a Social Security benefit. Instead, it's a cash assistance or welfare program that you qualify for based on financial need. This is a big difference from basic Social Security benefits, including SSDI (see the preceding section).

You contribute to the basic Social Security programs, including SSDI, through the payroll tax, and then you qualify for benefits you've earned through work credits that add up over time.

SSI, on the other hand, is financed by general tax dollars. People don't need to build up work credits or demonstrate a work history to qualify. They just have to demonstrate an extreme level of need. The rules on income and assets are strict, however. To get SSI in most states, people must earn below the federal payment standard of $783 per month for an individual and $1,175 per month for a couple (as of 2020). *Assets* (the things people own, such as cash or property other than your home) generally can't exceed $2,000 in value for an individual and $3,000 for a couple.

REMEMBER

Social Security is social insurance for people of all income levels. SSI is an assistance program for people with very little income.

IN THIS CHAPTER

» Recognizing that when you claim affects what you get

» Considering your life expectancy

» Remembering your spouse

» Working for greater security

» Making your decision on when to start collecting

Chapter 3

Deciding When to Start Collecting Retirement Benefits

I know people who are sick of their jobs, fed up with the demands of the work world, and ready to begin collecting Social Security the very first day they can get it. I also know people who love their jobs, see themselves as forever young, and are pained even to think about collecting retirement benefits. Where do *you* fit on the spectrum?

Of course, the decision on when to start collecting Social Security is personal. Your priorities and needs, your spouse's needs, your financial resources, your health, and your expected longevity all can shape your attitude about collecting Social Security.

Your decision on when to begin collecting Social Security retirement benefits may be the most important financial decision you ever make. Starting too early can cost you tens of thousands of dollars. Worse, jumping the gun may hurt the most in your final years, when it's too late to do anything about it.

In this chapter, I fill you in on the most important factors to consider in order to make the right decision for you. There is no one right answer. My goal is for you to make the decision about when to collect Social Security fully armed with all the information you need.

Paying Attention to Your Full Retirement Age

A key consideration in choosing a start date for collecting Social Security is something called your *full retirement age*. The Social Security Administration (SSA) gives you a window of several years before and after your full retirement age in which to begin collecting your retirement benefits, starting at 62. In the following sections, you find out how to determine this age (based on your year of birth) and how it affects the amount of your monthly benefit.

Determining your full retirement age

Your first question is probably this: How much Social Security am I going to get? The answer: It depends. The first step is knowing your full retirement age. If you collect Social Security *before* reaching your full retirement age, you'll get less each month — potentially a lot less, for the rest of your life. If you collect Social Security *after* reaching your full retirement age, you'll get more each month.

REMEMBER

Your full retirement benefit is the amount you get if you wait until your full retirement age to begin collecting. But what the SSA calls your full benefit is not the biggest benefit you can get. You can actually get a lot *more* than your full benefit by waiting until you're 70 to begin collecting — 32 percent more if your full retirement age is 66, and 24 percent more if it's 67. The SSA uses your full benefit as the starting point when it decides how much you or your dependents will receive (see the next section for details).

The earliest age at which you can start collecting retirement benefits is 62, and the latest is 70. Your full retirement age falls somewhere in between. Table 3-1 shows a person's full retirement age based on his or her year of birth.

TABLE 3-1 Full Retirement Age Based on Year of Birth

Year of Birth*	Full Retirement Age
1937 or earlier	65 years
1938	65 years and 2 months
1939	65 years and 4 months
1940	65 years and 6 months
1941	65 years and 8 months
1942	65 years and 10 months
1943–1954	66 years
1955	66 years and 2 months
1956	66 years and 4 months
1957	66 years and 6 months
1958	66 years and 8 months
1959	66 years and 10 months
1960 and later	67 years

** If you were born on January 1, refer to the previous year. Full retirement age may be slightly different for survivor benefits.*

Estimating how much you'll get each month based on when you retire

After you figure out your full retirement age (see the preceding section), you can get a ballpark idea of your monthly benefit. Currently, the average retirement benefit is $1,503 per month (this is being written in January 2020), but benefits go much higher, depending on your earnings history and when you begin collecting.

TIP

It's easy to get at least a rough estimate of your retirement benefits. Just use one of the SSA's online calculators — the Social Security Quick Calculator at `www.ssa.gov/oact/quickcalc` or the Retirement Estimator at `www.ssa.gov/estimator`. They can give you projected amounts for retiring at different ages, such as 62, waiting for your full retirement age (according to Table 3-1), or delaying all the way until 70. You also can get estimates customized to your personal situation by using AARP's Social Security Benefits Calculator at `www.aarp.org/work/social-security/social-security-benefits-calculator`. See Chapter 6 for more details on calculating your benefits.

If you use the SSA's Retirement Estimator, you'll see roughly how much Social Security you could get, especially if your earnings don't skyrocket or crash between now and the time you retire. If you haven't yet done so, you can use the Retirement Estimator as a starting point to think about how much money you can count on in retirement. (I talk more about planning for retirement in Chapter 14.)

Online calculators are not the only tools you can use to get an idea of your benefit amount. You also can sign up for a personal "*my* Social Security" account with the Social Security Administration at `www.ssa.gov/site/signin/en/`. This online statement offers estimates of your future benefits for retirement, for your survivors, and for disability. For an in-depth discussion of "*my* Social Security" accounts, turn to Chapter 7.

Whether the Social Security numbers look small, large, or in between, remember that Social Security is meant to be just *one part* of your financial foundation.

As I mention earlier, you stand to get much more money each month if you can delay collecting Social Security past your full retirement age. For example, if you were born between 1943 and 1954, your Social Security payment at 62 is 25 percent lower than if you wait until 66 (your full retirement age). If you hold off to age 70 — four years past your full retirement age — the benefit balloons by 32 percent.

These differences can add up to real money over the years — or decades. Consider the following example:

> Elisa was born in 1957 and wants to know how she would be affected by choosing different dates to retire. She goes to SSA's Quick Calculator (`www.ssa.gov/OACT/quickcalc/index.html`) and plugs in the $160,000 she earned last year. If Elisa waits until her full retirement age of 66 years and 6 months, she'll get about $2,881 per month. If she waits until 70 to collect benefits, she'll get about $3,756 per month. And if she wants to start as soon as possible, at 62, she'll get a more modest $2,044 per month.
>
> Elisa knows that longevity runs in her family, so she wants to find out how much she'll collect from Social Security if she lives to 90. To get the answer, she calculates the number of months she would receive benefits in three different cases: starting at 62 (336 months), starting at 66 and six months — her full retirement age — (280 months), and starting at 70 (240 months). Then she multiplies the number of months by the estimated benefit provided by the online tool.

If Elisa starts the benefit at 62 and lives to 90, she could end up with more than $686,784 over her lifetime, not even counting increases for inflation (336 months between 62 and 90, multiplied by the estimated benefit of $2,044 per month for benefits starting at 62). If she starts at 66 and 6 months, her lifetime collection would exceed $806,680. And if she starts the benefit at 70, she ends up with more than $901,440. The difference between starting benefits at 62 and at 70 comes to $214,656 for Elisa.

Figure 3-1 shows that your decision on when to begin retirement benefits makes a real difference in your monthly income. The numbers here are based on a retirement age of 66 and a monthly benefit of $1,000. They may differ based on your year of birth and other factors.

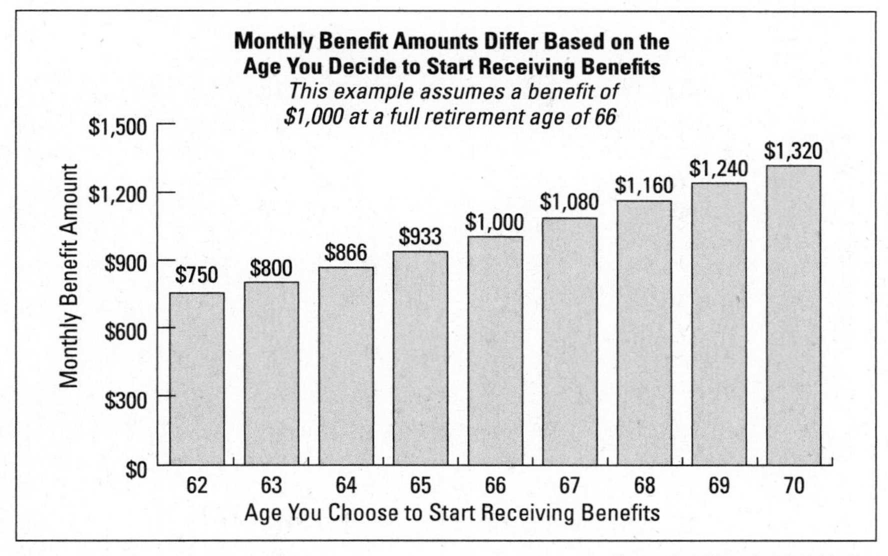

FIGURE 3-1: The amount of your monthly benefit depends on the age you start receiving it.

Source: Social Security Administration

TIP

Waiting to take retirement benefits beyond your full retirement age could prove especially important for Baby Boomers and, right behind them on the age ladder, members of Generation X. For people born in 1943 or later, the retirement benefit expands at a rate of 8 percent per year (or ⅔ of 1 percent per month) for each year you delay claiming (up to age 70) after reaching full retirement age. Check out Table 3-2 for the numbers.

TABLE 3-2 Increase for Delayed Retirement

Year of Birth*	Yearly Rate of Increase	Monthly Rate of Increase
1933–1934	5.5 percent	11/24 of 1 percent
1935–1936	6.0 percent	½ of 1 percent
1937–1938	6.5 percent	13/24 of 1 percent
1939–1940	7.0 percent	7/12 of 1 percent
1941–1942	7.5 percent	⅝ of 1 percent
1943 or later	8.0 percent	⅔ of 1 percent

* *If you were born on January 1, refer to the previous year.*

USING YOUR NEST EGG TO DELAY CLAIMING

If you're fortunate enough to have a nest egg and you want to retire, you can consider withdrawing more savings up front as a way to hold off starting your Social Security benefit. But does the strategy make sense? It well may, and there are some important things to keep in mind.

Social Security benefits go up about 7 percent for each year they are not claimed between age 62 and your full retirement age. Wait longer and the reward grows even more: Benefits increase 8 percent annually for each year they are not claimed between full retirement age and 70.

Are your financial resources adequate to support your lifestyle without Social Security, so you can delay claiming and lock in the income gains I just described? The issue can get complicated, and those interested may want to talk it over with a financial advisor. Among the considerations are the following:

- **The tax bite:** A portion of your Social Security benefit may be subject to income tax (though at least 15 percent is tax free for everyone). Withdrawals from (non-Roth) Individual Retirement Accounts will surely have tax implications. But some research has shown that withdrawing more up front may reduce the tax bite later. Check your situation with an expert.
- **Family income:** Is your spouse eligible for Social Security based on his or her work record? This increases your options. Just know that your total income may affect whether your Social Security benefits are subject to income tax, how much, and

whether it makes sense to delay claiming. (See Chapter 13 for a discussion of income tax rules and Social Security, including provisional income.)

- **Your investments:** Consider reasonable rates of return, including your appetite for risk, in weighing the pros and cons of delaying a claim for Social Security. It's extremely difficult to beat Social Security's guaranteed returns.

Finally, a note of caution (and common sense): If your nest egg is modest, the strategy of withdrawing savings to delay Social Security may be unwise, because it's important to have a cushion. Be realistic when calculating how much of a cushion you need.

Looking at Life Expectancy When You Claim Benefits

When figuring out how much to reduce people's benefits if they take the benefits early, the SSA considered average longevity. But you could live a lot longer than average — and that makes your decision on when to claim benefits that much more important.

No one can predict exactly how long you'll live. You should also consider how old your parents lived to be and your personal health, including chronic conditions that may shorten your life span.

TIP

You can use an online calculator to assess your life expectancy. Go to `www.livingto100.com` and click on "Take the Calculator" or take the Longevity Test at `www.bluezones.com`, and you'll be given an estimate. The Longevity Illustrator, developed by the American Academy of Actuaries and the Society of Actuaries, highlights how long you might live at different ages of retirement; visit `www.longevityillustrator.org`.

In the following sections, I cover two topics related to longevity and Social Security: completing a break-even analysis and handling the possibility of exceeding your projected life expectancy. Neither is as complicated as it sounds.

Doing a break-even analysis: The payoff from different retirement dates

A *break-even analysis* compares what you get in your lifetime if you pick different dates to collect Social Security. It's a way to estimate your total payoff from retiring at an earlier date (with reduced monthly payments) and retiring at a later date (with higher monthly payments). This approach gets some criticism, because it can lead to a costly decision if you end up living longer than expected. Factors such as your health and other financial resources also should be weighed in deciding when it makes the most sense to claim retirement benefits.

But I also know that many people care — understandably! — how much Social Security they may get in a lifetime. In general, if you die before reaching the break-even age, and you started collecting benefits at the *earlier* date, you come out ahead. If you live beyond your break-even age but started benefits at the *later* date, you also come out ahead, because those bigger payments add up over time. Where you lose out is if you die before reaching the break-even age (and you started collecting larger benefits at the later date) or if you die after your break-even age (and you started smaller benefits at the earlier date).

The break-even approach is a common tool recommended by financial planners, and it can provide perspective. But it's just one consideration. The more you care about how your benefits add up over a lifetime, the greater weight you may give a break-even calculation. The more you care about ending up with the biggest monthly benefit, the greater weight you may give to delaying your claim for Social Security.

TIP

Your break-even age will vary based on your earnings record and date of birth, but estimating it isn't too difficult. Here's how to compare how you'll come out over your lifetime if you start benefits at age 62 versus your full retirement age:

1. **Determine your full retirement age (refer to Table 3-1).**

   For example, say your full retirement age is 66.

2. **Determine your full retirement benefit at that retirement age by going to** `www.ssa.gov/estimator`.

   For example, say your full retirement benefit at 66 is $1,500 per month. (***Note:*** The estimator assumes you keep working until age 66.)

3. **Determine your benefit at 62 by going to** `www.ssa.gov/estimator`.

   In this example, if you claim benefits at 62, your monthly payment is $1,125.

4. **Figure out how much you would take home in the 48 months between age 62 and your full retirement age (66) if you start collecting at age 62.**

   In this example, you're taking home $1,125 per month, and you're doing that for 48 months, so multiplying $1,125 by 48 months gives you $54,000.

5. **Now figure out how many months you would have to survive beyond age 66 in order to break even.**

   In this example, the difference in monthly payments taken at age 62 ($1,125 per month) and 66 ($1,500 per month) is $375. So, divide the amount from

Step 4 ($54,000, in this example) by the difference in monthly payments ($375, in this example), and you get the number of months you'd have to survive beyond age 66 in order to break even (in this case, 144 months, or 12 years). So, in this example, if you live past age 78, you come out ahead by starting your benefits at the full retirement age of 66.

TIP

If doing all that math doesn't appeal to you, and if you were born between 1943 and 1954, here are some general guidelines:

- **If you're comparing retirement at 62 with full retirement at 66, your break-even age is typically around 77 or 78.** In other words, if you die earlier, you could end up with more money by claiming early retirement benefits. If you live longer, you could be better off taking your benefits at 66.
- **If you're comparing full retirement at 66 with delayed retirement at 70, your break-even age is typically several months after your 82nd birthday.** In other words, if you die before 82 or so, you could end up with more money by beginning benefits at 66. If you live past 82, you could be better off delaying your retirement benefits until you turn 70.

REMEMBER

Social Security provides a kind of insurance against running out of money for however long you live. The guarantee of inflation-protected income makes Social Security different from a typical investment. For many people, a range of considerations affect the timing of a claim. The break-even analysis is just one piece of information.

Considering what'll happen if you live longer than you expect

Half the people in any given age group will exceed their life expectancy, in some cases by a lot. Does longevity run in your family? For older couples in decent health, the odds that at least one spouse will survive to a ripe old age are very high. Life expectancy may be higher if you have a good education, if you make a nice living, if you're closely connected to your friends and family, and if you're careful about keeping in shape.

The possibility of living a very long life can be a big factor when you're deciding when to start Social Security. You could live a lot longer than you expect. That means your price tag for retirement will keep going up, while financial resources may dwindle. How much will the cost of living be 20 or more years down the road? What about doctors' bills or long-term care needs? How long can you realistically expect your savings to last? The bigger Social Security payment you get by delaying benefits until you're 70 could come in very handy in those later years.

Here's some food for thought: A man who turned 65 in 2015 can expect to live about another 17.9 years. A woman who turned 65 in 2015 can anticipate another 20.5 years. At age 75, he can expect another 11.2 years, and she can expect another 13. If that man and woman make it to 85, each is projected to live past their 90th birthday. Among today's 65-year-olds, one in three will make it past 90. Almost one in ten will reach 95.

REMEMBER

Knowing your life expectancy isn't enough. You also need to know what gives you peace of mind when it comes to money. What do you think is worse: living longer than you expected and running short of money, or living shorter than you expected and feeling secure until the end (even if you didn't max out your lifetime Social Security benefits)?

To illustrate, I present Eager Edgar and Steady Betty, two pre-retirees who are thinking about the next phase of their lives in very different ways. Both are 61 and have had virtually identical earnings in their careers.

> Eager Edgar dreams of retiring from his job as a warehouse manager and trekking through the wilderness while he still has the energy. His parents died young, and he views early retirement as his last sure chance to really live. He has a couple hundred thousand dollars in an individual retirement account (IRA), and his rent is modest. The month after he turns 62, Edgar collects his first Social Security payment of $1,600.
>
> Steady Betty sees the world differently. She likes her accounting job, even though the commute is increasingly stressful. But Betty doesn't want to worry about money when she's older, and she knows her mother lived until 90. Betty decides to wait until she reaches 66 (her full retirement age) before claiming Social Security. The prospect of getting a bigger monthly payment and building her nest egg further gives Betty peace of mind.
>
> Fast-forward a few years. Eager Edgar's arthritis is getting worse, and his medications are costing more and more. After a couple of adventures in the Rocky Mountains, his hiking equipment begins to gather dust. Unplanned costs for healthcare, a loan to his unemployed son, and the rising cost of living reduce Edgar's savings. A long stint in a nursing home costs him $30,000. For the last three years of his life, Edgar is obsessed with the fear that his savings will run out and he'll lose his independence, all because he has to survive on the reduced Social Security benefits he chose. He takes to splitting pills in half, which increases his pain. He dies at 84, a lot later than he expected.
>
> Steady Betty sticks to her plan, putting away savings every month. At 66 she begins collecting her full retirement benefit of $2,133 and enjoys a fulfilling new chapter. A fatal aneurysm brings her life to an abrupt end, midway through her 74th year, much earlier than she expected.

TAKE THE MONEY AND RUN? THINK AGAIN

Maybe you doubt the wisdom of waiting to start collecting Social Security. Studies have shown that age 62 — the earliest age of eligibility — is the most common age for retirement claims. But is it the best? Taking the money as soon as possible may seem sensible — it's a sure thing. You may need the money. Or you may have reason to believe you won't live much longer because of a serious illness, for example. In such cases, the logic of claiming reduced, early benefits may be undeniable. But certain arguments in favor of early claiming are shakier. Here are a few of the less persuasive reasons to begin collecting benefits early:

- **"I can make the money grow and come out ahead."** This is the economic principle that money today will be worth more tomorrow, through investments and a helpful boost from rising interest rates. You may be able to come out ahead, but there's a guaranteed reward for collecting Social Security later — several percent a year between age 62 and your full retirement age, and 8 percent per year after that up to age 70. And remember: That's on top of inflation protection. Years ago, retirees could, at the least, plunk down money on risk-free certificates of deposit (CDs) and look forward to steady gains. These days, CDs barely pay anything — and you're aware of the uncertainties of the stock market. But maybe you're blessed with financial savvy. Maybe you have the skill to outperform the markets year after year and the discipline to stick to your program. To come out ahead, that's what you'll need to do, especially if you live a long time. For most people, relying on a bigger Social Security benefit as a firm foundation of retirement security is easier.
- **"I want a new life."** If you hate your job or you've been waiting for a chance to reinvent yourself (say, by launching a small business), a guaranteed Social Security payment may seem like just the ticket to get started. Of course, you should try to pursue your dreams. Just be aware that your interests may change and business ideas may fail.
- **"I could get hit by a bus. Why leave money on the table?"** Yep, you could get hit by a bus. But however fatalistic your view, the reality is that a 60-year-old man has a greater chance of dying in his sleep at 85 from various ailments than coming to an accidental finale much earlier. Why not make sure that you have the finances you need in the meantime?
- **"I'd better get my share before Social Security goes bust and there's nothing left."** This belief strikes a chord with some people. After all, you've been hearing doom and gloom about Social Security for years. But as a strategy for collecting your benefits, it's a bad idea. Most proposed reforms would not hit retirees or near retirees. When Congress voted in 1983 to raise the full retirement age, for example, the impact came far in the future, affecting people who reached full retirement age in 2000 and beyond.

Things turned out differently than either Eager Edgar or Steady Betty planned. The point is that you can't be sure how long you'll live. When you're deciding when to begin collecting Social Security, keep different possibilities in mind and consider the implications for your standard of living and sense of well-being.

Considering Your Spouse When You Claim Social Security

Earlier in this chapter, I focus on how timing your collection of Social Security affects your *own* bottom line. But the issue of timing is even bigger than that. You and your spouse could face decisions on when to collect benefits that could affect your household for many years. I'm talking about benefits that go to a dependent spouse, based on a breadwinner's work record, and benefits that go to a survivor after the breadwinner dies. Women are more vulnerable than men to poverty in old age, so these decisions may be of great consequence to many wives, but the same principle applies to everyone: Choices on when to begin Social Security benefits could have a lasting impact on you and your spouse's financial well-being.

If you're eligible for Social Security as a dependent spouse, you face a real choice about when to begin benefits. You may claim this benefit if you have reached 62 and your partner has begun collecting retirement benefits. But your own spousal benefit is reduced for each month you claim it before you've reached your own full retirement age. At your own full retirement age, your spousal benefit can be 50 percent of the breadwinner's full retirement benefit. But if you don't wait, and you claim it as early as 62, it's reduced significantly.

By the way, if you've established your own earnings record with Social Security, that could change things. In that case, your payment is the greater of the benefit you've earned yourself or the amount you qualify for as a dependent spouse.

For workers with a full retirement age of 67, claiming the spousal benefit early reduces benefits by as much as 17.5 percent for those claiming at 62 to a little over 4 percent for those claiming at 66. Suppose your spouse has begun collecting his or her full retirement benefit of $1,000 per month. If you wait until you reach your full retirement age of 67, you get $500 per month in spousal benefits. If you start as soon as possible, at 62, you get about $325. You can get more details on what the spousal benefit means to you, and how your amount is affected by when you claim it, at `www.ssa.gov/oact/quickcalc/spouse.html`.

Social Security applies a monthly reduction rate to spousal benefits taken before full retirement age. The rate is $^{25}/_{36}$ of 1 percent per month for each of the first 36 months before full retirement age, and $^{5}/_{12}$ of 1 percent for each month before then.

If a dependent spouse starts collecting before reaching his or her full retirement age, the amount is reduced. But unlike some benefits, it doesn't work the opposite way: Social Security provides no "bonus" for waiting past full retirement age. The upper limit of a dependent spouse benefit is 50 percent of the benefit that would go to the breadwinner at full retirement age. (The breadwinner can't push the spousal amount higher by delaying collection of benefits past his or her own full retirement age.) ***Note:*** A spouse who has reached full retirement age will get 50 percent of the breadwinner's full retirement benefit, *even if the breadwinner begins collecting before full retirement age.*

Table 3-3 shows the monthly reductions that affect spousal benefits taken by a dependent spouse before reaching full retirement age. It also shows that the monthly reductions differ, based on year of birth.

Your decision about when to collect benefits also has a major effect on the amount of Social Security you leave behind for a surviving widow or widower. If you die, your spouse (at his or her full retirement age) can get 100 percent of your benefit. That means the bigger a benefit you wait to receive, the more you leave your surviving spouse. You could look at it this way: A retirement benefit you claim at 70 is 76 percent more than what you get if you start at 62. That much larger benefit is what you could leave a surviving spouse, who may rely on it for a long time.

Widows and widowers also face timing decisions. They can collect their survivor benefit as early as 60, but with a substantial reduction. (I'm speaking here about aged widows and widowers who are not disabled or raising children — factors that allow for earlier eligibility.) Generally, it will cost the surviving spouse about 30 percent of the benefit to take it at 60, when compared to waiting until full retirement age.

Social Security offers a lot of material online about survivors' benefits and other categories of benefits. To find out more about survivors' benefits, go to `www.ssa.gov/pubs/10084.html`.

TABLE 3-3 Primary and Spousal Benefits at Age 62*

			Primary		Spouse	
Year of Birth	Normal or Full Retirement Age	Number of Reduction Months	Amount	Reduction	Amount	Reduction
1937 or earlier	65 years	36	$800	20%	$375	25%
1938	65 years and 2 months	38	$791	20.83%	$370	25.83%
1939	65 years and 4 months	40	$783	21.67%	$366	26.67%
1940	65 years and 6 months	42	$775	22.5%	$362	27.5%
1941	65 years and 8 months	44	$766	23.33%	$358	28.33%
1942	65 years and 10 months	46	$758	24.17%	$354	29.17%
1943–1954	66 years	48	$750	25%	$350	30%
1955	66 years and 2 months	50	$741	25.83%	$345	30.83%
1956	66 years and 4 months	52	$733	26.67%	$341	31.67%
1957	66 years and 6 months	54	$725	27.5%	$337	32.5%
1958	66 years and 8 months	56	$716	28.33%	$333	33.33%
1959	66 years and 10 months	58	708	29.17%	$329	34.17%
1960 and later	67 years	60	700	30%	$325	35%

** Based on a $1,000 primary insurance amount*

Recognizing the Potential Payoff of Working Later in Life

Suppose you're approaching 62, so you're still years away from full retirement age. You're still on the job, and you like it that way. Maybe your employer's health plan is cheaper than any healthcare coverage you could get on your own, because you're still too young for Medicare. Maybe you're making good money. If so, you may be increasing your future Social Security benefit, if your current earnings are higher than some of the earlier years on your record.

At 62, you could face a decision on whether to work *and* start to collect retirement benefits. You already know that Social Security pays less each month for early retirement. But there's another consideration: You're likely to smack right into the earnings limit.

The earnings limit is a potential issue for individuals who claim retirement benefits before their full retirement age (see Chapter 13 for a more complete discussion). What it means is that if you begin Social Security while still earning money and you haven't reached full retirement age, the SSA will withhold part, or even all, of your benefit if you earn above a certain amount per year. At full retirement age, though, you can say goodbye to the earnings limit. The SSA will raise your payment to give back the money it withheld.

For early retirees, the SSA holds back $1 for every $2 earned above a certain amount ($18,240 in 2020). The limit changes for the year in which you reach full retirement age. For individuals in this category, the SSA withholds $1 for every $3 earned above a certain limit ($48,600 in 2020). The withholding stops during the month that you reach full retirement age. The earnings limit rises each year to keep up with rising wages.

REMEMBER

The earnings limit, combined with early retirement reductions, creates a potential double whammy: You temporarily get a smaller benefit because of working, and — more important — you *permanently* get a smaller payment because you claimed retirement benefits early. Does that make sense for you? It could. You may need the money. You may be improving your earnings record, which will boost your Social Security benefit. (You can get insight on this point by working with Social Security's online calculators or by calling the SSA.) But think it through. Think about how long you could live. Think about whether you really need the early Social Security benefit. If you make enough money on your own, you may be better off working (even part time) without collecting Social Security. Later, you can enjoy a larger retirement benefit for the rest of your life.

REMEMBER

You don't permanently lose the money withheld because of the earnings limit. At your full retirement age, the SSA returns the withheld money in the form of higher benefit payments.

Putting It All Together: The Right Time to Begin Collecting Benefits

TIP

Selecting the right time to begin benefits is a personal matter. Only you know what makes sense for your family. But you should keep in mind some key points when you make this critical choice:

- **Make sure that you know when you qualify for full benefits, but remember you have broad discretion about when to claim.** Refer to Table 3-1.

- **Know your benefit.** By using the Social Security retirement calculators (see "Estimating how much you'll get each month based on when you retire," earlier in this chapter), you can quickly get an idea of the benefit you'd receive before, at, and after your full retirement age. Each year you wait to collect beyond your full retirement age will add 8 percent to your benefit. Each year you begin collecting before your full retirement age will reduce it between 5 percent and 7 percent. In other words, the earlier you retire, the less Social Security you get each month. For many people, that's a powerful argument to hold off claiming benefits.
- **Be realistic about your life expectancy.** If you don't like to think about how long you'll live, get over it. Your life expectancy, and the possibility that you may exceed it, should be factors when you make plans for Social Security and retirement in general. Of course, no one knows how long you'll live. But there's plenty to consider:
  - Do people in your family tend to live long?
  - How would you grade your own lifestyle in terms of fitness, exercise, diet, and other personal habits that affect health?
  - How healthy are you? Do you suffer from a chronic condition that is likely to shorten your life?
  - Do you have a lot of stress? If so, do you have ways of managing that stress that make you feel better?
  - Do you lug around a lot of anger and worry? If so, can you do anything about it?
- **Think about all your sources of income and your expenses.** Consider your savings, including pensions, 401(k)s, IRAs, and any other investments. Make realistic calculations about how much money you need. Look at several months of statements from your checking account and credit cards to review what you spend on and look for waste, while you're at it. Ask yourself: Do you have the option to keep on working? Are you physically up to it?
- **Think about your spouse.** If you die first, it could determine how much your spouse gets for the rest of his or her life. Consider your spouse's life expectancy and financial resources. Does he or she have a chance of living for many more years? If so, what are the household finances (beyond Social Security) to support a long life? Does the spouse have health issues that could cost a lot of money in the future? Husbands should bear in mind that wives typically outlast them by several years, because wives are typically a few years younger and because women have a longer life expectancy than men. Is that the case in your marriage?

SOCIAL SECURITY BECOMES MORE IMPORTANT THE OLDER YOU GET

You can't make the stock market go up or control whether someone will give you a job. You can't make your house jump in value if the whole neighborhood is sinking. You can't go back in time and start an early nest egg if you spent like crazy when you were younger. You can't make your employer keep a pension plan. And you can't prevent the cost of living from rising.

But you do have some influence over the size of your Social Security benefit, based on when you claim it. This matters for a little-recognized reason: The older you become, the more likely you are to depend on Social Security.

The more years pass, the more you need Social Security's protection against inflation, known as the *cost-of-living adjustment.* This provision is a big deal (even if the adjustment is small some years) because the effect of inflation over time can be drastic. At a rate of 3 percent inflation, the buying power of unprotected income plunges by *half* over a 20-year period. Even if you're fortunate enough to get a private pension, it's probably not shielded against inflation, and rising prices erode it over time.

Other resources can boost your retirement security but are far from a sure thing. Earnings from even part-time work may go a long way. But work may become undesirable or physically difficult in later years. Older Americans have the highest rates of home ownership. But older people still may have mortgages and other debts to consider — their debt levels have actually risen over the years.

Social Security benefits compare favorably with many other sources of income, because they're protected partially from taxation (see Chapter 13). Most seniors don't have to pay a penny on their benefits. Even the most affluent pay income taxes on 85 percent of their benefits, not 100 percent.

A 2019 report by the Economic Policy Institute found that nearly half of working families have no savings at all. Findings like that help explain why so many people are afraid they'll last longer than their money does. If their fears are borne out, Social Security will play a critical role in filling the vacuum.

» **Talk it out if necessary.** Couples should discuss this topic together, even though, in many marriages, one person may be the one who makes most of the financial decisions. You also may want to discuss your finances with a financial planner, especially if you've built up a nest egg and you have questions about how Social Security income will fit in.

» **Be clear on the trade-offs.** You can choose between a smaller amount sooner or a bigger amount later. It often makes sense to talk with a financial advisor, especially if you have investments to help support your lifestyle in retirement. Your decision about when to start retirement benefits will affect your family income for the rest of your life.

REMEMBER

Experts agree that it is often unwise to claim Social Security retirement benefits as soon as possible (age 62). But that is not always the case. Early claims may make sense for individuals who need the income for necessities and lack other financial resources to pay for them or who do not expect to live much longer.

» Taking care of your Social Security card

» Safeguarding your Social Security number

Chapter 4

Protecting Your Number and Securing Your Card

Your Social Security number is a key to your identity — and that makes it valuable in all kinds of ways. In this chapter, I cover the ABCs of Social Security numbers and cards: how to get them and when, how to replace them, the different types of Social Security cards and who needs which kind, what to do if criminals get ahold of your number, and more.

Getting a Social Security Number

Technically, you aren't required to have a Social Security number, but it sure comes in handy. You typically need a Social Security number to get a job and earn money — your Social Security number is how employers report your income to the Internal Revenue Service (IRS). And you need a Social Security number to collect Social Security benefits. All kinds of institutions — from banks to schools to healthcare providers — ask for your Social Security number. Even if you aren't a U.S. citizen, you may find it extremely useful to have a Social Security number. That's right — you don't have to be a citizen to get a Social Security number, if you meet the requirements.

Generally, applicants for a number are expected to present at least two documents to prove their age, identity, and U.S. citizenship or lawful status. In this section, I go over the rules for adults and children who are citizens, as well as noncitizens.

TIP

Social Security has technical rules that govern who gets a card and what you need to show. For a good overview, go to www.ssa.gov/ssnumber.

For U.S. citizens

U.S. citizens typically have a Social Security number before they reach adulthood. In this section, I walk you through how to get a Social Security number if you somehow made it to adulthood without one, as well as how to get a Social Security number for a child.

For adults

To get a Social Security number, you must complete Form SS-5, available at www.ssa.gov/forms/ss-5.pdf. The form asks for basic information, such as your name, gender, place and date of birth, and the names and Social Security numbers of your parents. (If you don't know your parents' Social Security numbers, you can check Unknown.)

You have to show up in person at a Social Security Administration (SSA) office to apply for a number. When you go to the office, be prepared to establish the following:

- **Proof of age:** An original birth certificate established before age 5 is best. If you maintain that it doesn't exist, the SSA will check with the bureau of vital statistics in the state in which you were born. In such cases, you can present other documents to prove your age, such as a hospital record, a religious record from birth, or a passport.
- **Proof of identity:** You need to present current evidence of your identity in your legal name, which will be used on your Social Security card. Social Security looks for documents issued in this country that confirm your date of birth and physical details such as height, eye color, and hair color. A U.S. driver's license, state-issued nondriver ID card, or passport are good examples. ID from the U.S. military, an employer, or a school may be accepted as backup proof.
- **Proof of citizenship:** Your birth certificate serves this purpose, but the SSA will consider other documentation, including a U.S. passport or religious record, preferably recorded soon after birth. If you were born outside the

United States, the SSA will require you to provide a U.S. passport or other documentation, such as a Consular Report of Birth Abroad, a Certificate of Citizenship, or a Certificate of Naturalization.

The SSA wants original documents. Copies generally must be officially certified by the issuing agency and cannot be photocopies. The SSA will not be impressed by a notary's stamp.

You now may be able to replace a Social Security card by going online. To see whether you are eligible, just go to `www.ssa.gov/myaccount`.

For children

Kids need Social Security numbers for many of the same reasons that adults do. You need your child to have a Social Security number to claim him or her as a dependent on your tax return. Plus, you may want your child to have a number so you can open a bank account or buy savings bonds in the child's name. A Social Security number can make it easier for you to get health insurance or other services for your child.

New parents typically apply for Social Security numbers at the hospital, soon after their babies are born. You can apply for the number when you apply for a birth certificate. State agencies that handle birth certificates typically will provide the information on the newborn to the SSA, and the SSA will mail you the baby's Social Security card.

If you wait until your child is 12 years old to apply for a Social Security number for him or her, you have to go through all the same steps that an adult has to go through when applying for a number (see the preceding section). The child will have to appear in a Social Security office, with a parent or legal guardian, to apply.

If you're adopting a child, the SSA may assign a number before the adoption is finalized. If the child's legal name is changing, wait until the name change is final so the right name appears on the card and matches up with the SSA's records.

For noncitizens

For many noncitizens and visitors to the United States, the key to getting a Social Security number is being authorized to work by the Department of Homeland Security (DHS). If that's you, be prepared to provide evidence of your identity. (In some cases, the SSA may be able to obtain some of what it needs through other government agencies you've dealt with already, but it never hurts to be prepared.)

Meeting the requirements as a permanent resident

If you're in the United States as a permanent resident, you may want a Social Security number. The good news is that you don't have to fill out extra forms with the SSA if you requested a card at the time you applied for a visa. (The Department of State, by way of DHS, will provide the SSA with the information required for your card.) After you arrive, the SSA will send the number and card to the mailing address where DHS sends your Permanent Resident card. The Social Security card should come in the mail within three weeks of your arrival in the United States.

REMEMBER

If the card doesn't show up within three weeks of your arrival, contact the SSA.

If you're a permanent resident who did not apply for a card when you sought a visa, you have to go to an SSA office. Calling ahead and making an appointment is a good idea, but it isn't required; you can contact the SSA at 800-772-1213 (TTY 800-325-0778) to make an appointment at the office nearest you. At the appointment, you'll be asked to present at least two original documents to prove your work-authorized immigration status, age, and identity. Be prepared to show the following documents:

- Your unexpired foreign passport
- Your machine-readable immigrant visa (MRIV) or Permanent Resident card (Form I-551)
- Your original birth certificate

For a replacement card, you'll just need proof of work-authorized immigration status and identity, such as your permanent resident card or MRIV card, visa, and current passport. For accepted documentation, visit www.ssa.gov/ssnumber/ss5doc.htm.

Meeting the requirements as a temporary worker

As Table 4-1 shows, certain visa classifications for work may enable you to get a Social Security number, even if you aren't a permanent immigrant to the United States.

If you're in the United States as a temporary worker, you must apply for a Social Security number at a local SSA office. The SSA will want you to have two original documents proving your work-authorized immigration status, age, and identity. Be prepared to show the following:

TABLE 4-1 **Visa Classifications That Allow You to Work in the United States**

Visa Classification	Definition
E1, E2	Treaty trader or treaty investor
F-1	Foreign academic student, when certain conditions are met
H-1B, H-1C, H-2A, H-2B, H-3	Temporary worker
I	Foreign information media representative
J-1	Exchange visitor, when certain conditions are met
K-1	Fiancé or fiancée of a U.S. citizen
L-1	Intra-company transferee
M-1	Foreign vocational student
O-1, O-2	Temporary worker in the sciences
P-1, P-2, P-3	Temporary worker in the arts or athletics in an exchange or cultural program
Q-1, Q-2	Cultural exchange visitor
R-1	Temporary religious worker with a nonprofit organization
TC	Professional business worker admitted under U.S. Canada Free Trade Act (NAFTA)
TN	Professional business worker admitted under NAFTA

Source: Social Security Administration (www.ssa.gov/people/immigrants/visa.html)

- Your unexpired foreign passport
- Your Form I-551, including an MRIV
- Your Arrival/Departure Report (Form I-94) or your Employment Authorization Document (Form I-766)

If you're a foreign student (with F-1 status) who's working in the United States, you also must provide your Form I-20 (Certificate of Eligibility for Nonimmigrant Student Status). If you're an F-1 student and you're eligible to work on campus, you must provide a letter from a designated school official that identifies you, confirms your student status, and identifies your employer and the type of work you are or will be doing.

The SSA also will want to see proof of employment, such as a recent pay slip and letter signed by your supervisor; this letter should describe the job, document the employment start date and hours you'll be working, and provide your supervisor's name and phone number. (If you're an F-1 student authorized to work in curricular practical training, you must provide your Form I-20 with the employment page signed by your school's designated official.)

If you're in the United States as an exchange visitor (J-1 status), the SSA will ask for your Certificate of Eligibility for Exchange Visitor Status (Form DS-2019). If you're a J-1 student, student intern, or international visitor, you must provide a letter from your sponsor. The letter should be on the sponsor's letterhead with an original signature that authorizes your employment.

Whether you're a foreign student or an exchange visitor, you're asked to first report to your U.S. school or program sponsor and wait ten days before applying for a Social Security number. You'll have to complete the Social Security card application (Form SS-5) and provide proof of your immigration status, age, identity, and work authorization from DHS.

Getting a card if you're not authorized to work

You can't get a Social Security number just for convenience — say, to apply for a driver's license, register for school, buy insurance, or apply for subsidized housing or a school lunch program.

REMEMBER

Social Security numbers often are not *required,* even when they're requested. In such cases, you simply have to explain that you don't have a Social Security number and ask whether you can be identified in another way.

Although getting a Social Security number is extremely difficult if you're a noncitizen and not authorized to work, sometimes it is possible. The SSA allows you to get a number if

- A state or local law requires you to provide a Social Security number to get welfare benefits that you're eligible for.
- A federal law requires you to provide a Social Security number to get certain government services or benefits.

TIP

You may apply for an Individual Taxpayer Identification Number (ITIN) if you need a number to file your taxes. The ITIN is a nine-digit number that is not a Social Security number. For more information, go to `www.irs.gov/individuals/article/0,,id=96287,00.html` or call the IRS at 800-829-3676 and ask for the Application for IRS Individual Taxpayer Identification Number (Form W-7). You also can download Form W-7 at `www.irs.gov/pub/irs-pdf/fw7.pdf`.

WARNING

Starting January 1, 2020, ITINs not used on a federal tax return at least once in the last three years will expire. Additionally, ITINs issued before 2013 with middle digits of 83, 84, 85, 86, or 87 (for example, 9NN-83-NNNN) expired at the end of 2019. For more information, go to www.irs.gov/individuals/itin-expiration-faqs.

REMEMBER

Notify the SSA if your immigration status changes or you become a citizen. This may affect the type of card you get.

Managing Your Social Security Card

When you're granted a Social Security number, you're given a card that has your name and Social Security number on it. There are three main types of Social Security cards:

- **Cards for U.S. citizens and lawful permanent residents:** If you're a U.S. citizen or a lawful permanent resident, you get the basic Social Security card featuring your name and Social Security number without any fine-print restrictions. You can work wherever you want, and you don't have to bother asking the government for permission.
- **Cards for lawful nonimmigrants admitted to the United States temporarily with permission to work:** This card not only features your name and number but also includes the restriction: "VALID FOR WORK ONLY WITH DHS AUTHORIZATION." This card is given to people who present a DHS document showing that they may work in this country for a limited time.
- **Cards for lawful nonimmigrants admitted into the United States temporarily who do not have permission to work:** This card has your name and number, like the others, but it also states clearly: "NOT VALID FOR EMPLOYMENT." You may receive this kind of Social Security card if you have an acceptable nonwork need for a Social Security number (see the earlier section "Getting a card if you're not authorized to work"). If you become a citizen or you get DHS approval to work, you can apply for a new card that doesn't have this restriction. (Your new card will have the same Social Security number as your original card.)

WARNING

You may think of your Social Security card as a basic part of your personal ID, like a driver's license. But the reality is that in most cases, it's the number you need, not the card itself. Because Social Security numbers are coveted by crooks, your Social Security card belongs in a secure place, not in the wallet you carry around with you. For the same reason, be careful about where you write down your Social Security number and whom you give it to.

After you obtain a Social Security card, it doesn't require a whole lot in the way of maintenance — you don't have to renew it periodically the way you do a driver's license. In the following sections, I cover two cases in which you may need to deal with the SSA regarding your Social Security card.

If your card is lost or damaged

It's not that big a deal if the dog eats your Social Security card or you run it through the washing machine. You can replace a card free of charge. Social Security has imposed some limits, however, because it doesn't want excess cards floating around in today's security-conscious society.

Here's the rule on card replacement: You can replace three cards per year and up to ten cards in your lifetime. (How many cards can one person lose anyway?)

But even this rule on card replacement has some exceptions:

- If you change your name, you can apply for a replacement card without it counting toward your replacement limit.
- A change in citizenship status also allows you to get a new card.
- The limit on card replacements may not apply in cases where you require a new card to avoid hardship. (In such a case, your employer or public assistance agency must provide a letter stating that you need to have a card to keep the job or benefit.)

TIP

If you are a U.S. citizen and 18 years or older with a U.S. mailing address and you are applying for a replacement card only, you can go online and use a "*my* Social Security" account in participating states to apply for a replacement card. Go to `www.ssa.gov/myaccount/` for details.

WARNING

If your card is stolen (as opposed to being chewed up by your dog or run through the washing machine), that's a more serious situation. When your Social Security number is in the wrong hands, you face the possibility of identity theft. For more information, read the later section "Protecting Yourself by Protecting Your Number."

If your name changes

A name change is a significant event for your Social Security record. You need your legal name to match up with the SSA's records to make sure that your earnings are properly credited and counted toward your benefits. A mismatch between the name you're using and the name the SSA uses for you also could slow down any tax refund coming your way.

To change your name with the SSA, you have to provide recent documents proving the change. The documents you're required to provide vary, depending on the reason for the name change:

- **Marriage, divorce, or annulment:** In cases of marriage, divorce, or annulment, you not only have to provide documentation of the marriage or its end, but you also are expected to provide an identity document with your old name and other information that identifies you. (In this case, it's okay if the document with your old name is expired.)
- **Adoption or naturalization:** In cases of a name change that involves adoption or naturalization, you must show documents with the new name, including the following:
  - An adoption decree or Certificate of Naturalization
  - Two other papers to establish your identity, such as an identity document in your old name and an identity document (unexpired) in your new name

Social Security may ask you for more evidence, especially if you changed your name more than two years ago.

ESCAPING DOMESTIC VIOLENCE WITH A NEW NUMBER

If you need a new identity to escape domestic violence or abuse, the SSA will provide you a new number. In such situations, you need to show up at an SSA office and provide evidence that you're being abused or harassed or that your life is in danger. This evidence may include accounts from police or medical personnel that describe the nature and extent of harassment, abuse, or life endangerment. Evidence also may include court restraining orders and letters from shelters, counselors, family, or friends who know about your problem. The SSA will help you complete the statement you must provide (including getting further evidence) and your application for a new number.

If you plan to change your name, do it *before* you get a new Social Security number.

Remember: If you get a new number, you aren't allowed to use your old number again.

Protecting Yourself by Protecting Your Number

Identity theft is a growing problem in the United States. Identity thieves will abuse — and damage — your credit by opening accounts in your name, making big purchases, racking up major debts, and even claiming tax refunds. They may do this by getting ahold of your Social Security number, which is why safeguarding your number is so important.

WARNING

In some cases, scammers have tried to open up phony personal accounts with the Social Security Administration in order to hijack benefits. If you hear from the SSA that you opened a personal "*my* Social Security" account, and you did not do so, contact the agency at once. By the way, establishing such an account is a good way to prevent that kind of fraud.

Protecting your identity

REMEMBER

Treat your Social Security card and number like valuable assets. Don't display your card carelessly or leave it lying around. Store it in a safe place, like a safe-deposit box.

You're entitled to know why someone asks you for your Social Security number. Providing your number in certain situations — such as when you're opening a bank account, applying for a credit card, or seeking a loan — is routine. But don't share it too casually. If you have doubts about why someone is asking for your number, ask what he needs it for, what he's going to do with it, and what will happen if you don't provide it.

IF SOMEONE ELSE IS USING YOUR SOCIAL SECURITY NUMBER TO REPORT INCOME

Sometimes another person may use your Social Security number for work purposes, possibly even by mistake. This can cause serious problems, especially at tax time. If you have any reason to suspect this may be happening — for example, if the IRS informs you incorrectly that you have unreported income — call the SSA right away at 800-772-1213 (TTY 800-325-0778).

Note: Employers are able to check the validity of their employees' numbers by making use of Social Security's Number Verification Service. For details, go to `www.ssa.gov/employer/ssnvshandbk/ssnvs_bso.htm`.

TIP

Even if you've carefully secured your Social Security card, be aware of other papers that may reveal your number. Be cautious in handling any document that contains your Social Security number.

WARNING

Previously, Medicare and Social Security numbers were the same, putting your Social Security number at risk. Between April 2018 and December 2019, however, the government issued new Medicare cards with unique "Medicare Beneficiary Identifiers" made up of 11 characters, including numbers and letters. But here are some other ways that scammers can get your Social Security number to steal your identity:

- **By stealing your mail:** Your mail may contain financial statements or tax envelopes that contain your number. Criminals know this. Don't leave your mail unattended for long.
- **By getting your information on the internet:** Most internet commerce is conducted through secure means, but some of it isn't. If you enter your Social Security number on an unsecured website, a scammer may get ahold of it. Don't let your number be hijacked electronically.
- **Through data breaches:** Everyone's data, including Social Security numbers, are exposed through data breaches and then bought and sold on the dark web. To protect yourself, freeze your credit and set up electronic access to all financial accounts so you can closely monitor them for suspicious activity.

TIP

Look for `https://secure.ssa.gov/` (as opposed to just *http://*) at the beginning of the web address. That one little letter *s* means that your information is being transmitted securely. If you don't see *https://* at the beginning of the web address, don't enter your Social Security number. Also, a legitimate web address for the government will typically end with *.gov.* Links within emails from SSA's marketing firms will be *.gov* followed by a forward slash, such as *`https://secure.ssa.gov/`*.

- **By scouring trash (both your household's trash cans and larger dumpsters) in search of personal records that you thought you'd gotten rid of:** Billing statements, receipts, credit card offers, bank information, anything with your Social Security number — all are hot commodities. Shred any documents that contain your Social Security number and/or other personal information before they hit the garbage. (You can buy inexpensive personal shredders at any major office supply store.)

TIP

Not all shredders are created equal. If you want to really make sure your documents can never be put back together, use a micro-cut or quality cross-cut shredder that will turn your papers into confetti.

- **By impersonating someone who may ask for such information, such as a credit card company representative or a landlord:** This con takes place over the phone or via email. Be wary. If it sounds fishy, it probably is. Tell the person you'll call back yourself, and then call the number on the back of your credit card or the phone number on your lease.
- **By collaborating with someone who has your information, such as an employee who has access to your credit application:** This type of scam may be hard to combat, but be careful when you choose to write down your number.

BEWARE SCAMMERS WHO SAY THEY'RE FROM THE SSA

SSA employee impersonation scams come in many forms. Someone may be inventing a new one even as you read this. Here are a few examples:

- **Email "phishing" to get ahold of your personal data:** Crooks send you an email, which directs you to a phony "Social Security" website — the website may look like the real thing. At this fake site, you're asked to provide personal information in order to receive a government check. This scheme has been used in connection with cost-of-living increases, tax refunds, and other government payments. ***Beware:*** Social Security does not send out such emails.
- **Telephone calls or even personal visits:** Crooks identify themselves as SSA employees and concoct various excuses to get you to reveal your private information. For example, scammers posing as SSA employees may say that the SSA needs to personally verify information that was lost in a power outage. Your caller ID may even show the number is SSA's. ***Beware:*** The SSA would not call with such a question. And don't trust your caller ID: Scammers can use technology in a method called "spoofing" to make it look like they are calling from the SSA or other places that you trust.
- **Official-looking letters:** An imposter may send you a fake letter claiming that you're qualified for more benefits or provide some other financial lure for you to reveal personal information. Sometimes the crooks try to scare you by warning that benefits will stop unless you answer their questions. ***Beware:*** The SSA would not approach you like this.

If you wonder whether a contact claiming to be from the SSA is for real, don't give out personal information. Just end the conversation and say you'll get back to them. Crooks have been known to provide toll-free numbers where you can call them back, but don't rely on those numbers — instead, contact the SSA by calling the fraud hotline at 800-269-0271 or going to your local SSA office. The SSA will want to know the caller's name, phone number, time and date of the contact, information the caller sought from you, and anything else you may find noteworthy.

The SSA's Office of the Inspector General looks into such complaints. You can fill out a fraud complaint form online at oig.ssa.gov, call 800-269-0271 (TTY 866-501-2101) from 10 a.m. to 4 p.m. Eastern time, or mail your complaint to:

Social Security Fraud Hotline

P.O. Box 17785

Baltimore, MD 21235

Remember: The SSA already knows your Social Security number. It will not contact you unexpectedly and ask for personal information that you provided when you applied for benefits or that it routinely gets from your employer.

Knowing what to do if scammers get your number

Say you've been a model of caution but something goes wrong anyway. You have reason to believe a stranger is using your Social Security number as part of a scheme to make purchases in your name. Maybe odd and costly charges are popping up on your credit cards or something is amiss in your credit report.

If this happens, the SSA can't fix your credit record. Instead, you can take a series of steps to protect your credit and your finances:

- **Report the crime online to the federal government at** www.identitytheft.gov/. This resource will walk you through the steps you should take. Or call 1-877-IDTHEFT (1-877-438-4338; TTY 1-866-653-4261).
- **Close any accounts that were tampered with.** Get on the phone with your credit card companies and banks right away, but be prepared to back up your concerns in writing. Save all correspondence.
- **Contact one of the three major credit-reporting agencies and tell it to place a fraud alert on your credit report.** You need to contact only one of

the three, and it doesn't matter which one — the other two will be notified automatically:

- **Equifax:** 888-766-0008; www.equifax.com
- **Experian:** 888-397-3742; www.experian.com
- **TransUnion:** 800-680-7289; www.transunion.com

» **Regularly check your credit report from the three major credit-reporting agencies.** You can obtain a free copy of your credit report every year from each of the three major agencies at www.annualcreditreport.com. Be wary of other websites, which may charge hidden fees to access your report.

» **File a police report.** The interest of your local cops may vary depending on the particulars of your complaint, but a police report may back your claim if creditors seek documentation of the theft.

» **Notify the IRS if you're concerned that the identity thief may file a tax return with your Social Security number.** You can contact the IRS Identity Protection Specialized Unit at 800-908-4490 and find info for taxpayers at www.irs.gov/uac/taxpayer-guide-to-identity-theft.

» **Report the crime online to the Internet Crime Complaint Center at** www.ic3.gov. This group may refer your complaint to law enforcement at the local, state, federal, or international levels. It's a partnership between the Federal Bureau of Investigation (FBI) and the National White Collar Crime Center (NW3C), a membership organization of police agencies.

You can't easily get a new Social Security number. For example, the SSA won't give you a new number just because your card is lost or stolen. It wants you to provide evidence that the number is being misused, and it wants you to try to fix the mess. If you prove that the problem is serious, the SSA may give you a new number.

REMEMBER

A new Social Security number is not a cure-all. You probably have many records that are based on your old number that will live on with other agencies, including the IRS and your state's department of motor vehicles, as well as banks and other private firms. In other words, the new number may not wipe out the old number (though it will for Social Security). Ironically, a new number may even make it harder to get credit because of your lack of a credit track record with the new number.

COMPUTING A NUMBER THAT FOILS IDENTITY THIEVES

Your nine-digit Social Security number is based on a plan devised in 1936, long before identity theft developed into the sophisticated art form it is today. Your number is divided into three sections (XXX-XX-XXXX):

- The first three digits are known as the *area number*. For years, they were based on geographic region (generally, people born on the East Coast have lower area numbers, and people on the West Coast have higher area numbers), but since 1972, the SSA has pretty much allocated area numbers based on zip code.
- The fourth and fifth digits are known as the *group number* (01 through 99). In the pre-computerized world, the SSA created the group number to help with record keeping.
- The final four digits are the *serial number*. They've traditionally been assigned in a straight numerical series, linked to the group number. You may have noticed that these four digits sometimes appear as personal identifiers on forms and applications that you're asked to fill out. For example, your doctor's office may ask for "the last four of your Social," meaning the last four digits of your Social Security number.

Scholars at Carnegie Mellon University showed that if crooks consult Social Security's Death Master File (DMF) and identify the numbers of individuals born around the same time and place as you were, they can come up with a number very close to yours, if not yours exactly. The first (geographic) section is a big clue. On top of that, the other two sections are assigned in patterns that may be possible to predict. If you were born in a small, less populous state, the vulnerability is greatest. Others have pointed out that the use of your last four digits as an identifier by private firms may give a further clue to scammers who want your Social Security number.

In a bow to modern realities, the SSA ditched the old way of assigning numbers in 2011, opting for a more random approach that's harder to figure out. The new process of assigning numbers is called *randomization,* and it was intended to make it impossible for a clever identity thief (and computer program) to figure out your number. The first three digits no longer have any geographic meaning. SSA officials also say it will prevent a possible shortage of new numbers in some parts of the country. (Unfortunately, randomization has had the unintended consequence of making it easier for scammers to create random Social Security numbers.)

Of course, your own Social Security number is not going to change. The SSA is using the new approach for new numbers and has no plans to replace those already assigned.

2

Taking the Plunge: Filing for Social Security

IN THIS PART . . .

Gather all the details on how to sign up for benefits. I walk you through applying for different types of benefits and give you information on when you can expect to start receiving payments.

Stay ahead of the game by estimating what you've earned so far and where you may be headed.

Know how to stay organized, provide proper paperwork, and meet deadlines. I give you tips on how to avoid problems when dealing with the Social Security Administration.

Discover how to manage the appeals process if a claim is turned down.

» Knowing where to go to apply

» Finding out what's required to apply

» Discovering how and when your payment will arrive

Chapter 5
Signing Up for Benefits

Applying for Social Security benefits is a big step, but it can be a smooth one if you know what to expect. In this chapter, I tell you what you need to know to file — the when, where, and how of it. Whether you're applying for retirement benefits based on your own work record or you're applying for survivor benefits on behalf of a dependent child, you find the information you need to apply. I end the chapter with information on how and when you can expect your payments to arrive.

When to Apply for Social Security Benefits

The Social Security Administration (SSA) generally recommends that you apply for a benefit three months before you want to receive it. Applying for Social Security can be a process rather than a quick event.

Starting your application without having all your supporting documentation assembled is perfectly normal. Plus, keep in mind that the SSA already may have some of the information it needs if an application involves someone who's already in the system (such as in the case of a survivor's benefit involving a retiree who dies).

WHEN THE TIME CLOCK IS TICKING: YOUR PROTECTIVE FILING DATE

When the SSA considers your application started, it will assign you a *protective filing date* that, in some circumstances, can mean you're owed back payments when your application is complete and approved. To secure a protective filing date, you don't have to submit a formal application for Social Security benefits. Instead, as long as an SSA representative records that you *intend* to move forward with an application for benefits, the protective filing date may go into effect, possibly opening the door to several extra months of benefits.

Because money may be at stake, some people recommend that beneficiaries who are deciding whether to file for benefits go ahead and file a *protective filing statement* to avoid potential loss of benefits. The SSA doesn't provide a form for such a declaration — you simply write down your intention to file for a particular benefit, sign it, and mail it to your local SSA office via certified mail (so you have proof that it was delivered), keeping a copy of the statement for yourself.

Note: While you may get a windfall of back benefits by using a protective filing date, depending on the rules of the benefit, you also may end up with a smaller monthly amount going forward. Your benefit will be based on your age at the protective filing date, potentially making it subject to an age-based reduction of up to six months.

If you're already receiving Social Security benefits, the SSA may make certain adjustments to your benefit without your having to file a new application. For example, it will automatically switch an individual getting disability benefits to retirement benefits when that person reaches his or her full retirement age. If you're getting a spousal benefit and the breadwinner dies, the SSA will adjust your status to a survivor's benefit after you've reported the death.

TIP

Benefits for retirees who are older than their full retirement age, the disabled, and certain dependents may be *retroactive* — that is, applicants may get some back payments for months prior to when they applied for benefits. For more information, see the later section "How to Apply for Social Security Benefits."

Where to Apply for Social Security Benefits

Depending on the type of benefit you're applying for, you may have three options for staking your claim: online, in person, or on the phone. (At the time of this writing, however, Social Security offices are closed due to COVID-19, and it may be difficult to get through by phone.) Each method has its pros and cons, and one may fit your needs better than another. Whichever method you choose, an application can move swiftly — in theory, as fast as a day — but it may take months if you have to track down supporting evidence.

In this section, I give you more information on each of the three application methods so you can choose the one that's best for you. (For more information, see the later section "How to Apply for Social Security Benefits.")

Online

The Social Security Administration encourages people to sign up online. You can apply online for retirement, spouse's, Medicare, and disability benefits. Gather the information you need (see the later section "How to Apply for Social Security Benefits" for a list), and then go to `www.ssa.gov/applyonline` to begin your application. ***Note:*** The online application system is available Monday through Friday, 5 a.m. to 1 a.m.; Saturday and holidays, 5 a.m. to 11 p.m.; and Sunday, 8 a.m. to 11:30 p.m.

TIP

You don't have to complete an application in one session. If you've started an application for benefits, but you need to stop and come back later, just make sure that you follow the instructions to save the pages you've worked on. When you're ready to get back to it, you'll need your application number to retrieve your unfinished application.

If about 25 minutes pass without any action on a page, you'll get a warning, and you'll have the chance to extend your time. You get three warnings. At that point, if you don't continue working (or sign out), you'll lose all work on that page.

WARNING

Filling out an online application without the personal guidance of an SSA representative can lead to errors, which will require the SSA to check back with you. If you have concerns about accurately filling out your application, you may want to apply by phone or in person instead, as explained in the next sections.

TIP

You can have a friend or relative guide you through an online benefit application. In fact, your helper can fill out the entire online application form for you, and the SSA will mail the application to you to sign. Your helper just has to indicate (by checking a box on the first page of the online application) that he or she is filling out the application on your behalf and whether you're present while the application is being filled out.

After you submit your online application, you can't just delete it. If you've changed your mind about applying or realized you made a mistake on your application, you need to contact the SSA. You may call the office that is processing your application (that information should appear on the "What's Next" page, which is part of your application), or call the SSA at 800-722-1213 (TTY 800-325-0778).

REMEMBER

By filing online, you don't have to mail in or drop off an application, but you may still have to deliver supporting documents.

TIP

You can check the status of your online application starting five days after you apply. Just go to `www.ssa.gov/applyonline` and click "Check the status of your application online." You'll need to provide your Social Security number and the confirmation number you were assigned when you applied.

In person

Should Social Security offices open after the COVID-19 pandemic (occurring at the time of this writing), you may want to apply in person. The upside to applying for Social Security benefits in person is easy, two-way communication. The downside is the time involved: It may take a while for you to get to the SSA office, and you may have a lengthy wait after you arrive. Typical waiting times in an SSA office, measured from when you take a number to when the interview begins, are approaching half an hour, but if you walk in at the wrong moment, you could wait more than an hour.

TIP

You can cut down your waiting time by making an appointment over the phone in advance. Call 800-772-1213 (TTY 800-325-0778) to make an appointment at the SSA office nearest you. If you want to save even *more* time, keep in mind that the SSA phone line is busiest in the morning, early in the week, and early in the month.

The SSA offers an online tool to help you find the office nearest you. Just go to `www.ssa.gov/locator`, scroll down to click on "Locate An Office By Zip," and enter your zip code. You'll be given the address of the nearest office, along with that office's hours of operation.

By phone

If you prefer to talk with a representative over the phone, you can call the SSA toll free at 800-772-1213 (TTY 800-325-0778). The phone lines are staffed Monday through Friday, 7 a.m. to 7 p.m., but during the COVID-19 pandemic at the time of this writing, it's been difficult to get through. If you call outside those hours, you can still get information about popular topics, such as benefits, eligibility, and online services.

How to Apply for Social Security Benefits

Social Security offers benefits for retirement, survivors, and disability, in addition to running the program of Supplemental Security Income (SSI) for people with little earnings (see Chapter 2 for more on each of these). Whatever benefit you're applying for, the SSA will seek information and proof of eligibility (though the burden may be lighter in situations where the SSA has some of what it needs on file already). Generally speaking, there are rules governing the age at which you become eligible for a particular benefit and documents you may have to provide. Certain rules also determine whether you or your dependents may be eligible for benefits you were owed prior to your application date and whether your benefit is reduced if you start it before you reach your full retirement age.

The SSA doesn't go by the honor system. The documents you provide to back up your claim generally must be originals or official copies certified by the issuing agency — notarized photocopies won't cut it. If you need to demonstrate birth, death, or marriage and you don't have the proper certificates, the SSA may consider other evidence, such as a religious record of birth, a funeral director's statement of death, or a marriage license.

In the following sections, I tell you what you should know and the information and documents you need to apply for each type of Social Security benefit.

Retirement benefits

When you're applying for retirement benefits, the SSA will need a lot of information about your recent earnings, your marital history, your military background, whether you qualify for a federal pension, and possible eligibility of any family members for Social Security benefits, based on your own work record. You have a multiyear window to apply, based on your desired start time.

In the following sections, I cover the details you need to know, whether you're applying for retirement benefits based on your own work record or applying for auxiliary Social Security benefits based on the record of a retired worker.

Based on your own work record

When to file: Three months before you want benefits to begin.

Your benefits are reduced if you start drawing retirement benefits before your full retirement age. For more information, turn to Chapter 2. And to figure out when you should start collecting retirement benefits, check out Chapter 3.

Where to file: In person, by phone, or online.

PROVING YOUR AGE: NO TIME FOR VANITY

Establishing your age is a key to many applications for Social Security benefits. The main evidence you need is an official birth certificate or authentic religious record, such as a baptismal certificate created before you were 5 years old. (A photocopy of your birth certificate, even a notarized one, won't pass muster with the SSA.)

But what if you can't find your birth certificate? Let's face it: Not everyone who's old enough to apply for retirement benefits keeps his or her birth certificate on top of a neat pile on the kitchen counter. No need to panic. If you end up in that situation, you have a few choices to establish your age with the SSA.

For starters, the state where you were born can probably provide you with an official copy, for a fee. Go to `www.cdc.gov/nchs/w2w/index.htm` to find the office for the state where you were born. Typically, all you need to provide is your name and Social Security number, plus the names of your parents, and you'll be able to order an official copy of your birth certificate.

In the unlikely event that a birth certificate or acceptable religious document can't be found, the SSA may consider secondary evidence to prove your date of birth, assigning more weight to the oldest documents. For example, you may be asked to provide at least two backup documents, such as a later birth certificate (recorded after your fifth birthday), school records, medical records (such as immunizations and hospital admissions), state census records, and insurance documents.

Keep it handy: The SSA advises that all or some of the following information and documents are needed to apply for retirement benefits (but don't wait to apply just because you haven't yet gathered all these materials):

- Your Social Security number.
- Your birth certificate (original or certified copy) or an acceptable religious record (such as a baptismal certificate) from earlier than age 5.
- Your Form W-2 earnings statements (one from each of your employers) or your tax return (if you're self-employed) from the prior year. Photocopies of these documents are acceptable.
- Military discharge papers, such as DD Form 214 (Certificate of Release or Discharge from Active Duty). Photocopies of these papers are acceptable.
- Proof of U.S. citizenship or lawful alien status if you were not born in the United States. Citizenship and naturalization papers must be original or certified by the office that provided them.

APPLYING FOR MEDICARE

The SSA handles applications for Medicare, too. If you're already collecting Social Security retirement benefits, you'll be enrolled in Medicare automatically when you turn 65, although you'll have the option of *not* enrolling in Medicare Part B (which includes doctor's services and charges a premium). If you reach 65 without collecting retirement benefits, you need to apply separately for Medicare.

If you're applying for Medicare and you have current healthcare coverage through an employer, the SSA may ask

- The date you started the health coverage
- The date of employment for that coverage
- Whether you're getting healthcare coverage through Medicaid

No matter what you decide about when to begin Social Security retirement benefits (see Chapter 3), you should file for Medicare during a seven-month window that begins three months before the month of your 65th birthday and ends three months after that. Confused? According to Patricia Barry, author of *Medicare For Dummies* (Wiley), if your 65th birthday is in mid-July, your sign-up window begins April 1 and ends October 31. If you wait longer, you may have to pay extra for Medicare Part B and Part D (prescription drug coverage).

You can get lots of information, including a link to file for Medicare online, at `www.ssa.gov/planners/retire/justmedicare.html`.

Back benefits: You may be eligible for up to six months of benefits prior to your application date if you're at least six months older than your full retirement age.

Based on the work record of a parent, grandparent, or current or former spouse

A person may be eligible for Social Security auxiliary benefits based on the work record of a retired parent, grandparent, spouse, or former spouse. For details on who's eligible, turn to Chapter 2. In this section, I fill you in on what you need to know to apply.

CURRENT OR FORMER SPOUSES

When to file: As early as three months before you want your benefits to begin. You can't apply more than three months before you turn 62. And the breadwinner must have filed for retirement benefits in order for you to apply for benefits yourself. (This requirement is waived for divorced spouses.)

Where to file: Online preferably and possibly by phone, especially during the COVID-19 pandemic (at the time of this writing). When offices open again, by phone and in person.

Keep it handy: You'll need to provide the same documents that someone applying for retirement benefits based on his or her own work record has to provide. (See the earlier section "Based on your own work record" for a list.) In addition, if you're still married to the breadwinner, the SSA may require proof of marriage in the form of a marriage certificate. (You may be able to provide other proof, such as a marriage license or sworn statement, if you don't have a marriage certificate.) If you're divorced from the breadwinner, you'll be asked for the beginning and ending dates of the marriage and your final divorce decree.

Back benefits: You may be eligible for up to six months of benefits prior to your application date, but not for any month in which your spouse is younger than his or her full retirement age.

CHILDREN OR GRANDCHILDREN

When to file: You should file for benefits on behalf of dependent children or grandchildren when the breadwinner files for retirement benefits. *Note:* A parent or guardian may file for benefits on behalf of a child who is under 18; under certain circumstances, children 16 and older who are mentally competent may sign their own applications.

Where to file: In person, by phone, or online.

Keep it handy: You'll need to provide the same documents that someone applying for retirement benefits based on his or her own work record has to provide. (See the earlier section "Based on your own work record" for a list.) The child's Social Security number also is required.

Survivor benefits

When to file: You can file for survivor benefits, for adults or children, as early as the month the covered worker or retiree dies. But rules on age affect when to file:

- Widows and widowers may get reduced benefits at age 60 and full benefits at full retirement age. (If survivors age 62 and up file for benefits based on their own earnings, they get the larger of their survivor benefit or any retirement benefit they have earned.)

Note: The full retirement age for widows and widowers is computed slightly differently than for workers and their spouses (see Chapter 2).

- Disabled widows and widowers may qualify at 50.
- Widows and widowers at any age if they are caring for the deceased worker's child who is under 16 or disabled and getting benefits.
- Unmarried children under 18 or up to 19 if still in high school. A parent or guardian may file on behalf of the child.
- Children of any age who were disabled before 22.
- Financially dependent parents at 62.

Where to file: In person or by phone.

Keep it handy: The following information and documents may be needed to apply for survivor benefits:

- The deceased person's Social Security number.
- Your Social Security number and the Social Security number of any dependent children.
- Your birth certificate (original or certified copy) or an acceptable religious record (such as a baptismal certificate) from earlier than age 5.
- Your Form W-2 earnings statement (one from each of your employers) or your tax return (if you're self-employed) from the prior year. Photocopies of these documents are acceptable.
- The deceased person's death certificate or a statement of death from a funeral director.
- Your marriage certificate or divorce papers (if you're applying for survivor benefits as a widow/widower or former spouse).

Dependent parents applying for survivor benefits on a deceased adult child's record must prove that they relied on the adult child for half of their financial support.

Back benefits: You may be eligible for up to six months of benefits prior to your application date (12 months for disabled widows/widowers ages 50 to 59) but not for any month before the breadwinner died. Benefits generally are not retroactive for widows/widowers without children who haven't reached full retirement age.

WARNING

The SSA expects you to return any payments sent to a deceased beneficiary. If the benefits were paid by direct deposit, notify the bank; if the benefits were paid by check, the check should be returned to the SSA.

REMEMBER

The SSA makes payments with a one-month time lag. If someone dies in February, it's the payment received in *March* (and anything after March) that must be returned. Be sure to contact the SSA soon after a person's death to avoid this situation.

REMEMBER

In addition to receiving survivor benefits, you may be eligible to receive the *lump-sum death benefit,* a one-time payment of $255 to survivors after the death of a covered worker. You must file for this benefit within two years of the worker's death. You may file in person or by calling the SSA.

Disability benefits

When to file: As soon as you become disabled. (Benefits may be payable if five full months have passed after the onset of a disabling condition.)

Note: Dependent family members may file for auxiliary benefits based on the record of a disabled worker. A parent or guardian may file for benefits on behalf of an unmarried child who is under 18; under certain circumstances, children 16 and older who are mentally competent may sign their own applications.

Where to file: In person, by phone, or online.

TIP

Some advocates believe that individuals with obvious impairments may improve the chances that their claim will be approved by showing up at an SSA office in person to apply.

Keep it handy: The following information and documents generally are needed to apply for disability benefits:

- Your Social Security number, as well as the Social Security numbers of your spouse and minor children.
- Your birth certificate (original or certified copy) or an acceptable religious record (such as a baptismal certificate) from earlier than age 5.
- Contact information for doctors, hospitals, and medical personnel who have treated you.
- Dates of your healthcare appointments related to this condition.
- Your prescription information.

- Your medical records and lab results related to this condition.
- A summary of your work history (the last five jobs you've held).
- Your most recent Form W-2 earnings statement (one from each of your employers) or your tax return (if you're self-employed). Photocopies of these documents are acceptable.
- Your military discharge papers, such as DD Form 214 (Certificate of Release or Discharge from Active Duty). Photocopies of these papers are acceptable.
- Information on other disability claims filed with insurance or workers' compensation.
- Name and contact information of a friend or relative who can help you with the application.

Back benefits: You may be eligible for up to 12 months of benefits prior to your application date but not for any month before you became disabled. (Back benefits also depend on when the SSA concludes that your disability began.)

If a worker is getting Social Security disability benefits and reaches full retirement age, the SSA will automatically shift the benefits from disability to retirement benefits. The benefit level will not change, however.

Wounded warriors who became disabled while on active military service on or after October 1, 2001, may receive expedited processing of their Social Security disability claims at `www.ssa.gov/woundedwarriors`. Benefits available through Social Security are different from those through the Department of Veterans Affairs.

Supplemental Security Income benefits

When to file: As soon as needed.

Where to file: In person or by phone.

Keep it handy: When you're applying for SSI, you may be asked for all or some of the following information:

- Your Social Security number.
- Your birth certificate (original or certified copy) or other proof of your age, potentially including a hospital record, a religious record from birth (such as a baptismal certificate), a passport, or another document that shows your name and date of birth.

- Documentation on where you live (such as a lease or utility bill with your name on it).
- Financial records, including payroll slips and bank statements.
- Asset information (for example, a list of the property and vehicles you own, and financial statements showing the balance on any investment or bank accounts). Generally, assets may not exceed $2,000 for individuals and $3,000 for couples (as of 2019), although certain resources are exempt, such as your car and home.
- Proof of citizenship, including documents that show you were born in the United States, such as a birth certificate. If you're a U.S. citizen who was *not* born in the United States, the SSA may accept a U.S. consular report of birth, U.S. passport, Certificate of Naturalization, or Certificate of Citizenship.
- Department of Homeland Security documents, such as Form I-551 (Permanent Resident card), Form I-94 (Arrival/Departure Record), or an order from an immigration judge granting asylum or withholding deportation.

If you're applying for SSI disability, you need to provide contact information for doctors, hospitals, and medical personnel who treated you; the dates of your healthcare appointments; your prescription information; and lab results.

Back benefits: Generally not available.

If you get SSI, you're usually eligible for Medicaid right away. Go to `www.medicaid.gov` for more information on Medicaid.

How You Get Your Money: The Check Is Not in the Mail

One term I've tried to keep out of this book is *your Social Security check* — for the simple reason that those paper checks are rapidly going the way of the dinosaur. Everyone who gets Social Security is now expected to receive an electronic payment, with the rare exception of those who are have been granted a waiver. Under the new system, you get your benefit through one of the following methods:

- **Direct deposit:** New applicants are encouraged to opt for direct deposit when they apply for Social Security benefits. To receive your payments via direct deposit, you need your bank account number and your bank's routing number. (You can find this information on one of your personal checks or contact your bank for the numbers you need.)

- **Direct Express debit card:** An alternative to direct deposit is the Direct Express prepaid debit card. This card is critical for individuals who don't have bank accounts. To sign up, call 1-800-333-1795 or 877-874-6347, or go online at `https://godirect.gov/gpw/`.

The U.S. Treasury has trumpeted savings of $1 billion over the next decade because it costs more to mail a check than to deposit money electronically. Officials also say that the move will protect beneficiaries, whose checks no longer can be lost or stolen. If you're already getting Social Security and you still need to make this shift, you can go to `https://godirect.gov/gpw` or `www.ssa.gov/deposit/` for information and links to apply, or call the helpline at 800-333-1795.

TIP

Not everyone has to get the payment electronically. The rule doesn't apply to individuals born on or before May 1, 1921. Also, people who would have trouble with electronic payments because of mental impairments, or those who live in isolated areas without banks, may be allowed to receive paper checks. The waiver application can be downloaded at `www.ssa.gov/deposit/`; click on the Waiver Form link.

SHOW ME THE MONEY: WHEN YOU'LL RECEIVE YOUR SOCIAL SECURITY PAYMENT

After you're approved for benefits, the SSA sends your payments on a particular schedule, based on the birth date of the person on whose record you're receiving benefits. If you get benefits as a retired worker based on your own work history, your benefit payment date is determined based on your own birth date. If you get benefits as a spouse, your benefit payment date is determined based on your spouse's birth date.

Here's when you can expect to receive your Social Security payment:

Birth Date	Benefit Date
1st through 10th of the month	The second Wednesday of the month
11th through 20th of the month	The third Wednesday of the month
21st through 31st of the month	The fourth Wednesday of the month

Remember: Payments come with a lag of one month. If your benefits are approved for August, you'll get your August payment in September, your September payment in October, and so on.

» Using an online calculator to estimate your benefits

Chapter 6
Determining How Much You've Earned

You shouldn't — and don't need to — wait until you apply for Social Security benefits to find out what you have coming. You have several ways to check on the amount you've earned so far and where you're headed if you keep it up. An estimate of benefits gives you a glimpse at a key building block of income you'll depend on in retirement.

One tool is your personalized Social Security statement, accessible online at `www.ssa.gov/myaccount`, or you can request a paper statement using Form SSA-7004 (available at `www.ssa.gov/myaccount/materials/pdfs/SSA-7004.pdf`). It should arrive in about four to six weeks. Beyond that, the SSA and others, including AARP, offer tools you can use online, free of charge, to get a ballpark idea of benefits. You can even plug in different variables to see how your benefits would be affected by changes in earnings or different retirement dates.

In this chapter, I cover these basic options and how you can use them to cast light on the future.

REMEMBER

What you're doing in this chapter is *estimating* your benefits. If you're in the workforce, the size of your Social Security benefit is a moving target. It may change if you earn more in the future than you did in the past. It may change if you're someone who had years of zero earnings in the past but tote up new years with even modest earnings.

But there's no need for a big surprise. Available tools can give you a pretty good idea of future benefits and how the steps you take may alter them. Knowing what's in store can help you plan wisely. The knowledge is easy to get — this chapter gives you the tools you need.

Your Social Security Statement

Think of your Social Security statement as your personal reminder from the SSA. The four-page statement lays out specific details about the benefits you've earned for yourself and family members. It also contains lifetime summaries of your annual earnings, as well as how much you've contributed in payroll taxes to Social Security and Medicare in your working career.

The statement also includes guidance targeted to different age groups: younger workers (25–34), mid-career (35–54), and closer to retirement (55 and up). Younger workers, for instance, are reminded of the importance of saving and financial planning.

How to access it

Increasingly, the answer will have to be online, where it is easy to print your own copy. Once upon a time, this information came in the mail to more than 150 million workers age 25 and up each year, about three months before the person's birthday. SSA later cut that back to every five years until a worker reached age 60, when it would mail his annually. But in an era of tight budgets, the written statement has been among the victims. In early 2017, the agency said it would mail written statements only to workers age 60 and over who are not yet getting benefits and who have not signed up for an online "*my* Social Security" account.

The same information is also available if you set up an online account, which you can do at `www.ssa.gov/myaccount`. For more information about online Social Security accounts, check out Chapter 7.

REMEMBER

If you get a copy of your personal Social Security statement in the mail, save it. The statement contains important estimates of your Social Security benefits, including retirement, disability, and survivor benefits, and also contains your earnings history on record with the agency. Regardless of your age or whether you have established an online account, you can still get a written statement by mailing in a form you can find at `www.ssa.gov/myaccount/materials/pdfs/SSA-7004.pdf`.

The statement is very useful, but it doesn't tell you everything. It doesn't explain the link between a worker's retirement benefit and the survivor benefit that same worker may leave for a spouse. Nor does it discuss the possibility that benefits for some individuals may be partially subject to income tax (check out the details in Chapter 13).

How to understand it

Your Social Security statement includes several key sections:

- An estimate of monthly retirement, disability, and survivor benefits that may go to your family members (page 2)
- Your year-by-year earnings record in the SSA's files, which it has used to determine your benefits (page 3)
- Basic information about how benefits are estimated (page 2) and descriptions of the main types of benefits (page 4)

The statement also offers guidance on keeping your earnings record accurate with the SSA (page 3); shows your lifetime payroll tax contributions for Social Security and Medicare (page 3); and explains the Windfall Elimination provision and Government Pension Offset provision, two policies that may reduce benefits for individuals who had jobs that were not covered by Social Security (page 2).

In this section, I walk you through a Social Security statement. If you have your own on hand, you can refer to that. Or you can download a sample of the Social Security statement for an imaginary person named Wanda Worker (catchy, huh?) online at `www.ssa.gov/myaccount/statement.html`.

Estimate of monthly benefits

If you look at the sample statement (or your own statement), you can see on page 2 that the age when you claim benefits can make a substantial difference in the monthly amount. The 2020 statement (for workers 55 and over) shows that if Wanda Worker maintains her current rate of earnings, she can expect retirement benefits of $1,376 per month if claimed at 62, $1,986 per month if she keeps working and claims at her full retirement age of 67 (a 44 percent boost), or $2,468 per month if she keeps working and claims at age 70 (an additional boost of about 24 percent for delayed retirement).

Although the personal Social Security statement uses your actual earnings to compute disability and survivor benefits already earned, it makes assumptions about your future earnings to estimate retirement benefits. The more years until your retirement, the more uncertain the forecast.

The statement also shows how you earn benefits that many people don't even think about. In the case of Wanda Worker, she's earned disability benefits of $1,956 per month if she becomes disabled right away. If she were to die, she's earned survivors' benefits of about $1,467 per month for a child and as much as $1,956 per month for a spouse (at the spouse's full retirement age).

Earnings record

Page 3 of the statement displays your earnings record. It documents the amount of earnings that were taxed for Social Security and Medicare year by year — in the case of Wanda Worker, from 1976 through 2018. Wanda Worker is credited with 43 years of earnings, but her Social Security benefit will be based on her 35 years of highest earnings. (If she had fewer than 35 years, the SSA would add zeros to the formula it uses to reach a total of 35 years.)

REMEMBER

Your earnings record is important because it provides the basis for your Social Security benefits. You should review the numbers with care and call the SSA if you spot any errors.

TIP

You don't need a Social Security statement to review the earnings history the SSA has on file for you. You can get the information by doing one of the following:

» **Going to your local SSA field office:** An SSA field office will supply you with a summary if you ask for one.

» **Filling out a form and mailing it to the SSA:** For more detailed information, including employers' names and addresses, go to www.ssa.gov, scroll down to "Forms," and plug in the number 7050-F4 to get the form. You will be charged a fee for this information.

Social Security Calculators

You don't need an official statement to get a ballpark idea of your Social Security benefits. Many user-friendly calculators are available online. You can use these tools to work through different scenarios for your future.

The calculators ask you for some information — such as your date of birth and earnings — and then they estimate your Social Security benefits. These tools vary in simplicity, the amount of details you need to provide, and the amount of information they make available. Many are free. I outline a few of them in this section. (My discussion here is limited to publicly available calculators you may use free of charge.)

Some online calculators are more easily customized to reflect your individual situation — your marital status, savings, and other factors all can affect your decision-making around Social Security. A few calculators even try to factor in your future tax liability to give a better idea of the financial realities that await you.

Many people turn to calculators when they start thinking about *when* to begin collecting retirement benefits. With that in mind, some calculators try to highlight the timing of your claim that will yield the greatest lifetime haul from Social Security for you and your spouse. Other calculators downplay the lifetime concept in favor of the greatest monthly haul. (For more on deciding when to start collecting retirement benefits, turn to Chapter 3.)

Whichever calculator you use, it should make vividly clear that your benefit amount will be smallest at 62, about 25 percent to 30 percent (for individuals with a full retirement age of 66 and 67, respectively) larger at your full retirement age, and 24 percent to 32 percent (for individuals with a full retirement age of 67 and 66, respectively) larger than that if you wait until 70.

When you're calculating your benefits, it helps to know your 35 highest-paid years of work. If you've saved your Social Security statements, you'll have a lot of what you need. (For more on accessing your Social Security statement, see "How to access it," earlier in this chapter.) You also can find the amount of your Social Security wages in Box 3 of the W-2 Wage and Tax Statement you get from your employer each year.

Your earnings for Social Security are the amount that is subject to the payroll tax. You may have earned more, but this is the maximum earnings that the SSA considers in its calculation of your retirement benefit. The Social Security earnings limit was set at $137,700 for 2020. If that's the limit and you earn $140,000, you make Social Security payroll tax contributions on only $137,700. You don't pay Social Security taxes on your remaining earnings of $2,300 (although you still pay the Medicare tax). See Chapter 1 for more details on the payroll tax.

You can find the latest maximum taxable earnings, as well as those going back many years, at `www.ssa.gov/OACT/COLA/cbb.html`.

Social Security's own tools

The SSA provides several different tools to give you an idea of your benefits without waiting for a statement. You can find the calculators at `www.ssa.gov/planners/benefitcalculators.htm`.

WARNING

Remember the saying "Garbage in, garbage out"? Calculators are no better than the information you provide. Most Social Security calculators, including some from the agency, rely on you to provide accurate information. Most do not link up with the SSA's own database to plug in your actual past earnings. So if you're making projections about future earnings, be as realistic as you can. If you're filling in earnings from past years, be as accurate as you can. Take a few minutes to dig out your own records, if you've kept them around. Otherwise, you may one day get a Social Security benefit that is much smaller or larger than you expected.

WARNING

Online calculators can provide a useful start in your planning for Social Security. But their findings may vary significantly, possibly by hundreds of dollars per month. Keep that in mind as you plan. It can make sense to look at more than one, including calculators from the SSA.

Here are some of the SSA's main online tools to help you get a sense of your future retirement benefits:

- **Social Security Quick Calculator** (`www.ssa.gov/OACT/quickcalc/index.html`): This calculator is quick and easy, but rough — it isn't linked to your earnings record on file with the SSA. Fill in your date of birth, current earnings, and projected retirement date. When the results pop up, you can click "See the earnings we used" to type in different earnings you may anticipate in the future. You may delete annual earnings figures that look off base and substitute more accurate numbers.
- **Retirement Estimator** (`www.ssa.gov/estimator`): This calculator uses real earnings. The virtue of this tool is that it's based on your actual earnings on record with the SSA. You plug in some personal information, including your name, Social Security number, birth date, the state in which you were born, and last year's earnings, and it estimates your benefits at 62, full retirement age, and 70. It also allows you to create scenarios by typing in different ages at which you stop work and different amounts of average future earnings.
- **Online Calculator** (`www.ssa.gov/planners/retire/AnypiaApplet.html`): This calculator takes a bit of time. You need a good idea of your past earnings to use this tool, because it requires you to enter them (increasing the chances of a mistake). It isn't connected to the SSA's earnings database.

TECHNICAL STUFF

One version of the Online Calculator (`www.ssa.gov/planners/retire/anyPiaWepjs04.html`) gives an idea of how much your benefit could be reduced for noncovered employment through the Windfall Elimination provision. Another makes estimates for those who may be affected by the Government Pension Offset provision (`www.ssa.gov/planners/retire/gpo-calc.html`). For details on these provisions, turn to Chapter 2.

» **Social Security Detailed Calculator** (www.ssa.gov/OACT/anypia/anypia.html): This calculator is not the choice for most folks. It's less user friendly than the others, and it still doesn't produce results that are certain. You have to download it, and even the SSA cautions that the calculator can be somewhat unwieldy to use. It also requires you to fill in your past earnings. One point in its favor: It provides the most accurate calculations for workers affected by the Windfall Elimination provision (which may apply if you had earnings under covered and noncovered employment).

You can learn a lot online. Beyond the benefits calculators listed in this section, the SSA has tools to help you estimate how earnings could affect your benefits before you reach full retirement age, reductions for early retirement, increases for delaying retirement beyond your full retirement age, and the impact of uncovered work on your benefits (through the Windfall Elimination provision) or the benefits your spouse and dependents may receive on your earnings record (through the Government Pension Offset provision). You can find these tools at www.ssa.gov/planners/morecalculators.htm.

AARP's Social Security calculator

Some calculators try to offer a more holistic and personalized approach to estimating your benefit than you get from the SSA's own tools. For example, you may want an idea of how far your Social Security payment will go toward covering your household expenses each month. Such knowledge can give you a better sense of when you should claim your benefit, because your payment will vary depending on your date of birth and when you start collecting.

Some calculators also make it easier to tweak the assumptions that go into an estimate, such as allowing you to plug in assumptions about your personal expenses. The more you're able to customize a calculator, the more meaningful its findings may be for you and your household.

One such tool is the AARP Social Security Benefits Calculator, available to the public free of charge at www.aarp.org/work/social-security/social-security-benefits-calculator. The AARP calculator offers more customizing choices than many other tools.

Notably, it addresses spousal concerns — offering action steps for a couple to maximize monthly benefits — and shows how earned income reduces benefits before you reach full retirement age. An interactive chart estimates how much of your benefit will be withheld if you work, based on different assumptions about your age and earnings, and shows how much monthly payments may increase after you reach full retirement age.

The AARP Social Security Benefits Calculator takes the view that, for most people, it's best to wait as long as possible to claim benefits. But it clearly displays amounts for claiming retirement benefits at different ages.

The AARP Social Security Benefits Calculator is designed to provide individual guidance to various kinds of individuals, including married, single, widowed, and divorced. To try it out, I invented Dori, a 56-year-old single woman who earns $80,000 per year as a human resources manager for a small company.

According to the AARP tool, Dori's estimated monthly retirement benefit is $1,562 at 62, $2,231 at her full retirement age of 67, and $2,766 at 70 (which assumes that she does not work past age 62 regardless of when she collects benefits). The calculator also gives Dori an idea of how far her Social Security income will go. By clicking "Maximize Your Benefits," Dori sees that if she delays Social Security until she's 70, the payment is enough to cover 80 percent of her projected expenses. If she takes Social Security as early as possible, at 62, the payment covers just 45 percent of her expenses.

In looking over the assumptions, Dori notices that the calculator assumes that she pays $1,619 per month for housing and utilities. But Dori already owns her condo, so she lowers that number to $800 per month. Based on that personal change, the calculator shows that if she claims Social Security at age 70, it will cover 100 percent of her monthly expenses. If she takes it at 62, the lower payment would cover just 60 percent of her expenses, leaving a big gap.

The calculator also offers some guidance on a question that many Baby Boomers are starting to face: how continued work and earnings may affect Social Security benefit payments. (Under the Social Security earnings test, earnings above a certain threshold result in withheld benefits if you haven't yet reached full retirement age; see Chapter 13.)

Dori is healthy and likes her job. She wants to know, in dollars, how much the SSA would reduce her benefits if she claimed her retirement benefit at 62 and continued to earn her $80,000 annual salary. The answer is that under the Social Security earnings test, it would withhold thousands of dollars a year — adding up to $87,842 in benefit payments until her full retirement age. After that, Dori would get back the withheld benefits in higher payments.

Other online calculators

A partial list of other online calculators includes the following:

- **The Consumer Financial Protection Bureau's Planning for Retirement** (www.consumerfinance.gov/retirement/before-you-claim): This calculator is simple and readable, with helpful background tips on Social Security survivors' benefits, the benefits of claiming later if you live a long life, and other matters.
- **Bankrate's Social Security Benefits Estimator** (www.bankrate.com/calculators/retirement/social-security-benefits-calculator.aspx): This is another easy-to-use tool that lets you make assumptions about future income and the rate of inflation.
- **The Center for Retirement Research at Boston College's Target Your Retirement calculator** (crr.bc.edu/special-projects/interactive-tools/target-your-retirement/): This is a more holistic retirement calculator that lets you factor in things like the impact of working longer and downsizing your home on your retirement income.

FIGURING YOUR BENEFIT THE OLD-FASHIONED WAY: DOING THE MATH

Maybe you're the paper-and-pencil sort and you don't want to bother with an online calculator. It *is* possible to estimate your retirement benefit. It just takes a bit of patience, some basic math skills — and a lot of motivation.

In today's world of online calculators, most people won't go through the exercise, so I don't lay it out here. Also, if you're younger than 62, you have to make some assumptions about future earnings. But if you want to see how it's done, you can get a basic idea by going to www.ssa.gov/pubs/10070.html.

Even if you don't want to do the math, it's worth knowing *why* Social Security came up with this computation. The goal is to give you a benefit based on your lifetime earnings, indexed in a way that reflects changes in average wages over the years. The formula also is designed to give back a larger share of pre-retirement earnings to lower earners than to folks with bigger salaries.

» Disclosing life events and keeping track of your earnings record

» Putting retirement benefits on hold

» Recovering a lost or stolen Social Security check

» Avoiding overpayment of your benefits and getting benefits from overseas

» Filing a complaint

Chapter 7
Navigating the System

Does the idea of dealing with a big bureaucracy raise your blood pressure? You're not alone. But it doesn't have to be a headache if you know what to do. In this chapter, I cover the most likely issues that could pop up between you and the Social Security Administration (SSA). I suggest how you can avoid problems and keep the benefits flowing, with a minimum of headaches, heartache, and wasted time. In many cases, your dealings can be a breeze — as long as you stay organized, meet deadlines, and provide materials that the SSA requests.

TIP

You can take care of (or at least start) many needed services, such as applying for most kinds of benefits, signing up for direct deposit, changing your personal contact information, or getting a proof-of-income letter, by calling 800-772-1213 (TTY 800-325-0778) Monday through Friday, 9 a.m. to 4 p.m., or by going online to www.ssa.gov. Even if you want to talk to someone in person, you can save time by calling the toll-free number and arranging an appointment at your nearest SSA field office.

TIP

The SSA has special services for the blind: It will send notices in Braille, large print, and audio CDs. The SSA no longer schedules in-person meetings outside its offices. But if you live far from the nearest SSA office, you may be able to arrange an official meeting over the telephone, possibly with a video hookup. Don't speak much English? Check out the SSA's Multilanguage Gateway (www.ssa.gov/multilanguage), which provides guidance in Spanish, Chinese, Vietnamese, Russian, Arabic, and other languages.

Being a Smart Consumer of Social Security

You can help keep your dealings with the SSA smooth by staying organized. If you're naturally diligent and well organized, you may want to skip the next few paragraphs. But believe me, staying organized doesn't come easy to everyone, and it sure helps. The SSA is about details, and bureaucrats are trained to follow procedure. If a time clock is ticking, you don't want to have a crisis because you forgot to get ahold of something that the SSA asked for several weeks before. In some cases, failure to complete an application on time could mean sacrificing money that you're eligible for.

This section offers a few simple suggestions to lower your stress, make sure that you receive everything you're entitled to, and help you stay on top of any issue that comes up with the SSA.

Keeping good records

Make a file. I'm talking low tech — a nice old-fashioned manila folder that fits in a drawer somewhere. This file is home base for all your Social Security papers. Include in the file your application number, if you applied for a benefit. Also, include any correspondence you have with the SSA. Make notes during or after phone calls and office visits, including the names of the people you talked to, and drop those notes in the file. Write reminders about unfinished business and deadlines by which you need to complete each task. If you've saved copies of your personal Social Security statements (which you should), keep them here. If you've set up an online account, keep a copy of your username and password right here.

TIP

Save in your file the SSA toll-free numbers (listed earlier in this chapter), as well as the phone number and address of your local office. You can find the address of your local office by calling the SSA, looking in the government pages in your local phone book, or going online to www.ssa.gov/agency/contact/ and scrolling down to Office Locator.

Making sense of the correspondence you get from Social Security

Read all correspondence carefully, and save it in your Social Security file (see the preceding section). Don't just skim correspondence — a letter may provide a deadline for action or clarify further documents you need to provide.

Although you may have good reason to call or make a personal visit, writing a letter can sometimes be a useful way to communicate with the SSA if the matter isn't urgent. A letter establishes a written record. If you write a letter, always include your Social Security number and the names of any SSA representatives you've been dealing with.

If you're sending important information or documents rather than delivering them, send them via certified mail and save the receipt. Make photocopies of what you mail and save them. Always attach your name and Social Security number to any documents you send or deliver.

The SSA doesn't want you to mail foreign birth records or any documents from the Department of Homeland Security. These records are hard to replace. Bring them yourself to your local Social Security office instead.

Making (and showing up for) appointments

Before you show up at an SSA office, make an appointment, and be sure to keep the appointment. When you have an appointment, you don't have to wait nearly as long to be seen. Plus, for some people, face-to-face meetings may prevent mistakes when filing applications.

During or after the appointment, write down what you found out, and save the information in your SSA file. Keep a record of your visit, even if it's the ticket you got at the kiosk in the office.

In recent years, Social Security has shuttered dozens of field offices around the country and closed an even larger number of mobile stations that served the public. Depending on where you live, this trend may make it less convenient for many individuals to receive face-to-face service.

Getting the Answers and Help You Need

When you're dealing with a bureaucracy as big as the SSA, questions may arise. Luckily, there are answers to be had — you just need to know where to look. In this section, I tell you how you can use the SSA website to find the answers you need. I also fill you in on your options when it comes to having someone help you deal with the SSA — you don't have to go it alone.

Finding answers online

The SSA website (www.ssa.gov) holds a vast amount of information about benefits and rules that may affect you. The website is far from perfect — much of the information is highly general, whereas your questions and issues may be highly specific. Still, there's a good chance that by investing a few minutes, you'll find out something useful about your issue and your benefits, which could focus your thinking when you contact the SSA.

By going online, you can do the following:

- **Apply for retirement and other benefits.** The SSA website provides direct links to begin applying for retirement and disability benefits. Survivor and Supplemental Security Income (SSI) benefits are located under Benefits Planner. You also can apply for Medicare and special aid for the cost of Medicare prescription drugs (for low-income people).
- **Set up a personal account with Social Security.** People who get benefits can use the account to check earnings records, change personal contact info, change direct deposit info, and get a benefit verification letter. Those not yet receiving benefits can use their account to get an estimate of future benefits and look at their earnings record. To get started, go to www.ssa.gov/myaccount. (Find more on this later in this chapter.)
- **Appeal an unfavorable decision on a disability application.** Just go to secure.ssa.gov/iApplsRe/start.
- **Download an array of forms free of charge, as well as guides to various Social Security rules.** For forms, head to www.ssa.gov/forms; for helpful publications, check out www.ssa.gov/pubs.

TIP

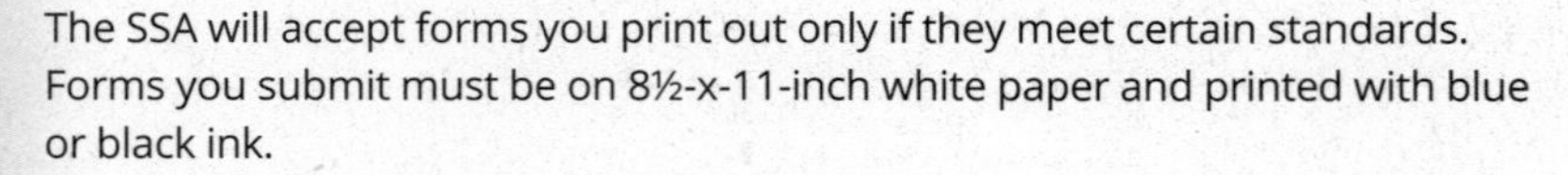

The SSA will accept forms you print out only if they meet certain standards. Forms you submit must be on 8½-x-11-inch white paper and printed with blue or black ink.

- **Get a rough idea of your benefit amounts.** The Social Security calculators are at www.ssa.gov/planners/benefitcalculators.htm. In addition, you can use an array of other tools designed to help you consider issues that could affect your benefits, such as the annual limit on earnings if you collect early retirement benefits and the impact of a government pension on your Social Security benefits. (I discuss these online tools, including AARP's Social Security Benefits Calculator, in Chapter 6.)

» **Apply for or replace a Social Security card.** Just go to www.ssa.gov/ssnumber. You will need to set up a personal "*my* Social Security" account.

In the following sections, I provide more detailed information on how to get the most value from going online with SSA.

Signing up for a "my Social Security" account

In a time when SSA field offices face a budget squeeze, it can be really worth your while to set up a personal "*my* Social Security" account — and more than 38 million Americans have done just that. A personal account provides a way to keep track of your earnings record, estimate future benefits, and accomplish various housekeeping tasks, ranging from changing your address or direct deposit information to replacing a Social Security or Medicare card — without using your valuable time on the phone or visiting a field office.

An online account also enables you to get a replacement SSA-1099, which is the annual statement that tells beneficiaries how much Social Security income to report to the Internal Revenue Service. (Some noncitizens living outside the country need the form SSA-1042S, which also can be replaced with an online account.)

To register for a "*my* Social Security" account, you have to be at least 18 years old and have a Social Security number, U.S. mailing address, and valid email address. If you have a security freeze or fraud alert on your credit report, you have to lift it temporarily to set up an account, and then you can reinstate it. If you don't want to temporarily lift your security freeze or fraud alert, you can go to an SSA office to open an account in person.

To set up a personal account, go to www.ssa.gov/myaccount. As an extra security measure, you must have either a cellphone with text messaging or email to use as a second identification for logging on. Using two identification methods protects against potential identity fraud.

WARNING

SSA has warned that scammers have tried to take advantage of private accounts to gain personal information or even to steal benefits (see www.ssa.gov/myaccount/security.html#h4). For example, crooks have sent emails inviting people to set up Social Security accounts, directing them to a bogus link where they can exploit the data. If you get an email out of the blue asking you to set up a personal Social Security account, delete it.

TIP

Email addresses from the Social Security Administration should end in dot gov/ (.gov with a forward slash). Don't be fooled by scammers.

TIP

You can block electronic access to your personal information. This step provides a strong protection for your data, but it means that you lose some of the convenience of online access: Neither you nor anyone else will be able to review or change your information online or through the SSA's automated telephone system. Typically, you would use this measure to prevent a serious problem, such as identity theft or domestic violence. You can take this step by going to `www.ssa.gov/hlp/block-access.htm` or by calling the SSA at 800-772-1213 (TTY 800-325-0778). To undo blocked access, you have to call or visit the SSA.

TIP

Social Security can give you an extra layer of security for your online account. Go to `www.ssa.gov/myaccount/security.html` and click "If You Want Extra Security." To get the added protection, Social Security will ask for the last eight digits of a Visa, Mastercard, or Discover credit card, or for some other financial information such as the direct deposit amount if you're currently getting benefits. When you have provided that information, a letter will be sent in the mail in five to ten business days. You need this letter to complete the voluntary process to add extra security. You can upgrade to extra security or disable it at any time. Adding extra security does not change the way that you sign in to your account. You must still sign in with your username, your password, and a unique security code that Social Security will provide each time you sign in.

WARNING

Social Security generally will not ask you for personal financial information, such as details about your credit cards. So this policy is a notable exception. Scammers sometimes seek such data by pretending they work for the Social Security Administration.

Finding out whether you're eligible

Wonder whether you're eligible for benefits? The SSA has put together an online screening tool to help you find out: `https://ssabest.benefits.gov/`. This is a five- to ten-minute exercise in which you answer a bunch of questions — stuff like birth dates (for you and a spouse), earnings, and dates of marriage and divorce. After you fill out the online questionnaire, you'll be told benefits you may be eligible for and given links for further information. This tool screens your eligibility for retirement, Medicare, disability, survivor, SSI, and special veteran benefits that may go to certain veterans of World War II.

Social Security has dubbed the exercise BEST — for Benefit Eligibility Screening Tool. Think of it as a preliminary guide. It's of greatest use if you know little about Social Security benefits. You certainly can find the information elsewhere, but you may find it convenient to have it in one place. BEST will base its findings and recommendations on the information you provide. It doesn't ask for your name or Social Security number, and it doesn't consider your actual record with the SSA.

REMEMBER

The screening tool does *not* provide benefit estimates. But it will suggest benefits you may apply for based on the information you enter.

Mastering the ins and outs of Social Security

If you're planning to get Social Security benefits, browsing the SSA website is a good idea. You may instantly spot topics that may affect you, such as links to retirement benefits, contact information, and answers to questions about Social Security issues that are currently in the news. The search function is prominently displayed, so if you don't immediately see what you're looking for, you can search for it.

At the SSA website, you can find out about the program's finances (`www.ssa.gov/OACT/TR/index.html`). No need to hear it secondhand from the politicians. You can even read the top ten names for boys and girls going back many years (`www.ssa.gov/OACT/babynames`).

TIP

You can find a full list of the SSA's online publications at `www.ssa.gov/pubs`. Here are a few of the publications that may give you a quick overview of benefits that could apply to your family:

- **"Understanding the Benefits":** `www.ssa.gov/pubs/10024.html`
- **"Retirement Benefits":** `www.ssa.gov/pubs/10035.html`
- **"Disability Benefits":** `www.ssa.gov/pubs/10029.html`
- **"Survivors' Benefits":** `www.ssa.gov/pubs/10084.html`
- **"Supplemental Security Income (SSI)":** `www.ssa.gov/pubs/11000.html`
- **"Benefits for Children":** `www.ssa.gov/pubs/10085.html`
- **"What Every Woman Should Know":** `www.ssa.gov/pubs/10127.html`

Having someone on your side when you deal with Social Security

In most situations, you can represent yourself perfectly well in dealing with the SSA. Your particular issues have probably popped up many times for others, and the system is supposed to know how to deal with them. Doing your homework, asking questions, and listening carefully to what the SSA representative tells you should be more than enough to dispel confusion and clarify your course of action. At least it *should.*

But sometimes you may end up in a situation in which you need extra assistance, either because of an unusual problem with the SSA, contradictory messages from SSA representatives (yes, this may happen), or personal difficulties such as health problems that make it hard for you to stay on top of matters by yourself. In this section, I fill you in on your options.

A friendly advocate

You're always allowed to bring a helpful companion with you when you meet an SSA representative. It can be a spouse, a friend, or whomever you like. The SSA is even set up to enable your helper to complete your online application in your absence or alongside you. (The helper will have to identify himself or herself.) Your helper can do a lot for you, although you have to sign the application. If you're not present during an online application process, the SSA will mail the application to you so that you can sign it.

Your helper also can complete the SSA online benefits screening tool on your behalf to help you find out whether you may be eligible for benefits (go to `www.benefits.gov`, click on Start, and fill out the questionnaire). If your helper accompanies you to a meeting with the SSA, the SSA representative may ask who the helper is, but the official SSA policy is to support your helper's efforts.

A professional advocate

In certain cases, you may want to appoint a representative to help you navigate an issue with the SSA — typically a lawyer, though not always. Hiring a representative isn't necessary for routine dealings with the SSA, but it's usually necessary in disputes over Social Security Disability Insurance (SSDI) claims, which are frequently turned down on the first try. If you want to challenge a benefits decision, a lawyer or other advocate who specializes in this area could help.

If you want to appoint an advocate, the SSA expects you to declare this decision in a signed and dated statement. It provides a form that you can download to provide the information at `www.ssa.gov/forms/ssa-1696.pdf`. Your advocate can charge you only up to a limit set by the SSA: $6,000 or 25 percent of past-due benefits, whichever amount is lower.

Disability is a particularly thorny area in which your claim for benefits may not be cut and dried. A technical grasp of the rules and appeals process often is crucial in getting what you want. See Chapter 8 to find out more about the appeals process and why it's often a critical step in winning claims for disability benefits.

OFFERING HELP TO A LOVED ONE

People with certain health issues, such as Alzheimer's disease, lose the ability to competently manage their money, and that includes Social Security payments. In such cases, the answer may be to appoint an official helper. The SSA calls such an aide a *representative payee,* and it has various rules governing that important role.

If you want to serve as a representative payee, the SSA will investigate the situation. Friends and relatives often fill that role, usually unpaid. You take on the responsibility for receiving the person's benefits. When you spend the money, you must follow strict guidelines intended to protect the beneficiary. The priority is using the cash to meet the individual's basic needs for food and shelter. If these needs already are met, you may spend the money to improve the person's daily living conditions or to pay for healthcare.

Representative payees must complete an annual form to explain how the Social Security money was spent the previous year. The SSA takes this responsibility seriously — helpers who misuse benefits risk fines and imprisonment. Representative payees also are required to inform the SSA of any changes that could affect the person's eligibility for benefits. The SSA offers a guide for such assistants online at `www.ssa.gov/pubs/10076.html`. SSA offers further background and a helpful video at `www.ssa.gov/payee/rep_payee_tech_training.htm`.

Life Happens: Keeping the Social Security Administration in the Loop

You need to inform the SSA when something happens that may have an impact on a payment going to you or to dependents who are getting benefits based on your earnings record. This may include income from work, changes in the makeup of your family, or more mundane housekeeping matters. You want to make sure you get the benefits that are coming to you and your loved ones — and you also want to stay out of trouble.

REMEMBER

You're supposed to tell the SSA about various changes involving your family, including the following:

» **Death:** If a loved one who received Social Security benefits dies, you should make sure that the SSA is informed as soon as possible. A grieving relative doesn't have to make the call, but someone does. In most cases, a funeral director will tell the SSA. This information is critical not only to stop future payments, but also because dependents of the deceased may qualify for benefits or payment increases.

- **Marriage, divorce, or remarriage:** Changes in marital status can potentially affect benefits, such as for widows, widowers, and divorced spouses younger than 60. Although divorce alone doesn't terminate benefits based on a former spouse's earnings record, you still must report the divorce to the SSA.
- **The birth, adoption, or move of a child:** If you're receiving Social Security benefits and you have a child, the child also may qualify. If someone else adopts a child who has received benefits, the benefits to the child may continue, but the SSA has to know about it.

  If you get spousal or widow/widower's benefits based on caring for a dependent child (such as due to your young age), and the child relocates for more than a month, you have to tell the SSA. Failure to report the move may cost you a month's benefit or more in the case of repeat violations.
- **A child leaves school:** You must inform the agency if a nondisabled child beneficiary over age 18 stops full-time attendance at secondary or elementary school.

You're also supposed to tell the SSA about the following, all of which have the potential to affect your benefits and your ability to receive them:

- **If you change your name:** Your name is a crucial piece of information to help make sure that the SSA properly credits earnings to your account.
- **If you move or if you change banks for benefits that are directly deposited into a checking or other bank account:** You want Social Security payments to reach you, right?
- **If you earn more money than you expected, or expect to earn more money than you originally thought:** For retirement and certain other benefits, earnings from work above a certain amount may trigger withholding of part of the Social Security benefit. As soon as you expect to earn more than you told the SSA you planned to earn, you should inform the SSA of the change. Don't wait, or you risk an overpayment charge.
- **If you get non–Social Security payments for disability:** If you're already getting Social Security disability benefits, you must tell the SSA if you apply for a different (non–Social Security) disability benefit, receive workers' compensation, or get a settlement. Such payments potentially affect Social Security benefit amounts for you and your family.

  Under the disability rules, your benefits may continue temporarily if you work and earn money above certain limits, but you must inform the SSA if you begin to work, your health improves, or there's some change in your ability to take a job.

TIP

If you seek SSDI benefits but also file a claim under the Americans with Disabilities Act (ADA), you could jeopardize your Social Security claim. Your ADA filing, in effect, says that you can work if your employer makes a reasonable accommodation. Before proceeding, get expert guidance on your personal situation.

» **If your citizenship status changes:** A change in status may affect the type of Social Security card you qualify for. To get a card, noncitizens usually must show that they're authorized to work by the Department of Homeland Security.

SHELTERING YOUR BENEFITS FROM DEBT COLLECTORS

Your Social Security benefits are protected from private creditors. Say you're in a mess financially and you owe money to a credit card company or fall behind on your mortgage. Private debt collectors may want to take the money you owe by garnishing your income. But under the law, they generally can't touch your Social Security benefits. The law is Section 207 of the Social Security Act (42 U.S.C. 407). If a court is prepared to allow garnishment, this law should be your trump card.

But be careful: If a bank carries out a garnishment order, freezing your account, and you've mingled Social Security benefits with other cash, you have a problem on your hands. One possible answer is to keep Social Security benefits in an easily identified account in which they aren't mixed up with other assets.

Still, protection from private debt collectors doesn't mean that your benefits are 100 percent immune from garnishment. The federal government is authorized to seize your benefits for several reasons, including the following:

- To collect child support or alimony (Section 459 of the Social Security Act).
- To collect unpaid federal taxes (Section 6334(c) of the Internal Revenue Code). The Internal Revenue Service (IRS) is allowed to seize overdue taxes by taking up to 15 percent of a monthly Social Security benefit until you've paid up.
- To collect debts owed to other federal agencies, such as student loans owed to the U.S. Department of Education.
- To pay restitution to a victim of a crime you committed.

Note: Benefits under SSI may not be garnished by the government.

» **If you work outside the United States and are younger than full retirement age:** This includes part-time work and self-employment. If you get early retirement benefits and work more than 45 hours outside the United States in a job that doesn't pay Social Security taxes, benefits may be withheld.

» **If you're convicted of a crime:** Benefits may be stopped if you commit a crime or have an outstanding arrest warrant, but payments to your family members generally continue.

» **If you receive pension benefits from work you did that was not covered by Social Security, including a government job:** Such benefits could possibly reduce your Social Security payment.

» **If you receive Railroad Retirement benefits:** This applies to you if you get both Social Security and Railroad Retirement benefits based on your spouse's working record and your spouse dies. After that happens, you'll end up with *one* of the benefits — the SSA will decide which one.

TECHNICAL STUFF

Federal rules provide some protection against garnishment of Social Security benefits that have been deposited directly into an account. Generally, banks may not allow creditors to seize benefits deposited within two months of a garnishment order. However, this protection doesn't cover child support or unpaid federal taxes.

Setting the (Earnings) Record Straight

Mistakes sometimes happen with people's earnings statements, potentially leading to incorrect Social Security payments. These mistakes don't happen very often, but they happen enough that you should pay attention to your own earnings statement.

The SSA used to mail out earnings statements to workers annually, but it cut back to save money. Now it mails them out more selectively. As of this writing, paper statements are mailed only to individuals 60 and older who have not established online "*my* Social Security" accounts (which I cover earlier in this chapter) and who have not begun to collect benefits.

Periodically look at your earnings record and carefully review the year-by-year summary of your earnings history. If you have any questions about amounts, check your other records, such as past tax returns. Missed earnings can result in reduced payments, so it's worth your time. (Don't worry if the most recent year is missing; it simply may not yet have been recorded.)

Your earnings record may contain errors for a few reasons:

- The SSA hasn't noted a name change.
- Your employer used an incorrect name for you when reporting your earnings.
- Your employer made a mistake in reporting your earnings.
- Your employer has an incorrect Social Security number on file for you.

Pay attention to the name and number your employer uses in reporting your earnings. Also, make sure that you, your employer, and the SSA are using the exact same name. Be especially vigilant in the case of a name change.

If you find any errors in your earnings history, you need to correct them — and that takes evidence. The SSA's preferred evidence is your Form W-2 Wage and Tax Statement (the SSA wants to deal with your employer on this, so inform your employer of the problem), a tax return, a wage stub or pay slip, your own personal records, or other documents backing up your claim. If you're really in a fix and you can't find such materials, the SSA will want you to write down some facts as best you can; these include the name and location of your employer, the dates you worked, your wages, and the name and Social Security number you gave your employer.

After you've organized your information as best you can, it's time to contact the SSA. If the SSA wants more information, it'll tell you what it needs, or it may contact your employer directly.

The time limit to correct your earnings record if you're self-employed may be as brief as 3 years, 3 months, and 15 days from the end of the tax year in which an error occurred. That deadline is important. But you may have a little wiggle room — the SSA will make certain exceptions to fix older mistakes. These include errors that the SSA considers "obvious," such as earnings mistakenly reported for another person but put on your record. The SSA also has the authority to check its records against your tax returns and fix certain mistakes, even when the deadline has passed.

The SSA uses your 35 years of highest earnings in computing your benefit. You can get earnings data by going to a local SSA office (be prepared to show photo ID) or by accessing your "*my* Social Security" account online. You also can request certified personal information by printing the form at `www.ssa.gov/forms/ssa-7050.pdf` and mailing it to the following address:

Social Security Administration

P.O. Box 33011

Baltimore, MD 21290-33011

WARNING

You may be charged a fee for this information. The form shows the fee schedule, depending on the number of years of information you seek.

It may come in handy to prove that you get Social Security or Supplemental Security Income, especially when you're applying for a loan or another government benefit. What you need is called a "benefit verification letter." You can quickly obtain such a letter online if you have a personal account (and sign in at `www.ssa.gov/myaccount`). You also can request the letter by calling Social Security toll free at 1-800-772-1213 (TTY 1-800-325-0778) or by visiting your local Social Security office. But be aware that going online may be the fastest way to get it taken care of.

Halting Your Retirement Benefits

In rare cases, you may start to collect Social Security benefits and then have a change of heart. Maybe you unexpectedly got an offer for that lucrative job you thought was out of reach. Maybe you decided that you want a bigger payment in the future and plan to live off earnings and your nest egg in the meantime. Yes, it would have been better to have known such things before you started collecting benefits, but it isn't necessarily too late to change your mind. Certain options may be open to you. They have potentially significant differences. If you go down the path of halting benefits, make sure that the SSA representative you deal with has a firm grasp of these rules:

- **Withdrawal of retirement benefits:** If you go this route, you have to pay back everything you received from Social Security during the time (less than one year) that you were collecting. Further, you must pay back any money that was withheld from your payments, such as Medicare premiums and tax withholding. On top of that, you have to pay back all benefits that may have gone to your spouse or other financial dependents, based on the application for retirement that you want to withdraw. (The SSA will require that such dependents agree in writing to the halt in benefits.)

  To apply for a withdrawal of retirement benefits, fill out form SSA-521, available at `www.ssa.gov/forms/`.

  WARNING

  You may withdraw benefits only within the first year of filing for benefits, and you may make only one such withdrawal in your lifetime. The SSA tightened up the withdrawal rules after some commentators touted the process as a way to get a "free loan" from Social Security.

- **Voluntary suspension of benefits:** You may request a voluntary suspension of your benefits when you've reached your full retirement age but have not yet reached 70. This move was part of a technique used by married couples to optimize their benefits that has largely been banned by the SSA. But it is still possible that an individual may decide it's worthwhile to turn off the benefits spigot at full retirement age and let benefits increase (at the rate of 8 percent a year) until they are restarted by age 70. For more information, go to `www.ssa.gov/planners/retire/suspendfaq.html`.

- **Waiver of benefits:** If you haven't reached full retirement age and you want to halt your retirement benefits, but not those of family members getting payments based on your record, you may request a waiver of benefits. You can make such a request to an SSA representative in person or over the phone.

  Note: If you waive benefits and earn enough money, the Social Security earnings test could lead to withholding of benefits to your dependents. (See Chapter 13 for more on the earnings test, as well as a benefit halt based on high earnings, known as a *work suspension.*)

Recovering a Lost or Stolen Social Security Check

Recovering a lost or stolen Social Security check is becoming a problem of the past as the SSA shifts existing beneficiaries over to direct deposit of benefits. (If you apply for benefits nowadays, you're given only two choices: direct deposit or a special debit card.) Electronic payments are supposed to be safer and more reliable than paper checks. But as of this writing, some beneficiaries still rely on getting a check in the mail. If that check doesn't arrive on time, you've got a problem.

REMEMBER

No matter how you're paid, it's worth knowing when the benefit is supposed to arrive:

- If your birthday is on the first through the tenth of the month, your benefits are paid on the second Wednesday of each month.
- If your birthday is on the 11th through the 20th of the month, your benefits are paid on the third Wednesday of each month.
- If your birthday is on the 21st through the 31st of the month, your benefits are paid on the fourth Wednesday of each month.

IF YOU THINK YOU'RE NOT BEING PAID ENOUGH

A good way to avoid getting underpaid is to make sure, in advance, that the SSA is crediting you with all the earnings you deserve when it computes benefits for you and your dependents; see "Setting the (Earnings) Record Straight," earlier in this chapter.

If you think your retirement payment is wrong, you may want to give yourself a reality check by using one of the online calculators. These tools do *not* provide exact benefits, but they may give you an idea as to whether the amount you're getting paid is in the ballpark.

In any case, if you have doubts about the amount you're getting, you have every right to call or visit the SSA and ask a representative to go over it for you.

The SSA requests that you wait three days past the payment date before reporting that a check or electronic payment is missing. If the benefit still hasn't arrived three days after the payment date, call the SSA at 800-772-1213 (TTY 800-325-0778).

For more information on direct deposit of Social Security benefits, go to `www.godirect.org`.

Getting Dinged for an Overpayment

Believe me, you don't want to be paid too much by the SSA. If the SSA decides that it paid you too much, it will demand the money back in a written notice of overpayment. Don't ignore this written notice. It'll state exactly how much the SSA believes you've been overpaid and when it sent you the money.

A common reason for overpayment is that you earned more than expected while also collecting retirement benefits. (It's perfectly okay to earn money while getting benefits, but restrictions apply if you earn over certain amounts and are under your full retirement age.) If this happens, the SSA may stop paying benefits until it has withheld a sufficient amount. It may even ask you to write a check.

But what if you don't believe you've received too much? You have certain options for challenging the notice of overpayment. For starters, respond promptly to the notice by setting up a meeting at your local SSA office. Then consider the following:

- **Waiver of recovery:** If you believe that the SSA is treating you unfairly in demanding the money, that it's not your fault you were overpaid, and you can't afford to pay it back — for example, you acted in good faith but made a mistake that now jeopardizes your benefit — you should ask for a waiver of recovery. The form you need to fill out is SSA-632 (OMB No. 0960-0037), available online at `www.ssa.gov/forms/ssa-632-bk.pdf`. This is a detailed form that asks not only why you seek a waiver but also for a bunch of personal financial information about your assets, income, and expenses.
- **Request for reconsideration:** If you think the SSA erred and you haven't been overpaid, you should file a request for reconsideration. The form is SSA-561(OMB No. 0960-0622), available online at `www.ssa.gov/forms/ssa-561-u2.pdf`.

You may want to file both forms if you believe both apply to your situation. Your appeal must be filed within 60 days of receiving the notice of overpayment. If you request a waiver of recovery within 30 days (10 days for SSI), you can stop any reduction in your benefits until you're able to show the SSA why you believe the overpayment demand should be dropped.

In reviewing your claim, the SSA will consider whether you've done anything wrong — even if the SSA made the mistake. It will reach conclusions about whether you acted responsibly, whether you understood the reporting requirements, and whether you have the competence and ability to follow the rules.

Under certain circumstances, such as when someone is unable to repay, the SSA may consider a compromise settlement or approve an installment plan. You may pay back an overpayment through various means, including money order, check, and credit card.

Getting Social Security in a Global Economy

What if you want to retire overseas? Will the SSA send you the money? What if you worked for a foreign employer? What if you've paid taxes into the Social Security systems of more than one country? What if you're a noncitizen who has lawfully worked in the United States for many years, contributing payroll taxes to Social Security? Do you qualify for benefits?

Welcome to the global economy. If those questions apply to you, they can be very complex to sort out.

WARNING

Be aware that the guidelines affecting Social Security payments to particular countries may change over time. If you fall into any of the categories discussed in this section, you'd be wise to consult with a lawyer or other expert to make sure that you're doing what needs to be done to comply with the rules and get the Social Security benefits you're entitled to. You also can keep up with changes by reading the online pamphlet "Your Payments While You Are Outside the United States" (www.ssa.gov/pubs/10137.html).

With that in mind, read on to get the information you need.

U.S. citizens

Most U.S. citizens work for U.S. employers and live their entire lives in the United States. If that's you, you can skip this section. If you either worked for a foreign employer or are now living abroad, however, keep reading.

If you worked for a foreign employer

If you worked for a foreign employer, you may have been protected from paying Social Security taxes to two countries (the employer's country and the United States) on the same earnings.

You also may have certain protections for your benefits if you worked in a country that has a treaty with the United States. The United States has reached agreement with many countries — including most of Europe, Australia, Chile, Japan, and South Korea — to simplify Social Security issues you may face.

For more information, go to www.ssa.gov/international.

If you live abroad

If you're living in one of many countries overseas, your Social Security payments will be sent to you, just as they would be if you lived in the United States. You even can get direct deposit in a lot of places; for a list, go to www.ssa.gov/international/countrylist6.htm or contact the SSA or the nearest U.S. embassy or consulate.

WARNING

If you're a U.S. citizen, you can travel to or live in most foreign countries except Cuba and North Korea, and still get your Social Security benefits. Restrictions apply in certain countries, however: Azerbaijan, Belarus, Kazakhstan, Kyrgyzstan, Moldova, Tajikistan, Turkmenistan, and Uzbekistan. You can get more information on restrictions that may apply to you by contacting the SSA or the nearest U.S. embassy or consulate.

REMEMBER

If you live overseas and collect Social Security, you still need to comply with the basic reporting requirements for changes in your circumstances that I list earlier in this chapter (see the section "Life Happens: Keeping the Social Security Administration in the Loop").

Noncitizens

You don't have to be a citizen to collect Social Security benefits. You have to have earned them properly and with a lawful immigration status.

If you don't meet certain residency requirements (generally, if you don't have a green card and haven't spent a prescribed amount of time in the United States during the past two years) and you're getting Social Security benefits, the IRS requires that the SSA hold back 30 percent of the taxable portion of your monthly payment. Some exemptions and reductions may apply, based on tax treaties between the United States and some other countries. A good way to find out about this is to review the SSA's nonresident tax screening tool at `www.ssa.gov/international/AlienTax.html`.

If you earned benefits as a noncitizen and now live *outside* the United States, the SSA will send your benefits to other countries, but certain restrictions may apply. Generally, the SSA is required to stop your benefits if you've been outside the United States for six consecutive months, unless you meet certain exceptions in the law, based on your country of citizenship, country of residence, and other factors. (In addition, five years of U.S. residency are generally required before you may be eligible to get benefits overseas as a dependent or survivor.)

WARNING

These rules can be complex. You can find out more by reviewing the SSA's Payments Abroad Screening Tool at `www.ssa.gov/international/payments_outsideUS.html`. You also may want to discuss your personal situation with a lawyer or other expert in Social Security benefits.

The SSA also has an online pamphlet called "Social Security Payment Requirements for Most North, Central, and South American Citizens Living Outside the United States." You can find it at `www.ssa.gov/international/61-011.pdf`.

MAKING SURE YOU GET THE RIGHT BENEFIT

The SSA usually does a good job of providing you the right benefits and giving you the right information. But it's hardly infallible. Smart consumers know that people sometimes make mistakes. Here are some tips to protect yourself, especially if you have a complex or unusual question:

- Call the toll-free line on two or three occasions to see whether you get consistent responses. Anecdotally (and in the preparation of this book), it's not unusual to get different answers to your questions from different SSA representatives. If you're getting inconsistent guidance, you have solid reason to question what you're hearing and to pursue the matter further.
- Ask the representatives for the official guideline from POMS, the Program Operations Manual System that provides guidance to SSA staffers. POMS guidelines are full of technical jargon that may be impossible to understand, but when in doubt, you want to make sure the representatives have done their homework.
- Get outside guidance from a lawyer or other expert in the technicalities of Social Security if important questions remain.
- Document the information you get from the SSA, either by writing it down right away or by sending the SSA a letter confirming what you've been told.

Registering a Complaint with the Social Security Administration

In the course of a year, the SSA has tens of millions of direct contacts with the public, in field offices and over the phone. These contacts range from simple queries for information to emotionally charged concerns about benefits that can have a huge impact on a person's monthly income. So it isn't surprising that people sometimes aren't satisfied with the process or outcome. You have options for registering your complaint, and they vary depending on how serious your complaint is.

If you'd like to give the SSA general feedback, you can do so online at `https://secure.ssa.gov/emailus/`. This online form takes just a few seconds to fill out and is *not* intended as a way to discuss personal matters. In fact, you may not use your Social Security number — the system will reject your message if you do. You can submit a complaint, suggestion, or compliment. The online form is an easy way to put in your two cents about customer service at the SSA.

You also can fill out a comment card to rate your experience at your local SSA office. This card, which should be available at your local SSA office, isn't an official complaint form. It's more like the little cards you may see at restaurants, asking what you thought of the service. It's not always available, but feel free to ask for it. (You can even use this card to say something nice if you're so inclined.) And of course, you have the right to speak to the office manager when you feel you have something to point out.

If you have a more serious grievance with the SSA, you need more than a comment card or online feedback form. Here are your options:

- **Contact your local SSA office in person or in writing.** You can get the address of your local SSA office by plugging in your zip code at the Office Locator link (secure.ssa.gov/ICON/) or by calling 800-772-1213 (TTY 800-325-0778).
- **Write to the national office of the SSA.** You can write a letter to the following address, detailing your complaint:
  - Social Security Administration

    Office of Public Inquiries and Communications Support

    1100 West High Rise

    6401 Security Blvd.

    Baltimore, MD 21235
- **Contact your elected representatives in Congress.** You can contact your congressperson at www.house.gov/representatives/find. To contact your senators, go to www.senate.gov/general/contact_information/senators_cfm.cfm.

If your complaint specifically has to do with discrimination or unfair treatment by an administrative law judge, the SSA has specific forms you can fill out. Here's the information you need:

- **Complaints of discrimination:** If you feel you were unfairly treated on the basis of your race, color, national origin, lack of proficiency in English, religion, gender, sexual orientation, age, or disability, you may file a formal complaint with the SSA. Such complaints should be registered within 180 days of the action you're complaining about.

  You can find the discrimination complaint form at www.ssa.gov/forms/ssa-437.pdf. Mail the signed, dated form, along with your written consent to let the SSA reveal your name in the course of its investigation, to the regional office nearest you. The offices with addresses are listed on page 8 of the complaint form PDF.

» **Complaints of unfair treatment by administrative law judges:** If you're fighting the SSA over benefit decisions, the hearing before an administrative law judge is a critical moment in your appeal (see Chapter 8). The appeals system depends on such hearings being fair, and the SSA provides guidelines on how to complain if you feel that you were treated unjustly. You may express yourself verbally, but you're better off writing down the facts and mailing them to the SSA.

Your complaint should include

- All your basic contact information
- Your Social Security number
- The name of the administrative law judge you're complaining about
- When the incident occurred
- Names and contact information of any witnesses

Your complaint should state your concerns as precisely as possible and what you considered to be unfair. Make clear the actions and words that you object to.

The SSA provides some background on complaining about an administrative law judge at `www.ssa.gov/pubs/EN-05-10071.pdf`. Send your written complaint to the following address:

- Office of Hearings Operations

  Division of Quality Service

  5107 Leesburg Pike, Stes. 1702/1703

  Falls Church, VA 22041-3255

REMEMBER

Don't confuse a complaint of *unfair treatment* by an administrative law judge with a step in your appeal. If you want to pursue your appeal after an *unfavorable finding* from an administrative law judge, your next step is to request a review by the Appeals Council. For more information on how to file an appeal, turn to Chapter 8.

SPECIAL ISSUES FOR VETERANS

If you're a veteran, you should be aware of certain rules that affect the amount of your benefits and what you may qualify for. Your military discharge form (DD Form 214) is the routine proof you need to clarify questions the SSA may have about your dates of service.

One important point to remember is that being approved for disability benefits by a separate agency does *not* mean that you're eligible for Social Security disability. The SSA has its own set of strict criteria to qualify for disability benefits (see Chapter 11). It does, however, offer expedited processing of disability claims for recent veterans (read on for more information).

Various aspects of Social Security apply specifically to veterans. Among the things you should be aware of are the following:

- **You may be eligible for extra earnings credits.** Soldiers on active duty have been covered by Social Security only since 1957. People on inactive duty in the armed forces reserves have been covered only since 1988. To help compensate for this, the SSA offers a boost in earnings credits to veterans of certain time periods, potentially raising the benefits you may receive.

  Veterans who served on active duty from 1940 through 1956 may receive an extra $160 in earnings credits for every month served during that time period.

  Veterans who served from 1957 through 1977 may receive an extra $300 for each quarter they served during that period. (If you served between 1957 and 1967, the SSA will add the credits to your earnings record at the time you apply for benefits. When the time comes, if it hasn't already, you should make sure that the SSA does so. If you served between 1968 and 2001, the special credits are supposed to be added automatically.)

  Veterans who served from 1978 through 2001 may be credited with an extra $100 in earnings (up to $1,200 per year) for every $300 in your active-duty pay. (Some restrictions may apply if you enlisted after September 7, 1980, and did not complete at least 24 months of active duty or your entire tour.)

- **You may be able to get expedited disability benefits if you became disabled while on active military service on or after October 1, 2001.** Veterans potentially qualify for multiple disability benefits, including SSDI, SSI, Department of Veterans Affairs, and Department of Defense programs.

  The SSA does not automatically reduce your benefit amount if you're receiving more than one disability payment. Be aware, however, that if you're approved for SSDI and you're also getting other disability benefits, including workers'

(continued)

(continued)

compensation, the SSA may reduce your disability benefit if your total sum of benefits exceeds 80 percent of your pre-disability earnings.

- **If you're an active-duty service member with a very serious health issue, you may be able to receive SSDI while still receiving your military pay.** The SSA has some discretion in deciding whether the duties you're performing for the military amount to substantial work that makes you ineligible for benefits. First, however, you must be approved for SSDI benefits, which requires a very serious health problem.
- **You can get Social Security and military retirement benefits.** Non–Social Security military retirement benefits do not generally reduce Social Security payments. Your military healthcare benefits under the Department of Veterans Affairs, TRICARE, or CHAMPVA could be affected if you qualify for Medicare. Consult with a military benefits advisor about your personal situation.

  You can find a lot online, but it may take time to sift through all the information. Here are some useful websites: `www.benefits.va.gov/benefits/`, `www.ebenefits.va.gov`, and `www.tricare.mil`.
- **Social Security survivors' benefits could affect benefits you receive under the optional Department of Defense Survivors Benefit Plan.** Check with the Department of Defense or your military retirement advisor if you think you fall into this category.

Social Security has a web page for wounded warriors that includes frequently asked questions, links to Social Security publications, and links to further information about government benefits. Go to `www.ssa.gov/people/veterans`.

» Seeking a hearing before an administrative law judge

» Bringing your challenge to the Appeals Council

» Suing Social Security in federal court

Chapter 8

When You and Social Security Disagree: The Appeals Process

You've filed for benefits and been turned down. You believe the Social Security Administration (SSA) made a wrong decision. You're frustrated, and you want to do something about it. Most often, these kinds of situations involve Social Security Disability Insurance (SSDI) benefits, and such challenges are the focus of this chapter. Be aware, though, that disputes can emerge over earnings amounts, family relationships that affect eligibility for benefits, and other matters. Whatever the issue, you can ask Social Security for a more favorable decision, and you can help your chances by understanding the system.

The appeals process has four distinct phases, depending on how far you take it. In most states, your appeal starts with reconsideration of the initial finding. It may continue with a formal hearing before an administrative law judge. Most challenges stop at that point. But you could take it further, first to the Social Security Administration's Appeals Council and, finally, into the federal court system.

REMEMBER

Each phase of the appeals process comes with its own rules and procedures. Understanding and following these rules and procedures is critical. If you need help in doing so, consider consulting with a lawyer or other Social Security expert. (See the later sidebar "Do you need a professional advocate?" for more information.)

In this chapter, I explain how to challenge Social Security if a decision doesn't go your way.

REMEMBER

As you read this chapter, weigh the pros and cons of undertaking an appeal, as well as the realities you may encounter at different stages of the appeals process. It isn't always enough to be right. You need to make your case and meet deadlines. And you may need to be patient — it can take a year or longer for a challenge to reach the hearing level, where statistics show you have the best chance of winning.

Reconsideration: Taking Your First Step

If the SSA denies your claim, you'll receive in the mail a notice of denial, which also informs you that you have a right to appeal. Now you face a series of questions: Did someone make a mistake in reviewing your application? Does it make sense to challenge the decision? If so, what's the next step?

WARNING

You have 60 days from when you receive the notice to tell the SSA that you want to appeal the decision. (You get five extra days for mailing time, but cutting it close isn't a good idea.) So you need to decide quickly whether you want to challenge the decision. Don't miss the deadline. The SSA may allow leeway for good cause — including a health emergency, miscommunication from the SSA, or other valid reasons — but late filing has the potential to kill your case.

If you decide to appeal the decision, you enter the first level of the appeals process, which is called a *request for reconsideration*. For the reconsideration request, a different evaluator from the state Disability Determination Services takes a look at the file. You may think of this as a "paper" review — it doesn't include your personal appearance or oral argument by an attorney. Critics call this stage of the appeals process a "rubber stamp" of the initial decision, because the vast majority of these appeals — approaching 90 percent in recent years — are turned down (see the later sidebar "Approval rates for disability"). But if you believe in your case and hope to get a hearing before an administrative law judge, you must first file a request for reconsideration.

DO YOU NEED A PROFESSIONAL ADVOCATE?

Your chances of winning an appeal are better if you work with a professional advocate instead of going it alone. Typically, your representative is an attorney who specializes in Social Security appeals, although some nonlawyers can provide the service. Recent statistics aren't available, but virtually every close observer agrees that claimants who use experienced representatives increase their chances of prevailing in a conflict dispute with Social Security.

Experienced advocates make sure that the proper evidence has been gathered and added to the record. This can include contacting your healthcare providers and developing effective evidence by asking them the right questions. They may even point to aspects of your mental or physical health that you didn't focus on in your initial application but that may strengthen your appeal.

Your representative should prepare you for the hearing conducted by an administrative law judge so you know what to expect and how to make the most of this critical moment in your case. At the hearing, your advocate has the opportunity to cross-examine witnesses the government may call, including vocational experts, whose testimony may not be favorable to you. An experienced advocate understands the SSA's medical and occupational guidelines and knows what you need to prove in order to be approved for benefits.

Your local SSA office can provide you with a list of organizations that can lead you toward representation. Start your search by contacting a legal-aid organization in your community. If it can't represent you, contact the National Organization of Social Security Claimants' Representatives (`www.nosscr.org`) or your state bar association for a referral to an attorney in your area. Another possibility: Allsup (`www.allsup.com`), an organization of nonlawyers who provide representation for Social Security claimants.

To use a representative to conduct your business with the SSA, you must fill out and sign Form SSA-1696, Appointment of Representative (`www.ssa.gov/forms/ssa-1696.pdf`). The SSA limits the fee that a representative may charge you to either 25 percent of back benefits awarded or $6,000, whichever is less, but the SSA must first authorize the fee. You and your representative can obtain approval using Form SSA-1693 (`www.ssa.gov/forms/ssa-1693.pdf`). Without authorization, the SSA will disapprove your fee agreement.

Your representative gets copies of all the correspondence the SSA sends you. The SSA has published pamphlets on getting representation, which are worth the read (`www.`

(continued)

(continued)

ssa.gov/pubs/10075.html and www.ssa.gov/representation/documents/Best%20Practices%20and%20Tips.pdf).

Here are a few tips to make sure that you make the most of representation, if you choose to get it:

- **Start early.** Very often, people don't hire an advocate until they've lost a request for reconsideration and want to take their appeal to an administrative law judge. You can strengthen your case by getting counsel earlier in the process. It also can increase your chances of success in an initial claim (though it's an uphill quest, to be sure) and help you build a strong record of evidence early, which can keep the process moving without delay.
- **Choose experience.** The SSA has its own guidelines and rules that largely determine whether an appeal succeeds. You should select a representative who has handled Social Security appeals before and knows the process.
- **Know what you're paying for.** Find out in advance exactly what services a representative provides and how often you may check in to make sure that your case is moving forward. If you have solid reasons to believe that your representative isn't paying enough attention to your case, say so. You also can file a complaint with your state bar association if your lawyer isn't returning your calls or is otherwise neglecting your appeal. You don't have to settle for second-rate service.

In this section, I walk you through the decision on whether to file a request for reconsideration, guiding you through some questions you should ask yourself to make the decision that's right for you. If you decide *not* to file for reconsideration, your work in this chapter is done. But if you decide that you want to go ahead with the appeals process, I tell you how to proceed.

TIP

You may benefit from expert guidance as you navigate the appeals process (or decide whether to appeal in the first place). A trained advocate, such as a lawyer or a nonlawyer who specializes in SSDI issues, should have a clear idea of whether you have a reasonable case to pursue and the sort of evidence you need to provide to prove your eligibility. For more on working with a professional advocate, see the nearby sidebar "Do you need a professional advocate?"

Deciding whether to file a request for reconsideration

Should you file for reconsideration? Start by asking yourself the most basic question of all: Are you disabled?

APPROVAL RATES FOR DISABILITY

The SSA has a high bar to qualify for SSDI — you have to have a very serious condition that is expected to last at least a year or end in death, and you have to be considered unable to work on a sustained basis, based on medical and vocational guidelines. (See Chapter 11 for an in-depth discussion of the SSDI program, including how the SSA defines *disability* and how it determines eligibility.) If you believe you have a legitimate case, you should pursue it. But know what you're getting into. About two-thirds of disability claims are turned down at first. Of those that are appealed, a significant number win at the hearing level, and a smaller number prevail at later stages of the process where the odds of success are tougher.

The following table shows the different rates of denial and approval at various stages of the appeals process for disability cases, which are the most common source of dispute. As you can see, denials are highest for reconsideration requests and lowest at hearings before an administrative law judge. (***Note:*** When an appeal is remanded, that means the Appeals Council has sent the case back to the administrative law judge with recommendations that may or may not be favorable. A denial means you lose. A dismissal also means you lose, because your case is thrown out.)

The majority of applicants for SSDI benefits get an individual version of a denial notice the first time they apply for benefits. The notice generally includes a brief explanation of why the claim for benefits was turned down, along with a brief summary of the SSA's criteria for disability. The notice also includes guidance on how to appeal the decision and notes that the claimant has the right to representation in mounting an appeal.

Stage	Allow	Dismiss	Deny	Remand
Initial application	34%		66%	
Appeals to reconsideration	13%		87%	
Appeals to administrative law judge	47%	21%	32%	
Appeals to the Appeals Council	1%	3%	86%	9%
Appeals to federal court	2%	8%	42%	48%

Source: Social Security Administration (`www.ssa.gov/budget/FY19Files/2019LAE.pdf`, *Table 3.49)*

Note: The appeals process is the same whether you were turned down for SSDI or other benefits. Much of the following information focuses on SSDI because it raises particular issues that often result in dispute.

REMEMBER

The SSA considers five areas in determining whether you qualify for SSDI benefits. Some of these steps entail technical considerations that may not be apparent, depending on how much research you have done or are prepared to do. Broadly speaking, the SSA wants to know several things about you:

- **Are you still able to earn a substantial amount of money from employment?** The SSA periodically revises the level it considers substantial (known as substantial gainful activity). (In 2020, it was set at $1,260 per month for the nonblind and $2,110 for the blind.) Earnings above that level are likely to disqualify you.
- **Do you have a severe condition that is likely to last for at least a year or end in death?** The condition can be physical, mental, or some combination of the two.
- **Is your condition included on the SSA's "Listing of Impairments"?** This list may be hard to decipher, but you can find it at `www.ssa.gov/disability/professionals/bluebook/AdultListings.htm`. ***Note:*** Your condition doesn't have to be on the list for you to qualify for benefits.
- **Can you still do your job or similar work?** The SSA may go back 15 years in deciding whether you're capable of doing work you're familiar with. So, even if you're not able to do your *current* job, if you're still able to do a job you had much earlier in life, you may not qualify for SSDI benefits.
- **Can you do any other jobs that exist in large numbers in the national economy?** The younger you are, the more the SSA expects you to find a new line of work that is compatible with limitations rather than get benefits. Applicants older than 50 have a better chance of qualifying for SSDI benefits than those who are younger; chances for approval increase with age.

TIP

You can educate yourself on qualifying for SSDI benefits by reviewing the material in Chapter 11 and by reading the information that the SSA puts out on the subject, starting at `www.ssa.gov/disability`. You'll find facts about the appeals process, technical details, and a link to frequently asked questions.

Taking the steps to file

You can file a request for reconsideration by filling out Form SSA-561 (`www.ssa.gov/forms/ssa-561.pdf`). If you're appealing a decision related to SSDI benefits, you also may file a request for reconsideration online (by going to directly to www.ssa.gov/benefits/disability/appeal.html or to www.ssa.gov and clicking Menu, scrolling to the Benefits section, and clicking "Appeal a Decision").

The SSA has a separate form if your issue involves the cutoff of benefits (as opposed to losing an initial claim). If benefits are being stopped, the form you need is SSA-789 (www.ssa.gov/forms/ssa-789.pdf).

WARNING

If you get a notice that the SSA is cutting off benefits, you have only ten days after you receive the notice to submit a written request that benefits continue while you appeal.

TIP

The request for reconsideration form gives you just three lines to state the reasons you're requesting a review. You don't need to prove your whole case on this form. What matters is that, in the course of your appeal (the sooner the better), you provide the SSA with all the background information it needs to consider your application, including detailed evidence about your medical treatments (doctors' visits and dates, lab results, prescriptions, names and phone numbers of all healthcare providers, and so on), along with your work history.

As part of your request for reconsideration, you also should file a new report on your disability and an authorization (Form SSA-1696; www.ssa.gov/forms/ssa-1696.pdf) for the individual who will represent you so he or she can see your file and talk about your case with the SSA. You may fill out forms authorizing other individuals, such as healthcare providers, to disclose information about you to the SSA. You can get the Disability Report at www.ssa.gov/forms/ssa-3441.pdf; the form requesting disclosure of your personal information is at www.ssa.gov/forms/ssa-827.pdf.

TIP

If you mail your request for reconsideration form, send it by certified mail so you have a receipt. If you hand-deliver the form to your local SSA field office, ask for a receipt. The receipt may prove valuable if the SSA loses your application while the clock is ticking.

REMEMBER

Stay organized at every step of the appeals process. Include your name, Social Security number, and telephone number on every document you send to the SSA. Keep photocopies and other records to help you keep track of what you've sent.

Requests for reconsideration are often decided within four months, give or take. The sooner you file your request, the more you can keep the process moving forward. This is important for a couple of reasons:

- The longer it takes to reach a decision, the more you risk losing back benefits.
- Requests for reconsideration usually lose. So, if you believe in your claim and you want to press on, you want to get to the next stage — a hearing before an administrative law judge — as soon as you can.

Going to an Administrative Law Judge to Solve Your Problem

If your request for reconsideration was turned down, you'll receive a notice in the mail. At this point, you may feel like throwing in the towel, but if you have good reason to believe that you qualify for benefits, don't give up yet! Most appeals are denied in that first stage, but your next option — a hearing before an administrative law judge — may be the pivotal stage in your challenge. Such hearings have a real chance of success: Judges have granted benefits in roughly half the cases they've heard in recent years.

After you receive the notice that your request for reconsideration was denied, you have 60 days (plus 5 days for mail time) to send in your request for a hearing before a judge.

WARNING

Failing to meet the deadline can mean the end of your appeal. But the SSA accepts certain excuses and may even hold a separate hearing to consider their validity. For example, if you suffer a serious health episode that interferes with your ability to file an appeal, the deadline may be extended. Other possible reasons for late filing include a death in your immediate family, a lack of understanding English, or not receiving the notice from the SSA. If you asked the SSA for more information and then asked for a hearing within 60 days of that information request, the SSA may accept a late filing. But don't count on the SSA making exceptions to that 60-day rule — file on time, if possible.

TIP

Most people need some support or guidance at this point in the appeals process, if not sooner. To give yourself the best chance for success, consulting an expert to represent you is usually a good idea. For more on working with an advocate, see the sidebar "Do you need a professional advocate?" earlier in this chapter.

TECHNICAL STUFF

If an evaluator has overlooked overwhelming evidence in ruling against your request for reconsideration, you may be able to get a favorable decision from an administrative law judge *without* a hearing, saving months of time. This is called an *on-the-record decision.* You may request an on-the-record decision only after you've filed for a hearing. On-the-record decisions are sometimes granted if you have a great deal of medical and vocational evidence on your side. If the request is turned down, you still get the hearing. (It doesn't make sense to make such a request unless your case is strong.)

Requesting a hearing

You request a hearing by filling out Form HA-501 (`www.ssa.gov/forms/ha-501.pdf`) or by writing a letter to the SSA.

REMEMBER

From the time you're notified that your request for reconsideration was denied, you have 60 days (plus 5 days for mailing) to request a hearing. Check for any timeline changes due to COVID-19 at www.ssa.gov/coronavirus/.

In addition to requesting a hearing on your rejected claim, the SSA may want you to fill out other forms at this point in the SSDI appeals process:

- **Disability Report—Appeal (Form SSA-3441):** www.ssa.gov/forms/ssa-3441.pdf
- **Authorization to Disclose Information to the Social Security Administration (Form SSA-827):** www.ssa.gov/forms/ssa-827.pdf
- **Claimant's Recent Medical Treatment (Form HA-4631):** www.ssa.gov/forms/ha-4631.pdf
- **Claimant's Medications (Form HA-4632):** www.ssa.gov/forms/ha-4632.pdf
- **Claimant's Work Background (Form HA-4633):** www.ssa.gov/forms/ha-4633.pdf

TIP

Get any new evidence to the administrative law judge as soon as possible, preferably within ten days of filing the request for the hearing. If you need more time to submit new evidence, ask the SSA for extra time to do so.

After your request is received, you'll get a letter from a Social Security Hearing Office that includes the hearing office's telephone number and mailing address. The Hearing Office should tell you (and your lawyer or other advocate) the date, time, and location of your hearing at least 75 days ahead of time. The Hearing Office sends a form for you to complete, indicating whether you'll attend the hearing. The hearing is usually within 75 miles of your home. Increasingly, the SSA offers people the opportunity to attend a video hearing, in which you and the judge are in separate locations but can see and hear each other through a video hookup. You may find this a convenient option (though it won't be in your own home).

TIP

Don't miss your hearing or leave it completely to others to speak for you. This is the one step in the process where an individual who judges your claim gets to see you as a human being. If you have a strong case, it can be more effective for a judge to hear it with you present than for a reviewer to make an assessment based on a stack of records. This is not only a chance to put a human face on what has been, until now, just another file, but it's also an opportunity to establish your credibility.

Preparing for your hearing

You (and your representative if you have one) should review your Social Security file well in advance of your hearing. You can ask your local SSA hearing office how you may see your file. You can find the phone number in the letter you received from the SSA's Office of Hearings Operations when it received notice of your appeal. Or just call the SSA at 800-772-1213 (TTY 800-325-0778).

If you filed your claim electronically and are working with a representative, that person can access your electronic folders (eFolder) on a secured website. You and your representative will need to complete an in-person enrollment process with a Social Security employee. SSA will then issue a USER ID and a REP ID (see `www.ssa.gov/ar/`).

The judge may seek more information before the hearing or even afterward. But you and your advocate should make your own assessment well in advance. In particular, look for the following:

- **Is all the healthcare information in place?** Make sure that records for all exams, consultations, lab results, and prescriptions are in the file, along with names and phone numbers of healthcare providers and dates visited. Check to be sure that your doctor has provided the necessary evidence, including an individualized statement that makes clear how your condition affects your ability to work, and that the record is up to date with your most recent treatments and exams.

TIP

  Healthcare records often fall through the cracks, so be persistent if providers are slow in sending them. You want to figure this out well before your hearing in order to prevent delay and to make the strongest case you can.

- **Is all the occupational information in place?** Your file should contain 15 years of employment information, including the tasks required at each job.
- **Are the physical and/or mental issues that prevent your ability to work on a sustained basis laid out clearly?** Don't just state the health problems. Make sure you explain how they prevent you from performing work tasks and holding down a job.

REMEMBER

This is *your* claim. It's your responsibility (and that of your advocate) to make sure that the full record of treatments, exams, and test results has been submitted to the record.

If you're working with an advocate, shortly before the hearing, he or she should tell you what to expect and advise you on how to make your case. Don't be passive. Ask your advocate everything you want to know. Think through the points you need to make when you speak to the judge. Your advocate should help you prepare.

Participating in your hearing

Your hearing will take place in a private room with your advocate (if you have one), the administrative law judge, an aide who runs the tape recorder, and possibly witnesses called by the SSA, such as a vocational expert and a medical expert. You may have your own witnesses as well. The atmosphere is serious but not very formal. The courtroom dramatics you see on TV — like shouts of "I object" or skirmishes over admissibility of evidence — aren't likely to happen. The hearing is a nonadversarial exercise in gathering information. The event will probably last less than an hour.

The administrative law judge runs the show. He or she is a fact finder, questioner, and decider of your case. The judge's job is to look at the facts with a fresh eye. The judge will ask you various questions about your daily life and activities, from the time you wake in the morning to the time you go to bed at night, even if that information is already in the record. The judge also may ask questions about your engagement in the world.

Here are some examples of questions the judge may ask:

- What sorts of tasks are you able to perform around the house?
- Can you handle your own grooming and hygiene?
- Do you work in the yard?
- How do you get around?
- Do you go to a house of worship regularly? If so, how do you get there?
- Do you have hobbies?
- Do you have an active social life?

Some of these questions are meant to draw out insights about your ability to do certain physical tasks. If you go to church, you presumably can leave your house and travel within your community. If you do yardwork, you may have some endurance. Other questions may elicit information about your mental and social adjustment. For example, having good, long-standing friendships says something about your social adjustment that is very different from having no friends.

REMEMBER

Eventually, the line of questioning will get around to the specifics of your condition and your claim for benefits. Employers don't just want you to be able to do certain tasks sometimes or some days. You're able to satisfy the requirements of a job only if you can do basic tasks on a *sustained* basis. You need to make it through shifts, and you need to make it through the week.

The judge also may question outside experts:

- **Vocational experts:** The SSA often calls vocational experts to offer their opinions about skills and exertion required to perform certain occupations. The judge could ask a vocational expert whether someone in your apparent condition can do certain jobs — or any job. If a vocational expert suggests that someone with your symptoms could do certain kinds of work, such as sitting at a desk or table most of the day, that testimony could hurt your claim.
- **Medical experts:** The SSA also may call in a medical expert if the judge wants to clarify questions about your health. A medical expert may be asked to weigh in on various issues, including whether the evidence in your case has conflicts, whether your impairments meet a listed impairment, and whether you've followed instructions in getting treatment.

For this part of the process, you may be most dependent on an advocate who knows the rules and who understands how your situation fits with the guidelines of SSDI. Your advocate also gets to question the experts and try to undermine damaging testimony they may provide. A good advocate can seize on mistakes or irrelevant points brought up by the experts and make clear to the judge why your claim is strong. (This is why having an advocate on your side is so helpful.)

The most important part of the hearing is your testimony. Your entire effort to get benefits has built up to this moment. You can help yourself, hurt yourself, or perhaps fail to make much of an impression, which may be a wasted opportunity.

REMEMBER

When you're testifying, be clear and detailed. Make sure that you know in advance what you need to get across about your limitations. You've waited a long time for this moment, but it's not about drama or emotion — it's about facts. You can paint the picture by honestly and straightforwardly presenting facts about your condition, backed up by details.

Here are a few do's and don'ts to keep in mind about how to make your case at the hearing:

- **Don't hype your symptoms.** The judge has heard it all before. If you raise doubts about your own credibility, you undermine your entire case.
- **Don't minimize your symptoms.** You need to make your limitations clear. If your condition makes it impossible to do work on a sustained basis — whether that means sitting, standing, concentrating, or any other critical ability — make that clear. You understand what you can and can't do better than the experts in the room.
- **If you're in pain, don't be stoic.** Let the judge know how much pain you have and what you take for it.

- **Don't go off topic.** You may be angry. You may be sad. You may want to make a speech about the government. But you're here to answer questions about your condition. That's the only way you can help yourself.
- **Don't make assumptions about the administrative law judge.** Whatever his or her style, the judge's professional duty is to follow the rules. If the judge makes a mistake or treats you improperly, you have recourse. (See Chapter 7 for how to file a complaint about an administrative law judge.)
- **Do respect the process.** Arrive early for your hearing, dress neatly, and come across as respectful and polite to the participants (whatever you may feel inwardly).
- **Do be prepared.** By now you should have an idea of what your strongest evidence is and the points you need to emphasize to establish your claim. If you aren't sure, discuss this with your advocate. State the facts as effectively as you can.
- **Do be specific.** Details from your life have the ring of truth. You can say that you're tired all the time, but if you (truthfully) say that some days you can't get out of bed at all, you leave a more lasting impression. You should point out whether you have severe back pain, but it helps to note that the pain makes it impossible for you to stay seated for more than a few minutes.
- **Do refer to the time you were insured for SSDI benefits.** By this point, you should know that you worked recently enough to be protected. Generally, that means you must show that you became disabled within five years of when you quit working.
- **Do highlight your own track record as a good worker.** If you were a reliable employee in the years before you claimed disability, that strengthens your case. If you've tried hard to keep working and, if possible, get better, that strengthens your case.

The SSA can take one to two months or longer to get you the administrative law judge's findings. If you win, benefits may start about two months later.

Knowing What to Expect from the Appeals Council

If the administrative law judge turns you down, your next option is to take your challenge to the Appeals Council, the highest level of the SSA's appeals process. The Appeals Council is mainly interested in whether the administrative law judge made a mistake. The odds for you aren't good at this point. Usually, the Appeals

Council concludes that the judge did *not* err. If the Appeals Council finds in your favor, it may send the case back to the administrative law judge and you may have a chance to win.

There are three ways to request an appeal. You'll need to act within 60 days of receiving the administrative law judge's decision:

1. You can request an Appeals Council review in writing. Fill out Form HA-520 (OMB No. 0960-0277) at www.ssa.gov/forms/ha-520.pdf. The form gives you just a few lines to say why you seek a review, but you or your advocate can attach a longer explanation. If you have additional evidence, include it at the time you submit this request.
2. You can file online at the iAppeal Online Appeals Application at www.ssa.gov/appeals/appeals_process.html#a0=0. You download the form by going to How to Ask for Appeals Council Review and click on Appeals Council Request for Review (iAppeals i520).
3. You can contact your local Social Security office's local hearing office by calling 800-772-1213 (TTY 800-325-0778) and filling out a request for review form.

Send your request for an Appeals Council review to the following address:

Appeals Council, SSA/OARO

5107 Leesburg Pike

Falls Church, VA 22041-3255

Or send your request online at the Getting Ready web page: https://secure.ssa.gov/iApplNMD/oao.

REMEMBER

Although the Appeals Council may consider new evidence, such evidence must relate to the time period before the administrative law judge ruled on your case. This may entail subtle considerations. For example, you may get a new lab result confirming that you have a certain disease, and this finding may have added insight into your condition at the time you were appealing your claim to the administrative law judge and at the hearing. But if you develop an entirely *new* illness after the hearing, such evidence isn't part of your appeal.

The Appeals Council will inform you that it has received your materials. But you're free to check for yourself either by calling the Council's Congressional and Public Affairs Branch staff at 703-605-8000 or by calling the SSA at 800-772-1213 (TTY 800-325-0778).

When the process begins, an SSA hearings and appeals analyst (a paralegal, law clerk, or attorney) reviews your file. If you've provided new evidence, the appeals analyst assesses whether it is material to the administrative law judge's decision and could affect the way your case should be handled. The analyst then makes a recommendation to an administrative appeals judge or appeals officer. This high-level reviewer makes a decision or asks the appeals analyst to make a different recommendation.

Be patient. It can take a year or longer for the Appeals Council to complete its review.

Requests that reach the Appeals Council tend to have four kinds of conclusions:

- **They're denied.** This result is the most common by far; it happens more than 85 percent of the time. You aren't out of options if your request is denied. If you want to keep fighting, your next stop is federal court (see the next section).

  You're allowed to file a new application for benefits with the SSA while your claim is pending in federal court. (Under limited circumstances, you may be able to file a new application while your appeal is pending at the Appeals Council if you have a new critical or disabling condition that began after the date of the decision by the administrative law judge.) But if you file a new application while an appeal is pending, the SSA can find only that your disability began as of the day after the date of the judge's decision.

- **They're sent back to the administrative law judge.** This action, known as a *remand,* is potentially favorable for the claimant, though it happens 9 percent of the time. It means that the judge made some kind of mistake, and the council wants the judge to fix it. The judge may have misinterpreted the law, failed to properly consider the evidence, or treated you unfairly. Potentially, it can lead to a new hearing, where you can try to make your case again.
- **They're dismissed.** This means your appeal is thrown out. Common reasons for dismissal are that you failed to comply with the rules, such as by filing after the deadline without a good excuse, failing to show up at the hearing, or otherwise not responding to requests from the SSA.
- **They're approved.** This is a complete victory for the applicant, and it's extremely rare.

In certain cases, signatures from two judges are needed for the Appeals Council to take certain action. These may include *remanding* (sending back the case to an administrative law judge with instructions about fixing a mistake) or the rare instances in which the council makes a final decision on the case.

Taking Your Claim to Federal Court

When you've run out of options inside the SSA and you still want to appeal, your next stop is the U.S. district court in the area where you live. At this point, you need a lawyer who knows how to sue in federal court. To prevail, your lawyer must show that the SSA made a mistake or was unfair in deciding your claim. Only a tiny percentage of Social Security claimants hang in for this step. Although prevailing remains difficult, your chances in federal court are somewhat better than at the Appeals Council.

To take this step, you must file suit within 60 days of receiving notice from the Appeals Council. You must file your case in federal district court, and you're required to send a copy of your suit (called a *complaint*) and summons to the SSA's Office of General Counsel that handles the area where the complaint is filed. To find information on the office associated with your area, see Program Operations Manual System, GN 03106.020 — Service of Process (`https://secure.ssa.gov/apps10/poms.nsf/links/0203106020`). ***Note:*** Copies should be sent by certified or registered mail.

Until now, you may not have faced out-of-pocket costs. But it costs money to sue in federal court (a $400 filing fee, as of 2019). If you can't afford to pay the fee, you may apply for a fee waiver; your lawyer typically handles this.

Much of the court process will be a battle of written briefs and responses between you and the SSA. After the SSA receives your complaint, summing up why you believe it was wrong to deny you benefits, the SSA sends its response back to the court. Your lawyer also sends in a brief that further argues your case. The SSA may respond to that brief, and your lawyer may send in a *reply brief*, responding to the SSA's response. The judge (often a federal magistrate) then may ask attorneys for both sides to argue in court. No witnesses or new evidence is permitted at this phase. The court's decision is based on the entire administrative record. You won't participate, but you may attend.

In the end, the judge can do one of a few things:

- Deny your claim.
- Send the case back to the SSA and order it to consider certain issues raised in your complaint.
- Approve your claim.

The length of time for this process varies, but it can take 18 months or more.

In recent years, the federal court has sent almost half of such cases (48 percent in 2017) back to the SSA for further review, thereby keeping the challenge alive. More than 40 percent are denied. A very small percentage wins outright victories in federal court, and the rest are tossed out. If you get a negative outcome in federal district court, you may challenge the ruling in the federal court of appeals for the judicial circuit that oversees your district court. But at that point, your chances for success are dwindling.

KEEPING THE APPEALS PROCESS MOVING

You need a lot of patience to mount an appeal, especially if you keep getting turned down along the way. An appeal can take years. That means you don't want to do anything that slows down the process. You want to do all you can to keep things moving along.

It never hurts to generate congressional interest in your disability claim. If you believe you've been wrongly turned down, you have every right to inform your local congressional office. It may not be easy to catch the interest of busy staffers (much less the actual politician), but don't be shy. Write a letter, and follow up with a phone call to make clear why you believe your claim is legitimate. Lawmakers and their staffs place a premium on constituent service. If a congressional staff member asks the SSA a question about your case, rest assured that the SSA will look at it. That doesn't mean you'll win, but you have nothing to lose. The SSA tries to be as responsive as it can to questions from Capitol Hill.

Here are some other tips to keep the process from getting any slower than it has to be:

- **File as soon as you can.** This step alone can save months of time compared to repeated last-minute filing if your appeal goes through a few stages.
- **Provide all the information the SSA asks for.** Fill out the forms completely and legibly. Respond promptly to requests for more information. If the SSA sets up a consultative exam, don't miss it.
- **Focus your effort.** Your goal should be to provide individualized, tailored evidence that ties in directly with the SSA's criteria for disability. It isn't enough for a doctor to say that you may have Alzheimer's disease. If possible, the doctor should provide specific details about your memory loss, signs of confusion, and other limitations that affect the ability to handle a job.
- **Assume nothing.** Keep in touch with your advocate to make sure that he or she is on top of the case. Periodically ask the SSA whether your file is complete or

(continued)

(continued)

whether you owe any information. Ask to inspect the file, and look for gaps. If healthcare providers haven't yet sent something, either you or your advocate should remind them to do so.

Under certain dire circumstances, you may qualify for fast-track consideration of a claim. If the system is working properly, the SSA should identify when these conditions exist, but you or your advocate shouldn't count on that. Make it clear to the SSA if you believe you qualify for a special, swift approval of your claim. Here are some situations in which a person may qualify for fast-track consideration:

- **If you fall into a "critical" category:** Critical categories may qualify for rapid processing of a claim, although the SSA retains some discretion. One such category is "dire need" of basic necessities, such as food, shelter, and medical care. Other critical categories include people with terminal illness; active military personnel injured on or after October 1, 2001; or individuals who are considered suicidal or homicidal.
- **Compassionate allowances:** Compassionate allowances include more than 200 grave conditions that have been specifically designated for rapid approval, when supported by the evidence. You can find more about compassionate allowances and find a list of these conditions at `www.ssa.gov/compassionateallowances`.
- **Quick Disability Determination (QDD):** This refers to an expanding effort in Social Security to approve claims, relying on computer analysis to highlight those applications that are likely to be approved.

3 Who Benefits and When

IN THIS PART . . .

Find out about spousal benefits: You may have earned benefits for your spouse, or your spouse may have earned benefits for you.

Gather the rules that affect benefits for children and parents, and discuss how the Social Security Administration defines dependent family members.

Examine disability benefits, and gain a clear overview of the rules that determine whether you may be eligible.

» Looking at how much a spouse gets

» Getting the most you can out of spousal benefits

Chapter 9

Spousal Benefits: Watching Out for Each Other

When you think about Social Security, you probably focus on your own retirement benefit, earned through years of working and contributing payroll taxes into the system. But if you are or ever have been married, you have more than that to consider. You also have earned (or may earn) benefits for your spouse, and your spouse may have earned (or may earn) benefits for you.

When you make decisions about filing for Social Security retirement benefits, you may not be making those decisions in isolation — your decisions may affect (or be affected by) your spouse or former spouse. Under the Bipartisan Budget Act of 2015, certain claiming strategies were restricted for married couples. But you still can maximize your retirement benefits — or leave the most for your spouse upon your death — by finding the strategy that's right for your unique situation. In this chapter, I show you how. But first, I start by telling you who qualifies for spousal benefits and who doesn't. If you're married, or you've ever been married, read on.

TIP

People sometimes confuse spousal benefits and survivor benefits, both of which may go to spouses but are different benefits based on different rules. The spousal benefit may be paid to a spouse when the breadwinner is still alive and getting retirement benefits. The survivor benefit may be paid to a spouse (or potentially other survivors) when the breadwinner dies. Important details on each appear in this chapter.

Who Qualifies and Who Doesn't

Spousal benefits are benefits earned by a breadwinner, based on his or her earnings record, not the earnings record of the spouse. Spousal benefits don't reduce the Social Security benefit that goes to the breadwinner. In fact, they can boost the income of an older household for many years — as long as the two partners remain alive.

Basically, you may be eligible for spousal benefits if all of the following apply:

- You're at least 62 years old.
- You are legally married to the breadwinner, and the marriage has lasted for at least one year.

TECHNICAL STUFF

  The Social Security Administration (SSA) allows several exceptions to the one-year marriage requirement to qualify for spousal benefits. Here are two of the major exceptions:

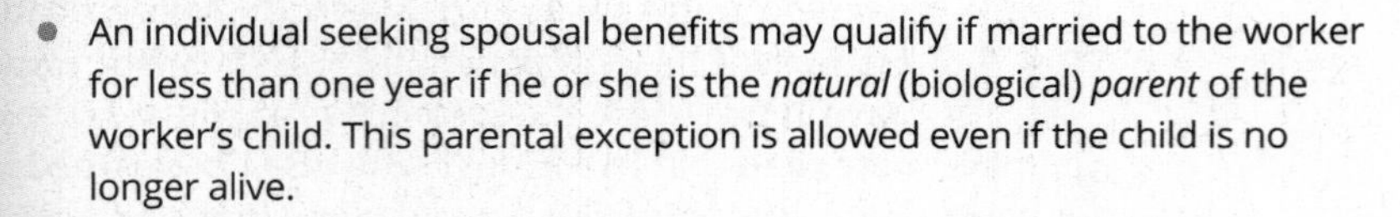

  - An individual seeking spousal benefits may qualify if married to the worker for less than one year if he or she is the *natural* (biological) *parent* of the worker's child. This parental exception is allowed even if the child is no longer alive.
  - An individual seeking spousal benefits may qualify if married to the worker for less than one year if he or she would qualify for a Social Security auxiliary benefit, such as an ex-spouse, widow, or surviving parent benefit, in the month prior to the month of marriage.
  - Say you're getting your own retirement benefit at 62, based on your own career, and then you get married. In such a case, you potentially qualify for spousal benefits through your new spouse, even if the marriage hasn't yet lasted a year. Of course, you want the spousal benefit only if it's bigger than the benefit you're already receiving.

- You don't already qualify for a larger benefit based on your own work record.
- Your spouse (the breadwinner) has filed for his or her own Social Security benefits.

You may be eligible for benefits as an ex-spouse if your marriage lasted for ten years. (*Note:* Your former partner doesn't have to file for benefits in order for you to potentially be eligible as an ex-spouse. But if your former partner hasn't filed for benefits, your divorce must have been in effect for at least two years.)

As with all Social Security benefits, you may have to provide certain evidence to prove you're eligible. For spousal benefits, this evidence may include proof of marriage (including proof that the marriage lasted at least one year) and proof of age. The proof of age requirement is waived if you're caring for a child who is under 16 or who gets Social Security disability benefits. See Chapter 5 for more information on the evidence required when filing for benefits.

TIP

When you file for spousal benefits, the SSA already may have some of the information it requires in its records, depending on your past dealings with the agency and whether you previously established an earnings record.

The SSA follows certain guidelines — including state and federal law — on who may receive spousal benefits. You may have a different definition of what constitutes a spouse or a legal marriage, but that won't change a decision on your claim. In the following sections, I fill you in on the details of who qualifies for spousal benefits and who doesn't.

Traditional spouses

If you have a traditional marriage (one man, one woman), the Social Security Act was written with you in mind. The spousal payment is based entirely on the earnings record of the breadwinner. It requires no earnings record on the part of the other spouse.

Same-sex spouses

In a historic turnaround, the SSA now processes spousal claims from same-sex marriages. While the agency initially placed great weight on whether a same-sex marriage was recognized as valid in the state where it took place, it has since broadened the policy and recognizes same-sex marriages if the initial claim for benefits was filed on or after June 26, 2015, or pending a final determination at that time — regardless of the state where the marriage occurred. (All U.S. states now recognize same-sex marriages as legally valid, although states reached that position on different dates.)

REMEMBER

While all states now recognize same-sex marriage, they do not all agree on the legal definition of a marriage, a fact that potentially applies both to unions of a man and a woman, as well as unions of the same gender. The SSA wants to know whether — under the law of the state where the worker lives — the worker's partner would be allowed to inherit a legal spouse's share of the worker's property if the worker died without a will. If the answer is yes, Social Security considers the couple (same sex or heterosexual) to be married, both for claims related to Social Security and for Medicare. If the answer is no, it does not.

Social Security lifted the longtime barrier on payments to spouses in same-sex marriages after the U.S. Supreme Court tossed out Section 3 of the Defense of Marriage Act. Until then, the agency had said the 1996 law prevented it from recognizing such marriages in allocating benefits. Implementing the law for Social Security has raised various issues. As of this writing, you can find the technical rules governing Social Security policy on same-sex marriage by going to `secure.ssa.gov/apps10/poms.nsf/lnx/0200210000`.

Common-law spouses

Common-law marriages are unions in which neither a religious nor a civil marriage ceremony took place, but the two partners live together and consider themselves to be married. A handful of states recognize common-law marriages entered into within the state's own borders as fully legal; most don't. The SSA goes along with the legal status of a common-law marriage in the state where you live.

Most states recognize common-law marriages that were validly entered into in one of the states that recognizes them. The following states generally recognize common-law marriage (but be aware that the list changes over time): Colorado, Iowa, Kansas, Montana, New Hampshire, Oklahoma, Rhode Island, South Carolina, Texas, and Utah. The District of Columbia also recognizes common-law marriage. Some other states recognize common-law marriage under certain circumstances.

Divorced spouses

The SSA allows spousal benefits for divorced spouses if the marriage lasted at least ten years and the former spouse who seeks benefits is unmarried. (It makes no difference to the SSA if the breadwinner on whose record the spousal benefit is based has gotten remarried.)

Benefit levels for a divorced spouse are the same as for a current spouse, but as with spousal benefits, the payment size varies according to the age at which the benefit is claimed (see the later section "How Much You Can Expect to Get").

If a divorced spouse and a current spouse each claim the benefit when each reaches full retirement age, their spousal benefit is the same size. A spousal benefit to an ex has no effect on the size of the benefit that goes to the current spouse. In theory, a worker could have a few former spouses, all of whom qualify for spousal benefits, as long as they meet the requirements.

Certain rules affect whether a former spouse may qualify for spousal benefits on the worker's record:

- **Unlike a currently married spouse who is raising the couple's child, a former spouse isn't eligible for spousal benefits before age 62, even if he or she is raising the once-married couple's child.** The rules do, however, provide one break based on the former spouse's age: If he or she is caring for the breadwinner's child and has reached age 62, he or she may qualify for spousal benefits with no reduction for age.
- **Unlike a currently married spouse, a former spouse may qualify for spousal benefits even if the breadwinner hasn't filed for Social Security benefits.** In such a case, however, the breadwinner must be *eligible* for benefits, even if he or she hasn't yet claimed them, and you must be divorced for two years.

  In addition, you don't have to be in contact with your former spouse. You don't even need to know your ex-spouse's Social Security number. Just provide the SSA with as much information as you can about your former spouse, and it does the rest to figure out your spousal benefit.

Widows and widowers

To get a Social Security widow or widower's (survivor) benefit, you typically must have been married to a covered worker for at least nine months and be 60 years old. Benefits also are provided for disabled widows or widowers who have reached 50. Divorced spouses may qualify for widow's or widower's benefits if the marriage lasted ten years and they didn't remarry before age 60.

The SSA provides for certain exceptions to the requirement that the marriage lasted nine months before the worker died. These include the same exceptions to the one-year length-of-marriage rule for spousal benefits (if the spouse is the biological parent of the worker's child or if the spouse qualified for different Social Security benefits in the month prior to the month of marriage).

In addition, a widow or widower may qualify for benefits if the worker died before the marriage reached the nine-month mark, if one of the following applies:

- The breadwinner died in an accident.
- The breadwinner died in the line of duty as a member of a uniformed service.
- The breadwinner and widow or widower had been married to each other previously, and their past marriage lasted at least nine months.

THE HISTORY OF THE REMARRIAGE RULES

The remarriage rules are rooted in a time when policymakers assumed that wives were financially dependent on their husbands. As a result, the rules treated women and men differently. Originally, survivor and spousal benefits were allowed for wives but not for husbands. But over time, the rules changed. In 1950, Congress made clear that husbands and widowers also were allowed to get spousal and survivor benefits. For either gender, the survivor benefit would stop if an individual got remarried.

Later, lawmakers voiced a different concern — that the remarriage rules were discouraging unmarried older couples from tying the knot, because they didn't want to lose their survivors' benefits from a previous union. In 1965, Congress voted to limit the remarriage penalty for survivors. Rather than face a complete loss of benefits, widows who remarry at 60 and widowers at 62 would lose 50 percent of their benefits, rather than the whole amount. Two years later, disabled widows were given the right to remarry at 50 and hold on to benefits.

But even with this liberalization, the rules still made it costly to remarry, and many older Americans acted accordingly. News accounts at the time pointed to the phenomenon of older couples choosing to "live in sin" and protect their benefits, rather than get married. In 1977, Congress and President Jimmy Carter agreed to ease the "living in sin" rule further by allowing individuals who remarry after age 60 to preserve the survivors' benefits they got from a previous marriage.

Restrictions on remarriage also affect divorced spouses. Congress has long assumed that divorced wives may face hardship. Over the years, it added spousal and survivors' benefits for former spouses who meet certain requirements. Spouses who lose benefits when they remarry may be able to get them back if the newer marriage ends because of death, divorce, or annulment. In any case, if you remarry, at age 62 you become eligible for benefits based on the earnings record of your new spouse. You may still be able to keep survivors' benefits from a former spouse, if those benefits are greater.

You may qualify for benefits as a married spouse *and* as a widow or widower. This could happen, for example, if you're eligible for widow's or widower's benefits from a deceased former spouse's earnings record, you remarry after age 60, and your new spouse files for Social Security retirement benefits. You may choose which benefit to take, but you can't take both.

TIP

When you're given the choice between two benefits, it shouldn't be hard. The SSA does the calculation for you, and if you're like most people, you'll take the larger amount.

How Much You Can Expect to Get

The maximum spousal benefit is 50 percent of the breadwinner's full retirement benefit. The actual amount of the spousal benefit depends on the size of the breadwinner's full retirement benefit and the age at which the spouse chooses to claim it. Suppose the breadwinner's full monthly retirement benefit is $1,000. The spousal benefit in this example can go up to $500, if the spouse claims it at full retirement age (currently at 66 and 2 months, gradually increasing to 67). If the spouse has no dependent child, he or she may claim a spousal benefit at age 62.

The spousal benefit is permanently reduced, however, for each month the spouse claims it before reaching full retirement age. If a spouse is still caring for the couple's child who is younger than 16 or disabled, the age limit doesn't apply. In that case, a spouse may qualify for a full spousal benefit (50 percent of the breadwinner's full retirement amount) at any age, as long as the breadwinner has filed for Social Security.

WARNING

Violating the child-in-care rules can cost you money. If you qualify for a spousal benefit because you're caring for a child, the SSA expects you to be doing just that. You're supposed to inform the SSA if the child spends more than a month not in your care, typically in the care of a nonresident parent. Payments are withheld — or you'll have to return them — for the number of months in which the child wasn't in your care. Note the important exceptions: If the child is with you for even one day during the month, that month counts as in your care. Also, a child is considered to still be in your care if he or she has gone to camp, is on vacation, or attends boarding school. You don't have to inform the SSA of such events.

When a child isn't in the picture, the reduction factors for early claiming can significantly reduce the spousal benefit. For example, a spouse whose full retirement age is 67 gets 50 percent of his or her partner's full retirement benefit at that age. If he or she receives benefits sooner, however, the reductions are made as shown in Table 9-1.

TABLE 9-1 **Reductions in Spousal Benefits**

Age at Which Benefits Are Claimed	Spousal Benefit
66	45.8%
65	41.7%
64	37.5%
63	35%
62	32.5%

TIP

The spousal reduction may vary depending on your date of birth and full retirement age. To get a calculation based on your own age of claiming, go to www.ssa.gov/OACT/quickcalc/spouse.html#calculator.

TECHNICAL STUFF

If you claim a spousal benefit before full retirement age, it's reduced by $^{25}/_{36}$ of 1 percent for each month, up to 36 months. If you claim the benefit more than 36 months before full retirement age, the benefit is reduced by $^{5}/_{12}$ of 1 percent for each additional month.

REMEMBER

Although a spousal benefit is reduced for claiming it before full retirement age, you get no reward for delaying it after you reach full retirement age. This is a notable difference from the Social Security retirement benefit, which goes up in value if you don't claim it until you reach 70. The maximum spousal benefit is 50 percent of the breadwinner's full retirement benefit.

You can get a rough idea of the spousal benefit you may qualify for by checking out the online calculator at www.ssa.gov/oact/quickcalc/spouse.html. It won't give you a dollar figure, but it will estimate the spousal benefit as a percentage of your marital partner's full retirement benefit, called the *primary insurance amount* (PIA; see Chapter 2). The percentage you see is based on your date of birth and when you expect to claim the spousal benefit.

If you're a spouse who wants to claim spousal benefits, be aware of the reductions for claiming benefits prior to your full retirement age. They make a difference, and the difference adds up over time. Here's an example of this situation in action:

> Melissa, who recently turned 62, is pleased to find out that she qualifies for a Social Security spousal benefit when her husband, Todd, begins to collect retirement benefits. Todd will begin to collect $1,800 — his full retirement benefit — shortly after he turns 66 and 2 months next month. Melissa's spousal benefit is based on Todd's full amount, but the size of her payment depends on the age when she begins to collect. Four years and 8 months from now, when she reaches her full retirement age of 66 and 8 months, Melissa will qualify for half of the $1,800 — $900 per month. But she isn't happy to find out about the reductions in store if she takes it sooner. If Melissa claims the spousal benefit right away, it's reduced to about 32.5 percent of $1,800, or $585 per month. If she waits until she's 63, the benefit goes up to about $630. If she waits until she's 64, it goes up to about $675. If she waits until she's 65, the benefit is about $750.
>
> Melissa and Todd both enjoy good health and are hoping for many years left with each other and the rest of their family. But with their modest life savings and in an era of low interest rates, they have little retirement income to fall back on, other

> than Social Security. Melissa and Todd talk it out over dinner. They decide it makes sense for Melissa to postpone her claim for a while. Instead, she'll continue working part-time at the prep school and putting away a bit of money each month. When she turns 66 and 8 months, she'll collect a spousal benefit of $900 per month.

Did Todd and Melissa make the right decision? Of course, that's something only they can decide. But they did *not* maximize their benefits, at least if they live to their average life expectancies. Melissa got the maximum spousal benefit by waiting until she reached full retirement age. But if he had waited until 70, Todd could have gotten 32 percent more — and enhanced the survivor benefit he may one day leave to Melissa.

WARNING

Early collection of spousal benefits may be costly for another reason, unrelated to the reduction for age: If you've earned Social Security retirement benefits based on your own earnings and you begin collecting a spousal benefit before you reach your full retirement age, your own (unclaimed) retirement benefit no longer can increase, as it otherwise would for every month you delay claiming after the full retirement age (and up until age 70). This could cost you thousands of dollars — possibly *many* thousands — and should be a factor in your decision of when to begin collecting spousal benefits.

How to Maximize Your Benefits

When you're collecting retirement benefits based on your own work record, you get the maximum monthly benefits by waiting until you're 70. If you're collecting based on your spouse's work record, you get the maximum monthly benefits by waiting until your own full retirement age. Certain strategies for claiming benefits make more sense than others, depending on the facts of your household.

But before you dive into strategies, first ask yourself:

> What matters more to me — the grand total of Social Security benefits that my spouse and I haul in over our lifetimes, or the size of our monthly payments?

If you care more about the lifetime haul, you may need a coordinated approach between the two of you. If you're more concerned with getting the largest monthly benefit, the strategy is simpler.

In the past, experts often suggested that you aim for the highest possible lifetime haul in benefits. But with increases in life expectancy and downward pressure on pensions and other sources of retirement security, you may just want the highest monthly benefit, even though this means waiting longer to claim Social Security. (This approach can add up to less than the highest lifetime benefit, depending on a multitude of factors, including how long you live.)

REMEMBER

You may live a lot longer than you think. There's no tidy way to factor that into a claiming decision except to consider the obvious: A larger Social Security benefit looks very good as those extra years add up. To get a general sense of your life expectancy, go to `apps.bluezones.com/vitality`.

Your financial (and emotional) needs may be quite different from your neighbor's. But here are some questions all couples should consider about when to claim their Social Security benefits:

- **Have you and your spouse both earned Social Security benefits?** Each of you should know your projected full retirement benefit (see Chapter 6).
- **Are the retirement benefits earned by the lower-earning spouse equal to at least *half* the full retirement benefit earned by the higher-earning spouse?** If so, the lower-earning spouse may get a larger benefit based on his or her own work record.
- **How long do you want to continue working?** This fact, along with the amount of savings and other income you have to live on, can make a big difference in when you should claim benefits.
- **Do you have health or longevity issues?** If so, those issues may argue in favor of your taking the money sooner rather than waiting for benefits to increase.
- **How urgently do you need the money?** In homes with two wage earners, it is possible you would want to claim one retirement benefit to get some money coming in, while delaying the second claim for as long as possible. But it depends on your ages and other factors. There is no one-size-fits-all answer.

In the following sections, I cover some strategies you can take as a couple, or as an individual, for maximizing your benefits.

Maximizing your lifetime benefits as a married couple

If you're a married couple and you have a little financial flexibility, you need to work together to maximize your lifetime benefits. You're not living in separate bubbles — who claims what and when affects the other.

Even though marital claiming strategies have been restricted, married spouses still have an advantage that single individuals don't enjoy: They can coordinate their Social Security claims in a way that works best for their household. Yes, it's common sense. Still, couples do not always stop and think about how their claiming decisions may affect each other.

Married or not, there are several variables for everyone to consider in claiming benefits, including age, financial need, how long you expect to live, and whether you get more peace of mind from locking in the income sooner or waiting for a bigger benefit later.

But couples have more flexibility than singles to create a strategy that involves two streams of Social Security. They also have more reason to think hard about survivors' benefits. Here are some things married couples can keep in mind about claiming Social Security:

- It sometimes makes sense for lower-earning spouses to claim their own retirement benefits sooner, while the primary earner holds off claiming, potentially until age 70. This approach works best if the main breadwinner has a much larger retirement benefit than the lower-earning spouse. (But keep in mind that there is a significant reduction for early claiming.)
- If both spouses have earned retirement benefits, and they can afford to wait, they will be rewarded with significantly higher Social Security income. It's simple math: The increases for delayed retirement claiming are magnified if they apply to two members of the family rather than just one.
- Life expectancy is always a consideration in when to claim, but it cuts both ways. If you do not expect to live much longer, it may make sense to claim Social Security sooner. If you expect to live a long life, this is an added reason to hold off claiming if possible.

But married partners have another question to consider: If the primary earner dies, how much will the widow or widower need Social Security to support his or her standard of living? The greater the need, the more reason the primary earner has to delay claiming. This may be a greater concern for wives than for husbands. The survivor is typically a woman, and women on average live longer than men do, so they need to finance a lengthier period of old age.

Getting the biggest benefit possible for your surviving spouse

If your main priority is to leave your spouse the biggest benefit possible, you just have to wait as long as possible (up to age 70) to claim your own retirement benefit. The survivor benefit that goes to your spouse after your death may be the same size as your own retirement benefit (if your spouse claims it when he or she has reached full retirement age).

In cases where a worker with a full retirement age of 66 claims benefits early, the rules provide a very slight cushion on behalf of the surviving spouse. That is because the benefit formula gives the widowed survivor *the greater amount* between the worker's benefit at the time of death *or* 82.5 percent of the deceased worker's full retirement amount. In this case, the worker's benefit comes to 75 percent of his full retirement benefit, because he claims at age 62, leading to a 25 percent reduction due to his age. If his widow claims the survivor benefit at her full retirement age, she receives 82.5 percent of the deceased spouse's full retirement benefit — slightly more than her husband was receiving when he was alive.

It's worth keeping in mind that when a retired worker dies, the total amount of Social Security going to the household generally declines if the household had been receiving two benefits — one for the retired worker and one for the spouse. The size of the drop varies, and it's true that expenses are less for one than for two. But the possible decrease in Social Security income faced by a widow or widower could be significant and is another reason that a worker may want to hold off claiming, in order to leave a larger survivors' benefit.

Consider this example: When Duane retired as an insurance claims adjuster, he claimed a Social Security retirement benefit of $1,800 a month, and his wife Amber began to collect a spousal benefit of $900 a month. But when Duane passed away a few years later, Amber's spousal benefit expired with him. The new Social Security benefit going to the house is a survivors' benefit of $1,800 a month (based on Duane's retirement benefit) — which is just 67 percent of the total that went to the house when Duane was alive.

Now suppose Amber had earned her own Social Security retirement benefit like a great many women today. Say she once earned as much as Duane but halted her career to stay at home with the kids, and she ended up with a Social Security retirement benefit of $1,600 a month. In their early years of retirement, the couple got a combined amount of $3,400 in Social Security each month (Duane's $1,800 plus Amber's $1,600). Upon Duane's death, Amber continued to receive a survivors' benefit equal to her late husband's amount of $1,800 a month. But her own benefit of $1,600 disappeared, reducing the monthly income total by 47 percent. That is quite a cut. In fact, many people believe Social Security treats widows unfairly, and there have been calls for change. But those are the rules for now, and if you're planning for the future, it's good to know them.

There is a wrinkle in this example worth noting. Say Amber had reached her full retirement age at the time of Duane's death but *had not yet applied for any Social Security benefits.* In such a case, she would have the option of restricting her application to the survivors' benefit and leaving her own earned retirement benefit unclaimed. Through delayed retirement credits, her unclaimed benefit would increase at the rate of 8 percent per year until she reached 70. Say that milestone is 3½ years away. At an 8 percent increase of $128 a year (1,600 times 8 percent equals 128) she could eventually add $448 a month to her benefit by earning 3½ years of delayed retirement credits (128 times 3.5 equals 448). Ultimately, that would get her a Social Security benefit of $2,048 (1,600 plus 448 equals 2,048), which beats the $1,800 she would otherwise receive.

TIP

Congress's action to restrict marital claiming strategies did not focus on survivors' benefits. If a surviving widow (or widower) has reached full retirement age and not claimed Social Security, she may still begin a survivors' benefit, while leaving her own retirement benefit untouched, so it can increase for a later claim (up to age 70).

Often, when older couples collect Social Security benefits, they focus on the income they'll get *today.* That's certainly understandable, but statistics show that in most marriages, a widow depends for years on her survivors' benefit. The survivors' benefit may be substantially larger than a spousal benefit because of the way the SSA calculates it. The survivors' benefit can have a major impact on the surviving spouse's standard of living for years to come.

REMEMBER

A spouse who waits until 70 to begin collecting retirement benefits leaves the largest possible Social Security benefit to a surviving spouse. If the survivor earned a larger benefit based on his or her own earnings, the survivor gets that benefit. The survivor doesn't get to claim both.

OLDER WOMEN HAVE A BIG STAKE IN SOCIAL SECURITY

If you're a woman, you'll likely have an extra need for Social Security as you get older. Social Security plays a crucial role in supporting men and women — middle class and lower income — yet for a variety of reasons, women rely on the program even more than men do. Single women rely on the program more than their married counterparts, and widows and divorced older women rely on it most of all.

If you're a woman and a Baby Boomer, these realities may have special meaning. Boomer women earned more money and are more educated than women who came before them. Those changes are helpful economically. But Boomers also are more likely to be single, which often creates a financial challenge. Despite their financial gains, Boomer women often are paid less than men. Disruptions in covered work, such as to raise kids, may reduce their Social Security earnings record and, ultimately, their benefits. More Boomer women got divorced or never married, when compared to their mothers' and grandmothers' generations. In many cases, that makes them extremely dependent on income from Social Security in their later years.

Part of the reason women rely so heavily on Social Security is that they tend to live longer than men do. (Female life expectancy at age 65 is about 21 more years; that's 2 years longer than for men.) Women make up 56 percent of Social Security beneficiaries age 62 and older. The pattern becomes even more pronounced at more advanced ages. By the time you get to the oldest age levels — 85 and up — women represent 65 percent of Social Security recipients.

Widows may face particular challenges. Their household income may plunge when a spouse dies, including a decline in total Social Security payments, private pension benefits, and earnings, if the deceased spouse was working. Further, if the spouse died after an illness, healthcare expenses may have reduced the family's nest egg.

For these and other reasons, a great many older women rely on Social Security to stay above the poverty line, although the margin may be narrow. Turn to Chapter 17 for a discussion of proposals to make Social Security more responsive to the needs of women in the 21st century.

» Recognizing how family members can benefit from your earnings

» Meeting the guidelines to count as a parent

» Computing the maximum family benefit

» Considering Social Security in child support

Chapter 10

Family Benefits: Who Gets What

Millions of people grow up in families where a Social Security check is a crucial element of monthly income. Maybe you're one of them. If not, you may know someone who is. Currently, about 4.1 million children get benefits, worth about $2.8 billion each month. Kids get these benefits because a parent (or two parents) has died, become disabled, or retired.

REMEMBER

The Social Security Administration (SSA) calls the payments that go to a dependent family member based on the earnings record of a living worker *auxiliary benefits.* It calls the payments that go to dependent family members when a worker dies *survivors' benefits.*

For the system to work, however, the SSA needs to know who qualifies and who doesn't. It needs to know whom to pay — and whom not to pay. Who's a real family member? Is the guy who moved in really the child's dad? Is a parent *really* caring for a kid who lives far away? Can a grandchild ever get benefits through a grandparent? Is the elderly mom unable to support herself, now that her son has died?

This chapter looks at how the SSA determines who's a child and who's a parent when it comes to allocating benefits. It also goes over other rules that are relevant to families, notably the *family maximum,* a provision that puts a cap on benefit amounts in homes where more than one person gets benefits based on the earnings of the same breadwinner. Kids and parents are the focus of this chapter, including issues that may arise when parents are estranged and a child is eligible for benefits.

TIP

In this chapter, I briefly cover the definition of marriage, but for an in-depth look at Social Security issues involving spouses, including rule changes that affect marital claiming strategies, see Chapter 9.

Defining Who's in the Family

When I say the word *family,* your mind probably goes to the people who are nearest and dearest to you — whether blood relatives or the inner circle of friends you've stayed close with for many years. Unfortunately, things aren't always that simple when it comes to Social Security. Assorted rules and state laws set the terms of who qualifies as a child, parent, spouse, and former spouse.

To define who is your child, and whether you're the parent, the SSA recognizes that families come in various forms. It has definitions for *natural child, adopted child,* and *stepchild.* It may recognize all these categories as eligible for benefits, often without a hitch, as long as you provide basic documentation, such as an acceptable birth record (see Chapter 5). It also has criteria that may enable a grandchild to get child benefits based on a grandparent's earnings record.

Note: As a general rule, a child must be unmarried and younger than 18 (or up to 19 if still attending high school full time) to qualify for child benefits.

In this section, I tell you what the SSA thinks of as a *family.* Its definition may not reflect who sits around *your* Thanksgiving table, but when it comes to collecting Social Security benefits, it's the only definition that counts. For more information on the benefits each category may be eligible for, see the later section "Identifying the Benefits Family Members Are Eligible For."

Spouses

In the past, the SSA recognized only marriages between a man and a woman in determining whether a spouse potentially qualified for benefits. However, in a significant change, it has begun to offer benefits to spouses in same-sex marriages, and the policy has become broader over time. Individuals in such marriages should contact the SSA if they have questions about their eligibility.

Often the worker has been married more than once, and it may not be clear if he or she has obtained a valid divorce before remarrying. In such situations, many states presume the most recent marriage is the valid one, unless this assumption is refuted with clear and convincing evidence.

TECHNICAL STUFF

In states that recognize common-law marriage, you need a formal divorce to dissolve it. There is no such thing as common-law divorce.

Spousal and survivor benefits have duration-of-marriage requirements (marriages are generally expected to last at least one year for spousal benefits and nine months for survivors' benefits), as well as restrictions on remarriage. See Chapter 9 for more on spousal benefits and marriage-related benefit rules.

Parents or grandparents

You may think it's simple to define *parent* or *grandparent*, but it actually can get pretty complicated. Generally speaking, the SSA considers you a parent if you're the mother or father as defined by the law in your state that governs inheritance of a parent's personal property. You may be the parent of a biological child, a legally adopted child, or a stepchild. Similar principles apply in determining whether you're the grandparent (the parent of the parent) of a child who is eligible for benefits on your record.

Note: The SSA draws the line at grandchildren. Great-grandchildren don't qualify for benefits on the earnings record of a great-grandparent.

Sometimes, the SSA must decide whether an individual is a parent when he or she isn't married to the child's other parent. In such a case, it may consider whether the breadwinner has "acknowledged in writing" that the child is his or hers. It may consider whether a court has decreed parental status. The SSA also may consider evidence that the breadwinner was living with the child or making regular and significant contributions to his or her living costs when the child applied for benefits. (Such evidence also may have to be supplied if the breadwinner has died.)

WARNING

The SSA wants to make sure that family benefits stay in the family. Dads are supposed to be dads, and moms are supposed to be moms. To help achieve that goal, the SSA has put together a series of internal guidelines, advising SSA employees of red flags to watch out for. If you fall into any of the following categories, your benefit ultimately may be approved, but not before further scrutiny. Here are some of the situations that get special attention:

- **If the parents' marriage isn't legal:** This situation raises questions about a child's legal status. (The SSA recognizes a marriage as legitimate if the couple believed they were taking part in a legal ceremony, even if it turns out something was technically wrong with it.)
- **If the child's mother is entitled to Social Security benefits through the work record of the father, but she hasn't filed for them:** The SSA may want to know why the mother hasn't filed. Certain explanations, such as the possibility that her claim would reduce a child's benefit, may be accepted. (The same is true in reverse — that is, if the child's father is the one entitled to benefits through the work record of the mother.)
- **If the parents weren't married when the child was born:** The child may still qualify for benefits as a child dependent, depending on state inheritance laws or evidence that the child is the biological child, adopted child, or stepchild of the breadwinner.
- **If the father's name doesn't appear on a birth certificate or other proof of a child's age:** This situation raises questions about paternity and the child's legal status as a dependent for Social Security benefits.
- **If the mother was over 50 when the child was born:** Although more common in today's era of assisted reproduction technologies, such births are still rare. The SSA may question whether the woman is actually the mother and whether the child is entitled to benefits. The SSA may seek additional evidence proving maternity, such as a physician's statement.

Natural children

A *natural child* is the natural (biological) offspring of a mother or father — a child you gave birth to or fathered. This relationship is the most common one, and in routine cases, such as when the child is born to legally married parents, the child becomes eligible for benefits without difficulty. It's just a matter of providing a valid birth certificate or other proof of the child's relationship to the parent who has earned the benefit (see Chapter 5). The SSA may seek more information when routine evidence isn't available, such as when the parent's name isn't on the birth certificate.

If questions arise about a child-parent relationship, the SSA turns to state inheritance laws. If the state law can be interpreted in more than one way, the SSA is supposed to interpret it in a manner that helps the child.

Adopted children

An *adopted child* is one who is not a biological child of the parent but was adopted through a legal proceeding, either in the United States or abroad.

A child may be eligible for Social Security child benefits if he or she is legally adopted by a covered worker. The SSA also may recognize a legal adoption by the covered worker's spouse that took place after the death of the covered worker. In such cases, the SSA follows state or foreign adoption laws (where the adoption took place) rather than state inheritance laws (see the preceding section).

TECHNICAL STUFF

A breadwinner may have planned to adopt a child but didn't complete the adoption, perhaps because of death. In such situations, the SSA may recognize an *equitable adoption* that wasn't legally formalized, thereby allowing child benefits. As in other questions of parent-child status, the SSA follows state inheritance law to decide whether a child filing for benefits would qualify as an heir if the deceased worker didn't leave a will.

Stepchildren

A *stepchild* is the natural or adopted child of a person's spouse.

A stepchild may qualify for Social Security benefits based on the earnings record of a stepparent under certain circumstances:

- After the child's birth, the child's natural or adoptive parent married the covered worker.
- A stepchild is conceived before a valid marriage between a natural parent and a covered worker and born after the marriage. In this case, the stepchild may be eligible for benefits if the marriage lasts for at least one year before the child applies for Social Security benefits.

If the covered worker is no longer alive, the stepchild-parent relationship is expected to have lasted at least nine months before the worker's death (subject to some exceptions, such as if the worker died in a sudden accident, if the worker died while on active duty in the armed forces, or if the parents had been married before and the new marriage was expected to last at least nine months).

In cases of divorce, a stepchild loses benefits based on a stepparent's earnings, unless the stepparent adopts the child.

Grandchildren

A *grandchild* may be natural or adopted. Step-grandchildren also may be included in this category.

Grandchildren may be eligible as dependents of a grandparent in certain situations when the grandparent supports the child. This can come up when the child's parents become disabled or die, and the child isn't getting benefits from either parent. Typically, the grandchild must be living with the grandparent for a year before the grandparent claims Social Security benefits, and the grandparent must provide at least half of the child's financial support.

The SSA also may consider a grandchild eligible for benefits if the grandparent adopts the child. If the grandparent dies, the grandchild may be eligible if he or she is legally adopted by the grandparent's surviving spouse.

Parents of a worker

If a worker dies, his or her older parents may qualify for benefits as survivors. The parents must have depended on their adult child for at least half of their financial support and prove this to the SSA.

Identifying the Benefits Family Members Are Eligible For

Earlier in this chapter, I give you the SSA's definition of *family,* spelling out who qualifies as a spouse, parent, child, grandchild, and parent of a worker. In this section, I tell you what kind of benefits each group is eligible for.

Dependent children under 18

Social Security payments may go to a child under the age of 18 whose parent has died, become disabled, or retired. The child must be considered dependent on the parent (natural children are generally considered dependent), and the child must not be married. If the parent is disabled or retired, the child may get 50 percent of the parent's full retirement benefit, also known as the *primary insurance amount* (PIA; see Chapter 2). If the parent has died, the child may get 75 percent. These amounts are subject to the family maximum, discussed later in this chapter.

Dependent children 18 and over

Benefits for unmarried, dependent children may continue to age 19 if the child has yet to graduate from high school. In this case, benefits may last either until the school term ends or for two months past the person's 19th birthday, whichever comes first. The SSA expects the child to provide a statement of school attendance that has been signed by an official at the school.

TECHNICAL STUFF

Depending on state requirements, the SSA's school attendance rule may be satisfied by a home school or online education program.

The benefit amount for dependent children ages 18 to 19 is the same as for dependent children under 18.

Disabled adult children

The benefit for disabled adult children pays the same as those for dependent children under 18. It may go to the child of a covered worker after the child turns 18, if the child becomes disabled (as determined by the SSA) before reaching age 22.

REMEMBER

The SSA has a strict definition of *disability.* It must entail a very serious physical or mental impairment that is expected to last at least a year or end in death.

This benefit may stop under certain circumstances (for example, if the individual's health improves).

If an adult child is getting this benefit based on the record of a living parent and the parent dies, the adult child disability benefit is switched to a survivors' benefit that potentially pays more — 75 percent of the worker's full retirement amount, rather than the 50 percent that the adult child may have been receiving previously.

Grandchildren

Under certain circumstances, grandchildren may qualify for kids' benefits on the earnings record of a grandparent. Benefits for grandchildren are basically the same as other kids' benefits. But in this case, they're based on the earnings of a grandparent, not a parent. Such benefits may go to a grandchild under 18 if the child's own parents have died or become disabled, or the grandparent legally adopts the grandchild. To qualify, the child must have lived with the grandparent before turning 18 and depended on the grandparent for more than half of his or her support for about a year before the grandparent filed for Social Security benefits. (The time requirement is modified for children who are less than a year old.) If the grandparent is already getting benefits, adoption is required.

As with other child benefits, Social Security could pay 50 percent of the full retirement benefit in the case of a living grandparent and 75 percent if the grandparent dies (with the amounts subject to a family maximum; find more information later in this chapter).

Parents of a worker

If an adult child who financially supported his or her parents dies, the parents may qualify for a benefit. The parent has to be at least 62 years old and not eligible for a larger Social Security benefit based on his or her own earnings record.

For a parent who qualifies and is single, this benefit pays 82.5 percent of the adult child's full retirement benefit. If both parents qualify, each gets 75 percent of the full retirement benefit. The parent's benefit is available only in cases of death, not retirement or disability.

REMEMBER

You have to prove to the SSA that you relied on your adult child for half of your financial support, either until your adult child died or until he or she became disabled before death. Such proof must be submitted within two years of the child's death. Also, you don't qualify for the benefit if you got married after the child's death.

Looking at How Having a "Child in Care" May Affect Your Own Benefits

If you're a parent who may be eligible for Social Security benefits, a key factor in whether you qualify may be whether you have a child in your care. Having a "child in care" also could determine the amount you receive. Two key areas where this comes up are the following:

- **Spousal benefits:** You typically become eligible for spousal benefits, which are based on a breadwinner's earnings record, at age 62 (if the breadwinner has claimed benefits). But if you have the breadwinner's child in your care, you potentially qualify for spousal benefits at any age. These benefits pay up to 50 percent of the worker's full retirement benefit.

» **Survivors' benefits:** These benefits pay a surviving spouse (age 60 and up) as much as 100 percent of the deceased worker's benefit amount, if you claim them at full retirement age. If you're caring for the deceased worker's child, you may qualify at any age (although benefits are capped at 75 percent if you're under 60).

TIP

An important and little-known exception to child-in-care guidelines applies to divorced spouses. If you're in that category, the SSA will *not* provide you divorced-spouse benefits (based on the earnings record of your ex) before you turn 62, even if you have your ex-spouse's child in your care.

The SSA has guidelines to determine whether you're exercising "parental responsibility" for a child in care in certain circumstances, such as when you don't live with your child. Here's the SSA in its own words on what the child-in-care requirements mean:

» **"Exercising parental control and responsibility for the welfare and care of a child under 16 or a mentally disabled child 16 or older."**

» **"Performing personal services for a physically disabled child age 16 or over."** Such services may include nursing care, feeding, dressing, and other special assistance.

REMEMBER

A child may be considered in your care during a month if he or she spends at least one day of that month with you. In addition, a child may be in your care under certain other circumstances, even when you and the child aren't living together.

The SSA may recognize a child in your care if you have a shared custody arrangement. The child may still be considered in your care if you continue to exercise control and responsibility when the child is with the other parent. If a child is living with the other parent for a month or longer, however, and that parent is exercising parental control and you aren't, then you may not have a child in care.

In deciding whether you exercise "parental control," the SSA considers whether you display a strong interest in properly raising the child, supervise the child's activities, and participate in key decisions about the child's physical needs and mental development. You can do this directly or indirectly.

You may have a child in care when the child is living away at school, as long as you continue to exercise parental control and participate in major decisions. If a child lives in an institution year-round, the child may still be considered in your care if you maintain contact with the institution and participate in decisions.

CALCULATING THE MAXIMUM BENEFIT FOR YOUR FAMILY

The SSA adds four numbers to determine the family maximum for retirement and survivors' benefits. (It uses a different procedure for disability.) These are percentages of prescribed dollar amounts that are known as *bend points.* Although the bend points may change annually, the following exercise gives you an idea how to do the calculation. To do this math, you need to know your full retirement benefit, also known as the *primary insurance amount* (PIA). For a ballpark primary insurance amount, go to the Social Security Quick Calculator (`www.ssa.gov/oact/quickcalc`) and plug in your information, including when you reach your full retirement age (currently 66 and 2 months, gradually increasing to 67). You then must compute some percentages and add up four amounts:

- 150 percent of the first $1,226 (bend point) of the worker's PIA, plus
- 272 percent of the PIA over $1,226 and through $1,770, plus
- 134 percent of the PIA over $1,770 and through $2,309, plus
- 175 percent of the PIA over $2,309

Your sum equals the maximum benefit amount for your family, based on your earnings.

Note: The preceding dollar figures are for 2020. You can keep up with the latest information at `www.ssa.gov/OACT/COLA/familymax.html`.

Understanding the Family Maximum

Suppose you have two children who qualify for Social Security benefits. Maybe you're eligible as well. You can't simply add up their potential benefits to know how much will be coming in. The SSA imposes a limit on benefits that go to a family based on one person's earnings record (generally between 150 percent and 180 percent of the breadwinner's amount, though potentially as high as 188 percent). This is called the *family maximum.*

If a family maximum applies in your case, the benefits going to all dependents are reduced proportionately to reach a lower total figure for the household. If another family member were to become eligible in the future (based on the breadwinner's earnings record), the family total would stay the same, and everyone's benefits would be reduced further. If a child who had gotten benefits turns 18 or 19 and no longer qualifies, the amount going to the remaining family members goes up, as long as the total stays within the cap.

The family maximum may come up when a worker with dependents is getting retirement or disability benefits, or when the breadwinner dies, leaving survivors behind.

The family maximum doesn't apply to everybody in the family. The benefit going to the breadwinner isn't reduced. Similarly, any benefits that go to family members based on their *own* earnings aren't affected. Also, spousal benefits going to a divorced spouse or a surviving divorced spouse based on the earnings record of his or her former spouse aren't affected by the family maximum.

The family maximum in the case of disability benefits is slightly different from the cap for retirement and survivors' benefits and is limited to no more than 150 percent of the disabled worker's full retirement benefit. For other benefits, the family maximum may hit up to 188 percent of the breadwinner's full retirement benefit.

Say a retired breadwinner dies, leaving behind a widow who has reached full retirement age and two elderly parents who depended on him for more than half of their support. Without the family maximum, the widow qualifies for 100 percent of his full retirement benefit, and each elderly parent qualifies for 75 percent of the full retirement benefit. If you add that all up, it comes to 250 percent of the deceased worker's full retirement benefit. But the family maximum reduces those benefits significantly, so the total adds up to no more than 188 percent of the deceased worker's full benefit.

Here's an example: Arnold, a well-paid architect, dies of a heart attack at 56, leaving behind three children and a widow. At the time he died, Arnold had 35 years of covered employment. His full retirement benefit, based on earnings of $80,000, would come to $2,821 (in 2020). Each of his three children is under 16, meaning that without a family cap, each would qualify for a survivor benefit of 75 percent, or about $2,116 (rounded up). In addition, because his surviving wife, Maddy, is caring for the children, she qualifies for an unreduced widow's benefit of the same amount. If you add it up, their benefits come to $8,463 per month. In this case, however, the family maximum kicks in, limiting the family to $4,993. To correct this, the SSA has to reduce the benefits of Arnold's survivors. Because Arnold's children and Maddy receive 75 percent of Arnold's full retirement benefit (each), their benefits are reduced equally. The maximum family benefit of $4,993 is split between the four of them, giving each $1,248.

The family maximum on occasion leaves some wiggle room when children's benefits are involved. This may take place when a child qualifies for benefits on the earnings record of more than one breadwinner. (The SSA calls this *dual entitlement.*) For example, a child may qualify on the accounts of a mother and a father, both of whom have earnings records with the SSA. In such cases, the child gets the higher-paying benefit. (The same happens with an adult beneficiary who qualifies under two different accounts.)

TECHNICAL STUFF

If more than one child in the family is getting benefits, and each of the children qualifies for benefits through two different workers, the SSA combines the family maximums for the two different accounts. But the combined family maximums are subject to a combined maximum limit. This may create a significantly higher cap, and each child's benefit may be higher than if he or she were eligible on only one worker's record.

Consider this example: Natalie and Julian die in a plane crash, leaving behind their three children, all under age 16. Julian, an interstate truck driver, had earned a full Social Security benefit of $2,524. Natalie, who helped manage a shoe store, had earned a smaller retirement benefit of $1,655. If their three kids all claim a 75 percent survivor's benefit based on Julian's earnings record (for a total of $5,679 in benefits), the payments exceed the family maximum, which comes to $4,467 based on his record alone. Because Natalie also earned a benefit, however, the SSA allows a higher family maximum. The family maximum based on Natalie's benefit alone is $3,085. If that could be added to Julian's amount, it would come to a much higher cap of $7,552. But it's more complicated than that, because the SSA caps combined family maximums. In this case, the actual limit that applies to the kids is $5,612 (this value changes each year). As a result, each of the three children qualifies for $1,893 (75 percent of Julian's benefit).

TIP

If you believe that your family's benefits may be affected by the family maximum, and if you have children in your family who are beneficiaries who qualify under more than one account, point this out to the SSA. It may result in higher payments to your household every month.

SCIENCE COLLIDES WITH SOCIAL SECURITY: WHEN A BABY IS CONCEIVED AFTER THE BREADWINNER HAS DIED

By the time Patti Beeler gave birth to her daughter, the father was dead — and he had been dead for almost two years. The Iowa mom used a modern technology (in vitro fertilization) that enabled the girl to be conceived after the father died from leukemia.

Patti sought Social Security survivors' benefits for her daughter, based on the earnings of the deceased father, Bruce Beeler. The SSA said no, setting off one in a growing number of legal disputes that the framers of Social Security couldn't have dreamed up. The basic question: Should a child who is conceived after the father has died qualify for Social Security survivors' benefits, based on the earnings of the deceased parent?

Appeals courts haven't agreed on the answers to such questions, which pose, as one court put it, "a host of difficult legal and even moral" issues. In deciding such matters, the SSA looks, in part, to state inheritance laws, and these laws vary. Many states have no law that specifically addresses the issue. Applications for survivors' benefits involving posthumous conception have reached the SSA.

You can't find answers to such questions in the Social Security Act or recent regulations. Does it make a difference how much time passes between a father's death and the child's posthumous conception? Should a child who is born two years after the father's death qualify for survivor benefits? What if 20 years have passed?

Patti sued in U.S. District Court and won. But the SSA challenged the ruling and prevailed in the Eighth Circuit Court of Appeals. (In response to Patti's legal travails, Iowa legislators changed the state law so that children like her daughter might qualify as heirs, if they are born within two years of their father's death. The new law didn't apply to her own case, however.)

In another case, a woman named Karen Capato sought survivors' benefits for her twin boys who (through in vitro fertilization) were born 18 months after the death of their father. The U.S. Supreme Court found that the children weren't eligible for benefits because they wouldn't be considered eligible in Florida, the state where the family resided when the father died. But by affirming Social Security's longtime reliance on state inheritance laws, the court seemed to allow for many different possibilities, depending on where such families live.

Who knows what questions assisted reproduction technologies may raise for Social Security benefits in the future? As a lower court noted in the Capato case, "The use of donor eggs, artificial insemination, and surrogate wombs could result in at least five potential parents."

You can bet they weren't considering matters like *that* when survivors' benefits were established in 1939.

Counting on Kids' Benefits When Parents Live Apart

If you and your spouse get divorced, and your spouse collects Social Security benefits, how does that income fit into the picture? Does it affect how much one spouse may owe in child support? The answer is yes — a spouse's Social Security benefit generally counts toward his or her income, and this may be significant in terms of paying child support.

But before I go further, I need to emphasize a couple of points:

- Divorce, including the matter of child support, is a state issue, and the laws vary widely.
- Even more important, you're bound by the court order setting the terms of your divorce.

You should be aware of certain rules if you end up in a dispute with a former spouse over Social Security benefits. Social Security benefits generally count toward the income of the worker who has earned them. In many states, this means that if a child receives Social Security benefits as a dependent of a noncustodial parent, those benefits may count toward the parent's child-support payment. This sort of situation can arise, for example, if a noncustodial parent begins collecting Social Security disability or retirement benefits and the child gets auxiliary benefits.

Suppose you're a dad who owes child support of $800 per month, but your child is getting $400 per month in Social Security benefits based on your earnings record. If your state allows a complete offset, you would have paid half of your $800 obligation through Social Security and still owe another $400. (Some states may allow less than a dollar-for-dollar offset. In other words, $400 of Social Security benefits would reduce a child-support obligation by a lesser amount. Other states leave more discretion to the judge, based on the child's need.)

If you're paying child support, be aware that your Social Security benefit can be garnished if you fall behind. (The same is true for delinquent alimony payments.) These are among the few exceptions to the general protection for Social Security against garnishment. The fact that Social Security may be garnished for delinquent child support and alimony is also a notable difference between Social Security and Supplemental Security Income (SSI). SSI generally can't be garnished.

Divorced parents also may get into conflicts if a child is potentially eligible for dependent Social Security benefits based on the record of a noncustodial parent but that parent declines to apply for those benefits. The uncooperative parent may fear — incorrectly — that dependent benefits will reduce the parent's amount. Or he or she may be avoiding the SSA for other reasons, such as not wanting his or her earnings scrutinized.

The SSA says it tries to help with an application for a child's benefit (based on the record of the noncustodial parent) even when that parent doesn't cooperate. The custodial parent should provide proof of the child's age and relationship to the other parent and, if possible, the other parent's Social Security number. (Anecdotally, such applications sometimes face an uphill climb.)

If a divorced parent potentially qualifies for benefits *but hasn't applied* (maybe he's over age 62 but hasn't claimed his retirement benefits), the child isn't eligible for dependent benefits. This is different from the way a dependent former spouse is treated. The SSA allows such a former spouse to file for spousal benefits at age 62, even if the ex — on whose record the spousal benefits are based — hasn't claimed benefits (if the divorce has lasted two years).

Managing Benefits on Behalf of a Child

When it comes to Social Security, children depend on others to make sure that they get what they qualify for and to make sure that the cash is handled properly after it arrives. The SSA appoints a type of helper, called a *representative payee,* to handle this responsibility.

Representative payees may be parents or other relatives. Institutions or foster care sometimes fills the role. Under certain circumstances, the SSA approves fees, as well as reimbursement for expenses, but most often the job is done for free by a relative. Overall, almost 6 million people (of all ages) who get Social Security rely on such helpers, and more than half of these beneficiaries are children.

If you're in that helping role, you have extremely important responsibilities. You have broad license to assess a child's needs and to make the right decisions about how to spend the benefits in the child's best interest. The money must pay for the child's current and foreseeable needs. Current needs include the necessities of life, such as food, clothing, and healthcare. Cash left over should be saved for the child, but savings aren't appropriate if the child has current unmet needs. You're required to fill out an annual form that documents how you allocated the money.

Payees also have reporting responsibilities. You're supposed to report to the SSA any developments that could affect benefit payments, such as a change in custody of the child, adoption of the child, or divorce of the child's parents.

- » Answering five key questions to qualify for benefits
- » Making your best case for disability benefits
- » Handling rejection
- » Transitioning back to work

Chapter 11
When You Can't Work: Social Security Disability Benefits

When you're healthy and working and leading a busy life, it may be hard to imagine yourself becoming disabled. But the risk is very real. According to the Social Security Administration (SSA), a 20-year-old today has a 26 percent chance of suffering a disability before retiring. If that happens to you, your whole life may be in crisis. How will you support yourself and your family? Social Security's disability protections were created to ease such hardship, but the benefits aren't easy to get.

The SSA has various rules that are intended to yield consistent decisions on who qualifies for disability. Applying for disability benefits is typically a lot more complicated than applying for retirement benefits. Assessing a disability claim takes a while — generally three to five months for an initial decision. If you're denied, there is a process in place for challenging the SSA's findings — the appeals process can take more than a year. (See Chapter 8 for a detailed discussion of the appeals process.)

In this chapter, I explain what the SSA means by *disability* and what you have to demonstrate in order to get (and keep) disability benefits. I offer some do's and don'ts in making your case. Finally, I tell you the rules about earning money and reentering the labor force after you've started receiving disability benefits.

WARNING

You can find out a great deal about disability benefits online, but be conscious of the type of website you're looking at. Many websites about Social Security disability have official-sounding names but are actually run by lawyers who are looking for business. Some of these sites are very informative, and you can learn a lot from them. Just be aware of whether you're looking at the actual SSA website (`www.ssa.gov`) or a marketing tool.

The Two Types of Disability Benefits

The SSA provides disability protections through two programs:

- **Social Security Disability Insurance (SSDI):** SSDI covers disabled workers and, in some cases, the family members who depend on them financially. For example, SSDI benefits may go to spouses of disabled workers, disabled widows, and disabled adult children.
- **Supplemental Security Income (SSI):** SSI is a program to assist low-income individuals, including those who are disabled, blind, or 65 or over.

REMEMBER

SSDI and SSI have important differences but one very important thing in common: the same, very strict definition of *disability* (see the later section "How Social Security Defines Disability"). To qualify for benefits in either program, you must be viewed as unable to work because of a very serious condition that has lasted or is expected to last at least one year or end in death.

SSDI and SSI consider the same health issues in deciding whether you're disabled, including medical evidence and limitations on your ability to function in the workplace. But they have different nonmedical requirements, pay different benefits, and have different rules for eligibility. (See Chapter 2 for an overview of their differences and Chapter 5 for details on how to apply.)

In the following sections, I elaborate on key differences between SSDI and SSI. Here are some highlights:

- **Eligibility of family members:** If you qualify for SSDI, certain dependent family members, such as a child, also may get payments based on your work record. By contrast, if you qualify for SSI, no one else in your family qualifies based on your individual application. (Eligible spouses may apply together as a couple and get a larger benefit.)

- **Work restrictions:** Working and earning money above certain amounts can cause a loss of benefits in both programs, but they have different income limits and rules for transitioning to work.
- **Asset limits:** SSI is a needs-based program, based on the disabled applicant's assets rather than how much they have worked. SSDI is part of Social Security and is an entitlement. It's available to those workers who have accumulated enough work credits.
- **Citizenship:** Noncitizens may qualify for SSDI if they've earned their benefits through covered work and tax contributions and if they had authorization to legally work in the United States. Noncitizens face certain restrictions in qualifying for SSI. It's generally harder for those who entered the United States on or after August 22, 1996.

Table 11-1 summarizes the differences between SSDI and SSI.

TABLE 11-1 A Comparison of the SSDI and SSI Programs

	SSDI	SSI
Source of payments	Disability trust fund.	General tax revenues.
Minimum initial qualification requirements	Must meet the SSA's disability criteria. Must be "insured" because of contributions made to FICA or SECA based on your own payroll earnings or those of your spouse or your parents.	Must meet the SSA's disability criteria. Must have limited income and resources.
Health insurance coverage provided	Medicare. Consists of hospital insurance (Part A), supplementary medical insurance (Part B), and Medicare Advantage (Part C). Voluntary prescription drug benefits (Part D) also are included. Title XVIII of the Social Security Act authorizes Medicare.	Medicaid. Medicaid is a jointly funded, federal-state health insurance program for low-income and needy individuals. It covers certain children and some or all of the aged, blind, and/or disabled who are eligible to receive federally assisted income maintenance payments. Title XIX of the Social Security Act authorizes Medicaid. The law gives the states options regarding eligibility under Medicaid.

(continued)

TABLE 11-1 *(continued)*

	SSDI	SSI
How your monthly payment amount is figured	The SSA bases your SSDI monthly payment amount on the worker's lifetime average earnings covered by Social Security. It may reduce the amount if you receive workers' compensation payments (including black lung payments) and/or public disability benefits (for example, certain state and civil service disability benefits). Other income or resources don't affect the payment amount. The SSA usually adjusts the monthly payment amount each year to account for cost-of-living changes. The SSA also can pay SSDI monthly benefits to dependents on your record, such as minor children.	To figure your payment amount, the SSA starts with the federal benefit rate (FBR), also referred to as as the federal payment standard. In 2020, the FBR is $783 for a qualified individual and $1,175 for a qualified couple. The SSA subtracts your countable income from the FBR and then adds your state supplement, if any. It doesn't count all the income that you have. The income amount left after the SSA makes all the allowable deductions is "countable income." The sections on SSI employment supports explain some of the ways that the SSA can exclude income. It usually adjusts the FBR each year to account for cost-of-living changes.
Provision of state supplemental payment	There is no state supplemental payment with the SSDI program.	Many states pay some people who receive SSI an additional amount called a "state supplement." The amounts and qualifications for these state supplements vary from state to state.

Source: Social Security Administration (`www.ssa.gov/redbook/eng/overview-disability.htm#4`)

Social Security Disability Insurance

SSDI is one of the protections that goes to everyone who is eligible for Social Security benefits. When a worker becomes disabled, this protection also may go to certain dependent family members. About 8.5 million workers get SSDI, and about 1.6 million of their relatives — mostly kids — also get disability payments. (See Chapter 2 for more information about eligibility rules for family members.)

REMEMBER

If a disabled breadwinner has earned Social Security coverage and qualifies for disability, benefits may go to dependents. These may include the following:

- A spouse who is at least 62 years old *or* is caring for the disabled worker's child who is younger than 16 or disabled.
- A disabled widow or widower who is at least 50 years old. (The disability must have begun no later than seven years after the breadwinner's death.)
- A child (including adopted children, stepchildren, and possibly grandchildren) who is unmarried and not yet 18 (or 19 if not yet graduated from high school), or an unmarried adult child who is 18 or older and became disabled before the age of 22.

The SSDI benefit amount depends on your earnings history with the SSA, but the average monthly payment to a disabled worker is $1,258. In determining the monthly payment, the SSA does a calculation similar to figuring your retirement benefit (see Chapter 6). You can get a rough idea of what your disability benefit may be at `www.ssa.gov/oact/quickcalc`. Just plug in your birth date, recent earnings, and when you expect to stop working.

TIP

If you're approved for SSDI, you generally become eligible for health benefits through Medicare after two years.

TIP

Find out how you can receive expedited processing of your disability claim from Social Security if you became disabled while on active military service on or after October 1, 2001. Visit `www.ssa.gov/woundedwarriors`.

To become eligible for disability benefits, you must meet certain requirements based on your earnings history. The SSA applies two separate tests to determine whether you qualify. These tests are based on what it calls *credits* (earnings you receive in the course of a calendar year). The dollar amount of a credit changes annually. (It was set at $1,410 for 2020.) You can get up to four credits in a year — and most full-time workers do. For example, in 2020, you get four credits by earning at least $5,640.

Here are two tests you have to pass to qualify for SSDI, based on your earnings history:

- **The recent-work test:** This test (also known as *disability insured status*) establishes whether you've worked recently enough to qualify, based on your age. (***Remember:*** You can get up to four credits per year, which most workers are able to do.) Workers under age 24 generally need one and a half years of work (six credits) in the three years leading up to their disability. Workers who are 24 to 30 years old need to have credits for half of the time between age 21 and the onset of their disability to get the credits they need. Workers who are 31 and older generally need at least 20 credits in the ten years immediately before onset of the disability.
- **The duration-of-work test:** This test (also known as *fully insured status*) establishes whether you've worked long enough in covered employment to qualify for disability benefits. The requirements vary significantly according to your age, with people under 28 needing just one and a half years of work and someone who is 50 needing seven years of work.

If you're an average wage-earning adult in decent health, you probably meet these requirements, but they do have pitfalls for some people. If you haven't worked very much in recent years, you may fall short on the recent-work test. Or maybe you've worked plenty, but your employer failed to make the required Social Security payroll tax contributions in your name. That could leave you with an insufficient earnings history to qualify. If you were self-employed and didn't pay your own Social Security payroll taxes, it could come back to haunt you if you suddenly need disability insurance.

Table 11-2 shows that the number of work credits you need to qualify for SSDI varies according to age.

TABLE 11-2 **Work Credits Needed for Disability Benefits**

Born After 1929, Became Disabled at Age . . .	Number of Credits You Need
31–42	20
44	22
46	24
48	26
50	28
52	30
54	32
56	34
58	36
60	38
62 or older	40

Source: Social Security Administration (`www.ssa.gov/planners/credits.html`)

Tables 11-3 and 11-4 show the rules for the SSA's recent-work test, as well as work requirements to meet the duration-of-work test.

The SSA may place a freeze on the earnings record of individuals who are entitled to disability benefits. This is to your advantage. It means that the period — potentially lasting years — in which a disability reduced or eliminated all your earnings isn't added in when the SSA computes your lifetime earnings record. The freeze may have the effect of propping up your earnings record, which otherwise would be harmed by disability, and preserving the amount of benefits you qualify for.

TABLE 11-3 **Work Needed to Pass the Recent-Work Test**

If You Become Disabled . . .	Then You Generally Need . . .
In or before the quarter in which you turn 24	One and a half years of work during the three-year period ending with the quarter in which your disability began.
In the quarter after you turn 24 but before the quarter in which you turn 31	Work during half the time for the period beginning with the quarter after you turned 21 and ending with the quarter you became disabled. Example: If you become disabled in the quarter in which you turned 27, then you would need three years of work out of the six-year period ending with the quarter in which you became disabled.
In the quarter you turn 31 or later	Work during five years out of the ten-year period ending with the quarter your disability began.

Source: Social Security Administration (`www.ssa.gov/pubs/10029.html`)

TABLE 11-4 **Examples of Work Needed to Pass the Duration-of-Work Test**

If You Become Disabled . . .	Then You Generally Need . . .
Before age 28	1½ years of work
At age 30	2 years of work
At age 34	3 years of work
At age 38	4 years of work
At age 42	5 years of work
At age 44	5½ years of work
At age 46	6 years of work
At age 48	6½ years of work
At age 50	7 years of work
At age 52	7½ years of work
At age 54	8 years of work
At age 56	8½ years of work
At age 58	9 years of work
At age 60	9½ years of work

Source: Social Security Administration (`www.ssa.gov/pubs/10029.html`)

TIP

If you've applied for disability, and you believe that your impairment has clearly reduced your earnings from what you earned before you had the disability, ask an SSA representative whether you qualify for a disability freeze. If so, you may end up with a higher benefit.

If you get multiple kinds of disability benefits, including SSDI, payment amounts are potentially affected. For example, if you get workers' compensation and SSDI, and if the total benefits exceed 80 percent of your pre-disability earnings, your Social Security payment could be reduced. Importantly, SSDI payments based on your work record that go to dependents also are counted toward the 80 percent cap. You also could run into this restriction if you're getting SSDI and a different public disability benefit that isn't job related.

SSDI benefits also may be reduced if you're receiving benefits from prior work for which you didn't contribute Social Security taxes, including government employment. (See Chapter 2 for a discussion of the Windfall Elimination provision and Government Pension Offset provision.)

REMEMBER

SSDI benefits are *not* reduced if you also get Veterans Administration (VA) benefits or certain state and local government benefits, as long as those benefits come from a job in which you paid Social Security taxes. The SSA won't reduce your SSDI payments if you're also getting private disability insurance.

Here's an example: Kimberly earns $40,000 annually as a dietitian in the county medical center. After she slips on a wet floor and suffers a serious head injury, she starts to receive $1,150 in monthly SSDI and another $2,000 in workers' compensation. Her combined benefits of $3,150 are 94.5 percent of the $3,333 she was taking home each month ($40,000 divided by 12) before the accident. The SSA wants the combined payments not to exceed 80 percent of Kimberly's former wages, which would mean $2,666. Therefore, the SSA reduces Kimberly's disability payment to $666. Because she is also getting $2,000 in workers' compensation, her total benefits now equal 80 percent of her prior monthly earnings.

WARNING

Private disability insurance policies may reduce their payments if you receive SSDI. Many policies have a provision stipulating that they'll reduce payments if you're approved for SSDI. Some companies even offer you legal counsel to pursue your Social Security claim. If you receive such an offer, proceed with care. Make sure that whoever represents you is working in your best interest. You may choose to hire an attorney or other representative of your own choice.

Supplemental Security Income

SSI provides cash assistance to people who are 65 or older, blind, or disabled, all of whom must have extreme financial need to qualify. Almost 5 million individuals who are under 65 get SSI; overall, about 8.1 million people get it. The program is funded through general tax revenues, and it isn't considered a basic social insurance benefit (such as retirement, SSDI, or survivors' benefits). That's because SSI pays benefits based on need and without regard to work history, earnings, or payroll taxes.

SSI imposes certain requirements to make sure that benefits go to those who meet its stringent income standards. Beneficiaries must have monthly income below the federal payment standard (set at $783 for individuals and $1,175 for couples in 2020). Personal assets, such as cash or mutual funds, are restricted to $2,000 for individuals and $3,000 for couples. A car may be excluded under certain circumstances, such as if it's used for work or to get needed medical care.

Different factors affect the income calculation, including varying state policies and personal circumstances, such as housing arrangements. Also, the SSA doesn't count all income. Exclusions include the first $20 per month in unearned income (a broad category of income other than wages you earn from an employer), the first $65 per month in earnings (plus one-half of the remainder), and a portion of certain assistance (such as food stamps).

SSI payment amounts also vary, based on state policies and personal circumstances.

Healthcare coverage is another difference between SSI and SSDI. SSDI beneficiaries typically qualify for Medicare after two years (a significant exception to Medicare's general rule of providing coverage for people who have reached age 65). In most states, SSI beneficiaries get healthcare benefits right away through Medicaid, which is a state-federal program of healthcare for the poor. (In some states, you need to apply separately for Medicaid.)

TECHNICAL STUFF

It may be possible to get both SSI and SSDI benefits if you've earned benefits under Social Security and you also meet the stringent financial limits of SSI. If your SSDI payment is below the SSI amount, but you're also poor enough to qualify for SSI, then SSI may make up the difference.

TIP

If you apply for SSDI, the SSA determines whether you qualify for SSI. But if you think you may be eligible for SSI, be sure to ask. The SSA should take applications for both SSDI and SSI at the time you apply.

How Social Security Defines Disability

REMEMBER

You're supposed to either be incapable of working for at least a year or have a condition that will end in death to qualify for disability benefits. This status can be hard to prove, and experts may not even agree. Claims involving pain, chronic fatigue, mood disorders, and other problems are hard to measure. Some people have good days and bad days. Some people have periods of apparent good health that are then disrupted by rough episodes.

The SSA weighs a lot in reaching a decision about whether someone's limitations are this serious. This includes an applicant's work experience, skills, education, and age, in addition to his or her health condition.

This section looks at the various steps the SSA takes to determine whether an applicant is disabled. Later in this chapter, I talk about what an applicant can do to simplify the journey through the process and help make sure that the SSA reaches the proper decision on a claim.

When you first apply, the SSA does an initial review to make sure that you meet the nonmedical requirements for coverage. The SSA also takes note of whether you're engaged in substantial, "gainful" employment, which it decides based on how much you're earning (along with possible work-related deductions because of your condition). Then the SSA moves the application to the Disability Determination Service in your state, which works with the SSA in assessing a claim.

The state evaluators focus on the medical and vocational realities surrounding your application. They should seek medical information from your physician and other medical professionals familiar with your condition, and they may arrange for a consultative exam if they want more medical input. An SSA field office then reviews the state's findings and informs you of its decision.

As the process unfolds, the SSA wants to answer five important questions. The answers to these questions determine how it rules on your claim. The questions are answered in order, and an application for disability can be derailed along the way. If you want to know your chances of getting disability benefits, it helps to know more about each of these questions.

Are you working for money?

If you're earning more than a certain amount of money, the SSA doubts that you're disabled because you're able to perform substantial work that an employer compensates you for. It makes no difference if the work requires you to haul crates or tap on a computer keyboard.

The SSA describes this level of work and earnings as *substantial gainful activity*. The amount of annual income that qualifies as substantial gainful activity usually changes each year. (In 2020, the level for most wage earners was $1,260 per month.) In determining whether your earnings are substantial, the SSA may deduct special expenses you need to work, such as a wheelchair or taxi. If you exceed that level, the SSA concludes that you're able to work.

In measuring gainful activity, the SSA has special rules for two categories of workers:

- **People who are blind:** Individuals with vision loss are given a higher level of allowable earnings before they exceed the limit on gainful activity. (In 2020, that level was set at $2,110 per month.) The SSA defines blindness as vision that can't be corrected beyond 20/200 in your better eye or a visual field limited to 20 or fewer degrees in your better eye.
- **The self-employed:** If you work for yourself, the SSA has a few ways of looking at whether your work activity should disqualify you for disability benefits. It wants to know the following:
  - Do you perform "significant services" for the business, and is your average monthly income above the gainful-activity limit?
  - Do you perform work tasks similar to healthy, self-employed individuals who work in the same kind of business in your community?
  - Is the work you provide worth the gainful-employment pay level? How much would you have to pay someone else to do it?

Do you have a severe medical problem?

The SSA defines *disability* as having a medical condition that prevents you from doing substantial and gainful work for at least a year or that will result in death. The disability must be serious and debilitating — the SSA doesn't provide partial benefits for limited health problems.

The fact that an individual may be diagnosed with a potentially grave illness, such as cancer, doesn't automatically mean that a claim is approved. The SSA uses the idea of "severe condition" to make sure that an applicant has a problem that is more than meaningless and to screen out those whose problems are minor. If someone has a serious impairment, but medical treatment is easing the symptoms, that person may be viewed as not disabled.

Disability evaluators want evidence that a person isn't capable of working — that routine activities, such as sitting, walking, and remembering, are too difficult. The SSA may arrange a consultative medical exam if it believes further information is needed about your condition.

Is your disability on "the list"?

The SSA maintains a long and highly detailed list of severe impairments that it considers to be disabling. The list lays out details of illness and gravity of symptoms that establish eligibility for benefits.

The list for adults includes 14 broad categories of disorders (such as respiratory, cardiovascular, digestive, and neurological) and specific disabling conditions within those categories. For example, the category of "respiratory system" includes asthma and cystic fibrosis. The category of "special senses and speech" includes different types of vision and hearing loss.

TIP

You can look at the list of adult impairments, as well as find links to extremely detailed explanations, at `www.ssa.gov/disability/professionals/bluebook/AdultListings.htm`.

TIP

The SSA has developed a sublist of more than 200 conditions considered so severe that they allow for fast-track approval of disability claims. This effort is called the Compassionate Allowance Initiative. It includes various cancers, brain disorders, and other severe conditions. (See Chapter 8 for details.) The complete list is available at `www.ssa.gov/compassionateallowances`.

The SSA has a list of 15 categories of conditions that are disabling for children under age 18. (In the case of a child, the SSA looks at "marked and severe functional limitation," as well as whether the condition will last at least one year or end in death.) You can find details about the child listings at `www.ssa.gov/disability/professionals/bluebook/ChildhoodListings.htm`.

REMEMBER

Children can't qualify for SSDI on their own, but they may be eligible for payments if they're the financial dependents of a breadwinner who has earned Social Security benefits. (SSI has its own income requirements for children who are disabled.)

It's not unusual for a person to have a combination of ailments or a particular problem that doesn't match up perfectly with the list. For example, an individual suffering from depression, a degenerated disc, and carpal tunnel syndrome may present a stronger case than an individual who has just one or even two of those problems. The SSA must consider the combined effects of a person's impairments at all levels of its evaluation process.

TIP

An impairment doesn't need to be on the list to qualify as a disability. If your condition is listed, however, that goes a long way toward getting a claim approved.

Can you perform the tasks required by your former job or a similar job?

Your age becomes extremely important at this stage of the process. Age is a factor in whether you should be approved for benefits. The SSA recognizes that an older worker with a serious health issue who lacks transferable skills and experience may find it impossible to get hired. So if you can't do the job you've done your whole life, you'll have an easier time getting approved if you're 50 or older.

If the SSA determines that you aren't earning a substantial amount and have a serious condition, but your problem doesn't match a listed condition, it goes on to the next question: Can you do the kind of work you did over the last 15 years?

Maybe your most recent job required a lot of traveling to meet with suppliers around the country, and you no longer can do that. But suppose you worked at a desk before that, and you're still able to handle the rigors of a desk job. It's possible that you would be able to perform that kind of work, despite your condition, and not be approved for benefits.

The SSA asks you for a detailed description of the tasks you used to perform. It won't rely on your description alone, but it may call on vocational experts to comment on what's expected in the workplace. It also may consult a vast online compilation of job descriptions, known as the *Dictionary of Occupational Titles* (`www.occupationalinfo.org`).

The SSA divides most occupations into five main categories of exertion, based on their physical demands. These demands include lifting certain amounts of weight, as well as other physical tasks, such as the ability to manipulate objects, use fingers and hands, sit, stand, bend, pull, and move your body in other common ways. The main categories of exertion are as follows:

- **Sedentary:** This is the label for jobs, including many office jobs, that mostly require sitting and no heavy lifting. Sedentary workers may have to carry files or tools, but they don't have to lift objects heavier than 10 pounds. Such jobs also may require some walking and standing. They often require certain repetitive motions using hands and fingers, such as typing or calculating.

- **Light:** This sort of work may include various sorts of light labor, such as lifting up to 20 pounds, lots of walking and standing (up to six hours), or even sitting while doing tasks that require the use of arms or legs. For example, light work may involve moving inventory in a store (but not hauling heavy containers), certain security jobs, working a cash register, and many other jobs.
- **Medium:** This work is more physical, requiring some lifting of up to 50 pounds and frequent lifting of up to 25 pounds. In addition, medium work may require other physical demands, such as bending, stooping, kneeling, squatting, or climbing. Skilled trade jobs, including electrical, plumbing, carpentry, and roofing, may fall into this category.
- **Heavy:** This work involves lifting up to 100 pounds and frequently up to 50 pounds. Think of demanding labor, typically done by brawny guys at a construction site or warehouse or loading dock.
- **Very heavy:** The SSA also has a category for "very heavy" labor for those jobs that require lifting of more than 100 pounds.

REMEMBER

Disputes over disability claims often center on whether a person can perform light or sedentary work that seems easy for healthy people. The demands of heavy labor are more clearly out of reach for many workers.

The exertion categories may be irrelevant, though, if the problem is mental (although some individuals have physical *and* mental impairments). In cases where physical ability isn't at issue, a person's capacity for work may depend on such factors as the ability to concentrate, understand, remember, pay attention, take orders, or interact appropriately with colleagues and the public.

If the SSA decides that you're still capable of doing the work you did before the impairment developed (or similar work), you won't get disability benefits. But if it decides that you no longer are capable of doing such work on a sustained basis, it moves on to the next question.

Can you do any other available work in the economy?

If you're younger than 50, the SSA is more likely to conclude that you can adapt to work you've never done before. This may include jobs that pay less, jobs you don't like, jobs that aren't conveniently located, jobs you may not be hired for, and jobs that are part time. By contrast, a disability applicant 50 or over, who is in similar physical shape, may get a more favorable decision, and an applicant 55 or over has an even greater chance. Broadly speaking, the SSA may conclude that someone with scant work history and no transferable skill is much less likely to engage in substantial work activity than someone of a similar age and condition who has a strong education and solid track record of skilled work. As a result, the individual lacking transferable skill and experience is more likely to be approved for disability benefits.

The SSA has put together lengthy tables (technically called *medical-vocational guidelines*, but often referred to as "the grid") that seek to boil down these considerations, based on broad categories of age, skill level, education, and work experience. The tables have been designed for different levels of exertion, such as sedentary, light, and medium work.

Under the guidelines, a worker who is 55 or older, with limited education and no transferable skills, may be considered disabled. Yet a worker who is 55 or older, has graduated from high school, and has transferable skills may be viewed as not disabled. A worker who is 45 to 49, illiterate and unskilled, and has a severe condition may be considered disabled. But a worker of the same age who went to college and has job skills may be ruled able to work and not eligible for benefits.

You can find more about the medical-vocational guidelines at `www.socialsecurity.gov/OP_Home/rulings/di/02/SSR82-63-di-02.html`.

REMEMBER

The grid is just one tool that plays into deciding an application when physical impairments are involved. The grid isn't designed to assess the work prospects of an individual with a mental condition. Providing the SSA with the fullest possible record from a qualified doctor who knows you, who clearly and specifically states your limitations, and who has phrased them in a way that fits with SSA guidelines can make all the difference in your claim.

How to Make Your Case

The SSA imposes a five-month waiting period after you become disabled before benefits may begin. But if you believe you qualify for disability, you should get the process started, because it can take a long time if there's a dispute. If you file soon after becoming disabled, benefits are payable starting with the sixth full month after the disability began.

Suppose the disability begins in January. The first possible payment could not come until June (paid in July). What if it takes you longer to apply? Back benefits are potentially available for the next 12 months. But you should apply within 18 months of the onset, or you could lose payments you would've been eligible for had you started the process sooner.

It's a good idea to begin your disability application even if you haven't gotten all your documents together yet. You can add documents along the way, and the process can take well over a year if you challenge an initial decision by the SSA.

The SSA considers it your responsibility to provide the information it needs. Evaluators may do fact-finding along the way, and they'll guide you in providing the required materials. But in the end, the burden is on applicants, or their advocates, to make a persuasive claim.

For most people, that requires some effort. It means pulling together a bunch of healthcare information, which could require multiple phone calls to your doctor(s) and following up if you need to. You need dates of appointments, tests taken, laboratory results, medications prescribed, and contact information for all of your medical providers. You need to obtain all recent hospital records. You also need to re-create your work experience over the last 15 years.

TIP

The SSA turns down disability claims all the time. You'll improve your chances by being as organized as possible. Keep copies of everything you provide to the SSA.

In the following sections, I offer specific tips to improve your chances of having your claim approved. I can't guarantee that your claim will be approved if you follow these suggestions, of course, but if you have a strong case to make and follow these guidelines, you stand a better chance.

Cutting through the red tape

To apply for disability, you may have to fill out several forms. You can start the application online, by going to www.ssa.gov and clicking "Disability." This leads you to a lot of information about disability benefits, including a link where you can apply.

TIP

If the SSA schedules meetings in the course of your claim or appeal, show up on time and come prepared. If you can't make it and you have a valid reason (such as a medical issue), inform the SSA as soon as possible.

Information you need to apply for disability benefits includes the following:

- Facts about a workers' compensation claim if you filed one, including the injury date, claim number, and payments you've received.
- Your birth certificate (original or certified copy) or proof of legal residency. (If you're a U.S. citizen who was born in another country, the SSA seeks proof of citizenship.)

- » Military discharge papers (DD Form 214; original or certified copy) for all periods of active duty.
- » Checking account number and bank routing number to sign up for direct deposit of benefits.

You also have to fill out other forms, which you can find online at `www.ssa.gov/online/#disability`. These forms and technical application requirements may evolve over time. Also, there may be differences between online applications and paper forms at a local SSA office. Potentially, they include the following:

- » **Disability Report — Adult (SSA-3368):** The Disability Report — Adult asks for highly specific information about you and your condition. It wants to know your name, how to reach you, and contact information for someone else who knows you.

  It asks you to list medical conditions, whether you're working, when you stopped working, and details of your job history and education. (For example, it asks if in previous jobs you had to walk, stand, sit, climb, stoop, kneel, crouch, crawl, handle large objects, handle small objects, write, type, or reach, and if so, for how many hours per day.)

  This report also asks details about your medical treatment, including names of doctors and healthcare facilities you went to, visits to doctors, visits to the emergency room, kinds of tests taken, including dates, and a list of your medications.

  You can download the form at `www.ssa.gov/forms/ssa-3368-bk.pdf`.
- » **Work History Report (SSA-3369):** The Work History Report asks you to list all the jobs you had for 15 years before your health problem, including how much you were paid at each job.

  You can download the form at `www.ssa.gov/forms/ssa-3369.pdf`.
- » **Function Report — Adult (SSA-3373):** The Function Report — Adult seeks details about your ability to handle routine tasks of daily life, such as bathing, preparing meals, shopping, getting around, and handling money. It asks, for example, whether you go outside, and if not, why not. It asks whether you're able to count change. It also seeks insight into your social activities, such as whether you spend time with others and whether you have problems getting along with family, friends, and neighbors.

  You can download the form at `www.ssa.gov/forms/ssa-3373-bk.pdf`.

» **Authorization to Disclose Information to the Social Security Administration (SSA-827):** This form authorizes healthcare providers, employers, and others to disclose information about you to the SSA.

You can download the form at `www.ssa.gov/online/ssa-827.pdf`.

REMEMBER

Keep track of your claim. Always make sure to put your name and Social Security number on all documents you send to the SSA and keep copies, if possible. Make sure that you get the name of the claims representative who takes your application and get a receipt for everything you submit. Keep a careful log of communications you've had with SSA representatives in the course of your application.

Gathering the best medical evidence: The role of your doctor

You need to establish a complete medical record of your condition, with material provided from a specialist in the field who knows a lot about your personal case, including your hospitalizations.

TIP

When it comes to your disability claim, all doctors aren't equal. The SSA accepts information from various healthcare professionals about your condition. But the more a doctor has treated you, and the more expertise the doctor has in your type of problem, the more influential that doctor's opinion will be. The SSA is supposed to make every reasonable effort to get its medical evidence from the doctor who treats you before it resorts to its own medical consultant. However, your doctor's reports should be highly specific. They must state specifically what your impairments are, the tests that were done, and how your impairments affect your ability to function.

Ideally, the doctor knows you well and has specialized expertise in your condition. (For mental issues, a psychologist or psychiatrist can provide valuable information.) The SSA is required to place great weight on the findings of such a physician. Federal courts have reversed the SSA in cases where it has ignored the reports of medical specialists — as long as those medical reports fall within SSA guidelines and don't appear inconsistent with other evidence. A medical specialist who has known you long enough also may offer credible observations about how your condition has changed over time.

WARNING

The SSA places less weight on the statement of a general practitioner, a doctor who gives an opinion unsupported by objective findings, or a doctor who isn't familiar with you (say, someone who saw you briefly in a clinic) and who doesn't have much experience in treating your type of problem.

Don't assume that a busy doctor knows everything about you. Patients react differently to conditions and treatments. When you visit your doctor, make sure that he or she understands details of your condition that affect your ability to perform basic job tasks *on a sustained basis.*

The doctor's statement should focus on the details of your condition and how it affects what you can and can't do. If your condition limits your ability to perform certain work tasks on a sustained basis, your doctor should back that up in clear detail. If an applicant has mental problems, the applicant's psychologist or psychiatrist and other therapists (like social workers or nurse practitioners) should provide evidence for the SSA.

Physical demands of the workplace include sitting, standing, walking, lifting, handling objects large or small, hearing, and speaking. Mental demands of the workplace include understanding, remembering, concentrating, following instructions, and adapting to change. Social and interpersonal demands include the ability to get along with colleagues and the public, accept orders, and control aggression.

The SSA isn't looking for your doctor's opinion on whether you qualify for disability benefits. It wants your doctor to give it all the details it needs to make that determination itself.

When your personal doctor's findings aren't consistent with other medical findings or otherwise raise questions, or if the SSA can't obtain the information it needs from a doctor who knows you, it may seek further information or another view. In such cases, the SSA may set up a consultative examination, conducted by a doctor it pays for.

If the SSA arranges a consultative exam, don't miss the appointment. The fact that the SSA arranged such an exam is a sign that your disability claim is progressing through the system. If you don't show up, it's delayed. During such an exam, the doctor observes you carefully and makes conclusions about the credibility of your claim.

Getting help

Most states have programs to help older Americans and people with disabilities apply for programs like SSDI and SSI, known as Aging and Disability Resource Centers. Contact your state Department on Aging to find a location.

TIP

You should seriously consider getting an experienced advocate if you want to win a claim for Social Security disability. Representatives include lawyers and trained nonlawyers. Representation becomes even more important if your initial claim has been turned down and you go through the appeals process (see Chapter 8).

Unlike most Social Security benefits, disability decisions turn on a range of evidence that may be interpreted differently by different people. Your case can be presented more effectively and less effectively. Your advocate can help guide your doctor to provide evidence that is most relevant to your case, instead of being vague and general. Further, challenges to SSA decisions must follow a set process for appeals and are considered in a type of administrative legal system that an experienced representative knows about.

REMEMBER

If you want to hire an advocate, don't pick just anyone. Find a lawyer or other expert who is experienced in the specialized area of Social Security disability claims. The right advocate helps gather the best evidence, understands how your circumstances fit with SSA guidelines and court precedents, and makes sure that you've obtained the documents you need to establish your claim. The lawyer can prepare you to make your best presentation at a hearing and know details of the process. (I discuss the need for representation in greater detail in Chapter 8.)

Showing that you've tried to solve your problem

Simple as it may sound, one way to help your case is to continue getting treatments you need and comply with your doctor's advice, including filling prescriptions and taking them on time. You can sabotage your case by failing to do so. This may be difficult if you're out of work and you don't have much money to pay for healthcare. But if you're in that situation, you still should try to find treatment, perhaps through a community clinic or another government benefit.

The SSA won't hold failure to get treatment against you in certain rare cases:

- If the treatment goes against your religious beliefs
- If you have a great fear of surgery
- If free treatment isn't available in the community or you otherwise can't afford treatment

But for most people, getting treatment while you're pursuing a disability application is very important. In addition, other factors also influence how a disability evaluator may assess your application for benefits. These include

» **Your credibility:** If you claim to be suffering from a serious condition, failure to get care raises questions. The SSA understandably wonders whether you're truly in bad shape.

» **Your documentation:** Documented medical care is the basis of the record the SSA relies on to assess your physical condition. By not going to the doctor or pursuing therapy, you're failing to build the record that can establish your disability — a record you may need later, as well, if you appeal a decision.

» **Your effort:** If you undergo testing and therapy that is uncomfortable or painful, you're showing that you want to get better. If you seek treatment and it doesn't cure the problem, that creates a clearer picture for the SSA to understand.

Telling the truth

You shouldn't exaggerate your problem, but you shouldn't trivialize it either. Don't minimize the serious nature of an impairment out of a sense of pride or to avoid embarrassment. Provide accurate, straightforward information to make your case.

WARNING

Disability lawyers are filled with tales of clients who downplay their own symptoms for reasons of personal dignity. By doing so, they hurt their chances.

One lawyer recalls how a client with serious mental issues informed an SSA hearing judge that he was in good shape and ready to work. The hearing judge listened — and turned down his disability claim. Another lawyer recalls applicants who exaggerated how much they could lift and how far they could walk because they had an unrealistic view of themselves. If you write on the Function Report that you clean the bathroom, when all you do is wipe the sink, the SSA may assume that you can get down on both knees and scrub the bathtub. If you say you can haul a "heavy sack" of dog food home from the supermarket, it's best to know how much weight you're actually talking about.

You also should be honest about work history. Embellishing the past can make you sound more employable than you may be and undermine a claim for benefits. If your job was washing cars, don't describe yourself as an automotive detail specialist.

REMEMBER

If you're approved for disability benefits, they could last until you reach your full retirement age. At that point, the SSA simply would shift you to retirement benefits, and you would get the same amount. But your disability benefits may not last that long. The SSA conducts periodic medical reviews, often every three years, to see whether a beneficiary's condition has improved. The review may include an interview, as well as current evidence of your condition and your activities. If the SSA concludes that you no longer are disabled, it can stop your benefits.

WARNING

Be aware of the image you're creating of yourself through social media. What you post on Facebook, Instagram, Twitter, and other social media may be noticed, and signs of vitality could be harmful to your application for disability benefits. If your online profile depicts you as a rugged adventurer or weekend golfer, while you're telling the SSA that you can't do any work, something doesn't add up. Your credibility matters.

What to Do If You Get Turned Down

For anybody who files for disability, the possibility that you'll be turned down is important to consider, because so many disability applications *do* get turned down. If you want to keep trying, you need to pursue the effort in the SSA appeals system — and you have 60 days to file an appeal from the time you get the bad news. The odds of winning an appeal are better than the odds of winning on the first try. So if you believe you have a valid case, it makes sense to press on. You may want to get professional assistance in pursuing an appeal.

The Social Security appeals system has several distinct steps. Turn to Chapter 8 for the details.

What Happens to Your Benefit If You Can Go Back to Work

If you've been approved for disability benefits, the SSA has determined that you can do little or no work. But in some cases, such as if your condition improves, you may be able to reenter the workforce after starting disability. The SSA encourages such a transition by offering certain incentives:

- **Trial work period:** You're allowed nine months to earn money with no income limit, provided you report earnings above a certain level to the SSA and still have a serious impairment. The monthly level rises over time. (It was set at $910 for wage earners in 2020; the self-employed were expected to report if they earned that much or spent more than 80 hours per month on their business.) The nine months don't have to come in a row; they're counted within a five-year period.

- **Deductible expenses:** Certain expenses you may need to work, such as a taxi, attendant care, and home modifications, may be deducted from your monthly earnings. This can make it easier to stay eligible for benefits and keep income below the level deemed "substantial." The SSA also may reduce the earnings amount for work performed under "special conditions," such as if you require extra supervision.
- **Extended eligibility:** If your nine-month trial concludes and you stop getting disability, benefits may still kick in for any months in which you earn below a certain amount. This amount was set at $1,260 per month for 2020 ($2,110 for people who are blind). This period of extended eligibility lasts for three years after the end of the trial work period. If you're in the period of extended eligibility, and you earn over the limit, the SSA allows you three months of benefits before cutting you off.
- **Possible continuation of benefits:** If the SSA cuts you off because of high earnings, but your condition later makes it impossible to keep working, you may request immediate reinstatement of benefits. You may receive payments for six months while the SSA determines whether you still qualify. This option is available for five years after your benefits stop.
- **Medicare coverage:** You remain enrolled in Medicare Part A (hospital insurance) for more than seven years after the trial work period. You continue to pay the premium for Medicare Part B (doctor and outpatient services).
- **Ticket to Work:** This voluntary program helps people who get SSDI find a path back into the workplace. It can include rehabilitation, training, job leads, and other support. Participants get help through employment networks and vocational rehabilitation agencies. The SSA doesn't conduct routine medical reviews of your disability for those participating in Ticket to Work. For more information, check out `www.ssa.gov/work/home.html`.

REMEMBER

You may work only within certain limits and continue to collect disability benefits from Social Security. If you show that you can support yourself on a continuing basis, earning above what the SSA considers a "substantial amount" to do what it calls "gainful work," the SSA ultimately cuts off benefits.

WARNING

An effort to work is commendable. Be aware of the rules, though, and make sure that there's no miscommunication between you and the SSA. If you earn above a certain amount of money, you could be hit with an overpayment notice — or the SSA may even garnish your wages.

WARNING

Sometimes people who are receiving disability believe they're allowed to go back to work and end up earning thousands of dollars beyond what the SSA believes they're eligible for. If this happens, the SSA may send an overpayment notice to recover the money. (See Chapter 7 for more on overpayments and your options if you receive a notice of overpayment.)

If you're getting benefits under SSI, the rules for work and benefits are different than if you're getting SSDI benefits. Generally, if you receive SSI, are disabled, and earn money, the first $65 in monthly earnings (plus one-half of the remainder) aren't counted, in addition to the $20 general income exclusion. Above that amount (and after certain deductions), SSI benefits are reduced by 50 cents for every one dollar earned over $85. SSI may deduct work expenses and certain spending toward an approved plan to support yourself. It also expedites restarting of benefits if medical problems once again make it impossible for you to work. Some of the technical rules vary from state to state.

DISABILITY BENEFITS AND SUBSTANCE ABUSE

The SSA's longstanding policy has been *not* to provide disability benefits for drug addiction and alcoholism (DAA). But if someone is disabled for another reason, and substance abuse isn't the cause, that person may qualify for benefits even if he or she has drug and/or alcohol problems.

This situation can get confusing, and it's the source of many disputes. Today's stricter policy is also a change from an earlier era when the SSA viewed DAA as a disease and individuals could qualify for benefits. The SSA allowed benefits if the DAA met the standard of being so serious that it prevented someone from working for a year or could end in the person's death.

Today, if DAA is considered "material" to a disabling condition, the applicant isn't eligible for benefits. But if someone has a condition that is disabling, independent of any substance abuse, he or she may qualify for benefits. If the person has stopped abusing drugs or alcohol but the disabling condition remains, he or she may qualify because the substance abuse isn't considered material.

Further, the DAA must be determined through medical evidence of signs, symptoms, and laboratory findings. If someone says he or she has a drug problem, that's not enough for the claim to be turned down on the basis of DAA.

4 Social Security and Your Future

IN THIS PART . . .

Discover the ins and outs of Medicare and how it relates to Social Security and, importantly, your wallet.

See how working longer may bolster your finances and affect your Social Security benefits.

Secure your financial future with key steps on how to prepare for life on a fixed income.

IN THIS CHAPTER

» Qualifying for and enrolling in Medicare

» Knowing your options for paying your Medicare premiums

» Paying penalties for missed deadlines

» Buying Medigap coverage

» Reaching out for financial help

Chapter 12

Enrolling in Medicare

Medicare is the healthcare program for more than 49 million people 65 and older (as well as millions of other people — more on that later). Social Security and Medicare are twin pillars of support for older Americans, and they work closely together.

The Social Security Administration (SSA) handles your sign-up for Medicare, figures the penalties if you miss Medicare deadlines, and assesses the premium surcharges paid by high-income beneficiaries. It also administers the Medicare Savings Program, which helps low-income individuals with the some of the out-of-pocket Medicare costs. The Extra Help program provides low-cost prescription-drug coverage for people with limited incomes.

Medicare gives you protections that most beneficiaries can't get elsewhere at anywhere near the price. It won't charge you extra (or exclude you) for preexisting medical conditions. At the same time, Medicare has several parts and different enrollment periods, and if you miss a deadline and want to enroll later, you risk financial penalties that could last the rest of your life. So understanding the ins and outs of the program is important.

In this chapter, I offer a quick and easy tour of Medicare, going over its main benefits, along with rules for eligibility and deadlines you should be aware of. The goal here isn't to be exhaustive (Medicare is very complicated) but rather to give you a basic primer for your future entry into the program.

Understanding the ABCs (and D) of Medicare

Traditional Medicare helps cover healthcare costs for doctors, hospitals, lab tests, medical equipment, home healthcare on a limited basis, hospice, and skilled nursing. It even includes expensive treatments like heart transplants. But Medicare does *not* cover continuous long-term-care services, such as an extended stay in a nursing home or in-home custodial care because of a chronic condition. Traditional Medicare generally does not cover checkups for vision or hearing (or corrective lenses or hearing aids), or dental care, although some Medicare Advantage plans may offer some coverage for those benefits.

The program is made up of four parts, conveniently named Parts A, B, C, and D. Parts A and B make up what is often known as the "traditional" or "original" Medicare program. Each part plays a distinct role and has its own fee structure. The following sections are a quick primer on the four parts of Medicare.

TIP

For a vastly more detailed explanation of how to navigate Medicare, written in clear, straightforward language, see *Medicare For Dummies* by Patricia Barry (Wiley).

Part A: Hospital insurance

If you have to check into the hospital, Medicare Part A covers some of the expense. This part may also cover temporary rehabilitation or skilled care in a skilled nursing facility, hospice, and some healthcare in your home. Most people don't have to pay a premium (set at up to $458 a month in 2020) because the premium is covered by payroll taxes they paid while working. You do face a deductible ($1,408 in 2020) for each "benefit period," which may mean an episode of illness but has a more technical definition.

A *benefit period* begins on the day you're admitted to the hospital or skilled nursing facility (SNF) and ends when you've been out of the hospital or SNF for 60 days in a row. If you're readmitted to the hospital after the benefit period ends, you owe a new deductible, unless you have a Medigap supplemental insurance policy that covers this cost (see "Buying Extra Insurance: Medigap," later in this chapter).

Part A helps pay for basic hospital services, including a semiprivate room, regular nursing care, hospital meals, and certain other hospital services (including medications, lab tests, medical appliances, and medical supplies furnished by the facility). Part A also partially covers stays of up to 100 days in a skilled nursing facility as part of recovery following a problem that required a hospital stay of at least three days. (It will not cover you for 100 days, however, if you're under observation status in the hospital; you must be admitted for at least three days.) Your doctor must approve nursing-home care as necessary. (Such rehabilitation isn't considered long-term care.) Under Part A, you can also receive certain home healthcare services and virtually free hospice care, if approved by your doctor.

REMEMBER

Part A does *not* pay for the services of physicians who treat you in the hospital or rehab facility; treatment by physicians is covered under Part B. Nor does Part A cover items you may find convenient but that aren't considered essential. For example, it doesn't pay for a private room (unless your doctor deems it medically necessary), a private nurse, a TV, a phone, or other conveniences.

Part B: Medical insurance

Part B covers 80 percent of the cost of most services, including doctor visits, outpatient care, certain tests conducted outside hospitals, mental healthcare, and an assortment of other medical services, including some done inside the hospital, such as surgery. Some preventive services come free of charge.

You pay a monthly premium for Part B, with higher-income seniors charged more. The standard Part B premium was set at $144.60 for 2020. Part B also has an annual deductible ($198 in 2020). After you've met the deductible, you typically pay 20 percent of the cost of approved services. Here's a partial list of these services:

- **Approved medical services provided by a physician who treats Medicare patients.** The treatment can take place in the doctor's office, a hospital, a clinic, or a rehabilitation facility.
- **An annual wellness visit and a one-time-only preventive checkup within the first year of signing up for Part B.** Both of these are free (no deductible or copay) if you go to a doctor who accepts the Medicare-approved cost as full reimbursement.
- **Preventive screenings, diagnostic tests, and lab tests in clinics and other nonhospital settings, some of which are free.**

» **Certain emergency-room services and home health services.**

» **Oxygen equipment, diabetic supplies, braces, wheelchairs, walkers, and other medical equipment.**

» **Outpatient mental-health services.**

Part B does *not* cover every service. For example, in addition to those previously mentioned (most vision, hearing, dental, and custodial long-term care), it doesn't cover routine chiropody services (such as toenail clipping) or home-safety equipment.

TIP

You can find more details about what Medicare Part B covers, as well as about the rest of Medicare, in the official handbooks "Medicare & You" (`www.medicare.gov/medicare-and-you`) and "Your Medicare Benefits" (`www.medicare.gov/Pubs/pdf/10116-your-medicare-benefits.pdf`).

Part C: Medicare Advantage

An alternative to traditional Medicare, Medicare Advantage plans under Part C are run by private insurance companies. They must offer all the benefits of traditional Medicare (Parts A and B). But they may charge lower copays for certain care and offer some additional services, such as routine hearing, vision, and dental care. Most Medicare Advantage plans include Part D (prescription-drug coverage). If you enroll in a Medicare Advantage plan, you deal with a particular healthcare organization and must accept its rules. You're still responsible for paying the Medicare Part B premium, in addition to whatever the Medicare Advantage plan charges you. (Some plans in some areas don't charge an additional premium.)

Most Medicare Advantage plans are health maintenance organizations (HMOs) or preferred provider organizations (PPOs) that offer managed care. They may restrict your choice of doctor or charge higher copays to see out-of-network providers, except in emergencies. In other words, you may give up some of your freedom to choose your own doctors (which is your right under traditional Medicare).

Medicare Advantage plans set their own fee structure, including deductibles and copays. These fees often, but not always, are lower than those charged by traditional Medicare. But by law, Medicare Advantage plans must put an annual limit on out-of-pocket costs. Traditional Medicare doesn't have an annual cap on costs you may have to pay.

REMEMBER

Medicare Advantage plans have the right to drop out of the Medicare program or change their costs, coverage benefits, and providers every calendar year. You may leave a Medicare Advantage plan and return to traditional Medicare during two periods of the year — October 15 to December 7, and January 1 to March 31 — or, if this is your first time in a Medicare Advantage plan, within 12 months of enrollment, which serves as a trial period.

TECHNICAL STUFF

A Medicare Advantage plan makes a calendar-year contract with Medicare. The plan, typically part of an insurance company, doesn't always renew. In such cases, individuals get a letter from the Centers for Medicare and Medicaid Services explaining their options to join another plan or return to original Medicare. If the individual does nothing, he or she has the protections of original Medicare. (In really rare cases, a Medicare Advantage plan goes out of business midyear or is shut down for violations.)

Part D: Prescription-drug coverage

This part of Medicare helps pay for prescription medications that you get from the pharmacy. Part D is handled by private plans that have been approved by Medicare. These include stand-alone drug plans, as well as broader Medicare Advantage plans that also cover prescription drugs under Part D.

To get Medicare drug coverage in a stand-alone plan, you must actively enroll and pay a monthly premium. Medicare Advantage plans that offer Part D coverage include it in their premiums, and some charge no premiums for either medical services or drug coverage. Part D plans vary widely, both in terms of the list of drugs covered (the *formulary*) and in terms of the premiums. Most premiums are in the range of $32 to $57 per month. Also, it's important to realize that cost-sharing like copays — even for the same drug — varies a great deal among different plans.

The Part D payment structure may be hard to understand. It has four separate stages:

1. **Deductible**

   You're responsible for this amount — up to $435 in 2020, although some plans have a lower or no deductible.

2. **Initial coverage**

   You pay the cost-sharing that your plan requires until the total cost of the drugs you've used since the beginning of the year (what you've paid *and* what your plan has paid) reaches a certain dollar limit ($4,020 in 2020).

3. **Medicare coverage gap (doughnut hole)**

   Once the total payment from your plan and out-of-pocket costs reaches $4,020 (in 2020), you reach the Medicare coverage gap. Originally, in the gap, you paid 100 percent of prescription drug costs. Now you will pay 25 percent of the drug cost. When you have reached a certain limit ($6,350 in 2020) in prescription drug costs, you enter the catastrophic phase.

4. **Catastrophic protection**

   In the catastrophic phase, Medicare generally pays 95 percent of your costs until the end of the calendar year.

This cycle of deductible, initial coverage, gap, and catastrophic coverage begins anew at the start of each year.

Picking the right Part D plan can be a confusing process, and the wrong choice can cost you a lot. You need to make an individual determination based on the medications you need (including whether cheaper generics provide a good alternative), the varied costs of a plan (such as premiums, deductibles, and cost-sharing), and the choice of local and mail order pharmacies. You can find out about different Medicare plans that serve your area by going to the Medicare website (`www.medicare.gov`) and clicking the "Sign Up/Change Plans" link and scrolling down to "Find health & drug plans." Just follow the directions for more details.

Before you start, put together a list of the prescription drugs you rely on. Research the costs charged by particular plans, because cost-sharing may vary widely, even for the same drug. You should also check to see whether your drugs are subject to "utilization management" such as prior authorization or quantity limits. If you don't take prescription drugs, it may make sense for you to pick a Part D plan with the lowest premium in your area. If your needs change, you can switch to a more suitable Part D plan during the proper enrollment period (see "Signing Up for Medicare," later in this chapter).

Qualifying for Medicare

To qualify for Medicare, you must meet certain conditions, which vary according to your circumstances. Here's a quick overview of how you may become eligible, depending on your personal situation:

- **You've turned 65.** You qualify automatically for Part A benefits, without paying premiums for them, if you've earned sufficient work credits under

Social Security or Railroad Retirement. Social Security awards one credit for a set amount of earnings ($1,410 in 2020) up to four credits per year. Social Security typically requires 40 credits, which most people attain through ten years of covered employment.

If your spouse has attained the necessary work credits, you can qualify for premium-free Part A coverage at age 65 (as long as your spouse is at least 62 years old), regardless of whether you've worked yourself.

If you've reached 65 but haven't earned enough Social Security credits, and you don't qualify under a spouse's work credits, this doesn't mean that you can't get Medicare coverage. It just means that you must pay a premium for Part A if you want it. This premium costs up to $458 per month (in 2020). This may sound expensive, but it's a lot less than what it costs to buy the same coverage in the private marketplace. You can get Part B and Part D coverage, regardless of work credits, by paying premiums under the same fee schedule as anyone else. (If you continue to work and build up enough Social Security credits, you can ultimately get Part A without paying the premium out of your own pocket.)

» **You receive Social Security disability benefits.** After 24 months of receiving Social Security Disability Insurance (SSDI), you're eligible for Medicare at any age. (See Chapter 11 for more information on SSDI.)

» **You suffer from certain diseases.** You're eligible for Medicare at any age if you're diagnosed with either of the following two conditions (see `www.medicareresources.org/medicare-eligibility-and-enrollment/medicare-eligibility-for-als-and-esrd-patients/` for more information):

- **Amyotrophic lateral sclerosis (ALS, also known as Lou Gehrig's disease):** You become eligible for Medicare the month you begin collecting Social Security Disability benefits, which is five months after being classified as disabled.

- **End-stage renal (kidney) disease requiring lifetime dialysis or a kidney transplant:** You become eligible for Medicare if you or your spouse has earned enough work credits for Social Security. The number of credits you need depends on your age when the illness began. A child with kidney failure may also qualify for Medicare coverage based on a parent's work credits. Generally, people with end-stage renal disease are not eligible for Medicare Advantage, although this will change in 2021.

Signing Up for Medicare

As your 65th birthday approaches, a giant milestone looms: your entry into the healthcare program for older Americans. That means you have certain decisions to make.

If you're already getting Social Security retirement benefits, the SSA signs you up automatically for the basic services of Medicare — Part A and Part B. If you aren't getting Social Security benefits, you need to apply for Medicare by contacting the SSA at 800-772-1213 (TTY 800-325-0778), ideally three months before your 65th birthday.

Note: If you live in Puerto Rico, enrollment in Part B is *not* automatic.

The SSA also signs you up for Medicare automatically if you've been receiving SSDI benefits for two years.

REMEMBER

You have the right to opt out of Part B instead of being enrolled automatically. But do your homework first, because you could incur penalties later if you change your mind. You can opt out of Part B and join later without penalty if you have group health insurance from an employer for whom you or your spouse is still working (see "Getting Hit with Late Fees," later in this chapter).

Deciding what parts to enroll in

Deciding whether to enroll in Medicare (and if so, which parts) requires a little thought. In this section, I walk you through each of the four parts and give you basic information you can use to make your own decision.

Part A

Just about everyone should sign up for Part A, even if you have other coverage. The only exception is if you're still working and have employer coverage that takes the form of a high-deductible plan paired with a health savings account (HSA). Under Internal Revenue Service (IRS) rules, you can't continue to contribute to an HSA if you're enrolled in Medicare.

Part A requires no premiums if you've paid enough Medicare payroll taxes at work, and you may need it to enroll in other parts of Medicare.

WARNING

If you have to pay premiums for Part A and fail to sign up when you first can, you may have to pay penalties if you want to enroll later.

TIP

If you are covered by health insurance you bought in the individual marketplace (rather than your employer) and are approaching 65, it still may make sense for you to sign up for Medicare when you become eligible during the initial enrollment period in order to avoid risking a future late enrollment penalty for Medicare Part B. In addition, if you stay with the marketplace plan, when your Medicare Part A coverage begins, you will have to pay full price for the plan, and you would no longer be eligible for a premium tax credit or other savings.

REMEMBER

If you have Part A *or* Part B, you become eligible for Part D. Enrollment in Part A *and* Part B is required to join a Medicare Advantage plan.

Part B

You should sign up for Part B at age 65 — *unless* you have health insurance from your own or your spouse's current employment that counts as primary coverage.

Here are certain situations to be aware of:

- **If you have health insurance through your (or your spouse's) job:** If you're covered by a group plan provided by an employer for whom you or your spouse is still working, you should find out how that plan interacts with Medicare.

  If your plan provides *primary coverage,* that means it pays the bills before Medicare; if your plan provides *secondary coverage,* that means Medicare pays the bills first.

  - **If you have primary coverage,** you can hold off on signing up for Part B until the employment or the health coverage ends (whichever comes first). At that point, Medicare gives you up to eight months to sign up for Part B without risking late penalties.
  - **If you have secondary coverage,** go ahead and sign up for Medicare Part B. Your work-related plan may require you to do so, anyway.
- **If you're retired by age 65:** Nobody can force you to sign up for Part B, but if you delay and want to enroll in the future, you'll face serious consequences (see the warning following this list), even if you have retiree health benefits or COBRA coverage that temporarily extends your former employer's plan.
- **If you aren't eligible for premium-free Medicare Part A, either through your own work record or your spouse's:** You're still allowed to enroll in Part B for the same cost as everyone else if you're 65 and a U.S. citizen or you've lived here legally for five years. You can also buy Part A services by paying

monthly premiums. You can enroll either during the initial enrollment period (a window of seven months starting three months before the month you turn 65) or within eight months of losing primary health coverage from your own or your spouse's job. (Otherwise, you face the consequences of failing to enroll, which I explain in the following warning.)

If you miss your deadline to sign up for Part B, you must wait for the general enrollment period that runs from January 1 to March 31. When that happens, your coverage doesn't start until July 1, so you may be uninsured for several months or have to buy expensive private insurance to fill the gap. You also have to pay a late penalty amounting to an extra 10 percent for every full year you delayed enrolling. This surcharge is added to your monthly Part B premiums for all future years.

If you have Part A *or* Part B, you become eligible for Part D. Enrollment in Parts A *and* Part B is required to join a Medicare Advantage plan or to buy Medigap supplemental insurance.

Part C

Medicare Advantage (Part C) plans offer the same benefits as Medicare Part A and Part B, while sometimes including extras. To qualify for a Medicare Advantage plan, you must be enrolled in Medicare Part A and Part B.

Medicare Advantage plans often provide prescription-drug coverage under Part D as well.

You need to choose a plan out of those available in your area. You can compare plans online to find the one that best meets your needs. Assemble a list of any medications you take, and then go to the Medicare website (`www.medicare.gov`), click "Sign Up/Change Plans" and then the "Find health & drug plans" link, and follow the prompts.

In deciding whether to enroll in Medicare Advantage, find out about the details that can affect your wallet: coverage limits, restrictions on choice of healthcare provider, the need for referrals, and out-of-pocket expenses you may face, such as deductibles and cost-sharing such as copays. The same Medicare website also tells you how Medicare rates each plan according to the quality of care it provides.

If you want to keep your current doctors, ask them which Medicare Advantage plans they accept before you sign up.

Part D

You can get prescription-drug coverage through a stand-alone Part D plan or a Medicare Advantage plan that already provides drug coverage (as most, but not all, Medicare Advantage plans do). To qualify for Part D, you have to be enrolled in Part A *or* Part B. You may *not* be enrolled in both a stand-alone drug plan *and* a Medicare Advantage plan that provides Part D coverage.

REMEMBER

Whether you should sign up for Part D may depend on a few things, including whether you already have what Medicare calls "creditable" drug coverage. *Creditable coverage* is defined as at least equal to the basic benefits required for Medicare Part D. (Your current plan must advise you on whether the coverage is creditable. If it is, you should get that answer in writing and save it.)

If you lack creditable coverage, it makes sense to sign up for Part D since you will face a late-enrollment penalty if you wait and sign up later. If you have alternative creditable coverage, however, you don't need Part D.

If you lose creditable coverage, you have a special enrollment period of two months to join a plan without penalty. If you voluntarily drop creditable coverage, you can sign up only during open enrollment (October 15 to December 7).

REMEMBER

You have various things to consider in selecting a Part D plan that's right for you. Most important, required cost-sharing may vary greatly among plans, even for the same drug. Also, premium cost, choice of pharmacies, and availability of mail-order services may differ in ways that matter to you.

TIP

If you already have drug coverage through an employer plan that also offers medical benefits, check with your plan administrator to find out the consequences of signing up for Part D, such as whether it jeopardizes your medical benefits. You need that information to make the right choice. (Joining a Part D plan doesn't automatically affect employer medical benefits. But dropping employer prescription-drug coverage could jeopardize benefits if drugs and medical benefits are part of the same package.)

If Part D is right for you, according to your own circumstances, you need to know when you can sign up and the penalties you may incur if you don't enroll at the right time (see "Keeping track of the enrollment periods" and "Getting Hit with Late Fees," later in this chapter).

Keeping track of the enrollment periods

You may sign up for the various parts of Medicare during one of several enrollment windows, depending on your personal circumstances:

- **Initial enrollment period:** This period runs for seven months around the time you turn 65. It's the window you should use to sign up for Parts A and B — unless you'll be covered, beyond 65, by primary health insurance from your own or your spouse's current employer.

  The initial period begins three months before the month you turn 65 and extends three months past the month of your birthday. (Say you turn 65 on August 15. In this case, the enrollment period begins May 1 and ends November 30.) If you're already receiving Social Security benefits, you're enrolled in Parts A and B automatically. Otherwise, you need to apply, as I explain in the next section.

  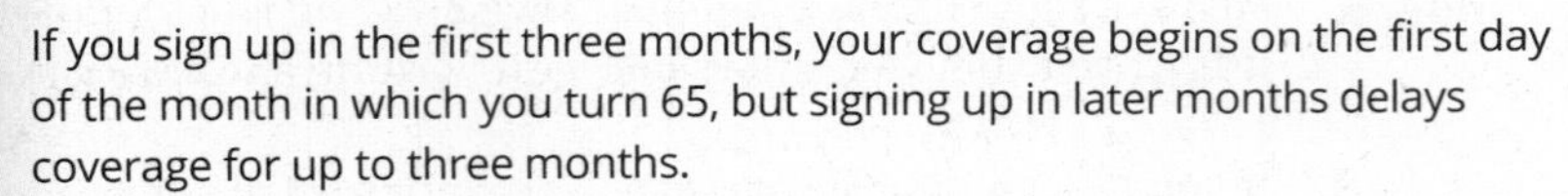
  If you sign up in the first three months, your coverage begins on the first day of the month in which you turn 65, but signing up in later months delays coverage for up to three months.

  Note: Medicare has a different initial enrollment period for people younger than 65 who qualify through disability. Generally, you must get disability benefits for two years before qualifying for Medicare benefits. In this case, the initial enrollment period is seven months long, starting three months before the month in which you receive your 25th monthly payment.

- **Special enrollment period for older workers:** If you're beyond age 65 and covered by a group health plan provided by an employer for whom you or your spouse is still working, you're entitled to delay Part B until the employment ceases (as I explain earlier in this chapter). At that point, you get a special enrollment period of eight months to enroll in Part B without penalty, but you can (and should) do so earlier to avoid a break in coverage.

  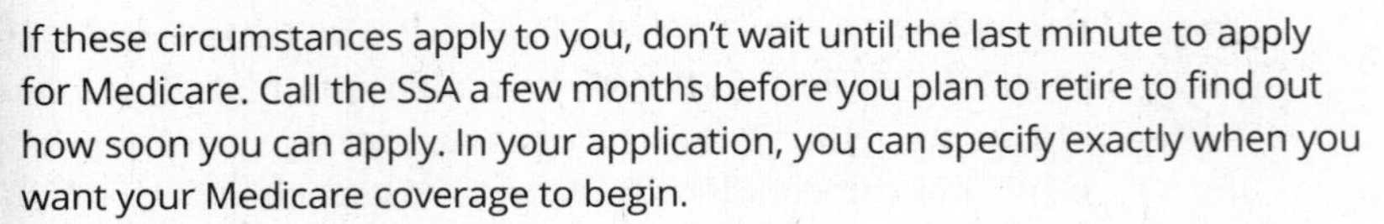
  If these circumstances apply to you, don't wait until the last minute to apply for Medicare. Call the SSA a few months before you plan to retire to find out how soon you can apply. In your application, you can specify exactly when you want your Medicare coverage to begin.

- **General enrollment period:** If you miss your deadline to sign up for Part B — at either the end of the initial enrollment period or the end of the eight-month special enrollment period granted to people with employer coverage — you can sign up *only* during a general enrollment period, which runs from January 1 to March 31 each year. In this case, your coverage begins July 1, and you may get permanent late penalties.

- **Open enrollment period to switch plans:** This seven-week period, from October 15 to December 7 each year, gives you the opportunity to make changes in your coverage — from traditional Medicare to a Medicare Advantage plan, and vice versa; from one Medicare Advantage plan to another; or from one Part D plan to another. If you make any of these switches, your new coverage begins January 1. This period also allows people to sign up for Part D if they missed their deadline earlier.

- **Special enrollment period for people working abroad and international volunteers:** If you work abroad and have health insurance from either your own or your spouse's employer or from the national health program of the foreign country where you live, you're entitled to a special enrollment period of up to eight months to sign up for Medicare without penalty when that employment ends. The same applies if you do voluntary service for at least 12 months overseas through a program sponsored by a tax-exempt organization that provides health coverage.
- **Medicare Advantage open enrollment period to switch or leave Part C plans:** You're allowed to leave a Medicare Advantage plan and switch to traditional Medicare, or switch from one Medicare Advantage plan to another, each year from January 1 through March 31. If your new Medicare Advantage plan doesn't have prescription drug coverage, you may also switch into a Part D plan during this same window.
- **Special enrollment periods for Part C and Part D:** Under certain circumstances, you may be able to sign up for Part C and Part D outside the usual windows. These include if you move out of the plan's service area or if the plan closes down. You can switch Part C and Part D plans at any time of the year if you move into or out of a long-term-care facility, become eligible for Medicaid, or qualify for special assistance with prescription drugs under the Extra Help program.

TECHNICAL STUFF

People who live abroad — without coverage while working or volunteering, as I explain earlier — or are in prison are expected to pay the Part B premium during their time overseas or while incarcerated, or they face permanent penalties when they return or are released. (This rule applies even though they can't use Medicare services abroad or in prison.)

Here are a couple of circumstances involving Part D that bear mentioning:

- **If you drop or lose a different prescription-drug benefit:** Suppose you drop or lose another drug plan that has been provided by an employer, a union, or a retiree plan. If you choose to quit your drug plan, you can sign up for Part D between October 15 and December 7. (You're expected to maintain coverage until that open enrollment period.) If you lose coverage — say, the plan is terminated — you have 63 days to start Part D coverage without getting a late penalty. The 63-day period starts either the day you get notice or the day your coverage ends, whichever comes later.
- **If you return to the United States or are released from prison:** You may turn 65 while abroad or incarcerated. If so, you have a seven-month initial enrollment period for Part D. The initial enrollment period begins three months before the month of your return or release and lasts three months

after it. If you reached your 65th birthday before you left the United States or went to prison, you get a special enrollment period of 63 days after your return or release to start Part D coverage without penalty.

TIP

The Centers for Medicare and Medicaid Services provides a useful summary of the various enrollment situations in Medicare, which you can find by going to www.medicare.gov/Publications/Search/Results.asp, and typing in the keyword 11219.

Knowing your options for applying for Medicare

You can apply for Medicare Part A and Part B online at www.ssa.gov/medicareonly, over the phone at 800-772-1213 (TTY 800-325-0778), or in person at your local SSA office. Applying for Medicare is a simpler process than applying for certain other benefits under Social Security. Generally, all you need to provide is your name, Social Security number, gender, and date of birth. (If you're applying for Part B beyond age 65 because you've had coverage from your own or your spouse's employer, you can't enroll online, and you need to provide proof and dates of that employer insurance.)

To enroll in a Medicare Advantage plan (Part C) or a prescription-drug plan (Part D), go to the Medicare website (www.medicare.gov), call the Medicare help line at 800-633-4227 (TTY 877-486-2048), or call the plan administrator directly.

TIP

If you have questions about applying for Medicare, such as when to start benefits and whether you need Part B, don't start online. Instead, call the SSA or go to a local field office. You can find out much more by dealing directly with an SSA representative than you can through the online application.

TIP

If you have limited ability with English, the SSA provides a translator to help you enroll in Medicare. You or a relative can request this, either over the phone or by visiting an SSA field office.

Paying Premiums

If you receive Social Security benefits (disability or retirement) and you're eligible for Medicare, the Part B premium is deducted monthly from your Social Security payment. If you don't receive Social Security benefits, Medicare bills you directly, three months at a time.

PAYING EXTRA IF YOUR INCOME IS HIGH

Medicare charges upper-income beneficiaries more for premiums in Part B (medical services) and Part D (prescription drugs). Only about 7 percent of beneficiaries are affected by these surcharges.

Medicare determines whether you owe a surcharge based on your modified adjusted gross income (MAGI), as shown on your latest tax return. MAGI is the sum of your adjusted gross income (AGI) and your tax-exempt interest income (both listed on IRS Form 1040).

The surcharges apply to individuals with MAGI above $87,000 and couples above $174,000. (The SSA looks at your past tax filings — up to a three-year lag — to determine whether you have to pay extra for Part B.) Medicare applies a similar approach to Part D.

To see the latest surcharge amounts in Part B and Part D for specified MAGIs, take a look at the factsheet "Medicare Premiums: Rules For Higher-Income Beneficiaries" at `www.mhaven.net/Docs/Medicare%20Premiums.pdf`.

Added costs can be steep (pushing up monthly premiums for the highest incomes as high as $491.60 for Part B and imposing a surcharge of up to $76.40 for Part D in 2020), but you can request a reassessment under certain circumstances, such as when the SSA is relying on outdated information about your income. For example, if you or your spouse cut back on working or stopped altogether, your income may have fallen significantly, and it's possible that you no longer have to pay a surcharge. Other life events that cause your income to plunge, such as a divorce, may also be reason for the SSA to amend your premium or even give you a rebate.

Tell the SSA if you've filed an amended tax return or your income falls. You can request an adjustment in your Part B premium using Form SSA-44, Medicare Part B Income-Related Premium — Life-Changing Event (`www.ssdfacts.com/forms/SSA-44.pdf`). It's possible that the SSA will adjust your premium based on the documented proof you provide. If you disagree, you should file a request for reconsideration (Form SSA-561-U2; `www.ssa.gov/forms/ssa-561.pdf`) and be prepared to document your case, such as with recent tax information. For more information, call the SSA at 800-772-1213 (TTY 800-325-0778).

You have different payment choices for Part C and Part D plans. (Automatic deduction from Social Security is one of them.) Just choose among the available options, and state your preferred method of payment when you first join a plan.

Getting Hit with Late Fees

Medicare has a simple way of encouraging you to enroll on time for Part B or Part D: It charges you extra money if you delay (a responsibility handled by the SSA). The longer you miss the deadline, the heftier the penalty. Like all insurance, Medicare needs the enrollment of healthier and younger people to keep it sustainable and affordable. If everyone waited until he or she became sick to enroll, the program would collapse. Just remember that these fees really add up, so you should avoid them if at all possible.

Part A

If you're eligible for premium-free Part A because you paid enough in payroll taxes at work, no penalties are applied to Part A even if you sign up late. But what if you don't qualify for Part A services without paying premiums for them, and you miss your enrollment deadline? In this case, after you finally sign up, you pay an extra 10 percent on top of the Part A premium for twice the number of years you were eligible for Part A.

Part B

You may sign up for Part B (and Part A for that matter) with no penalty after your initial enrollment period if you're still working and covered by a group plan through your employer or union, or if your working spouse has such coverage that includes you. In such cases, you're given a special eight-month enrollment period that begins the month you or your spouse stops work or loses employer health coverage.

But if you're already retired when you turn 65 (or when you're just about to), you could pay a penalty under certain circumstances, even if you have retiree health benefits from your former employer or union. You get a penalty if your initial seven-month enrollment period after you reach 65 has expired *and* more than 12 months have elapsed between the end of that initial enrollment period and the end of the general enrollment period in which you sign up.

In an important policy change, people who are in same-sex marriages and who have health benefits through their spouse's job-related coverage are now entitled to the eight-month special enrollment period. Therefore, they may now delay enrolling in Part B beyond the initial enrollment period without penalty (provided other requirements are met).

After you miss your initial seven-month enrollment period to sign up for Part B, you run the risk of a 10 percent penalty, unless you're entitled to enroll in a special enrollment period. Each year that passes costs you another 10 percent. For example, if you delay five years, you pay 50 percent more for the same coverage.

If you're over 65, this penalty continues for all future years. If you incur the penalty when you're under 65, it ceases when you turn 65 and become eligible for Medicare on the basis of age rather than disability.

REMEMBER

If your deadline for enrolling in Part B has passed, your next opportunity to sign up comes during the yearly enrollment window that runs from January 1 to March 31, and your coverage won't begin until the following July 1. In some circumstances, this means going without coverage for several months — an even more significant concern than the financial penalty.

TIP

You can get an estimate of the penalty you face for late enrollment in Part B at `www.medicare.gov/eligibilitypremiumcalc`. But always view calculators with caution, because they may miss the nuances of your personal situation.

Part C

Although Medicare Advantage plans have no enrollment deadlines, many offer prescription-drug coverage under Part D. If you enroll in such a Medicare Advantage plan but miss the Part D deadline, you get a late penalty for Part D (see the next section).

Part D

The size of the penalty for late sign-up varies based on how many months you had neither Part D coverage nor creditable coverage from elsewhere (such as a retiree plan) after turning 65. The penalty comes to about 1 percent of the national average Part D premium multiplied by the number of months you went without coverage. (A full year comes to 12 percent.)

For example, the national average Part D premium for 2020 was about $33. So, if you signed up that year but had delayed five years, your surcharge would be about

$33 multiplied by 0.6 (0.01 multiplied by 60), which equals $19.80 per month, or $237.60 per year. If the national average premium goes up, so does the penalty.

Missing a deadline can be costly because the surcharge is permanently added to your plan's premiums for all future years.

TIP

Say you don't need much in the way of prescriptions right now. You can avoid a late-enrollment penalty for Part D by signing up for the Part D plan that has the lowest premium in your area when you're first eligible. Later, if you need different coverage, you can switch to another plan that better meets your specific needs during the annual open enrollment period (October 15 to December 7).

REMEMBER

Lower premiums don't necessarily mean poorer coverage, and high premiums don't necessarily mean better coverage. Plans with the highest quality rating (earning the maximum five stars) tend to be in the middle range of premiums. The specific drugs you take — not the premiums — have the most effect on your out-of-pocket costs.

Buying Extra Insurance: Medigap

You may buy private insurance to help cover some or most of your out-of-pocket expenses in traditional Medicare, such as Part B copays and hospital deductibles. Such insurance is called *Medicare supplemental* or *Medigap*. It comes in different standardized packages, and you pay a premium (on top of your Part B premium).

Some policies cover more than others. Each of the ten standard packages is labeled with a letter — A, B, C, D, F, G, K, L, M, or N. (The missing letters belonged to Medigap policies that have been eliminated. Plans C and F have been eliminated for those enrolling after January 1, 2020.) The better the coverage, the more you usually have to pay.

REMEMBER

Insurers charge different premiums based on various factors, even though each lettered Medigap policy is standardized by law and must offer the same benefits as another policy of the same letter.

You may not purchase a Medigap policy if you're enrolled in a Medicare Advantage plan. Here are other issues to keep in mind:

- **If you want to buy Medigap insurance and you're at least 65, the best time to do so is within six months of enrolling in Part B because you get important federal protections.** In this time frame, an insurer can't charge you more (or reject you) for past or current health problems.

» **The protections I describe earlier (against extra charges or refusal of coverage because of health problems) may apply in certain other situations.** These include if you're enrolled in a Medicare Advantage plan that shuts down or you move out of its service area. In addition, you may be assured of Medigap coverage for your preexisting condition if you lose employer health coverage, COBRA, or retiree benefits that provide secondary coverage to Medicare. In such cases, you have about two months to buy a Medigap policy.

» **If you're younger than 65 and enrolled in Medicare, the federal protections I describe earlier do *not* apply.** But some state laws give similar protections — check with your state department of insurance.

» **Generally, Medigap won't cover your out-of-pocket costs for outpatient prescription drugs.** The exception is for people who are still enrolled in H, I, or J Medigap policies that they bought before 2006. These can no longer be sold and don't count as creditable coverage.

REMEMBER

Some people confuse Medigap with Medicare Advantage. They're entirely different:

» Medigap is supplemental insurance coverage you can buy to cover certain out-of-pocket expenses if you're enrolled in the traditional Medicare program. Premiums and coverage vary, according to the plan you pick.

» Medicare Advantage refers to an assortment of private health plans that provide an alternative way of receiving Medicare benefits.

TIP

To find out more about Medigap, go to `www.medicare.gov` and under the heading "Supplements & Other Insurance," click the drop-down arrow to find "How to compare Medigap policies." Doing so will lead you to a page with lots of information about coverage choices and enrollment details. You can also find a wealth of information in the Medicare publication "Choosing a Medigap Policy: A Guide to Health Insurance for People with Medicare." For a free copy, call 800-633-4227 (TTY 877-486-2048).

Getting Financial Help If You Need It

You have several options to pursue if your income is low and you can't afford the care you need. They include those I describe in this section.

Extra Help for Part D

This program provides low-cost drug coverage — reduced or no premiums and deductibles, low cost-sharing, and coverage throughout the year (no doughnut hole) — for people with limited incomes who qualify. You have to be enrolled in a Part D plan (or a Medicare Advantage plan that offers drug coverage) to receive Extra Help.

You can apply through the SSA over the phone, at your local office, or online. Find information at www.ssa.gov/medicare/prescriptionhelp/forms.html.

Medicaid

This is the federal-state healthcare program for people with very low incomes. Importantly, Medicaid covers long-term care, which Medicare doesn't cover. Eligibility rules vary among the states, although income requirements are strict everywhere. You can find more information about Medicaid in your state by going to medicaiddirectors.org or www.medicaid.gov/index.html and clicking on the "Medicaid" menu at the top of the page.

Medicare savings programs

These state-run programs provide help with premiums for Part A and Part B, as well as certain out-of-pocket costs. They're for people with little money, and they impose strict limits on income and assets. (Specifics vary by the type of benefit and the state you live in.) If your Part B premiums are paid by your state, you're automatically eligible for the Extra Help program.

You can find contact information for the Medicare savings programs in your state at www.medicare.gov/Contacts/#resources/msps.

Pharmaceutical assistance programs

These programs are aid efforts run by drug companies. To find out whether you may qualify for help based on your ability to pay and the medication you take, go to www.medicare.gov/pharmaceutical-assistance-program.

Programs of All-Inclusive Care for the Elderly

Programs of All-Inclusive Care for the Elderly (PACE) is a federal program that tries to help people stay in the community rather than move into a nursing home. You have to be 55 or older and have a chronic condition that requires an institutional level of care. These programs provide valuable benefits but aren't available everywhere.

TIP

You can find out more by reading the fact sheet at www.medicare.gov/your-medicare-costs/get-help-paying-costs/pace or by going to www.npaonline.org for a link to PACE programs by state.

State pharmaceutical assistance programs

You can find out whether your state offers help with the cost of medications at www.medicare.gov/pharmaceutical-assistance-program/state-programs.aspx.

State health insurance assistance programs

These programs, known as SHIPs, provide free, personal guidance from trained counselors on all Medicare and Medicaid issues. You can get help reviewing your Medicare options and finding a Medicare Advantage plan that meets your needs and preferences. To find contact information for your state, go to www.shiptacenter.org/.

IN THIS CHAPTER

» Understanding the Social Security earnings test

» Going back to work after you've retired

» Getting special advice if you're self-employed

» Paying taxes on your retirement benefit

Chapter 13

Working in "Retirement"

Once upon a time, work and retirement meant two different stages of life. You worked until you got older, and then one day your employer gave you a little keepsake and you walked out the door. Forever. But as you know, those days are gone.

If you're a Baby Boomer or Gen Xer, work may be part of your life beyond what people once thought of as retirement age. If you like to work and have decent choices, you're ahead of the game. Work can be healthy and rewarding on many levels. But millions of other people are hanging in there for the simple reason that they need the money. Work is becoming an increasingly important fact of life for older Americans. And that raises a question as you approach age 62: Does it make sense to work *and* collect Social Security retirement benefits?

In this chapter, I talk about how working later in life meshes with Social Security and the trade-offs you face. If you're an older worker, you need to approach Social Security with care. You may have good reason to work and collect Social Security benefits, but you should keep certain things in mind. Be aware that benefits are reduced significantly — and permanently — if you take them much before your full retirement age. For that reason it may make sense to wait (as late as age 70) if you can and rely on income from work and savings to get by in the interim.

Working longer to replace enough years of weak earnings (perhaps from when you were young or unemployed) with later years of strong earnings may also increase your Social Security benefit. But the exact impact varies, and it may not be significant.

You should also be aware of Social Security's annual earnings limit for those who claim retirement benefits, a rule that may significantly reduce your benefit payments if you collect them in early retirement (although the withholding is made up after you reach full retirement age). This chapter goes over how the Social Security earnings test works, what it could mean for you and your dependents, and why it was created. I also explain what kinds of income you don't have to worry about.

REMEMBER

Unless you're really set financially, it can make a lot of sense to work later in life if you have the option. I don't want to make work sound easier than it is or exaggerate the availability of good jobs. But be realistic about your financial realities. Whatever you decide, it's important to know how Social Security and work fit together to meet the individual needs of your household.

The Pros and Cons of Not Retiring at Retirement Age

Suppose early retirement isn't for you. You're not ready for Social Security, and you want a few more years of a steady paycheck to make sure that you'll end up with the lifestyle you want in retirement. You have skills to offer, and you know how to be a good worker.

By taking this path, you potentially bolster your resources for the long term and win a bounty of peace of mind down the road, when you finally do choose to stop working. At this point, you have a clear sense of how your wages can fit into a life plan. You may be following a smart, forward-looking strategy. You probably have more opportunity to save than when you were younger, and you may be less inclined to waste money on forgettable purchases. The future is getting a lot closer, and you're thinking about it. But be prepared — being an older worker isn't always a picnic.

Facing the challenges of working later in life

Older workers sometimes run into obstacles that make it a lot harder to earn a living, and there's no point in denying it. If none of these challenges comes your way and your path turns out to be a breeze, all the better. I cover some of the possible challenges in the following sections.

Age discrimination

Age discrimination is a lurking, often subtle reality in many workplaces. Employers may see older workers as costly because of healthcare costs and wages. They may view you as wary of new technology, or they may assume you're ignorant about it.

In a weak economy, companies often offer buyouts to cut costs, a perfectly legal strategy. But older workers may feel that if they don't grab a buyout, they'll get pushed out the door anyway, with no payoff.

Older job applicants sometimes complain that potential employers rule them out as "overqualified" or as not likely to stay in their jobs very long. When an older worker is laid off, it takes much longer to find a new job than it takes a younger worker to find one. According to the Equal Employment Opportunity Commission (EEOC), three in five workers have seen or experienced age discrimination in the workplace. It appears in three main areas: recruitment and hiring, when younger applicants are shown favor due simply to their age; on-the-job bias, when older workers are harassed or get fewer training opportunities, promotions, or rewards; and termination, when a company "freshens" its workforce or trims its budget by targeting senior employees.

Unexpected events

Surveys of retirees have found that 40 percent or even more feel that they were forced to retire before they expected to. Older individuals cite various reasons that they hang it up earlier than planned, including layoffs, a company (or job) relocation, an employer going out of business, and reduced demand for their skills.

Health problems

Chronic health issues become more common the older you get. Among people over 50, for example, four out of five have at least one chronic health condition. That's more than 70 million people. Moreover, older workers may face a difficult conflict between the demands of the workplace and caregiving for an ailing spouse.

An unsteady job market

Your ambition to stay in the workforce may be rewarded with a job that is below your expectations. You may like your current job, but you may not be able to keep it. On top of that, continual restructuring by U.S. businesses adds instability to many jobs. New technologies, changes in management priorities, or an economic downturn can all heighten job pressures and prompt an unexpected layoff.

Youthful co-workers

You may face a big age gap between yourself and your colleagues, some of whom may be young enough to be your children. Perhaps some of these "kids" make more money than you do and have more influence. Maybe one of them writes your performance review. You have to deal with it. And don't forget that your youthful boss may feel awkward about giving you orders or criticizing your work.

REMEMBER

As an older worker, use your maturity to keep relations easygoing and stress free. Your experience in dealing with others is an asset.

Reaping the benefits of working later in life

So much for the challenges. You may have very good reasons to persevere in the working world. You could push up your monthly retirement income by 25 percent if you retire at 66 instead of 62, according to scholars at the Center for Retirement Research at Boston College. In large part, the reason is that your Social Security benefit grows if you delay taking it. In addition, you strengthen your long-term security by adding to your nest egg and reducing the length of retirement you have to finance.

Working later in life can help you in other ways, too. Here are some of the reasons, in addition to the incentives provided by Social Security:

- **Health insurance:** Many employers offer health insurance, which can add up to thousands of dollars in annual benefits.
- **Workplace savings programs:** If your employer offers a 401(k), you may benefit from some matching contributions, which build savings. If you're over 50, you can make your own catch-up contributions to a 401(k) ($6,500 in 2020). If your employer offers no plan and you can set aside some money, you should put as much as possible into an individual retirement account (IRA). In 2020, a $1,000 catch-up was allowed for traditional IRAs beyond the $6,000 maximum contribution, or $7,000 if you're age 50 or older.
- **Opportunity to save:** For many people in their late 50s and 60s, the kids are out of the nest, the house is paid off, and the medical expenses that may be in store when you're older haven't hit yet. If you're in this fortunate position, you have a window of opportunity to plow as much of your wages into savings as you possibly can to prepare for the long haul.
- **The chance to wipe out debt:** Maybe you still have maxed-out credit cards and a big mortgage. If so, you don't need me to tell you how important your wages are. By preserving that income for a few extra years into your mid-60s or even beyond, you can pay down your debt and strengthen your finances.

The Earnings Test: How Your Payments Are Calculated When You Work

Social Security has an *annual earnings limit,* a rule that may significantly reduce your benefit payments if you collect them in early retirement (although the withholding is made up after you reach full retirement age — that is, once a person reaches full retirement age, the monthly payment increases accordingly).

The annual earnings limit may apply only if you're collecting Social Security benefits and haven't yet reached full retirement age (currently 66 and two months, gradually increasing to 67). This rule may also hit spouses as well as widows, widowers, and others getting survivor benefits. After you reach your full retirement age, the earnings limit vanishes. Then you can earn as much as possible, and the Social Security Administration (SSA) doesn't care.

I discuss a different restriction on earnings that affects disability benefits in Chapter 11.

How the earnings limit works

Here's how the basic earnings limit works: If you get benefits before you reach your full retirement age and you also earn money, the SSA generally reduces your benefit by $1 for every $2 you earn above a certain amount. The amount typically goes up every year; it was set at $18,240 in 2020. The limit eases for the year you reach full retirement age. In that year, the SSA withholds $1 for every $3 you earn over the limit. The cap on earnings while also receiving retirement benefits typically goes up annually; in 2020, it was $48,600.

When you reach full retirement age, your earnings no longer affect your benefits. Starting with your birthday month, the income is no longer a concern. Say your birthday is May 18. The SSA considers your earnings only through the month of April in determining whether you exceed the limit.

TIP

If you're working and getting Social Security, contact the SSA at the start of the year you reach full retirement age. Because less money is withheld from your benefit that year, it's possible that the SSA won't have to withhold anything (depending on how much you earn and your date of birth).

The withholding works like this: Suppose it appears, based on the information the SSA has, that your wages for the year will exceed the earnings limit. If so, the SSA takes the money in excess of the limit by withholding entire monthly payments until you've paid up. Suppose you earn enough to trigger $3,000 of withholding ($6,000 in earnings above the limit, divided by two). Now suppose your monthly

Social Security benefit is $1,000. The SSA may hold back each of your $1,000 payments for January, February, and March to get $3,000 and meet the requirement. Your benefits then resume in April.

You can sometimes meet the withholding requirement by spreading it over a year rather than giving up entire monthly payments. This is called *prorating*. You may qualify for prorating if you don't owe the SSA money from receiving an overpayment. If you want to prorate the withholding into June of the following year, you have to explain that it's needed to avoid financial hardship or that it disrupts your retirement plans.

Here's an example: Elena, 64, plans to begin her Social Security benefits in January and qualifies for a payment of $1,500 per month, which comes to $18,000 per year. Elena's employer values her graphic-design skills and makes her an unexpected offer to stay — $40,000 to continue working for another year on a reduced weekly schedule. Elena wants to know, however, whether working would affect her Social Security benefit. If the earnings limit is $18,240, that means her $40,000 in income would put her $21,760 above the cap. The SSA withholds $1 for every $2 over the limit, which in this case comes to half of $21,760, or $10,880. After withholding, Elena's Social Security benefit for the year would total $7,120. She'll ultimately get back that withholding after she starts benefits at her full retirement age. But unfortunately, by starting her Social Security at 64, Elena's benefit is reduced by about 14 percent — permanently — because of the normal reduction for starting benefits before full retirement age. Elena is glad she ran the numbers, because they make it clear that in her case, it makes more sense to take the good offer and start Social Security benefits later.

Suppose for a moment that Elena would earn less money at work. How does that change the equation?

Say Elena's employer offers her $22,000 for the year. In this case, her pay would put her $3,760 over the $18,240 cap. The SSA would withhold half of the $3,760, or a total of $1,880. Elena considers her modest living expenses and the fact that she doesn't have much other income. She believes that her employer may be willing to keep giving her work for a few more years. She also knows that she'll get the withheld money added on to her Social Security benefit in a couple of years, when she reaches her full retirement age of 66 years and 2 months. Elena decides to collect Social Security, continue working, and accept the fact that she has a lower benefit until she reaches full retirement age. The SSA withholds Elena's entire January payment of $1,500 and just $380 of the February payment to recover the $1,880 of earnings over the limit. Before that happened, Elena could have asked the SSA in writing to prorate the deductions over the course of the year, to spread them out and make each one smaller. But she decided to get it over with and resume her full Social Security payment in March.

These examples illustrate the earnings limit for work performed in the years *before* you reach full retirement age. But the rule is different if you work during the year in which you reach full retirement age.

In the year you reach full retirement age, the SSA withholds $1 in benefits for every $3 you earn above a higher cap. In 2020, the cap on your earnings is $48,600, but the SSA counts only earnings before the month you reach your full retirement age. Beginning with your birthday month, the withholding rule no longer applies.

How exceeding the limit may cost your family

Be aware that if you bust the earnings limit, the SSA may withhold not only your benefits but also the benefits of a dependent, such as your spouse. In such cases, dependents' benefits are withheld in proportion to their share of the family's total benefits. This can temporarily wipe out everyone's benefits.

Say Melissa gets $900 per month in Social Security retirement benefits. She's still working at age 63 as a retail-store manager and anticipates $2,000 in earnings above the limit. Melissa's husband, Bryan, is collecting a spousal benefit of $450 per month. The SSA withholds money from each of them, because Bryan's benefit is based on his wife's earnings record. For one month, the SSA withholds each of their payments completely — $900 from Melissa and $450 from Bryan, for a total of $1,350. But the SSA still wants to withhold another $650 to recover the full $2,000. It does so in proportion to each spouse's share of the total benefits paid to the family. So, the following month, the SSA withholds $433 from Melissa and $217 from Bryan to get the $650. At this point, the couple has satisfied the withholding requirement. For the rest of the year, each gets his or her normal monthly benefits.

If a lower-earning spouse exceeds the earnings limit, based on benefits collected through that spouse's own work record, the SSA withholds benefits from that individual — but not from the breadwinner or from any other relative who may be dependent on the breadwinner.

Take the example of Bryan and Melissa. If Bryan earns a lot of money and exceeds the limit, the SSA withholds only his benefits from him and does not reduce Melissa's benefits. That's because Melissa's benefits are based on her own earnings record.

Table 13-1 shows exempt amounts that workers are allowed to earn while also collecting Social Security benefits. The amounts change periodically. The higher amount applies to the year in which you reach full retirement age.

TABLE 13-1 **Annual Retirement Earnings Test Exempt Amounts**

Year	Lower Amount [1]	Higher Amount [2]
2000	$10,080	$17,000
2001	$10,680	$25,000
2002	$11,280	$30,000
2003	$11,520	$30,720
2004	$11,640	$31,080
2005	$12,000	$31,800
2006	$12,480	$33,240
2007	$12,960	$34,440
2008	$13,560	$36,120
2009	$14,160	$37,680
2010	$14,160	$37,680
2011	$14,160	$37,680
2012	$14,640	$38,880
2013	$15,120	$40,080
2014	$15,480	$41,400
2015	$15,720	$41,880
2016	$15,720	$41.880
2017	$16,920	$44,880
2018	$17,040	$45,360
2019	$17,640	$46,920
2020	$18,240	$48,600

[1] *Applies in years before the year of attaining full retirement age.*

[2] *Applies in the year of attaining full retirement age, for months prior to such attainment.*

Source: Social Security Administration (`www.ssa.gov/oact/cola/rtea.html`)

How the earnings test affects benefits

If you earn above a certain amount and haven't reached your full retirement age, the SSA withholds benefits. Table 13-2 provides examples of the impact of that earnings test for different levels of benefits and earnings.

TABLE 13-2 For People Younger than Full Retirement Age during the Whole Year (2020)

If Your Monthly Social Security Benefit Is . . .	And You Earn . . .	You Receive Yearly Benefits of . . .
$700	$18,240 or less	$8,400
$700	$20,000	$7,520
$700	$22,000	$6,520
$900	$18,240 or less	$10,800
$900	$20,000	$9,920
$900	$22,000	$8,920
$1,100	$18,240 or less	$13,200
$1,100	$20,000	$12,320
$1,100	$22,000	$11,320

Source: Social Security Administration (`www.ssa.gov/pubs/10069.html`)

Getting a break for your first months of retirement

If you earn enough money and begin collecting benefits during the year, the SSA could withhold *all* your benefits to satisfy the earnings rule. To avoid that kind of situation, the SSA allows for a special monthly earnings limit, typically used during the first year of collecting benefits. This exception allows you to collect your full benefit, as long as it's greater than your monthly income.

Say your annual salary puts you $14,000 over the annual limit, and you want to begin collecting Social Security in October. Now suppose your Social Security benefit is $2,000 per month. You would collect $6,000 in Social Security for the final three months of the year. But without this special provision, you could end up with zero benefits — the SSA could withhold half of the $14,000, which is a larger number than your Social Security benefits of $6,000. The special monthly rule would save you, though. Under the rule, the SSA may consider whether your earnings fall below a monthly cap, which is calculated as $\frac{1}{12}$ of the annual limit. In other words, if the annual cap is $18,240, the monthly cap is $1,520.

BEING PENALIZED FOR WORKING

Why does the SSA care if you work while getting retirement benefits? Isn't it a good thing if older people take the initiative to earn some money for their own well-being? What business does the SSA have holding back one penny of the benefit you earned just because you continue to work?

Many people ask these questions when they first hear about the Social Security earnings test. The answer is that Social Security retirement benefits were designed to help cover *retirement.* They were approved as a way to help people live out what time they had left with dignity and financial independence. Social Security benefits weren't intended to supplement work. To some early supporters, Social Security also established an incentive to retire. When Social Security was created in the 1930s, unemployment was skyrocketing. One of the ideas behind the new retirement benefits was that helping older workers move on would open up job opportunities for desperate young people.

In the early 20th century, work was different than it is today. More jobs required physical labor. Health and safety standards were weaker, if they existed at all. Older workers would cling to dangerous and grueling jobs because they had no other way to support themselves.

Withholding of Social Security benefits through an earnings test made work somewhat less appealing and gave workers a reason to retire completely or to hold off collecting benefits. It's important to remember that a worker's benefits aren't truly reduced on a lifetime basis. Later, you get the money back through a higher monthly payment.

Nonetheless, many people have long argued that the earnings limit is unfair. The first earnings test, which was included in the original Social Security Act, was much stiffer than today's. It applied to all workers, no matter how old they were, and to all earnings. Congress gradually eased it over the years. In 1950, lawmakers agreed to exempt beneficiaries age 75 and older (effective 1951). Congress later reduced the age to 72 (effective 1955), to 70 (effective 1983), and to full retirement age in 2000 (65 at the time), as part of the Senior Citizens' Freedom to Work Act. That law left the limit in place for early retirees. It means that you can earn all you want after you reach full retirement age, without the SSA withholding any of your benefits.

Lawmakers considered getting rid of the cap altogether. But they decided that eliminating it may encourage more people to start collecting Social Security early at reduced payment levels, which wouldn't be a good thing when many older Americans are feeling the squeeze of limited retirement income.

Now say you're earning $14,000 over the limit before retiring at the end of September. But you decide that leaving the workforce cold turkey is too extreme, and you land a part-time job that pays $1,000 per month. Your new monthly earnings are below the SSA's monthly cap of $1,520, so you're able to get your monthly Social Security payment of $2,000 with no withholding for earnings. (Self-employed individuals are expected to work less than 45 hours per month to qualify under the special monthly rule, or less than 15 hours if they're in a highly skilled occupation.)

What if you earn more each month? You could be out of luck. Say your employer lets you negotiate a phased retirement plan, in which you gradually ratchet down your hours and wages. Suppose your annual salary goes down from about $28,000 to $20,000. Now you take home about $1,670 per month. In this case, you still exceed the monthly cap by $150 (that is, $1,670 minus $1,520). As a result, the SSA withholds your payments for each month you work while collecting benefits. Your choices aren't great in this situation. You can negotiate a lower salary, or you can wait until the SSA makes up the money in the future. For example, if your monthly pay is $1,100 — which is under the SSA's monthly ceiling — your benefits flow in without the extra withholding. In any case, the SSA applies the annual limit the following year. You receive those lost monthly benefits after you reach full retirement age.

If you're using the monthly earnings test and for certain months you don't exceed the monthly cap, the SSA won't withhold anything for those months. This generally can happen only in one year, which the SSA calls the *grace year,* and it's typically the year you retire. After the grace year, if your annual earnings trigger withholding, the SSA withholds for all months until it has recovered the amount you're estimated to exceed the limit.

REMEMBER

The earnings limits are usually revised every year. If you're under full retirement age and collecting Social Security benefits, it's important to know the current limits and to report your expected income. You can find the current earnings limits at `www.ssa.gov/pubs/10069.html`.

Reporting earnings to the Social Security Administration

Usually, your regular income-tax filings provide the SSA with all the information it needs about your earnings — but not always. You may need to contact the SSA about your earnings.

If you haven't reached full retirement age and you get benefits, you need to tell the SSA if you expect your pay to exceed the earnings limit. The SSA wants to know in advance so it can withhold benefits. The SSA may also want you to file an earnings report for other particular circumstances, some of which involve self-employment. If you do have to file an annual report, the deadline is April 15 for calendar-year filing; otherwise, it's three months and 15 days after the end of the fiscal year.

You can submit your report by writing, calling, or mailing your local SSA office. In addition, the SSA may send you a letter requesting an updated earnings estimate.

Your first opportunity to inform the SSA of your expected income comes when you apply for benefits. When you apply in October or later, the SSA wants to know how much you may get paid during the following year.

After that, you may not have to make a separate annual accounting of your earnings to the SSA. The SSA generally relies on your filings with the Internal Revenue Service (IRS) to decide whether you should have extra withholding to meet the earnings test. If for some reason the IRS doesn't have information about your earnings that could affect your benefit eligibility, you need to inform the SSA.

WARNING

Bear in mind that there is a time lag between when you report income to the IRS and when the SSA finds out about it. If your earnings jump unexpectedly, and you don't inform the SSA, it could under-withhold — and ask you later to send the money back.

In the following sections, I fill you in on which income should be counted and when.

Which income should be counted

The SSA applies limits to certain kinds of pay — wages from a job, including bonuses, commissions, and stock options — or income from your own business.

You may have income, even a lot of income, that's not subject to the cap. If you hit it big on Wall Street, that doesn't count. Government benefits, such as unemployment or worker's compensation; interest; pensions; annuities; rental income; and capital gains don't count. Inheriting a bunch of money doesn't count. Distributions from an IRA or 401(k) plan don't count.

TIP

As more people work later in life, some lose jobs and qualify for unemployment benefits, and many receive Social Security. It's important to know that jobless benefits do *not* count as earned income toward the Social Security earnings test. But several states consider your Social Security payments in figuring out the size of your unemployment benefit. The list of states that offset jobless benefits to some degree by Social Security benefits has changed in recent years. But if you're potentially affected, you should check to see whether your state continues this practice. You can find contact information for the unemployment office in your state at `www.dol.gov/dol/location.htm`.

SPECIAL PAYMENTS

If you retire from your job and later get money you earned while still working, the SSA wants to know. The good news is that this income may not be counted toward the earnings limit. The SSA calls this sort of delayed compensation a *special payment.* Bonuses, unused vacation leave or sick pay, severance pay, sales commissions, and other earnings, such as deferred compensation earned in a year before your employer reports it on Form W-2, may fall into the category of special payments.

The self-employed may also get special payments. Say you have your own business. You performed a service before you retired, but you got paid after you began getting Social Security. That may count as a special payment that won't count against your Social Security benefits.

Special payments come in various forms. Suppose a farmer harvests and stores 100 tons of wheat before he starts Social Security. Later, he gets income from the wheat. That's a special payment. Say an insurance salesperson gets a commission after retirement for a whole-life policy sold before retirement. That's a special payment. Say an employer owes you back pay for work performed before you retired. That's a special payment.

If you get a special payment, make it clear to the SSA. Otherwise, the SSA may chalk it up to regular earnings and potentially withhold your benefits or even ask you for some money. If there's any disagreement about when you did the work, ask your former employer to clarify the matter for the SSA.

When your income should be counted

For regular wage earners, income counts when you earn it, not when you receive it. This policy may be confusing in some cases. Say you earn a bonus one year, but you get the money the following year. You have to count the bonus the year you *earn* it, not the year you *receive* it. (Exceptions may apply to compensation that you earn during the year you apply for Social Security but before your benefit begins.)

The SSA generally counts stock options as wages when you receive them, so even if you exercise them in retirement, they may not count against the earnings test. Royalties, sick pay, travel expenses, and business expenses all potentially count toward the earnings limit, but the rules are highly technical.

The deadline for filing an earnings report

The deadline for filing an earnings report is three months and 15 days after the end of your tax year. The SSA typically gets the information it needs from the IRS, though you can personally provide the information (and you should if you anticipate a change in the coming year). The SSA accepts information from Form W-2 (Wage and Tax Statement), as well as your tax filing to the IRS, if you're self-employed.

REMEMBER

The SSA sometimes mails requests to individuals to provide updated estimates of earnings, but don't wait. You're encouraged to contact the SSA and provide an earnings estimate. You can do this over the phone, by visiting your local SSA office, or in writing.

WARNING

If you don't file the information the SSA seeks within the deadline, you risk the loss of payments, potentially costing you thousands of dollars.

When You Go Back to Work after Retirement

What if you retire, decide to start your Social Security retirement benefit, and *then* you go back to work? It's easy to see how this could happen. Maybe you're an older employee who was laid off. You apply for dozens of jobs and nothing comes through. The bills are adding up. You need some income, so you begin your early retirement Social Security benefit. A few months later, an employer offers you a good job. If the pay is high enough, earnings limit withholding could gobble up 100 percent of your benefit. A lot of good that would do you.

In such cases, the SSA suspends your benefit if you haven't yet reached your full retirement age. Payments are stopped until your income is once more low enough that you again qualify for payments. (If your income stays very high, your benefit can remain suspended until you reach your full retirement age.) At full retirement age, your benefit is recalculated so that, in the long run, you recoup the suspended amount.

TIP

Another option that you have within the first year of benefits is to withdraw your application for benefits — in effect, to stop being a beneficiary. The downside of withdrawal is that you have to pay back whatever you received (as well as any benefits that went to others based on your earnings record). At one time, some experts recommended this strategy of terminating benefits and repaying them as a way to get an interest-free loan, while enabling your retirement benefit to get larger. The SSA has clamped down, however, and restricted such withdrawals to the first year of receiving benefits.

REMEMBER

The SSA reduces your benefit by $1 for every $2 you earn above a certain amount, if you haven't reached full retirement age. In the year you reach full retirement age, the SSA withholds $1 for every $3 earned over a (higher) limit. After you reach full retirement age, the earnings limit vanishes.

Consider this example: Antoine loses his job at 63, when the private security firm he helps manage goes belly up. He sends out dozens of job applications and doesn't get a single reply. Finally, he gives up and begins collecting a Social Security retirement benefit amounting to $17,000 per year. Six months later, he's amazed to pick up the phone and receive an offer from a former colleague to become vice president of a start-up security firm for $55,000. He says yes right away. But when Antoine calls the SSA office, he has a less pleasant surprise: The representative explains that Antoine's entire benefit is suspended. The math works out like this: His new salary of $55,000 is $36,760 over the Social Security threshold of $18,240. Divide $36,760 by two, and you get $18,380 — more than $1,000 above his annual Social Security benefit of $17,000. As a result, the entire benefit for the year is withheld. The work suspension isn't an entirely bad thing, though. Antoine can afford to live without Social Security. Meanwhile, as long as his retirement benefit is completely suspended, it grows at a rate of about 7 percent annually, until he reaches his full retirement age three years later at 66 years and 2 months.

REMEMBER

Benefits are most commonly suspended because of high earnings, although there are other reasons. For example, say you qualify for benefits as a young parent or young widow or widower who is eligible because you care for a child. If the child isn't under your care for a month — for example, because the child is living elsewhere and being cared for by a different parent — your benefits could be suspended. (A kid's visit to summer camp or boarding school won't disqualify you.) If you're a spouse, widow, or widower who gets a government pension unrelated to Social Security, two-thirds of the pension may offset your Social Security benefits and could cause a suspension.

Special Considerations for the Self-Employed

In business for yourself? The SSA considers you self-employed if you operate a trade, business, or profession. You can be a one-person operation, or maybe you have partners. Either way, you face a particular set of Social Security rules — and realities.

Many self-employed people are admirably independent and thrive on running their own show. The SSA is about rules and documentation. Keeping that in mind may help you have a good relationship with the SSA when the time comes to claim your benefits.

Unlike the typical wage earner who earns Social Security coverage, a self-employed person occupies two roles: employer and employee. Nobody's going to take care of your deductions for you. You report your own earnings and pay your own taxes to the IRS. You pay a different payroll tax, and you may qualify for Social Security credits through a different calculation than the one used for wage earners. You can read an overview of issues for the self-employed on the Social Security website at www.ssa.gov/pubs/10022.html.

The SSA has certain special requirements when you work for yourself, as well as a level of scrutiny that may exceed the norm. The fine print applies to deductions, earnings credits, and reporting.

TIP

If you're self-employed, keep good financial records — and be prepared to back them up. The SSA may review the earnings information you provide with more care than is applied to the average wage earner. Make sure that you can justify *everything* you say about your earnings.

Tax deductions

Self-employed people pay Social Security taxes on their net earnings from self-employment. This is basically your net profit from your business, plus or minus some additional adjustments. Because self-employed people occupy the role of employer and employee, they have to pay both shares. But you can reduce your taxable income by half of your Social Security tax on the 1040 IRS form. This is so the self-employed are treated similarly to employees who don't pay any income tax on the share of Social Security taxes paid by their employers.

Work credits

If you're self-employed, you may be able to use an optional method to obtain the credits you need to qualify for Social Security benefits. (Individuals typically need to earn 40 credits to be fully insured for retirement benefits. The amount may be lower for disability and survivor benefits.) There are two optional methods: one for earnings from a farming business and one for earnings from a nonfarm business. You may use both methods, if you're eligible.

Under the optional methods, a self-employed individual with low earnings may be able to obtain credits toward Social Security coverage that otherwise wouldn't be available. You can use the nonfarm optional method five times in a lifetime. For details on how it works for nonfarm businesses, go to www.irs.gov/pub334. For farm businesses, go to www.irs.gov/pub225.

You need to have gross income of not more than $8,160, or net profit of less than $5,891, to use the farm optional method (based on initial IRS guidelines for 2019). You may report two-thirds of your gross income, up to $5,440, as your net earnings by using this method. Note that using the farm optional method can increase or decrease your net earnings from farm self-employment, so you want to pay attention to the details if you use this method. For the nonfarm optional method, you need to have net profit of less than $5,891 and less than 72.189 percent of your gross nonfarm income. You may report two-thirds of your gross income, up to $5,440 (less the amount reported, using the farm optional method), as your net earnings by using the nonfarm optional method. Unlike the farm optional method, under this method you can't report less than your actual net earnings from nonfarm self-employment. (By the way, you are limited to using the nonfarm optional method five times in your lifetime.)

These calculations may sound complicated, but the directions on the IRS 1040 Schedule SE should help you do it without too much trouble. And it may be worth the effort, because even with low earnings, you can potentially get the maximum of four Social Security credits in a year by employing this method.

Earnings limit

If you're self-employed and getting early retirement benefits, the SSA wants to see firm evidence that you reported your income properly. It wants to confirm that you haven't made your income look like less than it is to evade the earnings limit.

The SSA may consider certain details you report to be red flags, worthy of closer scrutiny. For example, if you're still spending a lot of time on the job, if you remain in control of the business, or if you say you've shifted control to a relative, the SSA may take a magnifying glass to your report.

Before it's satisfied, the SSA may take a close look at your previous tax returns and other documents, such as expense records.

Reporting requirements

If you're self-employed, you meet the SSA's reporting requirements by filing the required tax forms on time with the IRS, if net earnings are $400 or more. These include Form 1040, Schedule SE (Self-Employment Tax), and normally Schedule C (Profit or Loss from Business) or Schedule F (Profit or Loss from Farming).

Complete the IRS paperwork regardless of whether you owe any income tax and whether you already get Social Security benefits. If you're self-employed, the SSA expects you to fill out forms 1040 and SE.

TIP

When a married couple is self-employed in a family enterprise, each spouse qualifies for Social Security earnings credits as a partner. But it's possible for the SSA to overlook one of the spouses (typically, the wife) unless each partner files a separate Schedule SE. It makes no difference if you file a joint income-tax return. If just one of you files a Schedule SE, that's who gets all the Social Security credits.

Uncle Sam Giveth and Taketh Away: How Benefits Are Taxed

A growing number of Americans owe income tax on part of their Social Security benefits. You typically won't owe income taxes on your benefits if they represent all your income. But significant income from work or investments or a pension — on top of Social Security — could be an income-tax liability. In addition to the feds, some states — predominately in the Midwest — tax Social Security benefits. (The states have a hodgepodge of tax rules and exclusions for Social Security, so check with your own state tax agency or accountant to figure out whether that applies to you.)

TIP

The state tax agencies go by different names, but you can find contact information for yours at `www.taxadmin.org/state-tax-agencies`.

Whatever your income, however, at least 15 percent of your Social Security benefit is protected from the tax collector. No one pays income tax on more than 85 percent of his or her benefits. Importantly, single filers are treated differently than married couples filing a joint return. You can go through a few steps to get a rough idea of how taxation of benefits may affect you:

1. **Get a rough idea of your provisional income, or what Social Security calls your *combined income.***

   Your provisional income is the sum of wages, interest (taxable and nontaxable), dividends, pensions, self-employment income, other taxable income, and half of your Social Security benefits, less certain deductions you may take when determining your adjusted gross income.

2. **See where your provisional income level fits into the tax rules.**

   Say you file as an individual, and your combined income is under $25,000. If so, you owe no taxes on your Social Security. If your provisional income level is between $25,000 and $34,000, you may have to pay income tax on up to 50 percent of your benefits. If your combined income is above $34,000, you may have to pay income tax on as much as 85 percent of your Social Security benefit.

For married couples, the levels are different. If a couple has provisional income of less than $32,000, you're in the clear. If provisional income comes in between $32,000 and $44,000 on your joint return, you may owe income tax on up to 50 percent of your Social Security benefits. Couples who earn more than $44,000 may have to pay taxes on as much as 85 percent of their benefits.

Married people who file separate tax returns and receive Social Security typically have to pay some tax on their benefits. This is because for people in this category, the limits are zero, meaning that up to 85 percent of Social Security benefits may be subject to the income tax.

3. **Determine exactly how much of your benefit may be taxed.**

   This can get complicated, depending on your personal situation, especially if you have to include 85 percent of your benefits as part of income for tax purposes. To do it right, you need to fill out a step-by-step worksheet, or rely on tax software or your accountant. You can find a worksheet at `www.irs.gov/publications/p915/ar02.html`.

TIP

Every January, you should receive a Form SSA-1099 that tells you your total Social Security benefits for the prior year. You need this information for your federal tax return.

Here's an example: Tom and Carol are a married couple who file jointly. Tom's Social Security benefit comes to $7,500, and Carol's spousal benefit adds another $3,500. Tom also gets a taxable pension of $22,000 from his former job with an automaker and interest income of $500 from some certificates of deposit. Tom and Carol figure out their provisional income by adding $22,000 plus $500 plus $3,750 (half of Tom's benefit) plus $1,750 (half of Carol's benefit) for a total of $28,000. Tom and Carol pay no federal income tax on their Social Security benefits, because their provisional income of $28,000 comes in below the $32,000 threshold for a married couple filing jointly. But suppose they had more income. What if Tom's pension came to $30,000? That extra $8,000 would boost the couple's provisional income to $36,000 — well above the $32,000 threshold for married couples. In this case, Tom and Carol would owe income tax on about 18 percent of their Social Security benefits.

TIP

As of this writing, U.S. citizens who live in certain countries, including Canada, Chile, Germany, Greece, Ireland, Italy, Japan, Switzerland, and the United Kingdom, don't have to pay income tax on Social Security or are subject to low rates, no matter how big their income. This is because of tax treaties between the United States and those nations. (The list may change over time.)

PAYING YOUR TAXES AHEAD OF TIME

You may be required to send quarterly estimated payments to the IRS if you have tax liability that isn't handled through withholding from an employer. Separately, you may request to have federal taxes withheld from your Social Security payments. You can get the IRS Form W-4V to request voluntary withholding at `www.irs.gov/pub/irs-pdf/fw4v.pdf` or by calling the IRS at 800-829-3676 (TTY 800-829-4059). There's also a link to the form at `www.ssa.gov/planners/taxwithold.htm`.

If you choose to withhold federal income taxes, you can select only among certain percentages: 7 percent, 10 percent, 12 percent, or 22 percent of your monthly benefit. You should return the signed form to your local SSA office.

» Tightening your budget before you retire

Chapter 14
Shaping a Financial Future You Can Live With

If you're thinking about retirement as the next phase in your life, you could use a road map. But the pathways that worked for our parents no longer seem to apply.

In our lifetimes, we've seen how 401(k) plans and individual retirement accounts (IRAs) can rise and plunge. We've seen how home values go down as well as up. We've seen how hard it can be to get a job even when the economy is growing. Employers have been dropping and freezing pension plans for years. If you count part-timers and the self-employed, roughly one in two workers doesn't have access to any job-related retirement plan. No wonder so many Baby Boomers and Gen Xers lack confidence in the future. And no wonder they'll rely heavily on Social Security in the coming years.

This chapter discusses how you can start right now to build on the foundation of Social Security and create your own road map for a secure future. You just need to find out how much Social Security and other income you have coming, figure out how much money you really need (or at least start to think about it), and adjust your plans accordingly — the sooner the better.

Envisioning Your Life with Social Security

REMEMBER

Social Security is just one part of your financial well-being. It is *not* meant to replace most of your pre-retirement income. (It covers roughly 40 percent for typical earners — less for the more affluent.) It was never meant to pay for an upscale lifestyle on its own.

You can get a sense of your future benefits by reviewing a recent Social Security statement, if you have one, or by checking out Social Security's online tools and plugging in your information. (See Chapter 6 for more on calculating your benefits.)

The future may seem hazy (especially when you're scrambling just to get through the day), but basic questions are clear. You can begin to imagine the next phase of your life by considering the following:

- **Where will you live?** Many people want to stay put. Maybe that makes sense for you. Consider how important your community roots are, the costs of your region, and whether you have family support nearby. If you want to relocate, you can't wait forever.
- **How long will you live?** The longer you survive, the more resources you need. See Chapter 3 for a fuller discussion of longevity, including links to calculators that can help estimate your life span.
- **How long will you work?** For many Baby Boomers and Gen Xers, the answer is "longer than expected." If you have the option to continue working, a few extra years of work can provide a big boost to retirement security.
- **What are your spending needs?** Do you expect to spend more for some things (say, travel and healthcare) and less for others (such as work-related expenses)?

REMEMBER

If you believe you need more money in retirement than you've saved, try to make changes while there's time, such as saving more or working longer. If your options are limited, try to bring your spending priorities into line with financial reality sooner rather than later.

Figuring out how much money you need

TIP

Envisioning your retirement is a chance to look at things freshly and creatively — but with a dose of reality. Here are some ideas to get the process rolling:

- **Follow the money.** Review several months or a year of checking account and credit-card statements to see where the money goes.
- **Look at your priorities.** How do you feel about where your money is going? Does your spending reflect your priorities? How do you want to use your time?
- **Visualize being older.** Some experts believe a 65-year-old couple should set aside more than $285,000 for future healthcare costs. You should also have an emergency fund large enough to cover three to six months of expenses.

  Will you opt for a change in housing? Consider potential costs, including transportation needs. Even if you stay put, your future quality of life may be aided by home renovations that support independence, such as extra-wide doorways, no-step entries (including the shower), grab bars in bathrooms, and a first-floor bedroom.
- **Write a budget.** On the income side, add up Social Security, any pension, expected earnings, and annual savings withdrawals, such as from a 401(k) or IRA.

  On the spending side, use your audit of monthly spending as a basis. How much of that spending is crucial? Do you plan to spend more for certain things? Now compare how your projected income and spending line up.

Determining how much income you need

Financial planners often say that your retirement income should replace 70 percent to 80 percent of your working income to keep up the lifestyle you're used to. That's just a rule of thumb, though. You may need more, or you may be able to get by with less (as many people do). You don't have to pick a percentage. You can build a spending plan from scratch.

REMEMBER

When you retire, you say farewell to certain expenses. You don't pay for commuting. You may buy fewer clothes. You may already have paid off the house and helped the kids through college. You're no longer setting aside money for retirement, such as in a 401(k) plan — now you're living off those savings. Your taxes may also decrease. (If you've stopped working, you no longer contribute payroll taxes.)

REMEMBER

You're an individual, not a rule of thumb. In projecting future income needs, ask yourself what's distinct about your own personal situation. Do you or your spouse expect to keep working for a long time? Do you expect to inherit money? Do you own valuable property? Can you generate rental income? Alternatively, do big expenses loom, such as caring for a child or an elderly parent? How are your own health and your healthcare coverage?

USING A RETIREMENT CALCULATOR

Retirement calculators ask you to fill in personal data, such as when you want to retire or how much of your current income you want to maintain when you do. They typically ask for (or provide) an estimate of your Social Security benefits. Then they project whether you're on your way to your goal or falling short.

Retirement calculators aren't an exact science — different calculators may produce very different numbers. But they can help you get a sense of how close you are to meeting your goal.

Here are two calculators you may want to try:

- **AARP Retirement Calculator** (`www.aarp.org/retirementcalculator`): The AARP Retirement Calculator aims for a holistic approach, factoring in your marital status, savings held by you and your spouse, and any anticipated windfall, such as from an inheritance or a property sale.
- **Ballpark E$timate** (`www.choosetosave.org/ballpark`): The American Savings Education Council, a program of the Employee Benefit Research Institute, produces this tool. It's designed to give you a bottom-line savings figure you need to reach your retirement goals. You fill in your expected retirement age and the amount you've saved so far to reach a savings target for the day you retire. You're also prompted to think about how long you could live by making assumptions about your longevity. (The longer you plan to live, the more savings you need.)

Narrowing the gap between too little income and too much spending

Life on Social Security is often a time to tighten the belt. This goal may be harder to achieve than you realize, especially if you haven't been disciplined in the past. There's no magic bullet to transform your finances, but a multifaceted effort can pay dividends.

Here are seven things you can do now to help your Social Security benefit (and other fixed income) stretch further tomorrow:

» **Save more.** If your employer offers a 401(k) plan, try to make the maximum contribution. If your employer offers another payroll savings plan, such as into a credit union, try to save there as well. If you're over 50, try to make the extra catch-up contributions allowed for IRAs and 401(k)s. (Contact your plan administrator to find out whether you qualify and how much you can add.)

See whether your bank will make monthly transfers from your checking account to your savings account.

- **Tackle debt.** Debt undermines your economic security in retirement, so you want to get a handle on it now. Can you pay off (or speed up paying off) your mortgage? (For many home loans, one or two extra payments per year can save tons of interest over time.) What about credit cards? Some experts say that you have too much debt if you spend more than 20 percent of your income on debt payments other than your mortgage. Compare finance charges from credit cards to see whether you're piling up extra-costly debt. You can consolidate multiple credit-card debts under the cheapest card (but make sure that you know the terms of a balance transfer, such as how long the interest rate lasts and what fees are involved). See whether a card issuer will reduce an interest rate.

TIP

If you're in over your head, get help. You can contact the National Foundation for Credit Counseling at 800-388-2227 or `www.nfcc.org`.

- **Watch healthcare costs.** Choose health plans with care. If your employer's plan offers a choice of deductibles, think carefully about which option makes the most sense. Before you schedule a medical test, find out whether your insurer expects you to wait a certain length of time before taking it. Look for savings on prescription drug costs, such as through generics. Also, find out whether your insurer offers a cheaper mail-order system for medications. You can't stop all illness, of course, but good diet and exercise may slow or prevent certain conditions, such as diabetes and heart disease.
- **Pay with cash.** The more you whip out a credit card, the easier it is to pile up unnecessary expenses. For many people, it's just a bit harder to hand over the actual cash in your wallet. If you do seek the convenience of plastic, try to make more purchases with a debit card, which comes straight out of your bank account, rather than a credit card, which may lead to hefty interest charges. A debit card has an immediate impact on your bank balance, so it lends itself more to discipline than a credit card that allows you to pile up thousands of dollars in debt. If you prefer to use your credit card, try to pay off the balance every month.
- **Review routine charges.** Some companies lure you in with cheap rates and then ratchet them up later. Check your monthly cable and internet plans to make sure you're getting the best price you qualify for. Find out whether your bank is charging fees for services it used to offer for free. Compare what you pay for auto and home insurance with other offers. Ask your insurance agent whether you can make modest changes to coverage that will lower your rates.
- **Save energy.** Waste adds up. Fix drafty windows and doors with weather stripping. Improve insulation wherever it's needed, including the attic, doors, and windows. (Curtains and blinds can help.) Seal leaking ductwork. Watch

where you set the thermostat in winter and summer — a few degrees can make a difference. Ceiling fans are a cheap way to cool things down in the summer. When you can, use the microwave rather than the stove. Turn off appliances when not in use.

- **Spend for value.** Do you still take your seven-year-old car to the dealer for routine maintenance? Look for a cheaper mechanic. Still use a travel agent? Try to book your own flights and hotels. Do you dine out frequently? Make use of online discounts. Be aware of bargains. No one of these choices will transform your finances, of course. But an awareness of value makes a difference over time.

Working with a financial professional

One way to plan for your life on Social Security is to consult a financial professional. He or she may offer guidance on when you and a spouse should begin to collect Social Security benefits, along with other important choices you face. (Some financial advisors even use software that considers the long-term impact of taxes and other not-so-obvious factors on your Social Security claiming decision.)

But be careful. You have a lot at stake here, and all sorts of operators want a piece of the action. The goal, of course, is objective advice uncolored by any self-interest on the part of an advisor. So where do you go? Who do you trust?

You may ask friends and relatives for recommendations. Another option is to look for online referrals from respected national organizations. You can plug your zip code into the following websites to search for a financial advisor near you:

- **Certified Financial Planner Board of Standards:** `www.cfp.net`
- **Financial Planning Association:** `www.fpanet.org`
- **National Association of Personal Financial Advisors:** `www.napfa.org`

Consider interviewing a few people to see who seems best for you. Here are some questions to keep in mind:

- **What services do you provide?** These services potentially include developing your retirement financial plan, monitoring the plan, meeting with you periodically, and managing your investments.
- **What are your credentials?** This field is loaded with confusing acronyms that sound alike and mean different things. You want someone with education,

experience, and an ethical code. Find out the individual's license or title and who granted it. Respected professional designations include

- Certified Financial Planner, from the Certified Financial Planner Board of Standards (www.cfp.net)
- Chartered Financial Consultant, from the American College of Financial Services (www.theamericancollege.edu/designations-degrees/ChFC)
- Registered Financial Consultant, from the International Association of Registered Financial Consultants (www.iarfc.org)

» **How do you get paid?** Financial professionals are paid in different ways, and you should understand the arrangement. If compensation is based more on commissions than your fee, take note. A broker may get hefty fees for selling you something you don't need. You want to be confident that the advisor is working for you, not exploiting you. Payment may also be based on a percentage of the assets under management, an hourly fee, a fixed fee, or some combination thereof.

» **Do you have a specialty?** If the planner is most interested in high-net-worth individuals and you aren't in that category, you may not get the attention you deserve. Your goal may be to preserve your assets or take on only limited risk. Ask how the planner feels about that.

» **How quickly do you respond to questions?** This question is a legitimate one for you to be clear on from the start. The answer may affect your comfort level with this person.

WARNING

Watch out for scams. You can check whether a broker has gotten into trouble in the past by getting in touch with the Financial Industry Regulatory Authority (FINRA), a nongovernmental oversight group. Either go to www.finra.org/Investors/ToolsCalculators/BrokerCheck or call 800-289-9999. You can find out more about scams by checking out the Senior Investor Resource Center (www.nasaa.org/1723/senior-investor-resource-center), which is run by the North American Securities Administrators Association.

Preparing for Life on Social Security

As the time to collect your Social Security benefits approaches, you face an array of strategic decisions. The same answers don't work for everyone. But the issues are clear, and it helps to think them through — early. In this section, I cover some of the major ones you may face.

TIP

If you're wondering when you should claim Social Security retirement benefits, turn to Chapter 3. There, I walk you through all the issues you need to consider to make the choice that's right for you.

Purchasing an annuity

If you want to add to the foundation of income that Social Security provides, one option is to buy an annuity. An *annuity* is a type of insurance contract that can turn your savings into a stream of income, potentially for the rest of your life.

WARNING

Annuities come in various forms. Many have fees that are hard to see and features that are hard to understand. Annuity fees are often high compared to other investments, and it may cost a lot of money to back out of a contract. If you have only modest savings, or if Social Security will already replace a significant share of your working income, you probably want to steer clear of annuities.

But you may want to consider an annuity if you approach retirement with income needs beyond Social Security and you have a chunk of money that you don't mind giving up. A good, transparent product can help you cover basic living expenses, perhaps making it easier for you to delay your claim of Social Security benefits. But don't forget that you lose control of your money, and you may have to pay a big penalty to get the money back.

An *immediate annuity* (sometimes called an *income annuity*) begins payments right after you purchase it. Such annuities often are the choice of people already retired. A *deferred annuity* pays off in the future. In each case, annuities (whether immediate or deferred) may pay returns that are fixed or variable:

- **Fixed annuity:** This type of annuity pays a steady amount for a prescribed number of years. Say you put down $100,000. Depending on your age and terms of the contract, it may pay you a set amount — for example, $600 per month, depending on your age — for as long as you live. Also, the contract may have terms for survivor payments, generally for a temporary period. Generally, a fixed annuity won't rise with inflation, so you don't want to tie up all your nest egg to get returns that are destined to fall in value over time.

WARNING

- **Variable annuity:** This type of annuity pays you a shifting amount based on the performance of underlying investments. Variable annuities offer the potential for growth but have been widely criticized for high fees and lack of transparency, and many experts consider them unsuitable for retirees.

REMEMBER

If you look into an annuity, make sure that you understand all the fees, including *surrender fees*, which apply if you want to get out of the contract. Make sure that you understand how much (if anything) goes to your survivors and for how long. Don't be swayed by high-pressure marketing.

TIP

Annuities can be a complex topic. Do your homework before committing money. One place to start is `www.investor.gov/investing-basics/investment-products/annuities`.

Signing up for Medicare

When your 65th birthday approaches, you face a range of decisions about signing up for Medicare. The healthcare program has four parts — A, B, C, and D. They have different fee structures, and different enrollment periods may apply. If you miss certain deadlines, you may get hit with financial penalties, so it's best to know the enrollment rules and avoid needless expense. (See Chapter 12 for a fuller discussion of Medicare, including its enrollment periods.)

If you're collecting Social Security, the Social Security Administration (SSA) automatically enrolls you for Medicare Parts A and B when you reach 65. If you aren't getting benefits, you need to apply. In either case, you face decisions about which parts of Medicare to enroll in. Your decisions may be affected by whether you have health coverage from your own or your spouse's employer.

TIP

Here are some tips to keep in mind about each part of Medicare:

- **Part A (hospital insurance):** This part is important coverage for hospital stays, temporary rehabilitation in a skilled nursing facility, hospice care, and some home health services. Part A comes free of premiums if you qualify for Medicare on the basis of payroll taxes you or your spouse paid while working. Most people sign up for Part A during the initial enrollment period around their 65th birthdays, even if they don't need Part B (keep reading).
- **Part B (medical insurance):** This part covers doctors' services (including those in the hospital), outpatient care, and medical equipment. The standard monthly premium for 2020 was set at $144.60; high earners pay more. You usually can delay Part B enrollment (and avoid the premium) after age 65 when you're covered by health insurance through your (or your spouse's) active employment. Otherwise, you face late penalties that add permanently to your Part B premiums.
- **Part C (Medicare Advantage):** Unlike traditional Medicare (Parts A and B), Medicare Advantage plans are run by private insurance companies. They usually have lower costs and may offer some extra benefits. You have to

decide whether to choose one of these plans, based on the choices available to you locally and the costs and benefits each plan offers. Plans differ in the premiums and copays they charge and your freedom to choose healthcare providers. You must be enrolled in Parts A and B to enroll in a Medicare Advantage plan.

- **Part D (prescription drugs):** To get Medicare drug coverage, you must have Part A and/or Part B. You also need to enroll in a private Part D prescription drug plan (either a stand-alone plan that offers only drug coverage or a broader Medicare Advantage plan that includes Part D coverage). You face late penalties if you delay signing up for Part D, unless you have drug coverage from another source that is considered *creditable* (a term used to describe coverage that is at least as good as Medicare's Part D requirements). Monthly premiums for stand-alone plans average about $33 per month (as of 2020), though high earners pay more.

Handling home equity

Home equity is the largest asset for a lot of Baby Boomers and Gen Xers. Prices may go up and down, but many people still derive great security from owning their homes.

That said, selling a home can provide options. You can downsize and have money left over for other purposes, such as saving for future emergencies. You can move to a cheaper part of the country. You also have the option of renting your home (or part of it) for income. If you can, paying off your mortgage is smart — it's a big step toward reducing your expenses in retirement.

Other, possibly less desirable options include home equity loans and reverse mortgages. With a *home equity loan*, you use your home as collateral to borrow money that you have to repay within a certain time frame. With a *reverse mortgage*, you use your home equity to get monthly payments, a lump sum, or a credit line without having to make monthly repayments as long as you live there. I call these "less desirable" because you're taking on debt at a time in your life when it's usually preferable to get rid of it. But such debt may make sense, depending on your personal circumstances.

TIP

You can find more information about reverse mortgages at www.aarp.org/money/credit-loans-debt/reverse_mortgages.

Getting long-term-care insurance

The cost of long-term care can wipe you out financially. A private room in a nursing home may cost more than $90,000 per year — or even more, depending on where you live. A home-care aide may cost more than $20 per hour or considerably more in some areas. Neither Medicare nor typical health-insurance policies cover long-term care, beyond brief rehabilitation.

By some measures, two-thirds or more of individuals over 65 will need some long-term care before they die. If you require extended institutional care, you'll have to use up most of your assets before you qualify for assistance through Medicaid, the government's healthcare program for the poor.

So should you buy a long-term-care insurance policy? The answer depends on a range of factors, including what brings you peace of mind, whether you can afford to pay for long-term care out of your own pocket if you need to, and whether you believe you have family support to count on.

TIP

A good, transparent long-term-care policy from an established insurer can help protect you — but understand the limits. Policies cost less if you start when you're younger, though future rate hikes can be jolting. Policies vary in daily benefits, waiting periods required before you can make a claim, and how long they'll pay for. Automatic, compounded inflation protection is an important feature to look for. Without it, coverage erodes over time.

TIP

You can find out more about consumer issues in purchasing long-term-care insurance at `https://content.naic.org/consumer/long-term-care-insurance.htm`.

Understanding how Social Security interacts with private pensions

Workers fortunate enough to qualify for private pensions may be in for an unpleasant surprise when the time comes to collect. In many cases — affecting perhaps two out of nine covered workers — private pension plans are designed to reduce your benefit, based on your Social Security benefit. This offset (called *Social Security integration*) can be costly, potentially reducing your private pension by thousands of dollars per year. It's perfectly legal, by the way.

If you qualify for a pension, you should find out in advance whether this provision applies to you. If so, someone who handles pensions for your company can guide you on what Social Security integration may mean for you, in dollars and cents, so you can plan accurately for your retirement income.

In certain cases (often involving past government work), your pension may reduce your Social Security payment. Workers who spent parts of their careers in jobs in which they contributed to pensions — but not to Social Security — face reductions from the SSA when they collect retirement benefits. (See Chapter 2 for details on the Windfall Elimination provision and the Government Pension Offset provision.)

Managing your investments

Whatever the size of your nest egg, you want it to help support you as long as possible. Certainly, you don't want it to be a cause of anxiety. Here are a few things to keep in mind when it comes to taking care of your investments:

- **Know your goals.** Do you want to preserve a lot of your savings and leave an inheritance for your children and grandchildren? Or are you content to spend most of your savings while you can? These priorities should influence your choice of investments, as well as how fast you withdraw your money.
- **Choose your risk level.** This decision is a personal one, and it goes right to your peace of mind. But generally, reducing risk as you get older is a good idea. The younger you are, the more risk you can take because you have more time to catch up if an investment crashes.
- **Mix it up.** One way to protect your savings is to avoid overexposure to any one investment. You may want to generate income through bonds. You may want a chance for growth and risk with some stocks. Cash equivalents, such as money market accounts and certificates of deposit (CDs), are safest and return the least.
- **Set a time frame.** Think ahead about when you'll want to withdraw the money. This may mean gradually shifting stock and bond investments to cash, well in advance, so you don't end up having to sell if the market is down.
- **Review and rebalance.** Periodically look at how your accounts have changed in value, and make sure that your overall portfolio is balanced the way you want. You should do this at least once a year, if not every six months. Major life events, such as having a child or getting married, are also good times to take a fresh look.
- **Limit fees.** Miscellaneous charges, such as fees and sales commissions, can eat into the growth of your nest egg and soak up thousands of dollars (potentially many thousands) over time. Some of the fees may be hard to see unless you ask about them or do extra homework. If you're interested in a mutual fund, look for its expense ratio in the prospectus, and see how it compares with others. You can get an idea of how your 401(k) plan shapes up by going to BrightScope (`www.brightscope.com`).

5 The Part of Tens

IN THIS PART . . .

Uncover some of the myths of Social Security that lead to public misunderstanding.

Check out ten reasons that young people have a big stake in Social Security and decisions that could affect their benefits for the long haul.

Find out the principal policy choices the nation faces about the future of Social Security.

IN THIS CHAPTER

» Dispelling wild tales about Social Security

» Keeping perspective about Social Security's finances

» Basing your views on facts

Chapter 15
Ten Myths about Social Security

Something about Social Security stirs the popular imagination. Rumors and phony stories have attached themselves to the program from the start. Sometimes you can identify the grain of truth that sprouts into a tall tale. Other times you can't.

Before Social Security got off the ground in the 1930s, newspapers in the Hearst chain spread the story that people would have to wear dog tags stamped with their Social Security numbers. (The dog tag idea actually *was* proposed but never approved.) Many people continue to believe that Social Security maintains an individual account with their contributions in it. The reasoning is easy to see, but the story isn't true.

Rumors swirl about the state of Social Security's finances, hidden meaning in the numbers, and other topics that find fertile ground on the internet and are spread through social media. Unfortunately, myths can be harmful because they undermine public understanding of Social Security and confidence in the program at a time when the nation needs a constructive, fact-based discussion.

In this chapter, I dispel ten myths, giving you the facts instead.

Myth: Social Security Is a Ponzi Scheme

This is a claim made by critics of the program who really are saying that Social Security is inherently unbalanced and doomed to fail. Their charge is based on a superficial comparison of Social Security with a type of fraud associated with Charles Ponzi, a charismatic con artist in the early 20th century.

Ponzi's infamous scheme involved speculation in international postal coupons. He lured his victim investors by promising returns of 50 percent at a time when banks were paying around 5 percent interest. Early investors were paid with money from later investors, a hallmark of Ponzi schemes. Such frauds may work for a little while, but inevitably they collapse. (Just ask Bernie Madoff.)

The misleading comparison of Social Security to a Ponzi scheme is based on the fact that Social Security does require one group (workers) to help support another group (retirees and other beneficiaries). This system is sometimes described as a *pay-as-you-go system.*

The Ponzi label falls apart, however, when you think it through. For one thing, Social Security doesn't rely on a soaring base of contributors, as Ponzi schemes do. Instead, it requires a somewhat predictable relationship between the number of workers and beneficiaries, along with adequate revenues. A lower U.S. birthrate starting in the 1960s and increasing life expectancy that has resulted in an aging of the population are significant causes of Social Security's expected shortfall.

Social Security has other fundamental differences from a Ponzi scheme. Importantly, it's transparent. Each year, the Social Security Administration (SSA) releases information about its financial state in exhaustive detail, along with projections 75 years into the future, based on different economic assumptions. Scams, by contrast, thrive on secrecy and deception. And unlike a Ponzi scheme, the money not used to pay current benefits has built up a surplus of $2.9 trillion.

Another basic difference between Social Security and a Ponzi scheme is in the goals. A crook hatches a Ponzi scheme to get rich at others' expense. Social Security provides social insurance to protect people. Money goes from one generation to help support another generation. Your tax contributions help support your parents. One day, the contributions of future generations will help support you.

Myth: Your Social Security Number Has a Racial Code in It

The nine-digit Social Security number has long fascinated people, because it is a unique, personal identifier in a nation that cherishes individuality. One myth is that the number contains a code that identifies the race of the cardholder. According to the myth, the code can be found in the *group number,* the fourth and fifth digits, in the middle. In one version of the rumor, a person's race could be determined by whether the fifth digit in the Social Security number is even or odd. (Group numbers range from 01 to 99.)

One explanation for this myth is that people have misinterpreted the meaning of the term *group number,* wrongly assuming that it referred to race. This rumor has caused some people to worry that their Social Security number makes them vulnerable to discrimination by potential employers or others who may spot the racial code in an application.

According to the SSA, however, the term *group number* refers simply to an old system of numerical grouping that traces back to Social Security's early days, when everyone's records were stored in paper files. Employees used the two-digit group number to help organize the files.

If you want to find possible meaning in your Social Security number, look to the first three digits — the *area number.* Before 1972, the first three digits were based on the state where the card was issued; after that, they were based on the mailing address on the application. This is no longer true, however. In 2011, the agency began assigning the first three digits randomly, as part of a strategy to protect people from identify theft.

Myth: Members of Congress Don't Pay into the System

This myth gets its strength by combining two rich symbols, Social Security and Congress. Variations of the myth include the idea that lawmakers get a special break on Social Security payroll taxes and that they're allowed to collect benefits at an earlier age than the rest of us.

In the past, Congress and the rest of the federal government were covered under the Civil Service Retirement System, which was created years before Social

Security. Under a 1983 law, however, all three branches of the federal government were steered into Social Security. As a result, since 1984, members of Congress, the president, the vice president, federal judges, and most political appointees have been required to pay taxes into the Social Security system like everyone else. And the same rules apply to them as apply to you.

TECHNICAL STUFF

Vestiges of the old setup endure for some federal employees. Those hired before January 1984 aren't required to participate in the Social Security system. All federal employees hired since 1984, however, make Social Security payroll tax contributions like everyone else. That includes lawmakers.

Myth: Social Security Is Going Broke

People have heard so much talk about Social Security's finances that it's easy to see why they may think the program is going off the cliff. That's not the case, however.

Social Security can pay full benefits until about 2035 — and it can continue to pay about 80 percent of benefits thereafter, according to the program's trustees. The gap is caused by the fact that a relatively smaller number of workers will be supporting a relatively higher number of retirees.

The large number of Baby Boomers retiring, combined with the smaller number of individuals paying into the system through the payroll tax (because of lower birthrates), has caused Social Security benefits to surpass the amount of payroll taxes coming in. To make up for this shortfall, Social Security will increasingly draw down its trust funds of $2.9 trillion to supplement the revenues that will continue to pour in (primarily through payroll taxes).

The funding gap can be closed through a combination of modest tax increases and/or phased-in benefit cuts for future retirees. Although it has been difficult for lawmakers to make a deal, various policy options show that it's possible. (Appendix C gives you a menu of some of the widely mentioned options and a chance to put together your own fix-it plan.)

Assertions that Social Security is running out of money erode the confidence of younger people, who will need Social Security one day. Polls have shown, for example, that substantial numbers of future beneficiaries — as high as 80 percent — worry Social Security won't be there for them when they reach old age. This undue pessimism helps reinforce the next myth.

Myth: The Social Security Trust Funds Are Worthless

Social Security revenues stream into U.S. Treasury accounts known as the *Social Security trust funds.* One trust fund pays benefits for retirees and survivors; the other pays benefits for people with disabilities. (The revenues come from the payroll tax and some of the income tax paid by higher-income retirees.)

Most of the trust-fund money is used quickly to pay benefits. But a big surplus has developed over the years — about $2.9 trillion. Under the law, Social Security is required to lend the surplus funds to the federal government, which is then obliged to pay the loan back with interest. This lending takes place through investment in special-issue, medium- and long-term Treasury securities that can always be redeemed at face value.

This sanctioned lending, by the way, is the reason you may sometimes hear claims that the government "raids" the Social Security trust funds.

Those who contend that the trust funds are worthless are really predicting that the federal government won't make good on that debt — even though the bonds are backed by the full faith and credit of the United States, just like other Treasury bonds held by the public. Investors throughout the world retain confidence in this nation to make good on the debt it owes, as demonstrated by the ongoing demand for U.S. Treasury bonds, even at a time of government deficits and budget battles.

In the coming years, Social Security will rely increasingly on income from bond interest and actual bond sales to pay benefits. That means the U.S. government faces a large and growing bill to pay Social Security back for the money it has borrowed over the years.

It's not the role of this book to suggest fiscal policy, and you won't find recommendations here on how the government should pay its bills. But if *you* consider those matters, just remember that Social Security isn't the cause of the nation's current deficits.

Myth: You'd Be Better Off Investing in Stocks

You hear this myth more often during boom times, but for the average person, it's highly dubious at any time. To be clear: It's important for people to save as much as they can, and stock investments may be an important element in your savings.

But the notion that you'd be better off *without* Social Security usually doesn't hold up. For one thing, Social Security and stock investing aren't substitutes for each other. Unlike stocks, Social Security provides broad protections for you and your loved ones, including benefits for disability, survivors, and dependent family members. These benefits may be payable if tragedy strikes at an early age, before you've had the many years needed to build up a nest egg.

Also, Social Security shields retirement income from risks that are inherent in the financial markets. Although stock returns may be greater, stocks are more volatile. If a market collapses at the wrong moment, your holdings can be hammered. Social Security, by contrast, provides a guaranteed benefit.

TIP

If you truly want to save for yourself, it helps to consider how much of a nest egg you need to match the protections you get from Social Security. You could buy an annuity to provide monthly income under certain circumstances. But what would it cost? Suppose you were trying to equal the average Social Security retired worker benefit (about $1,500 a month in 2020). You would need hundreds of thousands of dollars to purchase a survivor annuity that matched the benefit, starting at age 66 and protected for inflation. A higher-paying annuity meant to equal Social Security's family maximum for top earners (more than $4,500 a month) would cost nearly a million dollars. Annuity price tags vary as interest rates change; also, insurance companies charge different amounts, so you can't find one lasting dollar figure.

Neither of the products described here equals Social Security's protections. They don't cover family members while you're alive, including a spouse or children, nor do they offer child survivor benefits when you die.

Could you save half a million bucks? Suppose you had 40 years to build up the nest egg. At a 3 percent rate of return, you'd have to set aside about $6,500 per year. Most people don't save that much. Many people have nothing left over by the time they pay the monthly bills. Of those who do save, many could set aside more. Also, many people take money out of their nest eggs when needs arise. Unfortunately, such withdrawals can do lasting harm. Saving requires long-term discipline and possibly short-term sacrifice.

About one in four adults who have yet to retire report *no* retirement savings or pension, according to a Federal Reserve study in 2019. While savings do increase with age, millions of older workers lack adequate nest eggs. Imagine how much more insecure your retirement would be if you had to depend completely on yourself to save for retirement. Maybe you could pull it off, but most people are better off with the guarantees of Social Security.

Myth: Undocumented Immigrants Make Illegal Social Security Claims

Tales that undocumented immigrants are soaking up Social Security benefits pick up steam periodically. As one popular version has it, Congress is about to consider a bill making benefits legal for workers who are in this country without authorization. This notion makes a lot of people angry. It's also possible that the myth is spread when people stand in line at a Social Security office and make assumptions about others around them.

Whatever the cause, the myth isn't true. Plus, the myth obscures an irony: Undocumented workers actually *add* revenue to the system through the Social Security taxes that are taken out of their pay, while most never claim benefits.

Under the law, undocumented immigrants are prohibited from claiming Social Security, as well as most other federal benefits. (Certain exceptions to this ban are allowed, such as for emergency medical treatment and emergency disaster relief.)

In reality, some undocumented workers use fake Social Security numbers to get jobs. Payroll taxes are then deducted from their pay, just as they are from everyone else's, and credited to the Social Security trust funds. Generally, these workers don't collect benefits. In fact, SSA estimates that undocumented immigrants contributed $12 billion net — that is, revenue paid into the system over benefits paid out — into the Social Security funds in 2010.

Myth: When Social Security Started, People Didn't Even Live to 65

This observation shows how the "facts" can be misleading. Its underlying point — that Social Security was designed to pay little in benefits because people wouldn't live long enough to collect them — isn't true.

Back when Social Security was created, life expectancy *was* shorter; a high rate of infant mortality meant that many people didn't reach adulthood, and life expectancy *at birth* was especially low. (In 1930, it was about age 58 for men and 62 for women.) If you survived childhood, though, you could expect to live many more years. Among men who lived to 21, more than half were expected to reach 65. If you reached 65, your life expectancy came to about 78. (Women lived longer than men, as they still do.) Life expectancy at 65 has increased since the 1930s, to be sure, but much less dramatically than life expectancy at birth.

The architects of Social Security knew the program would serve many millions of beneficiaries as time passed. They concluded that age 65 fit with public attitudes and could be financed through an affordable level of payroll taxes.

The notion that Social Security was designed to cost little because people died early is simply not true.

Myth: Congress Keeps Pushing Benefits Higher than Intended

Commentators sometimes assert that, over the years, generous lawmakers have hiked Social Security benefits far beyond the intention of the program's founders. These heaped-on benefits, the story goes, explain why Social Security faces a future shortfall.

It's true that Congress has enhanced benefits on several occasions since the program's initial approval in 1935. But such changes were consistent with the intent of Social Security as a social insurance program for *all* Americans.

By the important measure of *replacement rates* (how much of your pre-retirement income you get back in benefits), Social Security has been stable over the decades. In fact, replacement rates are now declining because of the gradually increasing age for full retirement benefits that Congress approved in 1983.

When Social Security first began, benefits were limited to payments to retirees. The intent of the program, however, was to provide meaningful social insurance for certain risks in life and to extend such protections to dependent family members. Family benefits (including for survivors) were added in 1939, followed later by coverage for disabled workers and their dependents. Automatic annual cost-of-living increases took effect in 1975 to replace the ad hoc approach to inflation adjustments that had been followed previously.

The fallacy is that these reforms undermined Social Security's long-term stability. Studies have shown that the addition of survivor and auxiliary benefits was offset to some degree by slower growth in benefits paid directly to workers. The anticipated shortfall reflects the fact that relatively fewer workers (because of a lower birthrate since the 1960s) will be supporting a bigger population of longer-living retirees in the coming years.

Myth: Older Folks Are Greedy Geezers Who Don't Need All Their Social Security

As some tell it, most older Americans spend their days being pampered in posh retirement villas or country clubs. According to the stereotype, these misers have no concern for young people — they prefer to take advantage of Social Security benefits they don't need.

Talk about myths! Over half of older Americans depend on Social Security for at least 50 percent of their retirement income. The benefits keep more than one-third of older Americans out of poverty, often by a thin margin.

Are benefits too generous? The average monthly payment for a retired worker is about $1,500 (as of 2020). That's about $18,000 a year. Not only do many millions of people struggle with poverty and near poverty, but recent estimates paint a bleaker picture than had previously been thought.

A U.S. Census Bureau alternative poverty measure in 2018 found a 13.6 percent poverty rate among Americans age 65 and up. Without income from Social Security, the poverty rate for older Americans would nearly triple — soaring to nearly 40 percent. Such figures make clear what common sense may tell you: A great many older people rely on Social Security to survive.

The myth of greedy geezers is further contradicted by the interdependence of generations, which may be growing. An increasing number of older people are helping to support their adult children and grandchildren, and studies have shown a big rise in the number of interdependent, multigenerational families. A U.S. Census survey found that slightly more than 7 million children — nearly 10 percent of all kids — live in families that include a grandparent.

Sometimes commentators try to argue that retirees and young people are at odds economically, as if older Americans are grabbing benefits they haven't earned and don't deserve. Think of the older people you know personally, people in your own family, and ask yourself: Does that ring true?

» Understanding the growing value of guaranteed benefits

» Appreciating Social Security's role in fighting poverty

» Recognizing that benefits for older Americans help everyone

Chapter 16

Ten Reasons Young People Should Care about Social Security

If you have years until retirement, you have a vital stake in the future of Social Security, and this chapter explores many of the reasons why. For starters, proposals to modify benefits — such as by raising the retirement age or reducing benefit levels — usually are designed with younger workers in mind. (Policymakers have traditionally felt that changing the rules for current retirees or workers who will soon join their ranks is unfair and that young people have time to plan.)

Whatever you may think of the nation's budget issues and how best to address them, it's worth knowing that future beneficiaries would feel the brunt of proposals aimed at curbing Social Security benefits. If you're a young person, that future beneficiary is you.

But younger Americans have a stake in Social Security that goes beyond even the benefits they'll get one day. Benefits that go to older family members — and others in the community — help all of us by fostering independence and reducing poverty. If such support were to be decreased, we would pay the price in other ways.

In this chapter, I offer ten reasons that young people have a stake in preserving a strong Social Security program — for themselves and for future generations.

If You're Lucky, You'll Be Old Someday

What kind of world awaits you in old age? Who can say? But if you believe in planning, you can't ignore sweeping trends that have eroded retirement security for hardworking Americans. Private pensions have become much less common. Wages have grown little. Financial markets are volatile. Healthcare gets more expensive all the time. Meanwhile, gains in longevity mean you may be old for decades. The odds of reaching 100 are better than ever.

Maybe envisioning old age is difficult if you're still young. But no matter how old you are, you can probably agree with the following:

- You want to be secure in your later years.
- You want to be as independent as you can.
- You don't want to worry about the necessities.
- You don't want to lean on others to help pay your bills.

That gives you a stake in preserving a strong Social Security program.

REMEMBER

Social Security benefits don't just go to someone else. Someday, they'll go to you.

Your Parents Will Be Old Even Sooner

Even if Social Security still seems like some far-off concern to you personally, it may already be helping support your parents. As a loving child, presumably you want your parents to have independence and dignity after a lifetime of hard work. For most middle-class families, Social Security makes that possible.

Yet that's not the whole story. By helping your parents stay independent, Social Security may offer you an advantage you don't much think about. There's no delicate way to put this: Do you want your folks to move in with you?

Of course, some adult children would be happy for that. Intergenerational families are a growing phenomenon, particularly during tough economic times. It's safe to say, though, that ideally such households should be created through voluntary choice, not as a last resort in desperate circumstances.

Besides, even if you're game for Mom and Dad moving in, who's to say *they* want that? Older Americans typically prefer to have their own space, as long as they can afford it and have the physical ability to manage on their own. That's the arrangement most adults — parents and grown kids — want.

Social Security plays a critical role in preserving your parents' independence — and yours as well.

You're Paying into the System Now

One easy-to-grasp reason young workers have a stake in Social Security is that they're helping to pay for it. Social Security payroll tax contributions come straight out of your paycheck and add up to many thousands of dollars over the years. Many people, particularly those of moderate income, pay more money in Social Security taxes than they do in income taxes.

The basic Social Security tax rate is 6.2 percent of earnings up to a certain limit ($137,700 in 2020), each paid by the employee and the employer, for a total of 12.4 percent.

The payroll tax means that young workers pay a lot of money into the system in the course of their lifetimes. In return, they earn Social Security benefits for themselves and their dependents — benefits they may need long before retirement if misfortune strikes.

Young workers have a personal financial stake — perhaps larger than they recognize — in keeping Social Security strong for the day they receive benefits.

You Benefit When Social Security Keeps People Out of Poverty

Social Security keeps more people out of poverty than food stamps, earned income tax credits for the poor, and unemployment insurance combined. As a result, all of society benefits.

Before Social Security, needy older Americans could end up in the county poorhouse, where they lived out their final days in misery. Social Security has become the nation's most successful anti-poverty program, keeping about 22 million older Americans out of poverty, and perhaps significantly more, according to some measures. That includes more than 1 million children and more than one-third of older Americans.

Helping people stay self-sufficient isn't just humane. It also solves problems that would have to be dealt with one way or another and at potentially significant costs to the public. If Social Security were to play a smaller role in easing hardship, demand would soar for other services provided by the federal government and the states, creating pressure to raise taxes.

If you're a middle-class worker, Social Security's role in combating poverty may not be the first thing you think about when it comes to the program. But you benefit as a result.

You May Need Benefits Sooner than You Think

Even when you're young, you may be covered by Social Security for important benefits. These protections may apply not only to you but also to your immediate family. It's natural to think of Social Security as a retirement program. But millions of people benefit from protections that were created with the young in mind.

For example, Social Security may provide survivor benefits to young families if a breadwinner dies. These benefits may last until the worker's child reaches the age of 18. A widow or widower who is caring for the child may get benefits until the child reaches age 16. Similarly, you can build up disability benefits that you also may need at a young age. Such benefits also may go to dependent family members.

The Social Security Administration (SSA) recognizes that cases of death and disability can create extreme need when you and your family are still young. As a result, the eligibility requirements are designed with that in mind. You can become eligible for certain benefits after a relatively brief period of covered work, compared to the rules for retirement.

If you're still in your 20s, you can build up some eligibility for survivor and disability protections with as little as six credits — typically, 18 months of work. (Requirements vary based on age and tenure in covered work, but the idea is to give some protection to workers *before* they're old.) By contrast, you have to work about ten years to build up the earnings credits required for retirement benefits.

Bottom line: Social Security is set up to protect people of all ages.

Social Security Ensures That Time Doesn't Eat Away at Your Benefit

I bet you've heard your parents or grandparents reminisce about the "good old days" when bread cost a quarter and candy cost a penny. Maybe they even told you how proud they were to get that first job that paid a grand total of $10,000 a year. (I sure was.)

Just as the prices and wages our parents experienced 20, 30, or 40 years ago seem quaint today, without certain adjustments that are built into the Social Security program, our benefits would seem like a pittance to us 20, 30, or 40 years in the future.

Social Security shields benefits from economic erosion in two primary ways:

- **The benefit formula makes sure that payments increase from one generation to the next with growth in average wages.** It achieves this goal through indexing and other adjustments that can add hundreds of dollars a month to future benefit amounts.
- **Social Security is designed to keep up with rising prices (a feature that isn't part of most pension plans).** This protection can make an enormous difference in your future standard of living, because inflation eats away at the dollar as the years pass. For example, if you're 35 years old, a 3 percent rate of inflation would mean that a dollar you have today will be worth only about 40 cents when you're 65. To shield your benefit from inflation, Social Security applies a cost-of-living adjustment (COLA) to benefits, so that a dollar in benefits today will still be worth a dollar 10, 15, or 35 years from now.

Social Security benefits are supposed to be meaningful, not quaint relics of the past. The built-in wage and inflation protections mean that the benefits you earn while you're younger will retain real purchasing power when you need them.

Social Security Benefits Are One Thing You Can Hang Your Hat On

Retiring with financial security is increasingly difficult. You probably don't have a pension. If you own a home, it may have dropped in value, possibly below what you paid for it. Healthcare costs continue to rise, as do other necessities of life, including energy costs and food. Meanwhile, the gift of longevity means that old age can last a very long time. How will you pay for all those years?

Hopefully, you have various resources to draw on, and you keep your living expenses in line with income. Hopefully, these resources can endure, rewarding you for years of hard work and thinking ahead. But for many older people, it's a struggle. Account balances decline. Income fails to keep up with inflation. And you can't control these things.

Social Security's guaranteed income stands out as the one thing you can count on — a reliable monthly foundation of income that will last the rest of your life. And Social Security's inflation protection helps preserve its value no matter how long you live.

Unfortunately, the trends undermining retirement security are well established, and there's little reason to believe that they'll vanish anytime soon. Young workers need something they can count on to help them achieve financial security when they're old. Social Security remains the bedrock.

The System Works

Social Security isn't perfect. But by and large, it makes the right benefit determinations. Its administrative costs are low. Payments go out on time. You know what you've got coming, and you get it. This predictability is part of the value of Social Security.

I'm not saying that young people today know precisely what they'll get in the future or that Social Security will never be modified. But the enduring outlines of Social Security are apparent:

- It's an efficient system of guaranteed benefits that can last a lifetime, with some inflation protection.
- It's designed to replace more income for modest earners, but some income for all who pay in.

» It will remain a foundation for retirement security that people can count on every month for as long as they live.

Social Security isn't based on theories of human behavior, such as the idea that you'll save more or that you'll save wisely, or expectations of how Wall Street will perform in the future. It isn't an experiment. Social Security works.

The Alternatives Are Worse

You can bolster your retirement security in many ways. It was never Social Security's intended role to do the job alone. Saving over a lifetime can make a tremendous difference. Postponing retirement and extending your work life is a powerful way to nurture your nest egg for the long haul. Investing with care (and patience) can help savings grow significantly over time. If you have many thousands of dollars, you may consider buying an annuity to guarantee more monthly income when you're older.

None of these strategies, however, can match the broad, guaranteed protections of Social Security. For most people, savings rates are too low to protect them in a protracted old age. About a third of workplaces offer no retirement savings programs at all. When programs such as 401(k) plans are available, many workers fail to take full advantage of them, despite tax incentives and payroll deductions to encourage enrollment.

Financial investments — important as they may be — come with risk. When markets collapse, they pull down retirement assets with them. If that's your fate, it can take years to recover. Working longer can be enormously helpful in boosting economic security later in life. But research has shown that many older people retire sooner than they had planned on. Various reasons account for this, including layoffs in a tough labor market, personal health problems that make it difficult to keep up the daily grind, and the need to serve as a caregiver for an ailing spouse.

An assortment of strategies can combine to strengthen economic security in retirement. Hopefully, some of them are part of your own family plan. For most people, however, Social Security remains the linchpin of well-being in retirement.

Life Is Risky

When you're young, the fact that life is risky may be hard to grasp, especially if you've been spared tragedy. But that's one of the reasons Social Security was created — as a form of insurance to help ease some of the bad things that can happen in life.

Out of all the young men entering the labor force, 35 percent will become disabled or die before reaching retirement age, according to an analysis by the SSA. Among young women, the figure is 30 percent. And the chances of becoming disabled are a lot higher than the chances of dying, for both men and women.

Bottom line: Devastating events happen, perhaps more frequently than you realize, especially when you consider a period of many years. And when bad things happen, the tragedy may affect not only the victim, but the victim's entire family, whose livelihood may also be put in jeopardy.

REMEMBER

The protections that Social Security offers for survivors and disabled breadwinners can be a lifeline for families of all ages. They help households stay afloat financially at a time of grave crisis, providing the foundation they need to rebuild their economic plans for the long haul. They're an important reason that young people have a stake in a strong program of Social Security.

» Creating a fairer program

» Weighing the pros and cons of tax increases and benefit reductions

Chapter 17

Ten Choices Facing the Country about the Future of Social Security

Social Security faces a shortfall. To pay benefits, Social Security will increasingly rely on its trust funds (see Chapter 15) because revenues from the payroll tax aren't sufficient. After about 2035, when the trust funds are exhausted, the program is projected to have enough income to cover about 80 percent of promised benefits. That means the country faces choices about how to close the gap.

Social Security issues aren't limited to its solvency, however. Changes in lifestyle since the 1930s have prompted other ideas to make the program more fair and helpful in the 21st century.

This chapter outlines ten major policy options the nation may consider for the future of Social Security. The menu of changes is potentially larger. But these are among the most prominent approaches that have been debated for years by experts of varying political views. Millions of people will be affected by how these issues play out. What do *you* think?

Whether to Increase the Earnings Base

You make payroll tax contributions to Social Security on earnings up to a limit ($137,700 in 2020). This cap is known variously as the *wage base, contribution and benefit base,* and *taxable earnings base.* It has historically served as a limit on the payroll taxes that you and your employer each pay to the program.

Most workers (more than nine out of ten) earn less than the cap. But in recent decades, a small percentage of workers has been receiving a growing share of total U.S. earnings. If you think about all earnings as a pie, the slice that goes untaxed for Social Security has been getting bigger. Raising the earnings base is a way to make the pie look more like it used to and boost revenues for Social Security.

For example, increasing the earnings base such that 90 percent of earnings would be subject to the payroll tax would reduce Social Security's shortfall by 26 percent (if higher earners got somewhat higher benefits) or by 35 percent (if additional taxed earnings weren't included in the benefit calculation), according to 2019 SSA projections. To bring in more or less money, the earnings base could be increased by a higher or lower amount.

TECHNICAL STUFF

Eliminating the cap altogether is a way to greatly decrease the shortfall, but such a measure could weaken the link between contributions and benefits if the additional taxed earnings aren't used in the benefit calculation.

The argument against increasing the earnings base is that high earners already get less of a return on their contributions than lower-income workers get, because Social Security benefits are progressive by design. Also, raising the earnings base amounts to a big tax hike on high earners. But supporters say an increase goes a long way toward fixing the problem, and the burden on high earners wouldn't be onerous.

Whether to Cover More Workers

You and the people you know probably are covered by Social Security. Most workers are. The largest group outside the system is about 25 percent of state and local government employees who rely on separate pension systems and don't pay Social Security taxes. Bringing newly hired state and local government workers into Social Security would raise enough revenue to solve about 6 percent of the long-term shortfall.

State and local governments may oppose such a measure since it could adversely affect the financial stability of their pension systems. The federal government would have to provide a large cash infusion to those pensions if Social Security siphoned off new public employees who aren't now covered.

Such a proposal, however, could bolster Social Security's finances and simplify administration of benefits. That's because the way the program is set up today, Social Security must adjust payments for former government workers who spent part of their working lives contributing to public pension plans but not to Social Security.

In addition, newly covered public employees would benefit from disability and survivor insurance that is either weak or nonexistent in some state and local plans.

Whether to Raise Taxes

Raising Social Security payroll taxes is one way to address the financial shortfall head-on. Even small increases in tax rates go a long way toward shoring up the program's finances over time.

For most recent years, wage earners have paid a Social Security tax of 6.2 percent up to a certain threshold of income ($137,700 in 2020). Employers have paid the same rate as wage earners. The self-employed have paid 12.4 percent (both the employer and employee share). Raising the Social Security payroll tax from 6.2 percent to 6.5 percent would eliminate about 20 percent of the shortfall; raising it to 7.2 percent could close just more than half the gap. A higher increase would have a bigger impact, and a smaller increase would do less. Any increase could be phased in.

This approach would eliminate much of the problem and polls well with the public. But it also raises questions. Critics voice concerns about the economic impact of higher payroll taxes and the possibility that employers may respond to a higher tax by cutting other payroll costs, such as jobs.

Tax revenues for Social Security could be raised in other ways, such as by dedicating revenue from the estate tax or increasing income taxation of Social Security benefits. Neither, however, would generate enough revenue to make a significant dent in the problem.

Another approach would be to tax contributions to all *salary reduction plans* (arrangements in which you're able to divert some of your pretax income to certain areas, such as transit, flexible spending, dependent care, and healthcare accounts). Extending the Social Security payroll tax to all such areas could reduce the shortfall by 9 percent (but such a move would hit consumers who use such accounts to help cover necessities).

Whether to Cut Benefits

Benefit cuts are nothing to cheer about, but they would save money. Further, they could be structured in a way that doesn't hurt current retirees, soon-to-be retirees, and low-income individuals. Any changes could be phased in after a long lead time, giving younger workers years to adjust their plans for the future.

The formula that calculates benefits could be altered in a manner that protects individuals who depend most heavily on benefits, while landing hardest on those who can afford the change. But of course, the fine print would determine the impact. And the more people who are protected, the less savings are achieved. ***Note:*** Policymakers usually include some combination of benefit cuts and tax hikes when they devise plans to strengthen Social Security.

Still, a targeted reduction in benefits could undermine the broad public support for Social Security as a program in which everyone pays in and everyone gets benefits. The more cuts fall on the middle class, the more they erode retirement security for people already facing a squeeze. The more cuts fall on high earners, the less support high earners may have for Social Security.

Whether to Modify the Inflation Formula

Social Security benefits are adjusted to keep up with the cost of living. This protection is extremely valuable to beneficiaries and becomes even more so the longer you live. Without the annual cost-of-living adjustment (COLA), the purchasing power of your benefits shrinks over time. Private pensions usually lack this protection.

The Consumer Price Index for Urban Wage Earners and Clerical Workers (CPI-W) is used as the guide in adjusting Social Security benefits to rising prices. One proposal to save money would be to use a different measure known as the *chained CPI.* The chained CPI builds in the idea that consumers switch their purchases if the price of a particular good goes up too much. The notion is that if the price of ice cream soars, you may switch from eating Fudge Ripple to munching on cookies. If filet mignon is getting too pricey, maybe you'll reach for pork chops.

The chained CPI rises about 0.3 percentage points less each year than the CPI-W. That means a chained CPI would save the Social Security program a lot of money — reducing the shortfall by about 20 percent because of slower-growing benefits.

Unlike most savings proposals, an index that brings smaller inflation increases would affect *current* beneficiaries, albeit gradually, as well as future ones. Those receiving benefits for many years would eventually be hit the hardest. For example, you would see your benefit reduced by a bit less than 1.5 percent after 5 years, 3 percent after 10 years, and 6 percent after 20 years under a COLA based on the chained CPI.

Opponents say a chained CPI may not reflect the reality of older consumers. They spend a lot more on healthcare than young people do, and healthcare costs are rising fast. Older consumers also may rely on various services that may be hard to substitute for. These reductions would mean a larger benefit cut over time. As a result, some proponents would cushion such reductions with a special boost in benefits for the oldest beneficiaries (see the section "Whether to Give a Bonus for Longevity," later in this chapter).

Whether to Raise the Full Retirement Age

The age you can get full Social Security benefits is gradually rising (see Chapter 3). One proposal to save money is to raise the full retirement age even further.

This proposal saves a lot of money for the system while providing an incentive for people to keep working. Pushing the full retirement age to 68 could reduce the shortfall by about 17 percent. Raising it higher, as some suggest, would save even more. Such increases can be implemented very gradually to protect older workers. Proponents say this approach makes sense in an era of increased longevity. A 65-year-old man, for example, is expected to live on average to 84 — and many will live longer than that.

This issue, however, is more nuanced than some people realize. It's true that when Social Security was created, a newborn male wasn't expected to reach 65. But for those who survived to adulthood, many lived into their late 70s and beyond — fewer than today, to be sure, but the gap isn't as wide as some imagine.

Nor has everyone benefited equally from increases in longevity. Many lower-income, less-educated workers haven't enjoyed the same gains in life expectancy as their more affluent, more-educated counterparts, and by some gauges have suffered actual declines. Also, a later age for full retirement benefits could prove onerous for older workers with health problems or in physically demanding jobs.

A related proposal would index Social Security benefits to increases in life expectancy (such as by linking the full retirement age to advances in longevity). This would put the Social Security program on sounder footing by providing lower monthly benefits to compensate for the fact that people are generally living longer.

How to Treat Women More Fairly

Social Security was designed with a 1930s-era vision of the family with a male breadwinner and a stay-at-home mom. Of course, many households no longer fit that model. The result is that some of Social Security's benefit rules raise issues of fairness — issues that often affect women.

For example, Social Security provides a nonworking spouse a benefit of up to 50 percent of the breadwinner's benefit. Yet a working, nonmarried woman potentially gets a smaller benefit (depending on her earnings history) because she can't rely on a higher-earning spouse for benefits. Benefits that go to single women, such as working moms, also may be reduced because of time spent outside the paid workforce, such as to raise a young child or take care of an ailing parent.

One way to make Social Security fairer for working women would be to provide earnings credits for at least some of the time spent caregiving and raising children. For example, a worker might be awarded a year's worth of Social Security credits for a year's worth of such work, up to a certain limit. (Such a measure would be gender neutral and would also help some men, but it would primarily affect women.)

The argument in favor of such a reform is that it would make Social Security more responsive to modern realities and support women who may have low benefits. It could be expensive, however. For example, providing annual earnings credits for five years of child-rearing could increase the long-term funding gap by 8 percent. Plus, offering credits for caregiving may be hard to administer. The cost of such credits could be adjusted up or down, based on their size and the number allowed.

Another proposal would credit each spouse in a two-earner couple with 50 percent of their combined earnings during their marriage. This approach, known as *earnings sharing,* attempts to equalize the treatment of two-earner couples with those of more traditional, single-earner couples. (Under a growing number of circumstances, a working wife gets no more Social Security than if she had never worked outside the home.) Earnings sharing, however, could create new problems.

Benefits for many widows could be reduced, unless such a proposal were designed to prevent that, adding to its cost.

Whether to Divert People's Taxes to Private Accounts

Free-market advocates have long pushed to make Social Security more of a private program, in which some of your payroll taxes go into a personal account that would rise and fall with financial markets.

Supporters believe that your returns in the stock market would make up for cuts in your benefits. You would own the assets in your personal account and could pass them on to your heirs. Historically, the stock market has produced solid, positive returns when measured over long periods of time. Personal accounts could be introduced gradually, so that they would become a choice for younger workers while retirees and near-retirees wouldn't be affected.

The argument against this strategy is that it would erode the basic strength of Social Security, which is a guaranteed benefit you can count on, and replace it with the uncertainties of Wall Street and other investments. Social Security was created as social insurance that protects workers and their families when they no longer can work because of death, disability, or retirement. Private accounts have no such mission, and workers couldn't rely on the same protections for themselves or their dependents.

Whether to Create a Minimum Benefit

Social Security no longer has a real minimum benefit. Even with Social Security's progressive benefit formula, low wage earners may end up with benefits insufficient to cover basic living costs. A higher minimum benefit can be achieved through various means. For example, a minimum benefit may be set at 125 percent of the poverty line (or some other percentage), targeting workers who have worked fewer than the 35 years that go into benefit calculations. In theory, the Social Security Administration (SSA) could set a higher floor for benefits or include credits for unpaid work, such as for caregiving (see the earlier section "How to Treat Women More Fairly"). Also, a minimum benefit could be indexed to wage increases, keeping the minimum benefit adequate over time.

The problem is that a minimum benefit would cost money at a time when Social Security needs more of it. Further, it would weaken the relationship between contributions and benefits that has been so important to the program's success. The total cost of a minimum benefit depends on the particulars, but by some estimates it could increase the shortfall by 2 percent to 13 percent.

Whether to Give a Bonus for Longevity

The oldest Americans are often the poorest. They may have little savings. Usually, they no longer work, they face significant health challenges, and if they have pensions, such income is usually eroded by inflation.

Hiking their benefits through a *longevity bonus* is one idea for how to help them. For example, a 5 percent benefit increase could be targeted to individuals above a certain age, such as 85. Like other proposals, the longevity bonus could be phased in and fine-tuned. It would directly help a segment of older Americans who have the greatest need for adequate benefits and have little or no way to strengthen their finances.

This proposal isn't about saving money. For example, if a longevity bonus were offered 20 years after eligibility (which is age 62 for most people), it could increase the long-term Social Security shortfall by 9 percent. That's the argument against the bonus or to limit its size.

6 Appendixes

IN THIS PART . . .

Turn to the glossary to find Social Security terms defined in plain English. Knowing some of these terms is useful if you need to talk to the bureaucracy or simply want a clearer grasp of the program.

Check out the list of resources so you can get even *more* information on Social Security and related topics.

Devise your own fix-it plan for Social Security's finances. You may find this exercise instructive for your own financial well-being.

Appendix A

Glossary

administrative law judge: A legally experienced official who presides over hearings and administrative appeals of Social Security Administration decisions.

AIME: *See* average indexed monthly earnings (AIME).

annuity: An insurance product that provides a stream of income, sometimes for life.

appeal: A procedure by which an applicant challenges a decision by the Social Security Administration. The appeals process has four main steps: 1) reconsideration, 2) administrative law judge, 3) Appeals Council, 4) U.S. federal court (both the district court and the appropriate court of appeals).

Appeals Council: The Social Security Administration adjudicative body that reviews appeals after hearings with an administrative law judge.

auxiliary benefits: Benefits that go to family members, based on a worker's earnings record with the Social Security Administration. Also known as *family benefits.*

average indexed monthly earnings (AIME): A dollar amount based on past earnings for 35 years that have been indexed for wage growth and averaged. The annual average is then divided by 12 to get the monthly average or the AIME. AIME is a key to the Social Security benefits computation.

bend points: The dollar amounts defining the average indexed monthly earnings brackets (in the primary insurance amount formula) or the primary insurance amount brackets (in the maximum family benefit formula).

beneficiary: An individual who receives benefits.

breadwinner: *See* wage earner.

break-even point: The age at which your total collected Social Security benefits would be equal, if started at two different times. The break-even point reflects the fact that benefits claimed later pay higher amounts than benefits claimed earlier.

child: A biological child, adopted child, stepchild, or dependent grandchild who is potentially qualified for benefits based on a worker's earnings record. The Social Security Administration is guided by state inheritance laws in resolving questions about a child's legal status.

COLA: *See* cost-of-living adjustment (COLA).

compassionate allowance: A Social Security Administration initiative in which certain extreme conditions are designated for fast-track consideration for disability benefits.

computation years: The years with earnings used to calculate a Social Security benefit. For retired workers, this will be the highest 35 years of earnings. However, for the disabled and those who die, the number of computation years could be lower.

consultative examination: A medical exam by a government-paid healthcare specialist who advises an administrative law judge, determining whether an applicant qualifies for disability benefits.

contribution and benefit base: *See* taxable maximum.

cost-of-living adjustment (COLA): Annual adjustment to Social Security benefits so that they keep pace with inflation. Although rare, cost-of-living adjustments may not be made in years with little or no inflation.

covered employment: Work in which you and an employer are required to make Social Security payroll tax contributions. Most jobs in the U.S. economy are covered employment.

credits: Units that count toward entitlement for Social Security benefits, based on earnings in covered work. You get up to four credits per year. Credit amounts were set at $1,410 per quarter for 2020 (up to four credits, or $5,640, for the year). Forty credits is the usual requirement to qualify for retirement benefits. Also known as *work credits* or *quarters of coverage.*

DDS: *See* Disability Determination Service (DDS).

deductible: The amount you pay out of pocket before Medicare or other insurance kicks in. Medicare's Part A deductible for a hospitalization was set at $1,408 per benefit period for 2020.

delayed retirement credits: Factors that increase benefits when claimed after full retirement age. Delayed retirement credits are awarded up to age 70.

dependent: A family member who may qualify for benefits based on a worker's earnings record with the Social Security Administration. Dependents include a spouse, children, and potentially others.

disability benefits: Benefits awarded to an individual whose physical or mental condition is so severe that the individual can't work for at least a year or may die from the condition.

Disability Determination Service (DDS): The state agency that works closely with the Social Security Administration to review applications for disability benefits.

doughnut hole: A coverage gap in Medicare prescription-drug coverage. This means that after a certain amount, you're responsible for all out-of-pocket drug costs up to a certain limit.

dual entitlement: When you're entitled to benefits on more than one earnings record. Dual entitlement has become common as more women work in the paid labor force and are eligible for benefits based on their own earnings as well as their husbands'.

earliest eligibility age (EEA): This is the earliest age at which individuals can apply for Social Security benefits. For retirement benefits, the EEA is 62. For nondisabled widows or widowers with no children, the EEA is 60. For disabled widows or widowers with no children, the EEA is 50. For widows or widowers with children under age 16 and for the disabled, there is no EEA.

early retirement benefits: Retirement benefits claimed before full retirement age, as early as 62. Early retirement benefits are reduced for each month claimed before full retirement age.

earnings history: *See* earnings record.

earnings record: Your past covered earnings on file with the Social Security Administration. Retirement benefits are based on your 35 years of highest earnings. Also known as *earnings history.*

earnings test: Required withholding of benefits if earnings exceed certain limits and you haven't reached full retirement age. The limits were set as follows for 2020: benefits reduced by $1 for every $2 in earnings above $18,240 if you're below full retirement age for the entire year; $1 for every $3 in earnings above $48,600 for months during the year in which you reach full retirement age. Also known as *retirement earnings test.*

EEA: *See* earliest eligibility age (EEA).

eligible: Meeting the age, credit, and relationship (such as spouse, child, and so on) requirements necessary to receive a Social Security benefit. Eligibility doesn't automatically enroll you in Social Security; when eligible, you need to apply for a benefit.

entitled: Having completed an application for Social Security benefits that you're eligible for.

ex-spousal benefit: A type of Social Security benefit paid to a lower-earning divorced spouse. The ex-spouse benefit can be up to 50 percent of the higher-earning spouse's primary insurance amount, when claimed at full retirement age. The couple must have been married for at least ten years in order for the lower-earning ex-spouse to be eligible for an ex-spousal benefit.

family benefits: *See* auxiliary benefits.

family maximum: The maximum amount of benefits that can be paid to family members based on a worker's earnings record, generally 150 percent to 180 percent of the worker's primary insurance amount. Also known as *maximum family benefit.*

FICA tax: The payroll tax for Social Security and Medicare, under the Federal Insurance Contributions Act (FICA). The Social Security portion has historically been set at 6.2 percent on earnings up to an annual cap for employees and employers, although Congress has approved temporary breaks for workers. The Medicare portion is 1.45 percent on all earnings, also paid by employees and employers.

FRA: *See* full retirement age (FRA).

FRB: *See* full retirement benefit (FRB).

full retirement age (FRA): The age at which you qualify for full (or unreduced) retirement benefits. The full retirement age is based on your year of birth and is gradually rising to 67 for individuals born in 1960 or later. Also known as *normal retirement age.*

full retirement benefit (FRB:) The benefit you receive at full retirement age. It is equal to 100 percent of the primary insurance amount. Retirement benefits increase if claimed after full retirement age, up to age 70.

gainful activity: Work you do for pay. The Social Security Administration sets a dollar amount of gainful activity it considers "substantial" and may not award disability benefits above that level. The substantial gainful activity threshold was set at $1,260 per month for 2020 ($2,110 for the blind).

government pension offset: A provision that reduces Social Security spousal and widow/widower benefits if they're based on the earnings record of a worker who spent part of his or her career in government employment not covered by Social Security.

hearing: An appeal that takes place before an administrative law judge. The hearing stage of an appeal is where an initial Social Security Administration determination is most likely to be reversed.

hospital insurance: *See* Medicare Part A.

insured status: Your status toward eligibility for Social Security, based on your total number of work credits. Generally, "fully insured status" is required for full protection; however, in certain cases, "currently insured status" with fewer work credits may allow for widow/widower or child benefits.

listing of impairments: An official compilation of highly severe conditions, including detailed criteria that enable an individual to qualify for Social Security disability benefits.

long-term care: Various long-term services required by individuals with chronic conditions, including help with basic activities, such as dressing and bathing. Medicare doesn't cover nonskilled "custodial care" for activities of daily living.

lump-sum death benefit: A one-time payment of $255 to the spouse or child of a covered worker who dies. The survivor must file for the lump-sum death benefit within two years of the worker's death.

marriage: A legal marriage, which may include state-recognized same-sex marriages and state-recognized common-law marriages.

maximum family benefit: *See* family maximum.

Medicare: The government healthcare program for individuals 65 and older, as well as some others, including those receiving Social Security disability benefits for two years or more. Medicare includes Part A (hospital insurance), Part B (supplementary medical insurance), Part C (Medicare Advantage), and Part D (prescription-drug coverage).

Medicare Advantage: Privately run plans that offer basic services and often extras, generally with a restriction on choice of providers. An alternative to the original Medicare program. Also known as *Medicare Part C.*

Medicare Part A: The part of Medicare that covers a portion of hospital expenses, temporary rehabilitation in a skilled nursing facility, hospice, and some home healthcare. Also known as *hospital insurance.*

Medicare Part B: The part of Medicare that covers doctors' visits, outpatient services, and other medical services. Also known as *supplementary medical insurance.*

Medicare Part C: *See* Medicare Advantage.

Medicare Part D: The part of Medicare that helps pay for prescription medications. Part D is handled by approved private plans, including stand-alone drug plans, as well as broader Medicare Advantage programs that offer prescription-drug benefits. Also known as *prescription-drug coverage.*

Medigap: Private, supplemental healthcare insurance designed to fill in gaps in Medicare coverage.

normal retirement age: *See* full retirement age (FRA).

OASDI: *See* Old-Age, Survivors, and Disability Insurance (OASDI).

Old-Age, Survivors, and Disability Insurance (OASDI): The formal name for Social Security, including benefits for retirement, survivors, disabled workers, and dependent family members.

overpayment notice: Formal notification that the Social Security Administration believes that you've been overpaid and owe it money. You may challenge an overpayment notice by filing a request for reconsideration or waiver of recovery.

PIA: *See* primary insurance amount (PIA).

POMS: *See* Program Operations Manual System (POMS).

prescription-drug coverage: *See* Medicare Part D.

primary insurance amount (PIA): An amount equal to your Social Security benefit at full retirement age. The PIA is the basis used to compute benefits that may go to you or your family members. It's based on a progressive formula applied to the average indexed monthly earnings.

Program Operations Manual System (POMS): Provides guidance for Social Security Administration employees in making determinations about benefits.

progressivity: Measured in different ways, the feature of Social Security designed to make benefits relatively more generous for low earners than for high earners. Progressivity is achieved mainly through the formula used to calculate the primary insurance amount.

protective filing date: The date you contact the Social Security Administration about making an application for benefits. The protective filing date may help you gain back benefits if much time passes before the application is complete.

quarters of coverage: *See* credits.

reconsideration: *See* request for reconsideration.

reduction factor: The monthly amount by which benefits may be reduced if claimed before full retirement age.

replacement rate: The percentage of pre-retirement earnings replaced by Social Security benefits. It is about 40 percent for average earners, more for low earners, less for high earners.

representative payee: An individual authorized to receive and manage Social Security benefits on behalf of a beneficiary. Payees must use the benefits to meet the needs of the beneficiary, save anything extra, and keep records.

request for reconsideration: In most places, the first step in challenging an adverse decision on your application for benefits. This step is usually required before you may request a hearing with an administrative law judge.

residual functional capacity: An individual's remaining ability to function in the workplace, despite the limitations of a physical or mental condition. This can be an important factor in assessing whether an individual can work or is disabled.

retired-worker benefits: *See* retirement benefits.

retirement benefits: Payments made to workers who've earned Social Security coverage, starting as early as age 62. The Social Security Administration sometimes calls such benefits *retirement insurance benefits (RIB)* or *retired-worker benefits.*

retirement earnings test: *See* earnings test.

retirement insurance benefits (RIB): *See* retirement benefits.

retroactive benefits: Benefit payments predating the time of application that sometimes may be made to individuals older than full retirement age, the disabled, and certain dependents.

RIB: *See* retirement benefits.

SECA tax: The payroll tax for Social Security and Medicare paid by the self-employed under the Self-Employment Contribution Act (SECA). The Social Security portion has historically been set at 12.4 percent on net earnings up to an annual cap, although Congress has approved temporary breaks. The Medicare portion is 2.9 percent on net earnings (uncapped).

social insurance: An idea imported from Europe that nations could adapt insurance principles for the benefit of all members of a society.

Social Security Act: A 1935 federal law that created the Social Security program. The original act included benefits for retirees and the unemployed, among other provisions.

Social Security Administration (SSA): The agency that runs Social Security, Supplemental Security Income, and enrollments in Medicare. The headquarters is in Baltimore, Maryland, although local field offices are located in communities across all 50 states and U.S. territories.

"Social Security Handbook": A comprehensive guide to Social Security and its regulations, written for the public. New versions of the handbook are only available online: `www.ssa.gov/OP_Home/handbook/handbook-toc.html`.

Social Security number: The nine-digit identifier for Social Security, usually assigned during infancy.

spousal benefit: A type of Social Security benefit paid to married spouses. The amount is up to 50 percent of the worker's full retirement benefit, when claimed at the spouse's full retirement age. Also known as *spouse benefit.*

spouse benefit: *See* spousal benefit.

SSI: *See* Supplemental Security Income (SSI).

statement: A personal summary of Social Security benefits you've earned and projections for the future. You may view your personal Social Security statement by registering online. Starting at age 60, if you do not have an online account and have not claimed benefits, Social Security will mail you a written statement three months before your birthday.

Supplemental Security Income (SSI): A cash assistance program run by the Social Security Administration for low-income individuals, including those who are age 65 and over, blind, or disabled.

supplementary medical insurance: *See* Medicare Part B.

survivor benefit: A type of Social Security benefit paid to surviving spouses, children, and dependent elderly parents, based on the earnings record of a worker who dies. Also known as *widow(er) benefit.*

taxable maximum: The maximum amount of earnings to which the Social Security payroll tax can be applied. Also, the maximum amount of earnings that can be used in the Social Security benefit calculation. The taxable maximum was set at $137,700 for 2020. Also known as *contribution and benefit base.*

treating doctor: A physician or psychologist who treats an individual who has applied for disability benefits. The Social Security Administration gives significant weight to the observations of a treating doctor.

trial work period: A span of nine months in which someone getting disability benefits may work without interruption of benefits. During the trial work period, the restriction on substantial gainful activity isn't enforced.

trust funds: Separate accounts in the U.S. Treasury in which are deposited the taxes received under the Federal Insurance Contributions Act (FICA) and the Self-Employment Contributions Act (SECA). The money used to pay Social Security benefits is paid out of the trust funds. The main trust funds are the Old-Age and Survivors Insurance (OASI) Trust Fund and the Disability Insurance (DI) Trust Fund.

trustees report: The detailed, annual disclosure of Social Security's finances, released by its board of trustees. The six-member board includes the secretary of the treasury, the commissioner of Social Security, the secretary of health and human services, the secretary of labor, and two representatives of the public.

VE: *See* vocational expert (VE).

vocational expert (VE): A government-paid occupational expert who may testify at a disability hearing about the type of skill and exertion required to perform an applicant's previous job or other jobs in the economy to determine if the applicant can still do his or her previous work or other work.

wage earner: The individual upon whose record a claim for benefits is made, including claims by dependents. Also known as *worker* or *breadwinner.*

waiver of recovery: A request to toss out a Social Security overpayment determination, if you think such a determination is unfair.

widow(er) benefit: *See* survivor benefit.

Windfall Elimination provision: A rule that may reduce Social Security retirement benefits for individuals who earned pensions through government work not covered by Social Security. This provision reduces Social Security benefits for many older government workers who were under the Civil Service Retirement System.

work credits: *See* credits.

worker: *See* wage earner.

Appendix B

Resources

You can find a lot of information out there about Social Security and related issues of financial stability in retirement. This appendix highlights some of the chief resources and puts them together in one place for your convenience.

Social Security

You can contact the Social Security Administration (SSA) by mail, by phone, online, or by visiting your local SSA field office:

- **Mail:** Whenever you write to the SSA, be sure to include your Social Security number and claim number (if you have one):

  Social Security Administration Office of Public Inquiries and Communications Support, 1100 West High Rise 6401 Security Blvd., Baltimore, MD 21235

- **Phone:** The SSA phone lines are staffed Monday through Friday, 8 a.m. to 5:30 p.m. Some automated services are available 24 hours a day. Call 800-772-1213 (TTY 800-325-0778).
- **Web:** The SSA home page is www.ssa.gov. From this page, you can take care of much of the business you have with the SSA, using the links on the page. For example, to get a form, click the "Forms" link; to get a publication, click "Publications." Click the "FAQs" link for answers to more than 600 questions.
- **Local office:** To find an SSA office near you, simply go to www.ssa.gov, click on "Contact Us," and then click the "Office Locator" link. Some offices may be closed due to the COVID-19 pandemic.

Note: If you or someone you're assisting isn't fluent in English and needs help from the SSA, you have a few options:

- You can access the Spanish version of the SSA website at `www.ssa.gov/espanol`.
- You can access versions of the SSA website in other languages by going to `www.ssa.gov/multilanguage`.
- You can request interpreter services, which are available in various languages free of charge. Call the SSA and tell the representative you need an interpreter.

Medicare

You can contact Medicare by mail, by phone, or online:

- **Mail:** You can write to Medicare at the following address:

  Centers for Medicare & Medicaid Services Offices of Hearings and Inquiries (OHI), Attn: Customer Accessibility Resource Staff, 7500 Security Blvd., Mail Stop S1-13-25, Baltimore, MD 21244-1850.
- **Phone:** Call 800-633-4227 or the TTY number for the hearing impaired: 877-486-2048.
- **Web:** For questions about Medicare services, coverage, claims, or expenses, go to `www.medicare.gov`. From the Medicare home page, you can find a wealth of information about Medicare, including answers to frequently asked questions. Click the "Forms, Help, & Resources" link to find Medicare doctors, compare hospitals and nursing homes, and read a variety of publications with more info on many Medicare services.

REMEMBER

For any of the following situations, contact the SSA (see the preceding section):

- To get help with questions on enrollment, eligibility, premiums, or the Extra Help program
- To replace a lost or stolen Medicare card
- To report a death

TIP

For more information on Medicare, check out the official Medicare handbook, "Medicare & You," available at www.medicare.gov/pubs/pdf/10050-Medicare-and-You.pdf.

TIP

If you need help with Medicare, State Health Insurance Assistance Programs (SHIPs) provide free, personal help from trained counselors on all Medicare and Medicaid issues, including help in selecting Medicare Advantage or Part D plans. You can find contact information for the SHIP in your state at www.medicare.gov/Contacts.

If you're having trouble getting what you need from Medicare, you may want to contact the Medicare Rights Center (800-333-4114; www.medicarerights.org), an advocacy group that keeps close tabs on the program and sometimes takes legal action on behalf of beneficiaries.

AARP

AARP is a nonprofit, nonpartisan organization that helps people 50 and older have independence, choice, and control in ways that are beneficial and affordable to them and society as a whole. AARP offers a great deal of pro-consumer information about Social Security, Medicare, and other programs.

TIP

You can find a lot of information on the AARP website (www.aarp.org). For a targeted information search, check out the following:

- **General information on Social Security** (www.aarp.org/work/social-security): This page offers a wide array of pro-consumer materials about Social Security, including expert advice on benefits, scams to watch out for, and the latest news.
- **AARP Social Security Benefits Calculator** (www.aarp.org/retirement/social-security/benefits-calculator.html): This easy-to-use tool offers a holistic approach to estimating your future benefits.
- **AARP Retirement Calculator** (www.aarp.org/work/retirement-planning/retirement_calculator): This tool helps singles and couples get an idea of how much they need to save to have the future they desire.
- **AARP's "Medicare Part D Guide"** (www.aarp.org/health/medicare-insurance/medicare_partD_guide): This is a user's guide to Medicare's prescription-drug program.

- **AARP Public Policy Institute** (www.aarp.org/ppi): This site features research and reports on economic security, healthcare, and other policy issues of importance to older Americans. You can access the institute's page at www.aarp.org/ppi/publications.

Other Sources

You can find all kinds of information on Social Security by searching online, but you can't be sure how accurate the information you're getting is. Here are some potentially valuable resources:

- **Administration on Aging** (202-401-4634; www.acl.gov/about-acl/administration-aging): Provides information and resources for seniors and caregivers on many issues related to population aging.
- **Allsup** (800-279-4357; www.allsup.com): Provides nonlawyer representation for Social Security disability applicants.
- **American Academy of Actuaries** (202-223-8196; www.actuary.org): Provides independent analysis of risk issues in Social Security, pensions, healthcare, and other areas.
- **Cato Institute** (202-842-0200; www.cato.org/social-security): Gives a perspective on Social Security from a public policy group dedicated to "individual liberty, limited government, free markets, and peace."
- **Center for Retirement Research at Boston College** (617-552-1762; crr.bc.edu): Offers research on Social Security and other issues.
- **Center on Budget and Policy Priorities** (202-408-1080; www.cbpp.org): Offers research and analysis on fiscal policy and government programs that are important to moderate- and low-income individuals, including Social Security.
- **Century Foundation** (212-452-7700; tcf.org/topics/economy-jobs/social-insurance): Offers a progressive perspective on social insurance issues, including Social Security and retirement security.
- **Economic Policy Institute** (202-775-8810; www.epi.org/research/retirement): A nonprofit, nonpartisan think tank created in 1986 to broaden discussions about economic policy to include the needs of low- and middle-income workers.
- **Eldercare Locator** (800-677-1116; https://eldercare.acl.gov): Offers access to local resources for a range of needs.

- **Employee Benefit Research Institute** (202-659-0670; www.ebri.org): A research and education organization that focuses on employee benefits and other issues related to retirement and health security.
- **Heritage Foundation** (202-546-4400; www.heritage.org/issues/retirement-security): Offers a conservative perspective on the issues of Social Security.
- **National Academy of Social Insurance** (202-452-8097; www.nasi.org): Seeks to promote understanding of social insurance and its role in promoting economic security and a strong economy. You can find Social Security–specific information at www.nasi.org/research/social-security.
- **National Committee to Preserve Social Security and Medicare** (800-998-0180 connects you with the legislative hotline; www.ncpssm.org): Advocates for strong Social Security and Medicare programs.
- **National Council on Aging** (571-527-3900; www.ncoa.org): A nonprofit service and advocacy group to help older Americans. NCOA has created an online tool to help determine eligibility for various government programs, including Social Security disability, healthcare, and food stamps: www.benefitscheckup.org.
- **National Organization of Social Security Claimants' Representatives** (845-682-1881; www.nosscr.org): An association of attorneys and other advocates. The website contains a lot of information about Social Security disability benefits. You can call the toll-free number for a lawyer referral.
- **Nolo** (www.nolo.com/legal-encyclopedia/social-security): Articles on various Social Security issues from an organization dedicated to making the legal system accessible.
- **Rest-of-Life Communications** (www.restoflife.com): Helpful commentary on a range of Social Security and retirement-planning issues by Steve Vernon, an authority on retirement planning.
- **Urban Institute** (202-833-7200; www.urban.org): Gathers data, conducts research, evaluates programs, and offers technical assistance on topics as varied as Social Security, health, justice, and philanthropy.

Appendix C

Strengthening Social Security

There's no mystery about Social Security's projected shortfall. Policy experts have a good idea of its size, and they have a good idea of the sorts of measures that would close the gap. Most measures fall into two broad categories: tax increases and benefit reductions. A package to address the gap can include both of these approaches, and it can rely more heavily on one than the other.

You don't have to leave it to the wonks in Washington to figure it out. In this appendix, you can create your own fix-it plan for Social Security, closing the money gap the way you think best. By going through the exercise, you can compare your own priorities to what you hear in the news. (See Chapter 17 for a more detailed discussion of the policy choices.)

Table C-1 lists major proposals to boost revenues coming into Social Security. Table C-2 lists major policy options for reducing benefits. In each table, you see estimates of how far each choice goes toward fixing the shortfall. For example, Row 2 in Table C-1 shows that raising the payroll tax to 6.5 percent each on employers and employees closes 20 percent of the gap. If you prefer that option, place a check mark next to it and write "20%" in the far-right column of Row 2; then you need to make additional choices, adding up to 80 percent, to solve 100 percent of the problem.

TABLE C-1 **Ways You Can Increase Revenue**

Row	Revenue Increases	Share of the Solvency Gap Filled
1	Increase the amount of earnings subject to the Social Security payroll tax (currently $137,700). ❑ Increase the tax base so that 90% of earnings are covered (savings: 29%). ❑ Subject all earnings to the Social Security payroll tax (savings 7%).	
2	Increase the payroll tax rate on employers and employees (traditionally 6.2% each). ❑ Increase to 6.5% (savings 20%). ❑ Increase to 7.2% (savings: 55%).	
3	Impose the payroll tax on contributions to salary reduction plans,[1] such as 401(k) plans (savings: 10%).	
4	Include newly hired state and local government workers in Social Security (savings: 6%).	
	Total revenue increases (add Rows 1–4)	

[1] *Salary reduction plans allocate some of your pay to transit, healthcare, flexible spending, and other programs.*

TABLE C-2 **Ways You Can Reduce Benefits**

Row	Benefit Reductions	Share of the Solvency Gap Filled
1	Increase the full retirement age (currently scheduled to rise to 67) to 68 (savings 17%).	
2	Implement longevity indexing of the full retirement age, linking future increases in the full retirement age to increases in life expectancy (savings: 20%).	
3	Adjust the benefit formula by cutting benefits for some earners while protecting others. ❑ Protect the bottom 30% of earners (savings 56%). ❑ Protect the bottom 40% of earners (savings: 47%). ❑ Protect the bottom 50% of earners (savings 38%). ❑ Protect the bottom 60% of earners (savings 27%).	
4	Use a different measure (the chained Consumer Price Index) to calculate the annual inflation increase for benefits, reducing the size of the cost-of-living adjustment (savings: 21%).	
	Total benefit reductions (add Rows 1–4)	

Add up your total revenue increases (from Table C-1) and your total benefit reductions (from Table C-2). The goal is for that number to be at least 100 percent to eliminate a future shortfall.

Simple enough, right? Well, I'd like to introduce another variable. Many people believe that, as part of fixing Social Security for the long haul, certain benefits should be *enhanced.* Of course, that adds expense. But in theory the costs could be covered by other measures. I list three such proposals in Table C-3. If you want to include any of these increases in your fix-it plan, you should look for ways to pay for them.

TABLE C-3 Ways You Can Enhance Benefits

Row	Benefit Enhancements	Additional Cost
1	Ensure that workers with substantial work histories receive a basic, minimum benefit (cost: 5%).	
2	Provide earnings credits to working parents who take time out of the paid labor force to raise kids (cost: 9%).	
3	Increase the inflation adjustment so that retirees can better keep up with the cost of living (cost: 14%).	
	Total benefit enhancements (add Rows 1–3)	

In Table C-3, I list three proposals for enhancing benefits. Check any of the increases you want to include in your fix-it plan and jot down the increase in the far-right column. Add up the costs of any enhancements you choose, and then subtract them from the sum of your amounts in Tables C-1 and C-2.

You don't have to limit yourself to only one table. You can choose your own mix of revenue increases, benefit cuts, and perhaps benefit enhancements. But the goal is for the total of your choices to add up to 100 percent. (If you select any benefit increases from Table C-3, your fix-it choices from Tables C-1 and C-2 should add up to more than 100 percent.)

The options in the preceding tables are among those most frequently mentioned by policymakers. Select or reject them as you want. Maybe you can dig up more ideas on your own. Whatever the case, if your choices add up to 100 percent or more, congratulations! You've shown one way to strengthen Social Security. The job has proven difficult for your elected leaders in Washington.

(All numbers are illustrative, and savings estimates change over time. Details of implementation affect their precise impact on solvency.)

Note: For ease of computation, some figures are rounded.

Index

A

B

C

D

E

F

G

H

I

J

N

O

P

Q

R

S

T

U

V

W

Y

About the Author

Jonathan Peterson recalls one of the first big stories in his journalistic career — the epic deal to strengthen Social Security in 1983. "That debate got me thinking about the aging of the Boomer generation, and what that would mean for our country one day," he says. "And now we've got the Gen Xers reaching a more mature stage of life. Retirement security is a big issue."

Jonathan never lost his interest in Social Security and the aging of U.S. society. During his award-winning career at the *Los Angeles Times*, he wrote groundbreaking stories about the challenges to financial well-being facing Boomers and the younger people who will follow them into the uncertain terrain of old age.

The journalist's mission, he believes, is to help readers make sense of a complex world. He won two *Los Angeles Times* editorial awards, one for an exposé of a securities broker who squandered the retirement savings of older workers.

He also won an Overseas Press Club award for an in-depth series about the collapsing Soviet Union, and he was on the *Los Angeles Times* team that won the 1993 Pulitzer Prize for spot news coverage of the L.A. riots. During his news career, he covered the White House, state and national political campaigns, and various facets of U.S. domestic and economic policy. He was a 2007 National Press Foundation fellow in the program "Retirement Issues in the 21st Century." For nine years, Jonathan served as executive communications director at AARP, where he pitched in with speechwriting and other strategic communications needs.

He lives in the Washington, D.C., area, where he enjoys spending time with his wife, Lisa, daughters Hannah and Sara, and son Sammy.

Dedication

For my father, Morton Peterson, who always knew what mattered most.

Author's Acknowledgments

Many people supported this project, including colleagues at AARP and outside experts who responded generously to queries from out of the blue. To all who helped in any way at all, a heartfelt thank you. Your support made months of writing a less solitary experience and, more important, created a better book. In particular, for this latest edition, I want to give a shout-out to my diligent and talented researcher, Susan O'Brian. Sincere thanks as well go to the National Press Office of the Social Security Administration, my project manager Michelle Hacker, and Tracy Boggier, senior acquisitions editor at Wiley.

Mikki Waid's expertise has strengthened many of the pages in this book. Special thanks also go to Jodi Lipson, Elizabeth Kuball, Erin Calligan Mooney, Mark Friedlich, William "BJ" Jarrett, Kia Green, Patricia Barry, Sheri R. Abrams, Elliott Andalman, Robert B. Friedland, Jonathan Ginsberg, Nancy Hwa, Rebecca L. Ray of Allsup, Robert A. Rosenblatt, John Rother, Julie Shapiro, Nancy Shor, Paul N. Van de Water, Steve Vernon, the Center for Retirement Research at Boston College, Gary Koenig, Mike Schuster, Robin Cochran, Jean Setzfand, Christina S. FitzPatrick, Alison Shelton, Victoria Sackett, Lori A. Trawinski, Kristina Gray, Fred Griesbach, Enid Kassner, Daniel Koslofsky, Cristina Martin-Firvida, Lynn Nonnemaker, Linda Brandon, Ashley Petry, and Stacy Kennedy.

A special thanks to those who updated this fourth edition: Susan O'Brian, who expertly took the lead, as well as Joel Eskovitz, Dave Landes, Keith Lind, Claire Noelle-Miller, Jim Palmieri, Leigh Purvis, Kathy Stokes, and Jane Sung within AARP, and Web Phillips of the National Committee to Preserve Social Security & Medicare.

Finally, thanks to my three beautiful (and patient) children, and my wife, Lisa, who tackled problems as varied as word usage, Social Security arithmetic, computer formatting, and one very distracted husband, always in a spirit of true partnership.

Publisher's Acknowledgments

Senior Acquisitions Editor: Tracy Boggier
Project Manager: Michelle Hacker
Development Editor: Georgette Beatty
Copy Editor: Christine Pingleton
Proofreader: Debbye Butler
Technical Editor: Mark Friedlich
Production Editor: Tamilmani Varadharaj
Cover Image: © Adam Voorhes/Gallery Stock

Take dummies with you everywhere you go!

Whether you are excited about e-books, want more from the web, must have your mobile apps, or are swept up in social media, dummies makes everything easier.

Find us online!